ANTITRUST
AND
TRADE
REGULATION

MARSHALL C. HOWARD
University of Massachusetts

ANTITRUST
AND
TRADE
REGULATION
SELECTED ISSUES
AND CASE STUDIES

Prentice-Hall, Inc., *Englewood Cliffs, New Jersey 07632*

Library of Congress Cataloging in Publication Data

HOWARD, MARSHALL C.
    Antitrust and trade regulation.

    Includes bibliographies and index.
    1. Trade regulation—United States.   2. Antitrust
law—United States.   I. Title.
KF1609.H68   343.73'072   82-5345
ISBN   0-13-038349-X   347.30372   AACR2

Editorial/production supervision and interior design: **Joan Foley**
Cover design: **Diane Saxe**
Manufacturing buyer: **Ed O'Dougherty**

Printed in the United States of America

10   9   8   7   6   5   4   3   2   1

ISBN 0-13-038349-X

Prentice-Hall International, Inc., *London*
Prentice-Hall of Australia Pty. Limited, *Sydney*
Prentice-Hall Canada Inc., *Toronto*
Prentice-Hall of India Private Limited, *New Delhi*
Prentice-Hall of Japan, Inc., *Tokyo*
Prentice-Hall of Southeast Asia Pte. Ltd., *Singapore*
Whitehall Books Limited, *Wellington, New Zealand*

Contents

Preface

This book was written as an effort to present as clearly as possible both the principal antitrust and trade regulation issues that have to be dealt with on a daily basis by government authorities whose duty it is to maintain the competitive health of the economy, and related issues that have been the subject of prominent private antitrust actions. The first chapter lays out the theoretical economic framework and rationale for the maintenance of a system of competition. The second chapter presents the fundamentals of the legal framework in enough detail to make clear the rules of the game to which competitors must adhere and the incentives and disincentives that have been built into this system of social control of business. The remaining chapters present the issues, the underlying reasons why they are issues, and the solutions and alternative proposed solutions to these issues.

The special feature of this book is the case studies that are presented throughout. They are designed to provide substantive material to accompany presentations of antitrust and trade regulation issues. Although some of these studies are built around only one court decision or enforcement action, more of them are drawn up around several together and are presented within their own special institutional framework. Price-fixing has been more than the conventional conspiracy in a smoke-filled room; corporate executives have devised complex schemes, and members of some professions have interacted within particular organizational structures with price-fixing results. The lessee gasoline dealers are not just retailers who tend to deal exclusively in the products of one supplier; they are independent businesspeople positioned between the forces of the retail market and the pressures of a large landlord-supplier. Cooperative advertising is not just the case of a supplier granting advertising allowances to customers, sometimes on a more favorable basis to some than to others; it is a marketing institution that can have several forms and different results. Efforts to ensure that consumers have full information on textile fiber products to prevent possible misrepresentation and to create better-informed buyers have encountered problems which have required a high degree of specification in the resulting trade regulation. And so each of the case studies has its own distinctive characteristics or qualities.

I am pleased to acknowledge the critical and helpful comments of Sanford V. Berg, University of Florida; F. Jay Cummings, University of Texas at Dallas; M. Bruce Johnson, University of California at Santa Barbara; Steven R. Holmberg, The American University; J. W. McKie, University of Texas at Austin; D. Stanton Smith, Washington State University; T. S. Ulen, University of Illinois at Urbana-Champaign; Stephen H. Strand, Carleton College; and Robert M. Costrell, University of Massachusetts at Amherst, each of whom reviewed and criticized one or more chapters. Each suffered the disadvantage of viewing only separate parts of the manuscript. Any deficiencies are, of course, the sole responsibility of the author. In addition, I would like to express my appreciation for the efforts of editor Joan Foley and copyeditor Jeannine Ciliotta of Prentice-Hall.

The author is also indebted to his wife, Agnes, and to Jennie Cashman and Doris Holden, all of whom provided secretarial assistance and contributed to the editing of the manuscript.

Marshall C. Howard
Amherst, Massachusetts

ANTITRUST
AND
TRADE
REGULATION

1 — Competition: A Policy Goal

Basic public policy toward business in the American economy has been to promote and maintain competition as the most desirable means of allocating resources. Antitrust laws condemn unreasonable restraints on competition, monopolizing and attempting to monopolize, and unfair methods of competition. A sizable number of trade regulations have as their basic purpose the protection of consumers and competitors against certain excesses of the competitive process.

The idea that the competitive process has significant advantages is a thoroughly accepted one: The Sherman Antitrust Act, for example, was passed by Congress in 1890 without hesitation as to the appropriateness of its objectives. Before that, the common law had generally failed to support instances of monopoly that came before courts of equity. As Justice Black of the Supreme Court wrote in an antitrust decision:

> [The Sherman Act] rests on the premise that the unrestrained interaction of competitive forces will yield the best allocation of our economic resources, the lowest prices, the highest quality and the greatest material progress, while at the same time providing an environment conducive to the preservation of our democratic political and social institutions.[1]

Antitrust and trade regulation do not generally represent government "intervention" in the conventional sense. Rather, they represent government intervention only to remove obstacles to the free flow of commerce

[1]*Northern Pacific Railway Co.* v. *U.S.*, 356 U.S. 1, 4–5 (1958).

and to facilitate the dissemination of product information to consumers. The Supreme Court has called the Sherman Act "the Magna Carta of free enterprise."[2] There need be no actual government intervention unless there have been undue restraints on competition or excessive obstacles to the exercise of reasonable judgment by consumers in their purchasing. Rather than limiting the free enterprise system itself, this kind of social control is designed to maximize the aggregate freedoms of those in the marketplace. Antitrust and trade regulation are supposed to facilitate business entry, expansion, or exit, with efficiency as the basic guide, and to assist in sound decision-making by consumers.

The basic objective of antitrust and trade regulation, therefore, is to protect the marketplace from abuses that may adversely affect the functioning of the competitive process. Firms that should be competing may combine in collusive agreements to restrain competition among themselves. Some firms may work themselves into or find themselves in a strategic position within a particular market structure that enables them to behave as a monopolist or to apply restrictive coercive pressures against other firms in the market. The misrepresentation of goods and services to buyers can also result in abuse of the competitive system by sellers. The goal of antitrust and trade regulation is to identify and remove any serious imperfections in the competitive process so that the system will work more effectively.

THE RATIONALE FOR COMPETITION

Competition is understood in general terms to be a desirable means of allocating resources. It is the heart of a free enterprise economy. Profits will reward the producers who are most efficient in serving consumers. Losses and bankruptcy will face those who cannot operate in an efficient manner. The general result of the competitive process is the lowest possible prices for goods and services plus choices for consumers among a range of types and qualities of goods and services.

Economists have developed a rigorous model that demonstrates the advantages of competition: that of perfect competition. This model actually does not fit more than a handful of real world markets. It cannot be used directly to determine or fashion antitrust or trade regulation policy. We cannot force actual markets into its mold. It can, however, be the source from which we can derive certain principles of competition. These principles, in turn, used carefully, can be helpful in fashioning public policy.

Equally useful is the economic model of pure monopoly. Being the opposite of perfect competition, it can also be helpful in deriving principles

---

[2]*U.S.* v. *Topco Associates, Inc.*, 405 U.S. 596, 610 (1972).

that are supportive of those learned from the model of perfect competition. Pure monopoly, again except for a very few instances, is hard to find in the real world. Where it is found, it is usually a case of competitors combining together in some fashion to control the market for and fix the price of some valued product for which there are no close substitutes.

These economic models are of markets, not of industries. There is a basic difference between the definition of a market and the definition of an industry, although in a particular instance they may be the same. A *market* is formed by a common group of sellers who are selling in competition for the business of a common group of buyers. An *industry* is formed by all the sellers who produce a given product. So an industry can be larger than a market. Where the cost of transport of a product is high, several separate markets can develop for the same product. We might, for example, speak of the American cement industry as being composed of all the cement manufacturers in the United States. Yet there are separate cement markets, each within its own particular geographic area.

Perfect Competition   The structure of a perfectly competitive market has several special characteristics: (1) a large number of sellers and buyers, (2) a homogeneous product, (3) no barriers to entry, and (4) full market knowledge by all actual or potential buyers and sellers.

How large a number of sellers and buyers must there be? Enough so that any one firm feels it is so insignificant with respect to the total market that its sales or purchases have no impact on total supply or demand, and therefore on price. All accept the going market price as one determined by impersonal market forces. In sum, there are enough sellers and buyers so that no one of them can manipulate or control the market price. This clear lack of market power by any one seller or buyer is often viewed as being a virtue in itself.

The fact that the market product is homogenous reinforces the concept that no one seller can control this market in any way. The product of each seller is a perfect substitute for the product of any of the other sellers. If any seller tried to charge more than the going market price, its customers would all leave it and turn to another seller. The fact that all in the market have full knowledge of that market would enable customers to obtain the product at the going price from another seller.

The situation faced by the individual firm under the market conditions of perfect competition is depicted in Figure 1.1. A firm's price, or average revenue (AR), appears as a horizontal straight line, simply because the firm's view is that as many units of output can be sold at the going price as it wants to. This means that the firm's marginal revenue (MR) coincides with this demand, since the added revenue from the last unit sold is the same as the added revenue from the sale of any previous units sold. Thus, $AR = MR$.

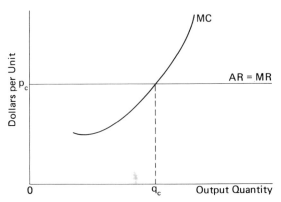

Figure 1.1 Output of the Perfectly Competitive Firm

At what level of output will the firm now produce, given that it can sell as much as it wants to at the going competitive market price, p_c? It is always assumed under the free market system that a firm will seek to maximize profits. It can accomplish this by producing at that level of output where its marginal revenue (MR) is equal to its marginal cost (MC). In perfect competition, since AR, or price, equals MR for the firm, the firm will supply that quantity of output where price = MC. In Figure 1.1 it will produce and sell quantity q_c. If the going market price were higher, it would produce and sell a higher quantity. Thus, the rising portion of the firm's MC curve is the *firm's* supply curve.[3] The added costs represented by the MC curve are the costs, considering any possible alternative opportunities of using those resources elsewhere, the firm will be willing to incur to produce added units of output.

The *market* supply curve S, as in Figure 1.2, is found by adding up the quantities supplied by all the separate firms in the market at each different possible price as determined by those firms' MC curves. In short, the market supply curve is the sum of all the individual firms' upward-sloping MC curves taken together. From the point of view of the economy as a whole, the costs incurred in any particular market represent the value of the resources used in that market rather than elsewhere in the economy. That is, the supply curve of the market represents the marginal cost to society of diverting resources to the market in question.[4]

The market demand curve D in Figure 1.2 represents the different prices consumers are willing to pay for different possible quantities. It

---

[3]Strictly speaking, the firm's supply curve is that portion of the MC curve which rises above the average variable cost curve. If the market price were not covering the firm's average variable costs, it would not produce at all.

[4]We omit the problem of externalities wherein some resource costs to society, such as air or water pollution, are ignored by the individual firms in their output decisions.

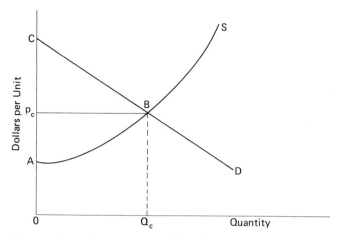

Figure 1.2 Consumer and Producer Surplus

almost invariably slopes downward to the right, indicating that consumers will purchase a larger quantity only at lower prices. Or, put another way, that the value of additional units of the product to society diminishes as there are more of them. Market price is determined by market demand and market supply together, and the market equilibrium price will be established where the quantity willingly supplied is equal to the quantity willingly demanded. In Figure 1.2 this competitive price is price p_c, and the quantity that will clear the market is quantity Q_c.

For every additional unit of output produced from zero up to quantity Q_c, it will be noted that the amount consumers will be willing to pay is greater than the marginal cost of the resources diverted from elsewhere used to produce it. This total surplus or gain to society is shown by the area ABC. It is shared by both consumers and producers. This is the distributional impact of perfect competition. Area p_cBC above market price is known as *consumer surplus;* consumers paid price p_c but were willing to pay higher prices for the units of demand between points C and B on the demand curve. The area p_cBA is known as *producer surplus;* producers received price p_c but were willing to supply those units on the supply curve between points A and B at lower prices. A key thing to note is that the total of these surpluses, area ABC, is maximized where price is the competitive price p_c and output is the competitive quantity Q_c. Any output less than Q_c would leave opportunities to create more surplus unexploited, and any output greater than Q_c would detract from this surplus, as supply costs would be greater than demand values. When the sum of consumer and producer surpluses is maximized, *allocative efficiency* is achieved.

Figure 1.3 shows the typical, or representative, firm's average total cost curve (ATC) and shows it as being tangent to the firm's AR curve. This

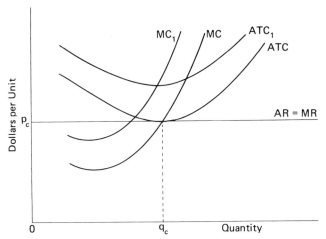

Figure 1.3 Long-Run Competitive Market Equilibrium:
The Firm

represents a long-run equilibrium condition. By that we mean that all
economic forces at work have completed their equilibrating functions, and
there are no economic forces at work to move away from this position. The
typical or "representative" firm in the industry is now using the most
efficient means of production and is earning only a "normal" profit, which
is included in the firm's *ATC* as a necessary cost of doing business. The
element of normal profit represents that minimum return on investment a
firm must earn if it is to continue to remain in the industry over the long
run. It represents a return the firm must earn if it is to be willing to replace
its fixed plant and equipment when it wears out and stay in the business.
When only normal profits are being earned, there is no incentive for firms
to leave or to enter the market (including expansion of productive capacity
by a firm already in the market). The resources being put to use here are
yielding a return equally as good as they could be earning elsewhere—no
more, no less.

The equilibrating forces in the perfectly competitive market operate
because there are no barriers to entry and there is full knowledge of all
profit opportunities. If demand were to increase, causing price to increase,
then new productive capacity would be induced to enter the industry
because there would now be *economic* profits (those above normal profits).
The free flow of resources to wherever economic profits show themselves
forces those profits back to a normal level. Economic profits are being
earned only in the period of transition before new entry can be completed.
The function of economic profits is simply to direct new resources to the
market in the economy where they are being earned. Once the new resources are in place, firms in that market will no longer earn any economic
profits; the new supply will have forced price back down.

6

No firm can be productively inefficient and survive under conditions of perfect competition. Managers are compelled by competition to use a minimum amount of resources, the least-cost combination, to achieve a given output. A firm whose average total cost appears in Figure 1.3 as ATC_1, for example, simply cannot survive. Competition will eventually drive that inefficient firm out of business. Competition is thus said to result in *productive efficiency*. It can also be seen in Figure 1.3 that, where $MC = MR$, it is also true that $AR = ATC$, and this all occurs at the minimum point of the ATC curve. It is part of the productive efficiency demanded by perfect competition that in long-run equilibrium firms produce where their average unit costs of production are at their lowest point.

Our analysis of the operation of the perfectly competitive model has illustrated the benefits that have caused it to endure for so many years. Remember, however, that the model cannot be applied directly to the real world. In fact, there are certain barriers to entry; market knowledge is not perfect; and the number of sellers or buyers in most markets is not likely to be large enough to meet the requirements of the model. Then too, it is a static model. It does not allow for product differentiation or a flow of new products. In short, it is not a dynamic market model. Most markets usually demonstrate continual change in products produced, resources used, and technology. In spite of these weaknesses, we should note the advantages of having minimum control over the market by sellers and buyers and the desirability of enjoying flexibility in the movement of resources as they move from a less to a more preferred position in the economy.

Pure Monopoly   The advantages we saw for competition can be viewed in reverse by analyzing the disadvantages associated with the model of pure monopoly. The pure monopolist, by definition, is the only firm in its market. Its product is unique to it. There are no close substitutes. Certain barriers to entry enable it to enjoy this position. Since it is the only firm in the market, the demand of the monopolistic firm is the demand of its market. Its demand curve (AR) therefore slopes downward to the right, in contrast with the horizontal demand curve of the firm in the perfectly competitive market. Its MR curve also differs from its AR curve; it declines more sharply since price must be reduced on all units sold in order to sell an additional unit.

We can now compare the favorable factors emanating from our analysis of the perfectly competitive market with the counterpart position of the pure monopolist. First, the firm does have some market power. It is not faced with a "going" market price; its sloping demand curve provides it with a selection of prices to choose from. It does have some control over the price it charges.

Second, the monopolist will not produce at a level of output where its marginal cost is equal to price. In order to maximize profits it will, of course, produce where $MC = MR$. But its MR is not its price. The level of production that will maximize its profits is one which represents a level of output less than and a price higher than those under competitive conditions. Price will be greater than *MC*. In Figure 1.4, the monopolistic level of output q_m is less than the competitive level of output q_c, and the monopoly price p_m is higher than the competitive price p_c. The monopolist has restricted output below the level that maximizes society's surplus. Instead of having a surplus represented by the area *ABC*, society has only the surplus represented by the area *ADEC*. There is a "deadweight loss" represented by the area *DBE;* this part of the surplus is simply lost to society. Resources have been diverted away from this market, with a resulting *allocative inefficiency.*

There are also *distributive* implications to this monopolistic restriction of output and charging of a higher price: Not only has the total surplus been reduced, but part of the remaining surplus, that represented by the area $p_c FEp_m$, has been transferred from consumer surplus to producer surplus. This too has been considered a disadvantage of the application of monopoly power.

Third, in a monopolistic market, barriers to entry prevent the flow of resources which, under competitive conditions, would keep profits down to a normal level. Economic profits can persist over long periods of time because barriers to entry prevent the emergence of new competitive productive capacity. In Figure 1.5, demand (*AR*) can continue to remain above the monopolist's average total cost (*ATC*). Over the long run, however, the monopolistic firm may begin to suffer losses if it does not face up to chang-

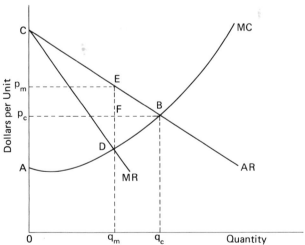

Figure 1.4   Monopoly Pricing, Welfare Loss, and Distribution Effect

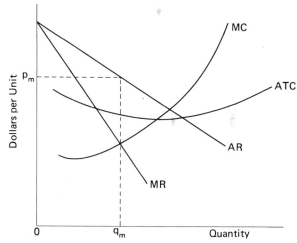

Figure 1.5   Monopoly Pricing and Profit

ing demands for its product or the development of other products that may begin to compete with its product.

Fourth, the monopolistic firm will not be forced to keep the overall level of its average costs down through the utmost in productive effort. To be sure, the greater its efficiency, the greater its profits. But it may trade off greater profits through greater efforts at efficiency for a slower, less demanding way of life. In short, it may suffer from *productive inefficiency*. In Figure 1.5, the level of the *ATC* curve might well be lower than it is shown.

Finally, the monopolistic firm may or may not produce at that level of output where its average total costs (*ATC*) are at a minimum, depending upon the strength (position) of the firm's demand. The point of production as determined by the maximization of profit where *MC* = *MR* may be on the declining or rising portion of its *ATC* curve. If it is producing on the declining portion of its *ATC* curve, as shown in Figure 1.5, it has not fully utilized the economies of scale that exist. If demand is strong enough, it could be producing on the rising portion of its *ATC* curve. In that case, the monopolist has more business than it can efficiently handle.

THE COMPLEXITY OF MARKETS AND COMPETITION

The models of perfect competition and pure monopoly can demonstrate the advantages to society of competition as a means of allocating resources. But they seldom exist in the real economy, in which are found various mixtures of the two. The types of markets for which economists have developed separate models are those of *monopolistic competition* and *oligopoly*.

In monopolistic competition, although there are a large number of firms, they have been able to create some slope to their demand curve and thus have been able to have a choice of prices to some minor degree through advertising, some product differentiation, and the use of brand names or trademarks. They do not have to accept a going market price. Yet because there is freedom of entry, they must be efficient to survive. They cannot earn monopoly profits to any significant degree.

In an oligopolistic market, there are only a few firms. They know exactly who their competitors are. They do not take market actions until they have reflected thoroughly on how competitors will react to those actions. Prices will be more stable or rigid than perfectly competitive prices. These competitors may be tempted to fix price collusively, or they may have tacit understandings as to what price behavior is to their mutual advantage. On the other hand, price wars can break out among them. Or, barring open price wars, there may be secret price-cutting. Then too they may compete actively in introducing new products and new processes. The market behavior of such competitors is not easily predictable.

Other markets may vary according to the number of sellers, the degree of concentration of market shares in the hands of the top few sellers, the degree of product differentiation, and the height of barriers to entry. Barriers to entry may vary in kind from market to market. The economies of large-scale operations may serve as a deterrent to entry. One barrier to entry into a particular market may be inability to obtain the necessary resources at a competitive cost. Patent rights or the technical knowhow required may be lacking. Predatory behavior, or threatened predatory behavior, on the part of firms already in a market can serve to delay or prevent the entry of others. Product differentiation and advertising may be perceived as a costly barrier. Yet in spite of these barriers, no real monopoly may exist since relatively close substitute products may abound.

Various versions of models of "workable" or "effective" competition have been developed to try to present some general principles that can serve as a guide to public policy application. For example, the number of sellers and buyers should be large enough to provide a reasonable number of alternative sources of supply to buyers and outlets for sales to sellers. Distinction should be made between natural barriers to entry and artificial barriers. The degree of substitutability of other products should be carefully considered before a firm can be said to be enjoying a monopoly. And a distinction should be made between the market knowledge generally held and that which is readily available if sought out. These principles can all be helpful, but there is considerable difference of opinion as to their application.

Take just one issue, product differentiation and advertising. One school of thought says this can be an artificial barrier to entry. If a firm is very successful in its advertising campaign or product differentiation, it can create consumer loyalties that are hard to break. The information function of advertising may be superseded by an effective program of buyer persuasion. Well-established firms may thus have an advantage over potential entrants and can often obtain a price which yields a higher profit than that of a new entrant even if unit total costs are higher. A newcomer to the market may find that the necessary advertising and promotion costs will be a financial drain, and there is great risk as to the successfulness of the promotion program.

This position was the one taken by the Federal Trade Commission (FTC) in its 1972 complaint against the four largest firms in the ready-to-eat cereal industry.[5] It alleged that the four companies had for at least 30 years established and maintained a highly concentrated noncompetitive market structure by erecting high barriers to entry through proliferating brands, differentiating similar products, and promoting the trademarked brands through intensive advertising.

A second school of thought is represented by those who hold that advertising is a means, not a barrier, to entry; a means of competing, not a method of monopolizing. How can a firm enter a market with a product unless it informs the public of the existence of the product? Advertising is a means of disseminating information, so as many buyers as possible can know about all the alternative possible purchases. The argument proceeds by saying that it is competitors who advertise, not monopolists. Real monopolists do not have to advertise because they are the only real source of a certain type of product. Further, goes the argument, the greater the amount of advertising, the greater the competition. And, even further, if advertising is successful, it means larger sales, and larger sales mean that overhead administrative costs and some distribution costs can be spread over more units of product, permitting the product to be sold at a lower price.[6]

The balance between these two positions has to be found in the nature and effect of the advertising. Is it truly informative, with the purchaser making a rational choice to satisfy his or her own desires better? Or is the advertising heavily "persuasive" (as well as informative) and perhaps even deceptive, with a resulting anticompetitive effect? Finally, if anticom-

---

[5]*In re Kellogg Co. et al.*, Docket No. 8883 (1972). The four largest firms held the following market percentages in 1970: Kellogg, 45 percent; General Mills, 21 percent; General Foods, 16 percent; Quaker Oats, 9 percent. The last firm was later dropped as a defendant.

[6]A principal proponent of this position has been Professor Yale Brozen of the Graduate School of Business of the University of Chicago. See the gist of his speech before the Commonwealth Club in San Francisco, "Advertising, the Consumer and Inflation," which was printed under Editorial Commentary, "No Scarlet Letters: Advertising Has Come under Dangerous and Unfair Attack," in *Barron's*, February 28, 1972. See also his "Entry Barriers: Advertising and Product Differentiation," in Harvey J. Goldschmid, H. Michael Mann, and J. Fred Weston, eds., *Industrial Concentration: The New Learning* (Boston: Little, Brown, 1974), pp. 115–37.

petitive effects are present, can they be eliminated without overly damaging the information effects?[7]

This brief analysis of just one issue shows that the competition of the marketplace is a complex institution. It is not a phenomenon that can be simply defined and described. It occurs with varying degrees of intensity and can appear in different forms. In most markets, elements of competition are mixed with elements of monopoly. As a result, different persons or different groups of persons may view a given market situation differently. Some may emphasize the competitive elements; others may emphasize the monopolistic elements. In any case, most markets unquestionably have unique features that have to be studied in depth before antitrust laws or trade regulations can be properly applied to them.

MAINTAINING EFFECTIVE COMPETITION:
ALTERNATIVE APPROACHES

Three possible basic approaches exist toward maintaining competition to ensure that it is effective. One is the structural approach; another is the conduct approach; a third is the performance approach. Any one of these approaches could be used for antitrust policy. But for unfair or deceptive acts of practices, the conduct approach has no real alternative. Let us look at each approach in some detail.

The Structural Approach   The structural approach makes sure that the structure of an industry is one from which effective competition will supposedly and inherently flow. As long as the structure is appropriate, there is little need for further surveillance. Certain structural standards can be established with respect to the minimum number of sellers and the concentration ratio of those sellers, such as the market share held by the four largest firms. If these standards are not being met, then government intervention would be automatically triggered to accomplish the necessary structural change.

The Concentrated Industries Act recommended by the White House Task Force on Antitrust Policy (Neal Report) in 1968 took the structural approach. It would have required the dissolution of oligopolistic industries so that no one firm in an industry would have a share of the market exceeding 12 percent. It defined such an industry as one in which four or fewer firms had an aggregate market share of 70 percent. Industrial reorganization acts before Congress in the 1970s would have restructured any

[7]William S. Comanor and Thomas A. Wilson, "Advertising and Competition: A Survey," *Journal of Economic Literature*, 22, no. 2 (June 1979), 472.

oligopolistic market where the four or fewer largest firms accounted for 50 percent or more of sales.

Forced changes in market structure have been accomplished through court decrees in antitrust cases where relatively large firms have been found to have abused the power of their size. Structural changes in an industry can also be brought about in this *ad hoc* manner.

The chief drawbacks to such a structural approach are two. First, there is a fear that economies of scale, with their resulting efficiencies, might be destroyed or their creation prevented. Some provision would have to be made for proving such efficiencies if they were believed to exist and allowing for their continuance if they were found to exist. Second, a large number of dissolution decrees reducing the size of some firms might have a disruptive impact on economic life and the growth of the economy.

The Conduct Approach   The second basic approach to maintaining effective competition is to establish rules of the game that zero in on the competitors' conduct. Wherever the market conduct of a firm or firms is having an adverse impact on the freedom of market action of other firms, whether actual or potential, or where other firms or consumers themselves are being adversely affected by misrepresentations or deceptive practices, the government can intervene to stop such conduct.

The conduct approach does not focus on size as such. Large firms that enjoy certain economies because of their size will not be disrupted by government intervention unless their market conduct is found to be objectionable. A large firm need not deliberately refrain from attempting to increase its market share—which, up to a point, is a form of competition itself. At the same time, a relatively large firm must recognize that its conduct is constantly under the eye of the antitrust authorities simply because of its size and the fear that a large firm can do more damage to a competitor than a small one if it attempts to skirt the bounds of legitimate competition. It should also be noted that the conduct of a firm or firms in the marketplace can affect the structure of a market. Exclusionary tactics, for example, can reduce the number of sellers.

Certain disadvantages are inherent in the conduct approach. First, it is *ad hoc*. Complaints are issued against a firm or group of firms on case-by-case basis involving the particular facts of the particular alleged offense. Further, although a complaint may be issued and litigated, the firms may be demonstrated as having not been guilty of the charge. The litigation in such a case represents a waste of resources.

Where a firm is found to have violated the rules of accepted competitive behavior, a legal precedent is being established or reinforced. Other firms can learn from this precedent that they too may be violating the rules. They may feel, however, that the particular facts of the previously litigated case vary from the facts of their own situation. As a result, litigation involving a particular form of conduct may become voluminous as different firms in different markets are charged with the same offense. This difficulty can be reduced by the creation, through the establishment of legal precedent, of *per se* rules—that is, rules that define clear-cut illegal forms of market conduct. And in the instance of direct consumer protection, trade regulation rules with the full force and effect of law have been issued to make clear just what market conduct is to be demanded of sellers.

In the legal world of antitrust enforcement, the conduct approach has predominated. The structural approach has been relied upon in a lesser number of cases. The conduct approach is the only real approach possible in the case of deceptive acts and practices.

The Performance Approach Policy-makers could examine market performance itself to decide whether or not government intervention is needed. Market performance is derived from market structure and the conduct that occurs within a market structure. A market performance test would examine whether there is production efficiency, prices flexible enough to reflect changing demand and supply conditions, prices and profits and selling costs which are not excessive, and a steady flow of improved processes and products.

The basic problem is this: How can we know what the desired best possible performance could be? Under an idealistic model such as that of perfect competition, we can know what the ultimate outcome of that structure and the conduct within that structure will be. But under imperfect forms of competition and their less than perfect structures, we cannot accurately predict either conduct or performance. All we can hope for is a best possible outcome, not a perfect outcome. In short, the ultimate state of desired performance itself cannot be perfectly clear. Even when applying a structural or conduct approach, the basic rule of thumb has to be that we will intervene only where by doing so we can see an improvement—a better result than there would have otherwise been.

The problem becomes clearer when we note the difficulty in trying to answer the subquestions that would have to be asked if we were to try to use a market performance test. How can we know when the price changes taking place are flexible enough? When are the firms in the industry doing a good enough job in keeping costs down? When are price/cost margins and profits reasonable? When are selling costs excessive? What actually constitutes the maximum possible flow of products and improvements in technology? Much subjective judgment would have to be employed in any attempt to answer these questions.

It is even possible that a shrewd monopolist, effectively entrenched in the market behind barriers to entry and able to exclude from the marketplace through various coercive tactics any significant competitors, could create the appearance of, or actually provide, successful market performance. The cost of permitting such a monopolist to remain is to permit the loss of a principle supposed to be inherent in the free enterprise system: freedom of entry and freedom of action within the marketplace.

IDENTIFYING THE RELEVANT MARKET

Where possible restrictions on competition are suspected, the first task is to determine who the competitors actually are. In antitrust cases, this is called defining the *relevant market*. Such a market will include all those sellers who are selling competing products to a common group of buyers. It is necessary to identify these competing sellers so that we can know just how many there are and just how concentrated the market in which they sell is. This is of special importance in monopoly cases, where we wish to know the percentage of the market accounted for by the largest firm or firms, and in merger cases, where we may wish to keep track of changes in the *concentration ratio*—the percentage of the market accounted for by, say, the largest four or eight firms. Antitrust litigation must first settle this issue before it can proceed further.

In identifying the sellers in a relevant market, one has to consider two basic dimensions of the market. One is the geographic territory in which the sellers operate, which is known as the "relevant geographic market." The second is the product being sold by these sellers to the common group of buyers. This is known as the "relevant product market" or, in purely legal terminology, the relevant "line of commerce." The competing sellers are those who are trying to sell a product in competition for the favor of the buyers of that product in a particular geographic area.

Geographic Market   The relevant geographic market may well be smaller or larger than the nation as a whole. Bureau of the Census industry data that tell us how many sellers there are of a given classification of products in the nation as a whole can thus be irrelevant in identifying competitors. First, the costs of shipping a product relative to the value of the product may cause a firm to confine its sales effort to only one region of the country, perhaps even to only a relatively small locality. Ordinarily, it does not pay to transport a given type of coal from West Virginia to California in competition with coal from Utah. Almost all cement is sold and used near the site of production since it is a heavy, bulky, relatively low value per unit of weight product which is ordinarily not practical to ship very far unless it can be done by water. A Federal Trade Commission investigation thus found that, out of the 50 largest metropolitan markets in the nation, 19 had five or fewer cement companies soliciting sales and an additional 19 had between five and ten cement suppliers.[8] Shoes, on the

---

[8]Federal Trade Commission, "Enforcement Policy with Respect to Vertical Mergers in the Cement Industry," 1967, mimeo, p. 4.

other hand, being a relatively high-value, lightweight product, can be sold in competition nationwide even though production may be concentrated in certain geographic areas. Second, the perishability of a product can limit the geographic dimension of a market. The products of an ordinary bakery in Portland, Maine, are not sold in competition with similar bakery products made in Portland, Oregon.

It should be noted that the competitive market territory is delineated by the area in which the firms' sales efforts take place or could economically take place; it is not determined by the location of the producing plant. In the *Bethlehem-Youngstown Sheet and Tube* merger case, the firms had argued that Youngstown Sheet and Tube plants were located quite centrally in the midcontinent area, whereas Bethlehem Steel's plants were located both west and east of these plants, not in the same location. Analysis showed, however, that steel sales were being made by both firms in areas that overlapped the plant locations.[9]

Product Market   The relevant product market can be more difficult to determine than the geographic market. The basic question here is exactly what products are actually in competition with one another. According to the Supreme Court in its *Brown Shoe* decision: "The outer boundaries of a product market are determined by the reasonable interchangeability of use or the cross-elasticity of demand between the product itself and substitutes for it."[10] In this merger case, the Supreme Court held that the relevant product market was not for shoes, but rather that there were, in effect, three separate products: men's shoes, women's shoes, and children's shoes. ". . . each has characteristics peculiar to itself rendering it generally non-competitive with the others."[11] The defense wanted the product to be narrowed even further, to infants' and babies' shoes, misses' and children's shoes, youths' and boys' shoes, and to differentiate between sex and age groups and low-priced and medium-priced shoes.

The Supreme Court in the *Brown Shoe* decision pointed to some seven different situations that might justify the legitimate existence of submarkets for antitrust measurement purposes. First, an industry or the public might recognize a particular submarket as a separate economic entity. Second, a product might have peculiar characteristics and uses. Third, the product might require unique production facilities. Fourth, the product might have distinct customers. Fifth, the product might have distinct

---

[9]*U.S.* v. *Bethlehem Steel Corp.*, 168 F. Supp. 576, 597–603 (1958).

[10]*Brown Shoe Co.* v. *U.S.*, 370 U.S. 294, 325 (1962). Cross-elasticity of demand describes the responsiveness in terms of the degree of change in the quantity demanded of one product given a change in price of another product. To say that there is a lack of significant cross-elasticity of demand is to say that the quantity demanded of one product is not appreciably changed by a change in the price of the other product.

[11]Ibid., p. 326.

prices. Sixth, the sensitivity of related products to price changes might be very small. Seventh, the submarket might involve specialized vendors.[12]

The outcome of an antitrust suit can sometimes hinge almost entirely on how the relevant market is defined. In the 1945 monopoly decision against Alcoa, the Court included only virgin aluminum ingot, which gave Alcoa a 90 percent share of the market.[13] If aluminum scrap had been included, Alcoa's market share would have been 64 percent. And if the ingot delivered by Alcoa to its own fabricating facilities had been excluded, Alcoa's share would have been 33 percent. In the 1956 cellophane monopoly case against Du Pont, the government argued that this firm, together with a licensee, had 100 percent of the market. The court, however, accepted the relevant product as being "flexible packaging material." This definition gave Du Pont only 18 percent of the market, and the government lost its case.[14] In 1964 the Supreme Court condemned a merger between the nation's second largest can producer with the nation's third largest glass container producer.[15] The defense had argued that cans and bottles represented two separate industries and that therefore the merger could not be increasing either firm's market share. The court held, however, that cans and bottles are directly competitive with each other. In a 1962 court merger decision involving Reynolds Metals Company, decorative florist foil (foil that is embossed and colored) was found to be a unique product not in competition with other aluminum foils because the buyers of this product were a distinct group of customers.[16] The market being defined by the Court so narrowly contributed to Reynolds Metals losing the decision.

DOG FOOD: MEASURING A PRODUCT MARKET—
A CASE STUDY

Defining a relevant product market has to be accomplished within the context of the structure and product characteristics of each particular industry. Each case can have its own separate peculiarities. For example, how many different kinds of dog food are there, and which of them are competing with one another?

In 1976 the FTC issued an antimerger order against Liggett and Myers (L&M) requiring that L&M divest itself of a dog food manufacturer, Ready Foods, which it had acquired in 1969.[17] Since a subsidiary of L&M (L&M–

[12]Ibid., p. 325.

[13]*U.S.* v. *Aluminum Company of America*, 148 F. 2d 416 (1945).

[14]*U.S.* v. *E. I. Du Pont de Nemours & Co.*, 351 U.S. 377 (1956).

[15]*U.S.* v. *Continental Can Co.*, 378 U.S. 441 (1964).

[16]*Reynolds Metals Co.* v. *FTC*, 309 F. 2d 223 (1962).

[17]*In the Matter of Liggett & Meyers Incorporated*, 87 F.T.C. 1145 (1976). The facts and quotations of this case study are taken from this Federal Trade Commission opinion.

Allen) was already selling several million dollars worth of dog food annually (Alpo label), the FTC held that the acquisition might substantially lessen competition or tend to create a monopoly in the production, distribution, and sale of dog food in the United States. There was no disagreement that the relevant geographic market was the entire nation. The delineation of the relevant product market, however, was subject to dispute.

Dog food has been categorized as being canned, dry, or semi-moist. It has also been argued that it should be further categorized as premium, regular, and economy. Is the competition among all these different forms of dog food? Or is the competition limited to certain submarkets represented by certain types of dog food?

Sales of L&M–Allen represented approximately 56 percent of all premium canned dog food sales, 22 percent of all canned sales combined, and 11 percent of all dog food sales combined. The acquired firm, Ready Foods, marketed no premium canned dog food itself, but did manufacture this type of dog food for L&M–Allen and for Safeway. Ready Foods also packed every major type of dog food for various chain store and dog food companies. Although Ready Foods was in the process of preparing to sell premium canned products under its own label, it was primarily a marketer of economy dog foods. It accounted for roughly 32 percent of economy canned sales, 4 percent of all canned sales, 4 percent of dry dog food, and an infinitesimal amount of semi-moist. Its market share of total dog food sales was 4.41 percent.

L&M argued that there were two separate product markets, premium and economy dog foods. Since L&M–Allen was primarily a marketer of premium and Ready Foods primarily a marketer of economy dog foods, their merger would not substantially lessen competition.

The FTC took the position that the relevant product market was all dog foods together. Both economy and premium, as well as dog foods of other categories, were interchangeable for the same use, "keeping a dog fed." All the two firms' products met the National Research Council's nutritional standards for a dog's main meal. The Commission further noted that, although Ready Foods did not market premium dog food, it did manufacture substantial quantities of the premium product for L&M–Allen. This production capability of Ready Foods to produce an economy or a premium product provided a flexibility of supply which was seen by the Commission to be sufficient cause by itself to assume that both firms were within the same line of commerce.

The FTC saw considerable evidence of competition between the premium and economy dog foods. The gap between the prices of the cheaper and the more expensive dog foods, although large, had been narrowing. The recession of 1974–75 had seen substantial growth in the sales of cheap dry dog food, whereas sales of the more expensive canned products had stagnated. The dog food market seemed to be in a state of flux, with new customers entering the market who had not yet established any brand loyalties. There had been a "slight trending together" in product characteristics because the premium and economy products seemed to be becoming a bit more alike as all-meat premium products became diluted to some degree with cereal and vegetable matter under the pressure of rising meat prices.

References had been made in this trade to an all dog food market and an all canned dog food market, and marketing successes were being measured against sales in these markets. L&M–Allen had promoted itself to retailers in the competition for shelf space against other dog food marketers, including Ready Foods, which were selling various types of dog food, including dry and semi-moist.

Firms in the industry seemed to have the ability to manufacture and market several kinds of dog foods, and often did so. The same management, research, and sales personnel resources were used to accomplish the production and selling of different types of dog food. A compelling factor in considering all dog foods together as being the relevant product market was that firms producing the different kinds of dog food had at one time or another given evidence in their advertisements that they viewed each other as being competitors. Advertisements directed to the consumer criticized the characteristics and ingredients of other types of dog food. Premium canned Alpo was touted over "cheap" canned, dry, and "burger-type" dog foods: "If you add a cheap canned dog food to a dry, you may be adding cereal to cereal." And "All those burgers on top of his dry would make a very heavy dog." L&M–Allen and Ready Foods had even challenged each other in advertising by name.

L&M had attempted to justify the existence of two separate submarkets, premium and economy products, through two arguments. First, L&M held that there was a lack of significant cross-elasticity of demand. The Commission's response to this argument was that L&M's short-run elasticity data were not developed on an adequate market test basis.[18] Further, short-run (six-week) data were not a measure of the long-run dynamic competition the FTC observed as being present. The FTC also

[18]"The data were derived from a market test in which some 480 families were asked to order their dog food needs during a six-week period from test catalogues.... Prices listed in the catalogues varied by 10 percent from the average prices measured in certain, but not all, stores in the test families' area.... While 10 percent is not an insignificant variation, in the context of dog food prices it represents a maximum variation of three or four cents from the store price for premium food, and one or two cents for economy food." 87 F.T.C. 1145, 1153. The criticisms of the test were that six weeks was too short a time period to measure consumer buying habit changes, especially where the consumer knew that the test was short-lived and the price differences were only a few cents and where there might be some difficulty in retraining the dogs to a new food.

held that cross-elasticity of demand is not governing in a situation where there is complete interchangeability of use, considerable supply-side elasticity, and evidence of direct competitive confrontation.

The second L&M argument against application of an all dog food market was that the *Brown Shoe* decision criteria of acceptable submarkets should be applied to find an appropriate submarket. The Commission's response to this reasoning—and it backed its position by citing a significant number of court decisions—was that you do not have to use a submarket when the broader market can be shown to be the one of economic significance. To be sure, there are price and quality differences among the several dog food products and there may be differences among dog owners and methods of marketing. But even if these differences may give credence to the finding of separate submarkets, these submarkets are nevertheless "associated in one market. In short, dog food is dog food."

SUMMARY

The antitrust and trade regulation laws are designed to promote and maintain competition. Their aim is to protect the marketplace against abuses that may adversely affect the functioning of the competitive process. They are intended to facilitate the flow of commerce and more rational decision-making by consumers.

The economist's model of perfect competition is not one to which real world markets can be readily fitted. But it can be used to demonstrate the advantages inherent in competition, and certain useful principles can be derived from it. These principles can be made clearer by comparing the model of perfect competition with that of pure monopoly. Competition can yield better allocative and productive efficiency.

Attempts have been made to develop market models of competition that are more directly applicable to the real world. Such models may be needed, but there are disagreements concerning their characteristics. In the last analysis, each market has to be examined on its own merits before deciding whether antiturst enforcement is called for.

There are three possible approaches to applying antitrust and trade regulation enforcement: the structural, the conduct, and the performance. Each has its advantages and disadvantages. The conduct approach is the one most frequently used today.

In analyzing any market to determine just how effective the competition within it is, it is first necessary to identify the geographic and product dimensions of that market. A Federal Trade Commission analysis of the market for dog food illustrates all the factors that must be considered in defining the product dimension of a market.

Selected Readings

ADAMS, WALTER, ed., *The Structure of American Industry,* 5th ed. New York: Macmillan, 1977.

BAIN, JOE S., *Barriers to New Competition.* Cambridge, Mass.: Harvard University Press, 1956.

BROZEN, YALE, ed., *The Competitive Economy: Selected Readings.* Morristown, N.J.: General Learning Press, 1975. Parts I and II.

HIRSCHLEIFER, JACK, *Price Theory and Applications,* 2nd ed. Englewood Cliffs, N.J.: Prentice-Hall, 1980.

McGEE, JOHN S., *In Defense of Industrial Concentration.* New York: Praeger, 1971.

SOSNICK, STEPHEN, "A Critique of Concepts of Workable Competition," *Quarterly Journal of Economics,* 72 (August 1958), 380-423.

2 — Antitrust and Trade Regulation Tools and Procedures

The Antitrust Division of the Department of Justice and the Federal Trade Commission (FTC) are the two principal agencies at the federal level that serve as antitrust and trade regulation enforcers. According to the language of the statutes over which these two agencies have jurisdiction, the Antitrust Division's basic function is antitrust (antimonopoly) in nature, whereas the FTC has two functions: antitrust and trade regulation, including direct consumer protection. Because the work of these two agencies clearly overshadows the efforts of the states, most of our discussion will be devoted to their actions.

Other federal agencies may also play a part when there is possible lack of consumer information, misrepresentation, or deceptive advertising. The Food and Drug Administration (FDA) can issue labeling and packaging rules with respect to food, drugs, and cosmetics. Various federal public utility regulatory commissions such as the Interstate Commerce Commission and the Civil Aeronautics Board have sections designed to protect consumers within their areas of jurisdiction. And the U.S. Postal Service can act to prevent use of the mails to defraud.

The federal antitrust and trade regulation arsenal is composed of a few key antitrust and trade regulation statutes, and supported by the rule-making power of the FTC. Antitrust and trade regulation by the states has been spotty, and enforcement has, at least until the late 1970s, generally been weak.

THE BASIC ANTITRUST STATUTES

The basic federal antitrust statutes, with certain exceptions, are quite short and are written in very general and simple language. They are negative in character: They tell business in very general terms what it should *not* do. They do not require a lot of paperwork—which is a major complaint of business against "regulatory interference."

The application of these statutes is on a case-by-case basis; they must be interpreted in the context of each particular situation. Some people have charged that the statutes are so vague they cause business much uncertainty as to whether or not the law is being violated in certain situations. The other side of the coin, however, is that the statutes, because of their nature, can be applied to changing economic circumstances. In their simplicity is breadth and flexibility.

The Sherman Antitrust Act (1890)   This foundation of the antitrust laws was passed as "An Act to protect trade and commerce against unlawful restraints and monopolies." It had two key sections, the basic provisions of which were these:

> *Section 1:*   Every contract, combination in the form of trust or otherwise, or conspiracy, in restraint of trade or commerce among the several States, or with foreign nations, is hereby declared to be illegal.
>
> *Section 2:*   Every person who shall monopolize, or attempt to monopolize, or combine or conspire with any other person or persons, to monopolize any part of the trade or commerce among the several States, or with foreign nations, shall be deemed guilty of a misdemeanor. . . .

The Sherman Antitrust Act was passed by an overwhelming vote.[1] Fears and complaints of growing concentrations of wealth and of the growing use of trusts and combinations in industry, combined with a feeling that the common law and state laws were inadequate to meet any problems that might arise, provided impetus to the passage of this legislation. Under the common law it was up to a party who felt injured by a monopoly to attempt to seek redress by taking a complaint to a court of equity. Not only was this an expensive proposition, but the legal precedents on which judges could rely in their decision-making were not all that clear-cut.[2]

[1]See Hans B. Thorelli, *The Federal Antitrust Policy: Origination of an American Tradition* (Baltimore: The Johns Hopkins Press, 1955), pp. 174–210.

[2]Hans Thorelli has expressed this situation well when he states that "The common law is mainly a body of traditions which have been applied and interpreted by individual judges in

The passage of the Sherman Act was a first clear-cut statement of national public policy toward monopoly. Statutory provisions of the act not only made it the duty of district attorneys and the attorney general of the United States to prevent and restrain violations of this statute, but gave injured persons the right to sue for treble damages. Today, the Antitrust Division of the Department of Justice is the governmental agency that enforces the Sherman Act. But private parties can and frequently do sue other private parties under the act. Indeed, there are many more private suits under the Sherman Act than there are government suits.

Note the uncertainties present in this statute. What is meant by the "every contract" of Section 1? Interpreted at one extreme, any supply contract could be said to be a contract in restraint of trade. If one firm agrees to supply another firm with materials for the next 30 days, then all other firms have been excluded from the possibility of making the sale to that buyer. Obviously, such an interpretation would put a large part of the business community in a bind in terms of violating the Sherman Act. The Supreme Court resolved this predicament when it applied the so-called rule of reason in the *Standard Oil of New Jersey* decision in 1911:[3] "As the contracts or acts embraced in the provision were not expressly defined . . . , it inevitably follows that the provision necessarily called for the exercise of judgment. . . ."[4] Thus, reasonable restraints are legal; unreasonable restraints are illegal. But what is reasonable and what is unreasonable?

Section 2 contains its uncertainties as well. What is to monopolize, or to attempt to monopolize? The Supreme Court took the position in *Standard Oil* that Section 2 of the Sherman Act complemented Section 1. The first section was to forbid the means of monopolizing trade. The second section was "to make the prohibitions of the act all the more complete and perfect by embracing all attempts to reach the end prohibited by the 1st section. . . ."[5] The rule of reason, therefore, was to apply to Section 2 as well as to Section 1.

Applying the rule of reason to differing instances of market behavior (or even market structure) leaves plenty of room for argument and debate. The complainant and the defendant may view the same situation in the different lights of their own logic and predispositions. The judge's views can, of course, be vital to the outcome of a particular case. As put by Richard A. Posner:

---

individual cases and are more or less continuously reapplied and reinterpreted in similar or seemingly singular situations by judges constantly under the influence, or sometimes pressure, of current economic and political opinions." Ibid., p. 51.

[3] *Standard Oil Co. of New Jersey* v. *U.S.*, 221 U.S. 1 (1911).

[4] Ibid., p. 60.

[5] Ibid., p. 61.

Not being trained to umpire the debates of the economics profession, judges invariably decide in favor of the school of
thought that coincides with their own preconceptions. More-
over, whatever the state of professional economic thinking, it
must be remembered that lawyers and judges are inveterate
amateur economists who display little reluctance to substitute
their own economic reasoning and evidence for that of the professionals.[6]

Only where legal precedent has become so clear through previous litigation can certain practices be clearly understood to violate the Sherman Act.
Such practices become *per se* violations; they are illegal in and of themselves, and no evidence as to economic impact is necessary.

The Federal Trade Commission Act (1914)   The establishment of the
Federal Trade Commission was mandated by the passage of the Federal
Trade Commission Act. This was to be a body of experts whose duties were
to be to gather and compile information and to investigate business organizations and practices, and to issue orders against unfair business practices.
Investigations were to be made on its own initiative or at the behest of the
president, either house of congress, or the attorney general. Its principal
enforcement duty was to prevent firms from using unfair methods of competition in commerce. The first sentence of the Federal Trade Commission
Act's most well-known section read: "Section 5: That unfair methods of
competition in commerce are hereby declared to be illegal." Uncertainty is
clearly present in this statute. What could be less clearly defined than an
"unfair" method of competition? It would be up to the Commission to
define the phrase in the context of different and continually changing
situations.

The expectation was that the FTC would act as a strong antimonopoly
agency. Staffed with economic and legal experts, having the power to
obtain information from business firms, making investigations and issuing
reports, and having the authority to issue cease-and-desist orders, the FTC
would define, case by case, the unfair methods of competition that violated
the law. Section 5 has turned out to be for the FTC the equivalent of what
the Sherman Act has been for the Antitrust Division of the Department of

---

[6]"Conglomerate Mergers and Antitrust Policy: An Introduction," in *St. John's Law
Review*, 44, Special Edition (Spring 1970), "Conglomerate Mergers and Acquisitions: Opinion
& Analysis," 530. On the assumption that court judges could profit from more training in
economics, the Law and Economics Center at the University of Miami School of Law has
offered a two-week seminar on economics several times a year to small groups of federal
judges. See Walter Guzzardi, Jr., "Judges Discover the World of Economics," *Fortune*, May
21, 1979. Even in this setting the particular economic models being imparted can hinge on the
training and views of the teachers.

Justice. It has covered a host of restraints of trade; it is the FTC's equivalent of the Sherman Act.[7]

In theory the Federal Trade Commission Act would protect the consumer by ensuring freedom of competition. If there were effective competition, then that process itself would ensure for the consumer the best-quality products at the lowest possible prices, with various options of price-quality combinations available. But in a 1931 decision, the Supreme Court took the stance that where a trade practice, although injurious to the consumer, could not be shown actually to injure any competitor(s), it could not be found to be an unfair method of competition under Section 5.[8] Although the Court admitted that consumers had been deceived by advertisements of a product sold as a remedy for obesity, it found that misrepresentation was common among the sellers of such products and therefore that competitors had not been injured. So in 1938, under the Wheeler-Lea Act, the wording of Section 5 of the Federal Trade Commission Act was expanded to read: "Section 5: Unfair methods of competition in commerce, and unfair or deceptive acts or practices in commerce, are hereby declared unlawful."

Under this amended Section 5, the FTC can take action against a firm if it feels the consumer has been deceived directly by the action of the seller. Injury to competition among sellers does not have to be shown first. This sets the stage for a double-track protection of the consumer: the indirect one through the maintenance of competition, and the straightforward one of protecting the consumer.

The added word, "deceptive," is not one to be easily applied to selling behavior. A particular selling tactic, especially certain advertising, may fool only a few consumers. Should the few who cannot see through, say, certain exaggerated claims for a product, be protected by a government agency spending tax dollars to intervene? This is a more complex question than appears on the surface, and it is discussed in Chapter 8. But it may be noted here that the Wheeler-Lea amendment to the Federal Trade Commission Act did recognize the problem of false advertising to the extent that new sections were added to the act to cover it. Section 12 states that false advertising of food, drugs, devices, or cosmetics falls within the prohibition of Section 5. And Section 15 tries to define this false advertising. The key element in the definition is that advertising is false where it is "misleading in a material respect." In trying to define further the latter, Section 15 states that representations made and failures to reveal material facts should be taken into account. Although differences of opinion can exist between regulators and regulated with respect to what is "misleading

---

[7]"It is clear that any activity that violates either the Sherman Act or the Clayton Act also violates §5(a)(1) of the FTCA." *Lippa's, Inc.* v. *Lenox, Incorporated*, 305 F. Supp. 182, 186 (1969).
[8]*FTC* v. *Raladam Co.*, 283 U.S. 643 (1931).

in a material respect," courts of appeal in misrepresentation cases almost always support the FTC position. For the FTC is a body of experts which it is presumed has examined these cases thoroughly from a public interest point of view.

Both Sections 5 and 12 of the Federal Trade Commission Act were amended in 1975. The phrase "in commerce" was found at law to limit the FTC in its efforts to reach down to the local level, where many of the unfair or deceptive acts or practices were occurring. Practices at this level either were beyond the jurisdiction of the FTC or required an inordinate amount of time and effort to gather evidence to satisfy purely jurisdictional technicalities.[9] This defect was remedied by substituting the words "in or affecting commerce" for the words "in commerce."

The Clayton Antitrust Act (1914)   Within a few days of the approval of the Federal Trade Commission Act, the Clayton Act was approved. Jurisdiction over the Clayton Act was given to both the Department of Justice and the FTC. This federal statute pinpointed four business practices that had been drawing antitrust attention: price discrimination, exclusive dealing, mergers, and interlocking corporate directorates. Except for the issue of interlocking directorates, however, the statute was written with the same general wording as the Sherman Act and the Federal Trade Commission Act. Price discrimination (Section 2), exclusive dealing (Section 3), and acquisitions of corporate stock (Section 7) were not to be automatically illegal (*per se* violations), but were to be illegal only "where the effect . . . may be to substantially lessen competition or tend to create a monopoly in any line of commerce."

It is clear from a reading of the language of the Clayton Act that several words have to be interpreted in each of these sections. What is a "substantial" lessening of competition? How is "competition" itself to be defined, since the analytically rigorous model of perfect competition cannot realistically be—and is not attempted to be—used in actual practice? How far a departure from some model of competition must there be before the effect is to "tend" to create a monopoly? And what is, in the real world, an illegal "monopoly"?

The word in this provisional clause that has had the greatest effect on the ability of enforcement agencies to apply antitrust law to business behavior has been the word "may," for it raises the issue of incipiency. Is the business conduct in question likely to substantially lessen competition or tend to create a monopoly? How likely? Is it a possibility or a probability? The courts have used both words, apparently interchangeably.[10] The logic

---

[9]*Consumer Product Warranties and Federal Trade Commission Improvements Act,* House Report No. 93-1107, 93d. Cong., 2d. Sess. (1974), Part 2, pp. 44–45.
[10]*H. J. Heinz Co.* v. *Beech-Nut Life Savers, Inc.,* 181 F. Supp. 452, 460–61 (1960).

they apply is usually that of probability, which they equate to high possibility. The key point to be made is that the enforcement agencies and the courts do not have to show that there has been an actual injury. One need not have to rely upon historical data to try to show an adverse effect on competition. One can try to build a case on anticipated eventual results. This has come to be known as the *doctrine of incipiency.*

The doctrine of incipiency inherent in the language of the Clayton Act illustrates a basic difference between the Sherman Act and the Clayton Act. Under the Sherman Act, to be found in violation one has to be shown to have damaged competition. Under the Clayton Act, no actual damage need yet have occurred. The analogy of gun laws is appropriate. Under a Sherman Act-like gun law one can carry a gun without concern of being apprehended for carrying it as long as one does not shoot someone or shoot up some property. Under a Clayton Act-like gun law the sheriff could take away a person's gun if the person were considered dangerous—if it were thought that one might very well shoot someone or something. The Antitrust Division of the Department of Justice, where a particular practice in question could fall under the Sherman Act as a restraint of trade or under the applicable section of the Clayton Act, has sometimes filed a suit under both acts. But where the behavior in question is found to violate the Clayton Act, then the Sherman Act charge need not be litigated.[11]

Eventually it was found necessary to amend Section 7 of the Clayton Act pertaining to mergers. The original section had referred only to the acquisition of corporate stock, because this had been the general way through which mergers took place. But suppose a corporation acquires the stock of a competitor and uses that ownership voting power to acquire the assets of the competitor. In a 1926 Supreme Court ruling the Court said, in reaction to a Federal Trade Commission effort to undo a merger that had been accomplished through the acquisition of assets through the voting of stock which had previously been acquired: "The Act has no application to ownership of a competitor's property and business obtained prior to any action by the Commission, even though this was brought about through stock unlawfully held."[12] After several years of congressional effort to close this gap in the antitrust laws, an amendment to Section 7 of the Clayton Act was passed in 1950 (Celler-Kefauver Amendment). The acquisition of assets was added to the acquisition of stock in Section 7 of the statute in order to cover both means of merger.

Section 7 was tightened further by the Antitrust Procedural Im-

[11]In *Standard Oil Company of California and Standard Stations, Inc.* v. *U.S.*, the Supreme Court said: "Since the decree below is sustained by our interpretation of Section 3 of the Clayton Act, we need not go on to consider whether it might also be sustained by Section 1 of the Sherman Act." 337 U.S. 293, 314 (1949).

[12]*Thatcher Manufacturing Company* v. *FTC*, 272 U.S. 554, 557 (1926).

provements Act of 1980. The word "corporations" was replaced by the word "persons." In this way, such business firms as large accounting partnerships and unincorporated joint ventures would be covered. The phrase "or in any activity affecting commerce" was added to the previous reference to "in any line of commerce." This change was comparable to the similar change made in the Federal Trade Commission Act in 1975.

The one *per se* violation of the Clayton Act was Section 8, pertaining to interlocking corporate directorates. The key words here are these:

> ... no person at the same time shall be a director in any two or more corporations, any one of which has capital, surplus, and undivided profits aggregating more than $1,000,000, engaged in whole or in part in commerce ... if such corporations are ... competitors. ...

These provisions being quite specific, the problems of interpretation of business conduct and their effects are considerably fewer. But the question of who is competing with whom remains.

The Robinson-Patman Act (1936)   The Robinson-Patman Act was an attempt to make the price discrimination section of the Clayton Act of 1914 more expansive and more specific. In the first place, it extended the "where the effect may be to substantially lessen competition" clause to add a clause reading ". . . or to injure, destroy, or prevent competition with any person who either grants or knowingly receives the benefit of such discrimination, or with customers of either of them." The reference to injury to a person singles out for special consideration the competitor—who is, of course, only a part of the competition. And the reference to the party receiving the discrimination emphasizes the price discrimination induced by the large buyer.

In the second place, the Robinson-Patman Act attempted to elaborate upon the kind of price discrimination which represented the presumed market evils that were to be eliminated. It provided for one particular prohibition and two particular mandates. The prohibition is represented by amended Clayton Act Section 2(c), which makes it unlawful for any firm to receive brokerage payments or allowances in lieu thereof if that firm is in any way affiliated with the buyer or the seller. The mandates are represented by Sections 2(d) and 2(e), which require that payments by suppliers to customers for services rendered by the customers or the furnishing by suppliers to customers of services or facilities be made to all customers on proportionally equal terms.

Section 3 of the Robinson-Patman Act, a criminal section of law calling for fines and/or imprisonment upon conviction, states that it shall be unlawful to discriminate in price in different parts of the country or to sell at unreasonably low prices for the purpose of destroying competition or eliminating a competitor. As a criminal statute, it is outside the jurisdiction of the FTC, and technically it is not considered an antitrust law.[13] It has lain largely dormant.

The theory of competition is that only the most efficient producer-sellers will survive. Advocates of the Robinson-Patman Act argued that to ensure equal competitive opportunity for the small business against the large, such specific and more elaborate legislation was necessary. Without such statutory protection, even the efficient small business is going to have a harder time surviving in the competition with the giants, especially those operating in the channels of distribution.[14] These advocates see small business as a necessary and important element in the structure of the economy, the survival of which should be assisted.

The opposing view is that the passage of this legislation represented Depression-born protectionist legislation to preserve the existence of the small business in the distributive trades, especially against the inroads of the then-growing chain stores. To protect the individual competitor is to confuse the competitor with competition. If a competitor is protected from full-fledged competition, then the competition itself no longer exists. That a competitor is forced out of business does not necessarily represent predation. And to foster such protectionism is to promote "soft" rather than "hard" competition. The cost is ultimately higher prices to consumers.[15] If there is real predation present, it is argued that the general wording of the old Section 2 of the Clayton Act, Sections 1 and 2 of the Sherman Act, or Section 5 of the Federal Trade Commission Act should be adequate to meet the problem.

The Robinson-Patman Act represents a departure from the basic antitrust statutes in the sense that it tried to make antitrust law less general and more specific. Experience under the act has demonstrated, however, that the built-in specificity has not greatly reduced the alleged "uncertainty" of the antitrust laws. Litigation has been quite voluminous in an attempt to obtain interpretation of the meaning of various words of the statute in their particular contexts. There being more words in the expanded price discrimination legislation, there have thus been more points to argue over in litigation.

PROCEDURES OF THE ANTITRUST DIVISION

The Antitrust Division was established as a separate division in the Department of Justice in 1933 as the need for a corps of specialists to handle

[13]*Nashville Milk Co.* v. *Carnation Co.*, 355 U.S. 373; and *Safeway Stores, Inc.* v. *Vance*, 355 U.S. 389 (1958).
[14]See U.S. Department of Justice, *Report on the Robinson-Patman Act* (Washington, D.C.: U.S. Government Printing Office, 1978), pp. 140–48.
[15]See ibid., pp. 37–100.

antitrust enforcement became evident.[16] Its antitrust functions are to enforce the Sherman and Clayton Acts. Its budget for fiscal year 1981 was $46.6 million.

The Department of Justice has sole jurisdiction over enforcement of the Sherman Act, which is both a civil and a criminal statute. The first decision is to decide which kind of suit to file. The general rule of thumb is to utilize a criminal suit where the alleged antitrust violation falls into the category of a "hard-core" offense. Such offenses are those that have come to be recognized as *per se* offenses, acts deemed inherently to be unreasonable restraints of trade, acts which through the establishment of legal precedent are in themselves illegal—in short, business conduct the courts over and over again have decided clearly violates the antitrust laws. Collusive price-fixing, dividing up the market geographically among competitors so that each would have its own territory, allocating customers so that business rivals do not compete for the same buyer's business, and the group boycotting of resellers all have been found by the courts to be illegal *per se*. Businesspeople and firms are supposed to know that such market behavior is illegal. Whenever businesspeople behave illegally under the antitrust laws in cases where they know they are violating such laws, criminal proceedings are in order.

Criminal Proceedings Criminal enforcement of the Sherman Act begins with a grand jury investigation. If the indictment submitted to the grand jury by the prosecution is returned by the jury as indicating sufficient evidence to justify a trial, the Antitrust Division will file a complaint with a district court. The defendants may wish to plead *nolo contendere* (I do not wish to contend). The courts need not accept such a plea from the defendant in a criminal antitrust case, but the record would seem to indicate that they usually do. It saves the time and expense of a court trial. What with court dockets being crowded, this provides considerable incentive for the court to accept the plea and dole out whatever fines or imprisonment (or nothing) it wishes. There is great incentive also for the defendant to plead *nolo contendere*, for by doing so the defendant will not have been found guilty. If found guilty by a court, that fact can be *prima facie* evidence (not requiring further evidence to establish its existence or credibility) in a private antitrust treble damage suit (discussed below).

Civil Proceedings Civil proceedings follow different procedures and have different possible outcomes from criminal actions. The objective

---

[16]The position of an assistant to the attorney general to handle all suits under the antitrust and interstate commerce laws was first established in 1903. For a digested statement of the organization and procedures of the Antitrust Division, see prepared statement of John H. Shenefield, Assistant Attorney General, Antitrust Division, *Hearings, Committee on the Judiciary, U.S. House of Representatives, Department of Justice Authorization*, 95th Cong., 2d. Sess., Serial No. 27, March 21, 1978, pp. 252–68.

is not to punish through fines and imprisonment, but rather to prevent and restrain antitrust violations by forbidding continuation of particular conduct or to restore competitive conditions by changing the structural characteristics of the market. Civil antitrust decrees have been utilized to break up corporations into several companies (dissolution), to force corporations to spin off some of their assets to create new competitors (divestment or divorcement), to make property such as patents or knowhow available to competitors, and to alter the terms on which goods and services are being bought and sold. For example, a court can order the time period of supply contracts reduced in length, or can order that a piece of machinery can be purchased as well as leased. Since such decrees are issued by a district court, the Antitrust Division's personnel have to convince the judge of the desirability and need of a particular structural change. The law has provisions for expediting a civil antitrust case at the district court level, and an appeal from the final judgment of the district court may go directly to the Supreme Court when it is requested and approved by the district court.

Facilitating Civil Proceedings   The use of civil proceedings by the Department of Justice was handicapped for several years by limits on its ability to obtain information to substantiate suspicions of possible antitrust violations. The Antitrust Civil Process Act of 1962 gave Justice specific power to demand any documentary material relevant to a civil antitrust investigation prior to the institution of a proceeding from any "person" under investigation. But "person" was defined to mean "any corporation, association, partnership, or other legal entity not a natural person." Furthermore, a court of appeals decision in 1965 held that such a civil investigative demand (CID) can be used to ascertain whether a "person" has been or is engaged in an antitrust violation, but not when the activity may be a violation in the future.[17]

Amendments to the Antitrust Civil Process Act in the Hart-Scott-Rodino Antitrust Improvements Act of 1976 remedied weaknesses of the 1962 law. First, a CID can be issued to a natural person. Second, a person may be ordered to answer written questions and to appear for oral examination (not just submit documentary material). Third, a CID may be issued to anyone who may have relevant information (not just the suspected party). And fourth, a CID may be issued concerning *"activities in preparation* for a merger, acquisition, joint venture, or similar transaction, which, if consummated, may result in an antitrust violation, which are under investigation and the provision of law applicable thereto" (italics added).

One way to expedite and keep down the costs of both parties in a civil antitrust proceeding is to have the attorney general and accused party come to an agreement as to how the issue should be resolved. If the two

[17]*U.S.* v. *Union Oil Company of California,* 343 F. 2d 29.

parties can agree, the proposed consent judgment is filed with the district court. The judge, if he or she approves, will then issue a *consent decree.* The court's approval has usually been perfunctory.[18] Most civil antitrust suits have been settled in this manner. One of the biggest advantages to the defendant is that he or she has not been found guilty of an antitrust violation; the consent decree cannot be used as *prima facie* evidence against the person in a private treble damage suit.

Although proposed decrees had to be made public 30 days before taken to court for approval, Congress was not satisfied that consent decrees were getting enough publicity before taking effect. The Antitrust Procedures and Penalties Act of 1974 thus built several publicity safeguards into consent decree procedures. Proposed consent judgments and written comments and any responses thereto by the government must be filed with the district court and published in the *Federal Register* at least 60 days prior to the effective date of the proposed judgment. Also to be filed and published is a statement indicating the competitive impact of the proposed judgment. To be published in newspapers in general circulation in the district in which the case has been filed and the District of Columbia are summaries of the proposed consent judgment and competitive impact statement, plus a list of the relevant materials and documents available for inspection and public comment and where they are located. Any written comments from other parties on the proposed judgment are then in order.

The required competitive impact statement is supposed to be fully informative. It must include (1) the nature and purpose of the proceeding, (2) the alleged illegal antitrust practices, (3) the anticipated effects on competition of such relief, (4) the remedies available to potential private plaintiffs damaged by the alleged violation, (5) procedures available for modification of the proposal, and (6) evaluation of alternatives to the proposal. The 1974 statute specifically states that this competitive impact statement is not admissible as evidence in a private treble damage suit.

PROCEDURES OF THE FEDERAL TRADE COMMISSION

The Federal Trade Commission is an independent regulatory agency. Its five commissioners are appointed by the president for terms of seven years, with the advice and consent of the Senate. No more than three commissioners can be members of the same political party, and their terms are staggered. The FTC budget for fiscal year 1981 was $71 million.

Scope of Responsibilities   The FTC has two principal operating divisions. Its Bureau of Competition enforces Section 5 of the Federal Trade

[18]Phillip Areeda, *Antitrust Analysis* (Boston: Little, Brown, 1974), p. 61.

Commission Act with respect to restraint of trade matters and the Clayton Act. Its Bureau of Consumer Protection litigates those acts or practices alleged to be unfair or deceptive to consumers. Its Bureau of Economics is a staff section that investigates, collects, and analyzes data; prepares economic reports and surveys; and advises the Commission on the economic aspects of its activities.

In addition to its responsibilities in enforcing the Federal Trade Commission and Clayton Acts, several other more specialized statutes are under the jurisdiction of the FTC. It must provide surveillance over and enforcement of the Webb-Pomerene Export Trade Act of 1918, which allows certain cooperative activity by export trade associations. Four labeling acts are under its jurisdiction, violations of which are held by statute to be violations of Section 5 of the Federal Trade Commission Act: the Wool Products Labeling Act of 1939, the Fur Products Labeling Act of 1951, the Textile Fiber Products Identification Act of 1958, and the Fair Packaging and Labeling Act of 1966. The FTC must implement the Lanham Trade Mark Act of 1946, which requires registration and protection of trademarks. Four credit-related statutes also fall to the FTC for administration and enforcement: the Truth in Lending Act of 1968, which requires full disclosure to consumers of credit terms; the Fair Credit Reporting Act of 1970, which is supposed to ensure the accuracy and confidentiality of consumers' credit reports; the Fair Credit Billing Act of 1975, which is concerned with correcting billing errors; and the Equal Credit Opportunity Act of 1975, which is supposed to ensure that consumers are not denied credit because of sex, marital status, age, race, religion, or national origin.

The Enforcement Process   In carrying out its anti-restraint of trade and consumer protection functions under the Clayton and Federal Trade Commission Acts, the FTC acts as a quasi-judicial body that hands down its own decision. Once a complaint is issued, an administrative law judge takes charge of the case and conducts any necessary hearings and review of documents, and then issues an initial decision. Administrative law judges operate under the Civil Service Commission and have tenure similar to that of federal court judges. The decision of the administrative law judge can be appealed by the defendant (respondent) or the Commission's complaint counsel to the commissioners. After hearing the appeals, the FTC will dismiss the case or issue an order, usually requiring simply cease-and-desist. In some cases, the FTC has gone beyond cease-and-desist and ordered positive corrective action. The respondent can appeal the FTC's order within 60 days to a circuit court of appeals. The case may eventually wind up in the hands of the Supreme Court for a decision.

Full litigation of an alleged illegal practice may be avoided by a consent order. Before or after the investigation has been completed, the consent order may be negotiated by the FTC and the respondent.[19] A consent order does not amount to an admission by the respondent of violation of the law, but it has the same force and effect of law as an FTC order that results from full proceedings. Consent order procedure is not a right a respondent can demand; if the public interest would seem to require full litigation of the issue, the respondent is denied this privilege. In any case, the FTC makes analyses of the consent order available for public comment for a period of 60 days. If letters of comment disclose information which indicates that the consent order is inappropriate or inadequate, the order may have to be revised.

The FTC can require reports from those who have been the subject of an FTC order indicating in detail how they have complied with that order. The FTC can also seek preliminary injunctions in district courts against anyone violating or about to violate any of the laws it enforces. Either the FTC or the Department of Justice can seek civil penalties from parties that have violated FTC cease-and-desist orders.[20]

Trade Regulation Rules   The Federal Trade Commission took a giant step in trying to make Section 5's "unfair methods of competition or unfair or deceptive acts or practices" more specific when it issued its first *trade regulation rule,* which became effective in 1963. A trade regulation rule typically will state that it is an unfair or deceptive act or practice, and sometimes as well that it is an unfair method of competition within the meaning of Section 5, to engage in the particular practice or practices cited in the rule. Having the full force and effect of law, the uncertainty of the law pertaining to various business acts or practices is thus considerably reduced. The number of trade regulation rules in effect as of June 1981 was 24. With two exceptions, all these rules are in the area of direct consumer protection with respect to misrepresentation and advertising.[21] Rules are issued only after lengthy public hearings and opportunity for industry and public comment.

Prior to use of the trade regulation rule, the Federal Trade Commission had used *trade practice rules* to provide guidance for members of many

---

[19]In a 1980 consent order with the FTC, two manufacturers of art materials agreed to pay $1.2 million in restitution to various school systems in a price-fixing settlement. This was the first time consumer restitution had been obtained by the FTC in an antitrust case. *In the Matter of Milton Bradley Co. et al.,* File No. 761 0087 (1980).

[20]A consent decree with the Department of Justice provided that a violator of an FTC cease-and-desist order against price-fixing dating all the way back to 1936 pay a civil penalty of $300,000. Department of Justice release, November 21, 1979.

[21]One exception pertains to discriminatory practices in men's and boys' tailored clothing, where the parties being protected are small apparel manufacturers, salespeople, and retailers. A second exception pertains to full disclosure of information to prospective franchisees by franchisors.

industries. A *trade practice conference* provided a forum for the exchange of views between members of an industry and the FTC as to what would be desirable rules of the game for an industry to help members determine that they were engaging in fair rather than unfair practices. The rules established as a result of these conferences were advisory only. In any possible litigation, the FTC had to prove a violation of Section 5; it could not rely on a violation of the rule itself. The FTC declared trade practice conference rules obsolete and repealed most of those still in effect in 1978; it reclassified the remaining seven as "industry guides" in 1979.[22]

The FTC's power to promulgate trade regulation rules was challenged by the National Petroleum Refiners Association in 1970. The trade regulation rule at immediate issue was a requirement that gasoline octane ratings be posted on gasoline pumps. A federal district court held that the language of the Federal Trade Commission Act gave the FTC a right to draw up only internal rules of organization, practice, and procedure; it did not therefore have the power to issue trade regulation rules.[23] But a circuit court of appeals reversed the lower court's decision, and the Supreme Court refused to review the decision.[24] That information regarding the octane rating of automotive gasoline be disclosed to consumers is now required by the Petroleum Marketing Practices Act of 1978. This statute required the FTC to promulgate a rule establishing uniform methods for determining, certifying, and displaying octane ratings.

The question of any doubts about the Commission's right to issue substantive trade regulation rules was addressed by the passage of the Magnuson-Moss Warranty—Federal Trade Commission Improvement Act of 1975. This statute gave the Commission specific authority to "prescribe interpretive rules and general statements of policy with respect to unfair or deceptive acts or practices in or affecting commerce."[25] Further, the Commission can prescribe "rules which define with specificity acts or practices which are unfair or deceptive acts or practices in or affecting commerce" and these rules "may include requirements prescribed for the purpose of preventing such acts or practices." Although these changes in the law emphasized the consumer protection aspects of rule-making by the FTC, Congress did not ignore the unfair methods of competition aspect. It in-

[22]*FTC News Summary*, No. 42-1978, p. 3; and No. 19-1979, p. 2.

[23]*National Petroleum Refiners Assn., et al.* v. *FTC, et al.*, 340 F. Supp. 1343 (1972).

[24]482 F. 2d 672 (1973); certiorari denied, 94 Sup. Ct. 1475 (1974).

[25]The explicit grant of rule-making authority now appears as a new Section 18 of the Federal Trade Commission Act. The Federal Trade Commission Improvements Act of 1980 amended Section 18 to prohibit the Commission during the fiscal years 1980, 1981, and 1982 from initiating any rule-making proceeding pertaining to commercial advertising that would designate an act or practice as being unfair (as distinct from being deceptive). The right of the Commission to promulgate any rule with respect to television advertising aimed at children as an unfair act or practice was specifically prohibited. Any rule on that subject would have to be based on its being deceptive.

cluded in the new statute a sentence to the effect that the FTC's authority to prescribe rules with respect to unfair methods of competition were not affected by this amendment. With the growing emphasis on use of trade regulation rules by the Federal Trade Commission, trade regulation has not only become more specific with respect to what business cannot do in the marketplace, but business can now be instructed by rules as to what it may have to do to avoid violating a rule. The FTC announced in 1976 its intention of putting into rule form, where appropriate, the principles of consumer protection law it had developed through individual cases and consent decrees.[26]

The FTC can, as provided for in the Magnuson-Moss Warranty— Federal Trade Commission Improvement Act of 1975, undertake civil action in the federal courts to seek redress for consumers where there have been violations of rules pertaining to unfair or deceptive acts or practices. The court, in turn, can award relief in the form of rescission or reformation of contracts, refund of money or return of property, or the payment of actual damages. In addition, the FTC can seek in the courts a civil penalty of $10,000 per day for a knowing violation of such rules or of a cease-and-desist order against such practices. This is so even though the person or firm in question was not the party against whom the cease-and-desist order had been issued; the criterion is that it must be a knowing violation.

MEANS TO REDUCE VIOLATIONS

Although the wording of the Sherman, Clayton, and Federal Trade Commission Acts is very general in nature, various means have been developed through which the uncertainty inherent in the provisions of these acts can be minimized. We have already seen how the FTC has utilized the trade regulation rule to make the law clearer and more specific. But there are other means by which these controls over trade can be made not only more understandable to the business community, but also more likely to be adhered to.

Per Se Violations   Certain business practices have come to be known as *per se* antitrust violations because legal precedent has clearly established that these practices are in themselves illegal. Collusive price-fixing, allocation of market territories or customers among business rivals (market sharing), and group boycotts of distributors all have had legal precedent clearly established against them. *Per se* illegality eliminates uncertainty as to legality. But education must overcome a certain amount of ignorance with respect to the *per se* illegality of certain practices.

[26]41 Fed. Reg. 3322, January 22, 1976.

Advisory Opinions   If firms are in doubt as to the legality of a particular course of action, they need but inquire of the Department of Justice or the FTC. Under the Department of Justice's business review procedure, the Antitrust Division will indicate whether or not an action would be challenged by the Division under the antitrust laws. The FTC has a similar program. Even if the advice of the regulatory agency is complied with, none of this advice is assurance that the firms will never have their actions subjected to trade regulation complaint, because the actions in question may turn out to have anticompetitive effects that could not have been foreseen.

Guidelines   The FTC and the Antitrust Division have provided guidelines with respect to certain business practices they would feel obliged to challenge. The Antitrust Division drew up detailed guidelines in 1968, using largely structural standards of market shares, to indicate which mergers it felt would be subject to antitrust attack. The Division announced publication of antitrust guidelines for international operations in 1977 and for research joint ventures in 1980. The FTC has guidelines on its enforcement policy with respect to vertical mergers in the cement industry (1967), mergers in the food distribution industry (1967), and mergers in the dairy industry (1978).[27] These FTC guidelines are based on market shares of the acquired and acquiring firms or on absolute volumes of a firm's sales or production.

The FTC has issued a whole series of industry guides on areas of possible consumer deception. These guides are interpretations by the FTC of the laws it administers and include topics such as bait advertising, use of endorsements and testimonials in advertising, use of the word "free," advertising allowances and other merchandising payments and services, and debt collection. Special guidelines have been issued to cover problems of misrepresentation for such products as dog and cat food, watches, ladies' handbags, law books, beauty and barber equipment and supplies, and feather and down products. These guides do not have the full force and effect of law; the FTC would still have to issue a complaint under Section 5 of the Federal Trade Commission Act. But any business that wants to avoid committing a deceptive act or practice can find help in these guides.

Fines and Imprisonment   The fines and prison sentences which can be imposed by a court under the Sherman Act have increased over the years. In 1890 the act provided maximum fines of $5000 and imprisonment not exceeding one year, or both. An amendment in 1955 increased the

---

[27]FTC merger guidelines for the textile mill products industry announced in 1968 were rescinded in 1975. Merger guidelines for grocery product manufacturing announced in 1968 were rescinded in 1976.

maximum fine to $50,000. Further amendment in 1974 through the Antitrust Procedures and Penalty Act increased possible fines from $50,000 to $1 million if a corporation and from $50,000 to $100,000 if a person, and possible prison terms were increased from one year to three years.[28] This last amendment also made criminal violations of the Sherman Act a felony rather than a misdemeanor.[29] A desire to create a deterrent force to hardcore antitrust violations has been the prime factor in these increases in fines and imprisonment. The Department of Justice has taken the position that fines and imprisonment should be meted out with enough force not only to remove the profit, but also to create a real deterrent. In 1977 it issued guidelines in the form of recommendations for sentencing in antitrust felony cases.[30] (These were only recommendations, for the court does the actual sentencing.)

For individuals, these guidelines view prison sentences as being more important than fines. They recommend an 18-month base, from which a sentence should be adjusted upward from one to six months according to certain aggravating factors, such as the amount of commerce involved, the position of the individual (the higher the position in a firm, the longer the sentence), the existence and degree of predatory or coercive conduct, the duration of participation, and any previous conviction. The guidelines recommend fines for individuals where prison terms are not appropriate. The recommended base fine is $50,000. If a $50,000 fine were to exceed 25 percent of an individual's net worth, then the latter figure would be used as the base point. Where a prison sentence less than recommended is imposed, a fine of a compensating percentage should be levied. The same aggravating factors applying to prison sentences would also apply to fines.

For corporations, the guidelines call for a minimum fine of $100,000. Hopefully, the fines would be large enough to remove the added profit gained from the illegal activity plus something as a punishment. It should hurt, but not hurt so badly as to remove the offending firm from the marketplace. The guidelines adopt a base point of 10 percent of the corporation's total sales in the affected line of commerce during the period of illegal activity. Elzinga and Breit argue against using a percentage of sales as a basis for fines because the profit-sales ratio can vary according to the nature of the firm. They point out that a firm with high inventory turnover would be much harder hit than one with low turnover. Making fines a percentage of profit would have a more consistent impact.[31]

[28]Separate fines can be imposed on each of several counts—the fixing of price of product A and the fixing of price of product B, and so on.

[29]The distinction between a misdemeanor and a felony is a matter of the seriousness and severity of penalties.

[30]U.S. Department of Justice, memorandum addressed to all attorneys and economists of the Antitrust Division, *Guidelines for Sentencing Recommendations in Felony Cases under the Sherman Act,* February 24, 1977.

[31]K. G. Elzinga and W. Breit, *The Antitrust Penalties: A Study in Law and Economics* (New Haven: Yale University Press, 1976), pp. 133–35.

One problem with jail sentences as a deterrent to antitrust violations has been that the courts have been reluctant to impose stiff sentences or actual jail terms. Data compiled by Elzinga and Breit for the years 1966 through 1973 indicate that suspended sentences and probation were much more common than actual imprisonment.[32] Actual time served was occasionally a 30-day term, but rarely more than that. Perhaps, as these authors suggest, there has been hesitation actually to commit to prison certain corporate executives when there exists uncertainty as to who within the corporation were the real organizers of the illegal activity—a position which they argue is a rational one.[33] But education of judges by the Antitrust Division on the need for jail terms for antitrust violators may be bearing fruit. In 1978, more jail time was imposed for antitrust violations than in the first 80 years of the Sherman Act.[34] Between 1890 and 1970, 19 persons served a total of 28 months in jail. In one year, 1978, 29 persons served jail time for the equivalent of 96 months.

Total fines imposed have also increased over the years. Whereas the fines for the five-year period 1965–69 totaled just over $5.3 million,[35] they were over $3.4 million in fiscal year 1977 and almost $13 million in fiscal year 1978.[36] In 1978 a forest products firm was fined $632,000,[37] a grain milling company was fined $750,000,[38] and two major construction companies each received the first maximum fines of $1 million ever levied under the antitrust laws (for rigging bids and allocating contracts).[39] These maximum fines were imposed after the firms had pleaded *nolo contendere*. A new high in aggregate fines imposed in one case totaled $6.1 million in 1979, when 7 major international shipping lines and 13 executives pleaded *nolo contendere* to charges of conspiracy to fix prices. The executives were fined $50,000 each.[40] These increases are not surprising given the new increased maximums set by the Antitrust Procedures and Penalty Act of 1974 and the attempts of the Antitrust Division to educate the courts on the need for stiffer fines.

The Department of Justice let it be known in 1978 that it would give

[32]Ibid., pp. 34–37.

[33]Ibid., pp. 38–39.

[34]Ky P. Ewing, Jr., Deputy Assistant Attorney General, Antitrust Division, "Antitrust Enforcement: Fighting Inflation in the 'Necessaries of Life and Business,'" remarks before the Legal Committee of the Grocery Manufacturers of America, Inc., Washington, D.C., May 1, 1979, mimeo, p. 2.

[35]Richard A. Posner, "A Statistical Study of Antitrust Enforcement," *Journal of Law and Economics*, 13, no. 2 (October 1970), p. 392.

[36]Richard J. Favretto, Deputy Director of Operations, Antitrust Division, remarks before the Twelfth Annual Antitrust Institute, Ohio State Bar Association, October 27, 1978, mimeo, p. 10. Fiscal year ends September 30.

[37]*Wall Street Journal*, November 14, 1978, p. 25.

[38]*Wall Street Journal*, November 15, 1978, p. 18.

[39]*Business Week*, January 8, 1979, p. 26.

[40]*New York Times*, June 9, 1979, p. 31.

serious consideration to lenient treatment of corporations' or firms' officers if they voluntarily reported wrongdoing prior to their being detected. Such consideration would apply in the case of a conspiracy only to the first corporation to come forward.[41] Although some corporations did respond, the number was far fewer than had been expected. One explanation has been that lawyers have been suggesting that the Antitrust Division might renege on its offer.[42]

Treble Damage Suits   Successful treble damage suits won by another private party can be the most expensive costs of an antitrust violation. Section 4 of the Clayton Act says that "any person who shall be injured in his business or property by reason of anything forbidden in the antitrust laws may sue therefor in any district court . . . and shall recover threefold the damages by him sustained, and the costs of suit, including a reasonable attorney's fee."[43] The antitrust laws are defined in the act as the Sherman Act, the Wilson Tariff Act amendment of 1904 (which applied to combinations, conspiracies, trusts, agreements, or contracts with respect to the importation of goods into the United States), and the Clayton Act. An amendment to Section 4 of the Clayton Act in 1955 provides statutory support for a federal government suit to recover actual damages and the cost of the suit wherever that results from anything forbidden in the antitrust laws.

Private treble damage suits under the antitrust laws are much more numerous than government antitrust suits. In 1978, 1435 new private antitrust cases were filed in federal courts, compared to only 72 Antitrust Division cases, both civil and criminal. In 1979, 1234 private cases were begun, compared with 78 government cases. And in 1980, 1457 private cases were initiated, compared with 78 government cases. The figure of only about 5 percent of all antitrust suits being filed by the government holds quite constant through the 1970s.[44]

Since the damages are trebled, and since the number of these private cases is greater than that of government antitrust suits, they pose a greater financial danger to a firm. The typical treble damage case is based on charges of price-fixing.[45] The amount of the calculated overcharges, multiplied by three, can be much greater than the fines imposed in a government-

---

[41]John H. Shenefield, Assistant Attorney General, Antitrust Division, "The Disclosure of Antitrust Violations and Prosecutorial Discretion," remarks before the 17th Annual Corporate Counsel Institute, Chicago, October 4, 1978, mimeo, p. 5.

[42]Tom Goldstein, "Antitrust Effort: Employee Role," *New York Times,* July 6, 1979, p. D3.

[43]Section 7 of the Sherman Act includes a similar treble damage provision applying to that act.

[44]New antitrust case filings in federal district courts can be found in the annual reports of the Administrative Office of the United States Courts.

[45]Areeda, *Antitrust Analysis,* pp. 69–70.

filed case. Settlements can amount to hundreds of millions of dollars. This emphasizes the importance to a firm of not having been found guilty by a court in a related government antitrust suit, whether civil or criminal, for such a conviction is *prima facie* evidence that can be used in a treble damage suit. A conviction can trigger a bandwagon effect of injured customers filing treble damage suits. And the convicted corporation can deduct on its income tax only one-third of any treble damage awards later assessed against it.[46] Taking the option of pleading no contest, even though the court may award heavy fines or even imprisonment, is likely to be the cheapest way out, for then there is no legal evidence of guilt.

Although charges of price-fixing may be the basis for most private treble damage suits as customers seek recovery of overcharges, other market practices or situations may also lead to such suits. In 1978 a group of 20 independent film producers filed a $180 million antitrust suit against the three major television networks, charging them with restraint of trade and monopolization of news and public affairs programming by refusing to purchase or program independently produced news or public affairs shows.[47] In 1976 the H. J. Heinz Company filed a $105 million antitrust suit against the Campbell Soup Company, charging predatory pricing of consumer soups. Campbell Soup countered this suit with one against Heinz for $46.5 million, charging that Heinz, with 80 percent of catsup sales, had been tying in sales of its other products with its catsup, requiring customers to deal exclusively with Heinz, and giving discounts to certain customers.[48] When the Antitrust Division sued International Business Machines Corporation in 1969 for having a monopoly position in the computer industry, this was just the beginning of the private antitrust suits that followed. Between 1970 and 1974, 12 separate private antitrust treble damage suits were filed against IBM.[49]

Some private treble damage suits have been looked upon as "nuisance suits," with the complainants testing their ability to use this channel as a source of additional revenue. This would cause the "misinformation effect," under which private parties would claim anticompetitive effects of rival parties where such had not been true in the hope of out-of-court settlements, or the "perverse incentive effect," where parties would knowingly allow monopoly behavior to persist with the idea of later suing for three times the damages.[50] With the attorneys operating on a contingency fee basis of from 15 to 35 percent of the verdict and with most such cases being settled out of court, there are additional incentives for filing these

[46]Shenefield, "The Disclosure of Antitrust Violations," pp. 8–9.
[47]*Wall Street Journal*, September 12, 1978, p. 7.
[48]*Business Week*, December 5, 1977, p. 44. This dispute was settled out of court. *New York Times*, July 5, 1979, p. A18.
[49]*Business Week*, February 10, 1975, p. 72.
[50]Elzinga and Breit, *The Antitrust Penalties*, pp. 84–95.

cases.[51] On the other hand, the private treble damage suit may help to reduce some of the "closeness" of the firms in industries where the number of sellers is not very great.[52] The curious paradox here would be that the legal rules to enforce competition would become a basis for part of the rivalry itself.

A related issue which has prompted bills in Congress is that of contribution. If only one of several conspirators has been sued for price-fixing and ordered to pay treble damages, why should not the other conspirators, who were not sued or settled out of court, help to pay for those damages? As a matter of law, the Supreme Court said in 1981 that no right of contribution exists.[53] Nothing in the legislative history of the Sherman and Clayton Acts relates to contribution. The Court had no authority to fashion a rule on this issue; it was a matter for Congress to decide.

Arguments pro and con contribution have been advanced. Proponents argue that forcing all the members of a conspiracy to contribute to the payment of damages ordered against one of the conspirators would be fairer. All would be liable and share the costs of the conspiracy. At the same time, this would be a more complete private enforcement of the antitrust laws. It would also force one conspirator to implicate the others and should thus serve as a deterrent. Arguments in opposition hold that if one participant in a conspiracy takes the risk of having to shoulder full liability for the damages resulting from the conspiracy, this would be a strong deterrent. Which argument is stronger would seem to hinge on what assumptions are made as to how risk-averse the possible conspirators are.

Consumer Redress and Civil Penalties   We noted in our discussion of the FTC's use of trade regulation rules that the FTC, since 1975, has had the authority to seek redress in the courts for consumers where there have been violations of rules pertaining to unfair or deceptive acts or practices. The court can then order refunds or return of property or can rescind or reform contracts. The court can also order the payment of damages.

The FTC can also seek civil penalties of $10,000 per day for violation of its rules or cease-and-desist orders. The Department of Justice can also seek civil penalties from the courts from parties that have violated an FTC cease-and-desist order.

Class Action Suits   Where sellers of goods know that the victim of any antitrust violation has a real incentive to sue for treble damages as redress for the injury, this knowledge can serve as a deterrent to improper

[51]Ibid., pp. 73–77.
[52]See Timothy D. Schellhardt, "Rivals Revenge," *Wall Street Journal*, December 29, 1976, pp. 1, 10.
[53]*Texas Industries, Inc.* v. *Radcliff Materials, Inc., et al.*, Trade Cases para. 64,020.

behavior. If individual damages are quite small, however, the treble damage recoveries would be too small to warrant the filing of a suit. One possible solution to this dilemma is the class action suit. This procedure permits one or more plaintiffs to sue in behalf of the several persons who may have been injured by the alleged wrong.

Class actions at the federal court level must satisfy Federal Rule of Civil Procedure 23. Some of the requirements of Rule 23 may not be so easily satisfied as to make a class action suit feasible. Several questions must first have satisfactory answers. Who are all the injured parties? How can they all be notified of their rights in the suit? Are the interests of all the injured parties adequately protected? How are the gains of the suit to be distributed? The court has to decide at the outset of such a suit whether the class action approach is manageable and the appropriate one.[54]

The courts in *Eisen* v. *Carlisle and Jacquelin* threw certain obstacles into the path of class action suits. A court of appeals in 1973 found the concept and practice of fluid recovery wholly improper and illegal as a solution to the manageability problem of class action suits.[55] *Fluid recovery* is a system of distribution of the damage awards applied in a situation where many members of the class are unidentifiable and under which particular parties who had never established their individual injury could receive some of the benefits.[56] The Supreme Court in the same case in 1974 took the position that the organizer of the suit should bear the cost of giving notice to the members of the class she was seeking to represent. Such notice must be given because absent members are legally assumed to be part of the class unless they "opt out."[57] The cost of giving notice may itself put an end to consideration of use of a class action suit.

The Supreme Court's 1977 decision in the *Illinois Brick* case threw still another obstacle in the way of class action suits.[58] It held that only direct purchasers from the alleged antitrust violator can sue for treble damages. In most cases this would prevent consumer class action suits, even though the costs of the antitrust transgression had been passed on to the consumer by the direct purchaser. *Parens patriae* suits by state governments in behalf of consumers (discussed below) could also be adversely affected. In decid-

---

[54]For discussion of the several pros and cons of class action suits and of the alternative legal procedures and requirements, see Legislative Analysis No. 8, *Consumer Class Actions* (Washington, D.C.: American Enterprise Institute for Public Policy Research, 1977).

[55]479 F. 2d 1005, 1018 (1973).

[56]An illustration of fluid recovery is that of a Los Angeles taxicab fleet which, because of defective meters, had overcharged riders 15 cents per mile. The taxi owners were ordered to lower fares for a long enough period of time so that riders would recover the overcharge. Cited in *Business Week*, January 24, 1977, p. 53. The recovery was fluid in that the riders who recovered were not necessarily the same as those who overpaid, although aggregate amounts of overpayment and recovery were presumably the same.

[57]417 U.S. 156 (1974).

[58]*Illinois Brick Co. et al.* v. *Illinois et al.*, 431 U.S. 720 (1977).

ing that the indirect purchaser does not have a right to sue for treble damages, the Supreme Court was thinking largely in terms of practicalities. If indirect as well as direct purchasers were allowed to attempt to recover treble damages, there could well be multiple litigation and multiple liability for the defendants. The damages allowed to wholesalers and retailers as well as consumers could be duplicated. The attempt to allocate the overcharge "would add whole new dimensions of complexity to treble-damages suits and seriously undermine their effectiveness."[59]

The Supreme Court in a previous decision had not accepted the argument by a defendant in a treble damage suit that the plaintiff had not been injured because he had "passed on" the higher costs to the next stage in the channels of distribution. It argued that to determine what costs, prices, and sales would have been if there had not been an antitrust violation overcharge would be an "insurmountable" task.[60] The 1977 *Illinois Brick* decision accepted this reasoning and pointed out that the defendant would also have to show the actual "passing on."

To blur the issue, the Supreme Court ruled in 1979 that consumers could sue to recover treble damages under the antitrust laws. The ruling came in a class action suit filed against five hearing aid manufacturers charging them with a variety of antitrust violations, including both vertical and horizontal price-fixing.[61] The defendants argued that the consumer who brought the class action suit had not been injured in her "business or property," as required under Section 4 of the Clayton Act. A court of appeals agreed with this position, holding that a consumer injury is not an injury of a commercial or business nature.[62] The Supreme Court reversed the lower court, arguing that as long as the consumer was being deprived of her money, her property was being injured. What the Supreme Court did not do in this decision was to spell out the relationship between the consumer being injured in her property, on the one hand, and the same Court's decision in *Illinois Brick*, on the other hand. The Court noted only in a footnote that the *Illinois Brick* issue was not before it.[63]

Proposed legislative remedies for creating a more manageable set of rules and procedures and for less protracted and expensive litigation in recovering damages for injured parties under class action suits have been advanced not only to give a damaged party proper due, but also to create a real deterrent to improper behavior. U.S. Attorney General Griffin Bell argued that the class action suit is an important part of the administration of justice and that "the primary interest [of small claim class action cases] is

[59]Ibid., p. 737.
[60]*Hanover Shoe, Inc.* v. *United Shoe Machinery Corp.*, 392 U.S. 481, 493 (1968).
[61]*Reiter* v. *Sonotone Corporation et al.*, 99 S. Ct. 2326 (1979).
[62]579 F. 2d 1077 (1978).
[63]99 S. Ct. 2326, 2330 fn. 3.

public: To prevent the unjust enrichment of wrongdoers and, by swift, effective legal action against them, to deter others from similar conduct."[64]

Dissolution, Divorcement, Divestiture   In a civil proceeding under the federal antitrust laws, a lower court may issue a decree compelling a firm to redistribute some or all of its assets through redistributing or altering ownership rights over those assets. This process or its results have come to be known as dissolution, divorcement, or divestiture: the three Ds of antitrust. The objective is to change the locus of the decision-making over use of particular business assets. Such change provides for a change in a market's structure. It therefore should provide for change in a firm's or firms' market conduct and, beyond that, in that market's performance. For this reason it is often cited as being the best solution to repetitive anticompetitive behavior of a firm or firms or to the constant danger of possible anticompetitive behavior in a market dominated by one or a very few firms.

Dissolution is the ultimate penalty. A firm may completely disappear in a dissolution proceeding. The Northern Securities Company, a holding company owning enough of the common stock of both the Great Northern and Northern Pacific railroads to centralize the decision-making of the two, was completely dissolved in order to return decision-making to the two separate would-be competing firms.[65] Standard Oil Company of New Jersey, a holding company, was ordered to distribute the shares of its 33 subsidiary companies to its stockholders.[66] Since this redistribution was made on a pro rata basis, the immediate result was not full decentralization of decision-making power. Power still remained in the hands of a small group of men who had constituted the central source of power before the dissolution.[67] If dissolution is to be an effective method for creating competitive market conditions, then how it is done must be carefully worked out.

The outright breakup of a corporation into several smaller parts has been a relatively rare event in the history of antitrust enforcement. The Supreme Court has considered it a remedy, not a penalty.[68] Judges have been reluctant to break up a corporation, especially for fear of destroying any economies of scale that may be present. Furthermore, there are many problems in deciding what plants or other assets should be the basis of the new corporations created and what is an equitable as well as an effective redistribution of the equity holdings in the new firms.

[64]Griffin B. Bell, *Hearings, Subcommittee on Judicial Machinery of the Senate Committee on the Judiciary, Reform of Class Action Litigation Proceedings*, 95th Cong., 2nd Sess., November 29, 1978, p. 4.

[65]*Northern Securities Co.* v. *U.S.*, 193 U.S. 197 (1904).

[66]*Standard Oil Co. of New Jersey* v. *U.S.*, 221 U.S. 1 (1911). A case study in Chapter 5 is based on this dissolution decree.

[67]Henry R. Seager and Charles A. Gulick, Jr., *Trust and Corporation Problems* (New York: Harper and Brothers, 1929), p. 123.

[68]*U.S.* v. *E. I. du Pont de Nemours & Co.*, 366 U.S. 316, 326–31 (1961).

Divorcement is the severing of integrated enterprises.[69] The case of the divorcement of production from the exhibition of motion pictures is a good illustration. Eight firms in the motion picture industry, including the "Big Five," were vertically integrated from production through exhibition. The small movie houses successfully made the argument that they were at a great disadvantage in competition with the large vertically integrated firms, which took advantage of their control of the better films and saw to it that they were able to exhibit these films under better time and cost conditions than the independent nonintegrated exhibitors. With the Supreme Court taking the position that divorcement was the best solution, consent decrees for that outcome were negotiated between 1948 and 1952.[70] No interlocking officers or directors were to be permitted for the separate production and exhibition companies, and dominant stockholders could retain stock in only one of the two stages of the industry.[71]

The concept of divorcement can also be applied to the divorce of firms previously married through merger. Since the active enforcement of the amended Section 7 of the Clayton Act, this form of divorcement has been quite common. A principal problem here has been how to re-create as a "going concern" a firm that had been acquired by another firm. A standard argument of those who have opposed such divorcement has been that it is difficult to accomplish—that once eggs are scrambled, it is practically impossible to unscramble them. This analogy, however, can be false.

The concept of *divestiture* encompasses several possible situations. Essentially it represents the forced "spinning off" of certain assets by a corporation. This could include the undoing of a merger, the creation of a new corporation from part of the assets of a corporation, or the forced sale of certain assets to another corporation. It could be represented by the compulsory licensing of a firm's patents to all other firms, at a reasonable royalty or royalty-free. It could include the ordered release of a brand name to general public use. Any of these possible forms of divestiture are equivalent to restructuring of a particular market. The "structural relief," in any case, is supposed to make the freedom of entry and operation better than it otherwise would be.

STATE ANTITRUST AND TRADE REGULATION

At the state level, antitrust and trade regulation commonly is in the hands of the state attorney general. Until the 1970s, state trade regulation had

---

[69]This definition is provided by Simon N. Whitney in *Antitrust Policies: American Experience in Twenty Industries* (New York: The Twentieth Century Fund, 1958), vol. II, p. 385.

[70]*U.S.* v. *Paramount Pictures, Inc.,* 334 U.S. 131 (1948).

[71]See Whitney, *Antitrust Policies,* chap. 15, for the whole story.

been weak, although it varied widely from state to state. Most of the states have statutory provisions against combinations, conspiracies, and restraints of trade, but these provisions have not generally been actively enforced. Direct consumer protection legislation aimed at shielding consumers from fraud has received considerable attention at the state (and even local) level since the late 1960s, but this area is still covered by a "patchwork" system of regulation.[72]

An increase in state antitrust activity beginning in the 1970s can be attributed to several factors.[73] New state laws have provided for expanded jurisdiction, more investigative powers, and stiffer penalties. State antimonopoly budgets have risen sharply. Beginning in 1977, federal grants have been made to the states to assist in antitrust enforcement.[74] Antitrust offices were created in about 25 states for the first time as a result of this federal funding.[75] Contributing to this increase in state activity have been the growth of the consumer movement, sizable increases in state purchases of equipment and supplies, inflation, and disclosure in federal cases of the extent of antitrust violations occurring at the local level.

The *parens patriae* provision of the Hart-Scott-Rodino Antitrust Improvements Act of 1976 gives statutory support to state attorneys general to bring civil suits for damages to the citizens of their states because of violations of the Sherman Act. Such suits would be in behalf of the state's consumers, not business units. This statute requires the attorney general of the United States, when initiating an antitrust action, to notify any state attorney general thought to be entitled to bring a suit based on this same alleged antitrust violation and to provide the state officer, upon request, with access to the investigative files "or other materials which are or may be relevant or material to the actual or potential cause of action under this Act." Under such circumstances, the state attorney general should have incentive to file such a suit.

Parens patriae suits are treble-action damage suits. The 1976 act also makes provision for the award of reasonable attorney's fees, but calculation of these private attorney's fees on a contingency basis is prohibited. In effect, these suits would be powerful class action suits, but bypass some of the weaknesses of class action suits. Price-fixing damages to consumers could fairly readily be calculated because the statute specifically provides that "damages may be proved and assessed in the aggregate by statistical

[72]Jonathan A. Sheldon and George J. Zweibel, *Survey of Consumer Fraud Law* (Washington, D.C.: U.S. Government Printing Office, 1978), p. 207.

[73]See *Wall Street Journal*, October 4, 1976, pp. 1, 16.

[74]Grant Program to Aid State Antitrust Enforcement, authorized in Sec. 309 of the Crime Control Act of 1976.

[75]Ky P. Ewing, Jr., Deputy Assistant Attorney General, Antitrust Division, "The Relationship of Federal and State Antitrust Enforcement: A Partnership in Making Competition Work," remarks before the 1978 Conference of Western Attorneys General, East Glacier, Montana, August 7, 1978, mimeo, p. 9.

or sampling methods" or any "other reasonable system of estimating aggregate damages as the court" may permit. And the court can distribute the damage monies in any way it chooses, including depositing them with the state as general revenues. There is, in short, no need to prove individual claims or to find some exactly equitable system of distribution of the proceeds. These suits can thus be considered much more "manageable" than a private class action suit, a lack for which class action suits can be thrown out of court. Public notice must be given, and individuals can still opt out to pursue their own remedies if they wish.

SUMMARY

The basic statutes that are the heart of antitrust policy are the Sherman Antitrust Act of 1890, the Federal Trade Commission Act of 1914, and the Clayton Act of 1914, together with their various amendments over the years. Their language is general in nature, outlawing restraints of trade, monopolizing and attempting to monopolize, unfair methods of competition, and, where they may substantially lessen competition or tend to create a monopoly, price discrimination, exclusive dealing, and mergers. Because of this general language, court decisions have been necessary to interpret their application to particular business situations. Some business practices, after repeated court decisions against them, have become illegal *per se.* A rule of reason has to be applied to other business practices to determine whether or not, under the particular circumstances of a case, they are illegal.

The two principal federal enforcement agencies are the Antitrust Division of the Department of Justice and the Federal Trade Commission. The Department of Justice has jurisdiction over the Sherman Act and the Clayton Act. The Federal Trade Commission has also been given enforcement responsibilities over several other trade regulation laws, such as the Webb-Pomerene Export Trade Act of 1918 and several labeling and credit information statutes.

The procedures of these two federal agencies differ in several major respects. The Department of Justice can use civil or criminal proceedings and must prosecute through the courts. The Federal Trade Commission is an independent enforcement agency and, as such, is quasi-judicial in nature. The Federal Trade Commission can also promulgate trade regulation rules that have the full force and effect of law. The great majority of these rules are designed to provide the consumer with direct protection against unfair or deceptive acts or practices.

Although the basic antitrust laws carry with them certain uncertainties as to their meaning and application, the Department of Justice and the Federal Trade Commission have established procedures to help remove that uncertainty. Guidelines have been announced to keep business informed of the regulatory agencies' views as to what they would consider illegal with respect to certain business practices. These agencies will also give an advisory opinion. Where certain business practices have become, through court precedent, illegal *per se*, the uncertainty of the law has been eliminated.

The threats of fines, imprisonment, private treble damage suits, civil penalties, consumer redress, and class action suits can force firms to act with care. Where other remedies are inadequate, the Department of Justice can seek to change a market structure by petitioning a court to break up a firm or to force the firm to divest itself of some of its assets.

State trade regulation, commonly in the hands of state attorneys general, has tended to be weak, although the 1970s has seen an increase in state enforcement activity. Federal legislation facilitating state class action suits, access to federal antitrust data, and provisions for federal seed money have served to accelerate state antitrust enforcement action.

Selected Readings

CIRACE, JOHN, "A Game Theoretic Analysis of Contribution and Claim Reduction in Antitrust Treble Damage Suits," *St. John's Law Review*, 55, no. 1 (Fall 1980), 42–62.

ELZINGA, K. G., AND W. BREIT, *The Antitrust Penalties: A Study in Law and Economics.* New Haven, Conn.: Yale University Press, 1976.

KATZMANN, ROBERT A., *Regulatory Bureaucracy: The Federal Trade Commission and Antitrust Policy.* Cambridge, Mass.: The MIT Press, 1980.

POSNER, RICHARD A., "A Statistical Study of Antitrust Enforcement," *Journal of Law and Economics*, 13, no. 2 (October 1970), 365–419.

THORELLI, HANS B., *The Federal Antitrust Policy: Organization of an American Tradition.* Baltimore: The Johns Hopkins Press, 1955.

WEAVER, SUZANNE, *Decision to Prosecute: Organization and Public Policy in the Antitrust Division.* Cambridge, Mass.: The MIT Press, 1980.

3 — Horizontal Price Relationships

The most common offense under the antitrust laws is behavior among competitors designed to avoid price competition. Where competing firms act together to control price, they are *per se* violating the antitrust laws, either Section 1 of the Sherman Act or Section 5 of the Federal Trade Commission Act. Although neither of these statutes specifically outlaws price-fixing, legal precedent of successive court decisions has made it clear that price-fixing is not to be tolerated under these statutes; it is a *per se* offense. In some states, however, statutes do directly prohibit collusive price-fixing.

It is important to understand the means by which price fixing can be accomplished and the forces at work which bring it about. It is likewise important to distinguish between a market price which has been fixed and one which has the appearance of having been fixed.

BASIC METHODS OF FIXING PRICE

The history of collusive price-fixing indicates that there are certain basic methods employed by competitors to avoid price competition. Price can be established jointly by the competitors either by agreeing upon the price to be charged or by controlling the quantity of the product which is supplied to the market. Indirect ways of avoiding price competition can be found in various forms of market sharing (division).

Controlling Market Price or Quantity   Price-fixing among business rivals may be accomplished in one of two possible basic ways, either of which is equally illegal. The conspirators may fix the price (including discounts and credit terms) directly, simply agreeing among themselves as to what the price of the product or service will be. Or, they may decide what quantity of the product they will permit to reach the marketplace. This is done on the assumption that a given quantity of product will clear the market only at a certain price. Price and the quantity demanded are almost always inversely related. A higher quantity of product will be demanded only at a lower price. And a lower quantity of the product will be demanded at a higher price. All the conspirators have to do is to estimate that quantity which will clear the market at the price they desire. They then can agree to limit the total quantity that reaches the market to that amount; the marketplace will take care of the rest.

As shown in Figure 3.1, the conspirators can decide among themselves to charge a price of p_1. At that price the quantity demanded will be q_1. On the other hand, the conspirators can attempt to achieve a market price of p_1 by seeing to it that the quantity reaching the market for sale is quantity q_1. The direct fixing of the price is a more certain procedure for fixing a particular price. What the colluding firms set to be the price will be the price (provided there is no break in the agreement). Controlling the quantity supplied at quantity q_1 in an effort to fix price at p_1 is a less certain method for achieving a particular desired price, since the exact shape and position of the demand curve can only be estimated.

The price (or quantity) selected by the members of the agreement will tend to be that which an individual monopolist would choose. The problem is one of joint profit maximization. All other things being the same, a monopolistic price will be higher than a competitive price. The whole history of monopoly furnishes evidence of the higher prices of monopolists,

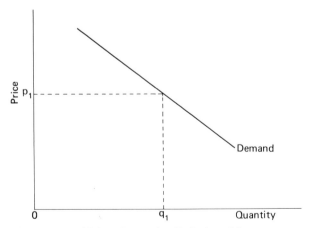

Figure 3.1   Price-Quantity Relationships

and theoretical analysis demonstrates that a monopolist will tend to select a lower rate of output and a higher price than would a truly competitive seller. The parties engaging in the price collusion will, however, have to consider the height of any barriers to entry that may be present when they set the price. There is some "limit" price that will yield a super-normal or economic profit, but any price above this will attract new competition.

Market Sharing Certain other selling practices that are closely related to and frequently accompany price agreements have likewise been determined to be illegal *per se*. These practices, which help to make the cartelization more complete, are territorial division, customer division, and product division. The phenomena are sometimes referred to as *market sharing*.

Territorial division occurs when two or more sellers decide to allocate the market between themselves on the basis of geographic territories. Seller A can confine its selling efforts to the area west of the Mississippi River, for example, while seller B restricts sales to the area east of the Mississippi. Or seller A can sell in one county while seller B sells in another county. If the firms are selling in world markets, seller A can sell in South America while seller B sells in Africa. The largest firms in an industry can in this way avoid direct confrontation with each other, and whatever competition there is in a given geographic territory will be between the large company and whatever small ones are also to be found in that territory.

A second form of market sharing is done by breaking down the marketplace, by individual customers, by type of customer, or by shares (percentages) of the aggregate business. Certain large buyers can be singled out as being the special customer of seller A, and other particular buyers can be reserved for seller B. Or one seller may confine its selling efforts to institutional buyers while the other seller considers its clientele to be retail stores. Or they can take turns submitting lowest bids on particular projects so that each seller gets its appropriate share of the total business available. In any case, competitive confrontation by the sellers is avoided.

A third form of market sharing is product division, which is represented by the situation in which seller A sells one particular type of product and seller B sells another, both in the same geographic territory. These products may be similar, but not perfectly substitutable. For example, one producer of razor blades back in the early 1960s sold close to 95 percent of the double-edge razor blades, while two other firms were the principal producers of the single-edge blade. A court observed that Gillette (Double-edge blades), on the one hand, and Shick Safety Razor Company and the American Safety Razor Company (single-edge blades), on the other hand, had made no serious attempt to invade each other's field by producing the other type of blade. The court saw a lack, therefore, of effective competition.[1] A major issue has not been made of product division because intent to avoid competition through this means may be exceedingly difficult to prove. Indeed, where the products are similar and yet different, this could be presented as evidence of attempt to compete more effectively by differentiation of products.

LEGAL PRECEDENT ON PRICE-FIXING

When collusive price-fixing first came before the courts under the Sherman Act before the turn of the century, the defendant firms attempted to show horizontal price-fixing as a legitimate economic practice. They argued that the price agreements were designed to prevent "ruinous" or "destructive" competition among themselves and that the prices being fixed were just and reasonable ones. Mutual protection was needed against ruinous competition. Otherwise, the weaker firms would be destroyed, and the survivors would raise prices as high as possible.[2]

Early Decisions   The Supreme Court rejected this general argument on several grounds. The first (*Trans-Missouri Freight Assn.*) decision (1897), which involved railroads fixing and enforcing rail rates, stated that the Sherman Act condemned "every" restraint of trade, and that the word "every" was to be taken literally.[3] The second (*Joint Traffic Assn.*) decision (1898), also involving railroads fixing rates, doubted that competition would necessarily lead to the destruction of the weaker railroads, and held that even if this possibility existed, competition should still be relied upon.[4] The Court was certainly not alarmed at the possibility of the "public calamity" the railroads argued would result if there were no agreements.[5]

The third (*Addyston Pipe & Steel*) decision (1899), involving producers of cast iron pipe who were dividing markets and customers and were rigging bids, took the position that this price-fixing was a general or nonancillary restraint of trade and was therefore unlawful.[6] If it were an ancillary restraint, there might be some justification for the restraint. For example, a restaurateur might sell his restaurant, including its good will, under the condition that he would not enter into competition with the buyer after the sale. Unless there were this restriction built into the contract

---

[1]*The Gillette Company* v. *White Cross Discount Centers, Inc., et al.,* Trade Cases para. 70,481 (Pa. Ct. of Common Pleas, Allegheny Co., 1962). This case involved an attempt by a manufacturer to enforce a state fair trade law. To enforce fair trade resale price maintenance under such a law, a manufacturer had to prove that "fair and open competition" existed.

[2]*U.S.* v. *Trans-Missouri Freight Assn.,* 53 Fed. 440, 451 (1892).

[3]*U.S.* v. *Trans-Missouri Freight Assn.,* 166 U.S. 290.

[4]*U.S.* v. *Joint Traffic Assn.,* 171 U.S. 505, 576–77.

[5]Ibid., p. 534.

[6]*Addyston Pipe & Steel Co.* v. *U.S.,* 175 U.S. 211.

of sale, the buyer would never have made the purchase; thus, the restraint could be considered reasonable and therefore lawful. In general price-fixing agreements, however, there is no such lawful purpose and therefore no way to measure their reasonableness. A *quid pro quo* cannot be determined.

In these decisions, competition clearly took precedence over the private interests involved. If one were to attempt to differentiate among and to decide which price-fixing arrangements were in the public interest, what would one use as a standard of measure? As a lower court in the third case had put it, such an administration of justice would be one of adopting a "shifting, vague, and indeterminate . . . standard."[7] Furthermore, one can readily imagine the chaos in the courts if all horizontal price-fixing conspiracies were to be subjected to a court test of their reasonableness. One could foresee the possibility, indeed perhaps the probability, that any price-fixing agreement found to be unreasonable by the courts would quickly and readily be replaced by another agreement. And each newly fixed price could well be subjected to litigation as to its reasonableness. From this viewpoint alone, it is clearly better to have competition be the judge rather than the man or woman sitting on the bench.

A Landmark Case The economic logic of the rationale against price-fixing was carried to its ultimate conclusion in the Supreme Court's 1927 landmark decision in the *Trenton Potteries* case.[8] This case involved 82 percent of the business of manufacturing and distributing vitreous pottery in the United States for use in bathrooms and lavatories. The defendants argued that the prices they fixed were reasonable prices and that they were, again, only trying to prevent "ruinous" competition. If the prices they fixed only yielded a normal profit, could they not therefore be considered to be reasonable prices? The court said, however, that reasonableness had to be judged by the effect of an agreement on competition itself. If competition were being restrained at all, then that was enough to judge it unreasonable: ". . . the public interest is best protected from the evils of monopoly and price control by the maintenance of competition." Further, "The reasonable price fixed today may through economic and business changes become the unreasonable price of tomorrow."[9]

Solidification of the Precedent A 1940 decision of the Supreme Court further solidified the concept of price-fixing as being a *per se* violation of the Sherman Act by condemning price-fixing achieved by controlling supply.[10] Several major oil companies in the Midwest had organized a

[7] 85 Fed. 271, 284 (1898).
[8] *U.S.* v. *Trenton Potteries Co.*, 273 U.S. 392.
[9] Ibid., p. 397.
[10] *U.S.* v. *Socony-Vacuum Oil Co., Inc.*, 310 U.S. 150.

program of purchasing the so-called distress gasoline being put on the spot market by relatively small independent refiners who had no regular outlets of their own. This "distress" gasoline was destabilizing the wholesale price of gasoline and contributing to price wars at the retail level. The major refiners were able to control and raise the wholesale price and thus influence the retail price by a concerted and well-timed program of purchases of gasoline from the independent refiners. By buying from assigned "dancing partners," the major refiners kept the marginal quantities of gasoline supplies emanating from the independent refiner sector of the industry from spoiling the price structure.

The argument that fairer competitive prices resulted when distress gasoline was removed from the market was entirely unacceptable to the Court. The avoidance of "ruinous competition," "financial disaster," or "evils of price cutting" provided no justification for avoiding the play of the forces of supply and demand.[11] The Court saw its decision as a continuation of 40 years of consistent adherence to the principle that price-fixing agreements were illegal *per se* under the Sherman Act.[12] "Under the Sherman Act a combination formed for the purpose and with the effect of raising, depressing, fixing, pegging, or stabilizing the price of a commodity in interstate or foreign commerce is illegal per se. . . ."[13]

Any collusive price behavior between or among independent firms is thus clearly illegal. This applies to vertical as well as horizontal relationships, as we will see in Chapter 6. As Chief Justice Warren said in a Supreme Court decision in 1956:

> It has been held too often to require elaboration now that price fixing is contrary to the policy of competition underlying the Sherman Act and that its illegality does not depend on a showing of its unreasonableness, since it is conclusively presumed to be unreasonable. It makes no difference whether the motives of the participants are good or evil; whether the price fixing is accomplished by express contract or by some more sub-

[11]Ibid., p. 221.

[12]Ibid., p. 218. Some analysts have argued that the Supreme Court's opinion in *Appalachian Coals, Inc.* v. *U.S.*, 288 U.S. 344 (1933), provided a clear break in the consistency of the Court's holdings that price-fixing is illegal *per se*. This case involved the formation of an exclusive selling agency by 137 producers of bituminous coal in Appalachian territory. The arrangement was not found to be in violation of the Sherman Act, even though it would eliminate competition among the defendants. The Supreme Court in *Socony Vacuum* viewed the Appalachian circumstances to be unique and attempted to differentiate that case. It was held to be a special genre and therefore not inconsistent with the principle of price-fixing as being *per se* illegal. It saw the exclusive sales agency as being not designed to fix market prices and unlikely that it could. The bituminous coal industry was seen as being a declining industry with overcapacity—a sick industry in distress. Furthermore, the agency plan had not actually been put into effect; if it were, and if it did control price, then the government could bring a suit.

[13]310 U.S. 150,223.

tle means; whether the participants possess market control; whether the amount of interstate commerce affected is large or small; or whether the effect of the agreement is to raise or decrease prices.[14]

The fixing of credit terms is considered the same as the fixing of prices and equally illegal.[15]

INDUCEMENTS FOR PRICE-FIXING

If collusive price-fixing is clearly illegal under the Sherman Act, why is it one of the most frequent antitrust crimes? Quite consistently over the past three decades, price-fixing cases have accounted for more than half the antitrust suits filed each year by the Antitrust Division of the Department of Justice. The Federal Trade Commission has also issued price-fixing complaints from time to time under Section 5 of the Federal Trade Commission Act. Since 1976 a criminal violation of the Sherman Act has been a felony rather than a misdemeanor, with much greater possible fines and terms of imprisonment, but the Antitrust Division continued to find it advisable and productive to emphasize price-fixing in the suits it filed. The assistant attorney general in charge of the Antitrust Division remarked in 1977 that he believed price-fixing had been "virtually institutionalized" in many industries.[16]

Price-fixing has been classified as white-collar crime in a manual prepared for the Enforcement Program Division of the Law Enforcement Assistance Administration of the Department of Justice.[17] Price-fixing is a subtle form of robbing the public. The higher prices of price-fixing are costs ultimately borne by the consuming public. Even the few cents of a higher price of a unit of good or service, multiplied by perhaps many millions of units sold, can add up to millions or hundreds of millions of dollars of income transferred from consumers to the price-fixing producers.

Price-fixing is represented in many facets of business: producers' and consumers' goods, service and commodities, and professional as well as commercial services. The dimensions of the market involved may be national, regional, or local. Price-fixing is often accompanied by the division of markets. In one year alone, 1978, press releases of the Department of

[14]U.S. v. McKesson & Robbins, Inc., 351 U.S. 305, 309–10 (1956).

[15]Catalano, Inc., et al. v. Target Sales, Inc., et al., 446 U.S. 643 (1980). In this case beer wholesalers agreed to eliminate short-term trade credit entirely. This was held to be the same as eliminating discounts and thus the same as price-fixing.

[16]John H. Shenefield, "Antitrust—Looking Ahead," remarks before the Financial Analysts Federation, Washington, D.C., June 29, 1977, mimeo, p. 3.

[17]U.S. Department of Justice, The Investigation of White-collar Crime (Washington, D.C.: U.S. Government Printing Office, 1977), pp. 12, 15, 278, 306.

Justice described price-fixing situations in violation of the Sherman Act such as the following: four prestressed concrete contractors rigging bids and allocating construction projects in New Mexico; a conspiracy to fix the price of land-surveying services; five corporations and two individuals conspiring to submit rigged bids and to allocate contracts for the sale of architectural hardware in New England; two large nationally known firms fixing the prices of gas meters throughout the United States; eleven New York City building maintenance service contractors allocating customers to permit submission of noncompetitive bids for contracts and compensating each other for customers lost to one another; five companies and four individuals conspiring to fix prices of paper products in South Florida; and three wholesale distributors of bakery products in the Gulf Coast area of Mississippi fixing prices and allocating territories. It was also during 1978 that an administrative law judge handed down a decision under Section 5 of the Federal Trade Commission Act condemning three medical associations for preventing their members from engaging in price competition and the Supreme Court ruled against price-fixing by the National Society of Professional Engineers.

The general conclusion from all this evidence is that it has paid to fix prices. Some price fixers have readily admitted balancing the possible profits against the risks of being caught.[18] To the individual corporate manager fixing prices of the products of a division, it may seem to be a way to show better performance and as a result to receive better pay and promotion. When top management directs the price-fixing, it may simply be viewed as a source of higher profits. Who actually initiates price-fixing schemes is not always clear. But regardless of who actually sets up a conspiracy, there are certain market characteristics which, if present, create a favorable economic setting.

Few Sellers   The fewer the number of sellers in a market, the greater is the likelihood of a price conspiracy. Walter Erickson views two types of market structure as being "prone to conspiracy": one contains a very small number of firms; the other has a somewhat larger number of firms but has one or two that predominate in size.[19] In any case, the fewer there are, the easier it is to reach an agreement. Beyond a certain point, the numbers become great enough to make it difficult to come to agreement. Or, if an agreement is made, there are more chances that it will fail because of recalcitrant action. Furthermore, agreements require joint discussion to arrive at a satisfactory profit-maximizing price. The fewer the sellers, the easier for them to get together in some convenient and unobtrusive place.

[18]*Business Week,* June 2, 1975, p. 42.
[19]Walter B. Erickson, "Economics of Price Fixing," *Antitrust Law & Economics Review,* 2, no. 3 (Spring 1969), 85.

A hotel or motel room, an obscure corner of a bar, or even a golf course can provide the necessary meeting place.[20]

Trade associations have been used effectively in some situations as an implementing device for price-fixing. Trade association meetings bring together the members of an industry. Where trade associations have been active and served as a central meeting place, they have sometimes gone beyond the performance of their legitimate economic functions and facilitated collusive agreements. One of the functions of trade associations has been to gather statistical information, including price data, and this can facilitate the discussion of prices. Where the associations have been strong and provided active leadership in price-fixing, the number of sellers can be larger than would ordinarily be considered possible for effective agreement and enforcement of an agreement.

Demand Conditions   Industries whose demand curves have certain characteristics make them prime candidates for price-fixing. If the industry demand is highly inelastic, there is an inducement for holding the price up or, better still, raising it. For with higher prices, there will be greater total revenue. At the same time, however, although industry demand may be inelastic, the individual firm's demand may be viewed as highly elastic. If the product is a fairly standardized one, such as a bag of Portland cement, an ingot of steel, or a thousand board feet of lumber, a small price cut by one seller may increase the quantity demand by a fairly large amount. This situation creates a fear of price-cutting.

If one firm cuts its price, others will feel obliged to meet that price cut. The more uniform and therefore substitutable the product of the industry is, the greater is this so. This factor is amplified if the product is uniform over a considerable period of time—if product innovation is slow. If all the firms cut their price in order to hold their market shares, they will all be worse off since, with the industry demand curve being inelastic, a lower price in all the industry means lower total revenues. By joining together in a price agreement, all the firms can gain the economic advantage of holding the price up or raising it. A price increase by all sellers in the industry will tend to lower the total quantity demanded, but total revenues will increase.

Figure 3.2 shows a market structure in which there is a small number of firms and in which product demand is generally inelastic. The curve DD represents a firm's share of the industry demand. Movements along DD occur when *all* firms change price in step. At price p_1, all firms would be hurt by any cutting that might bring price down to level p_2. The lower price of p_2 will increase the quantity demanded from q_1 to q_2, but because the

[20]Adam Smith in 1776 in his famous *Wealth of Nations* summed it up as well as anyone when he wrote: "People of the same trade seldom meet together, even for merriment and diversion, but the conversation ends in a conspiracy against the public or in some contrivance to raise prices." Book I, chap. X, part II.

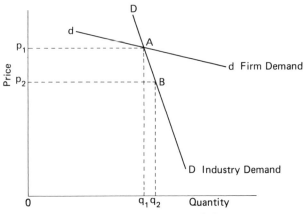

Figure 3.2   Oligopolistic Demand Curves

industry demand is inelastic, the increase in the quantity demanded will not offset the fact that price has been lowered on all the units to be sold. Total revenue for all members of that market will decline. Each firm may maintain its share of the market, but each share will bring in less revenue. The total revenue represented by area Op_2Bq_2 is clearly less than the total revenue represented by the area Op_1Aq_1.

The individual firm may nevertheless be caught in a conflict. Although realizing that a reduced market price makes each firm worse off in terms of revenue received, it may see an advantage if it alone can cut price. Its own demand would appear, as in Figure 3.2, as firm demand dd, which represents an elastic demand. A cut in price below p_1 by one firm alone would increase the quantity demanded of that firm by more than enough to offset the lower price, and that firm's total revenue would increase. Its price cut would draw business away from its rivals. There is an incentive for the firm to cut price if it thinks it can do so at the expense of its competitors without their following with a retaliatory price cut. This provides a spur to secret price cuts and discounts. The recognition that price-cutting cannot be concealed for long, however, provides an inducement for collusion among the competitors to hold price up.

Collusion under these conditions is also a more certain way to achieve an increase in price. If an individual firm independently were to try to increase its price above p_1, the competitors may very well not follow. If they do not, the firm will lose business to its competitors and suffer a decrease in total revenue. If all firms increase price together, they can all enjoy the increase in total revenue that will accompany the inelasticity of the industry demand.

In many industries, demand for the industry's product is inelastic because it is a demand derived from the demand for some final product of which it constitutes only one component. Suppose that the copper tubing going into the construction of a residential home is only 3 percent of the total cost of the house. If the price of the copper tubing is raised by 20 percent, this means that the cost of the house has gone up by only six-tenths of 1 percent (20 percent of 3 percent). It is unlikely that such an increase in cost will cause a home builder to revise his plans to build a house. There is, of course, the risk that in the long run builders will seek some less expensive substitute for the copper tubing.

Supply and Cost Conditions When an industry with a small number of sellers is experiencing considerable overcapacity relative to demand and that industry's demand is inelastic, there is a special incentive to engage in collusion to avoid unprofitable price-cutting. Demand may have contracted cyclically, or it may have declined for a protracted period of time. Or the industry may have overbuilt in expectation of future demand growth.[21] The temptation to use idle fixed resources may now prompt some firm or firms to sell at lower than previous quoted or book price. This is likely to trigger retaliatory price cuts and price warring. Collusive price agreements can help prevent this deep price-cutting. On the other hand, the greater the idle production facilities, the weaker may be the price agreements.

Spiraling price-cutting can drive price down in the short run to where it barely covers average variable costs. As long as price covers the immediate costs of raw materials, labor, and transportation, plus at least some contribution to the fixed costs associated with plant and equipment, it would pay the firm to continue to produce and sell at this level. If the firm were to cease operations, it would be making no contribution to overhead costs, which continue even when the firm is not producing any product at all. To continue to operate and make some contribution to these fixed costs is better than ceasing to operate and making no contribution to them.

This problem is exacerbated in the so-called heavy or capital-intensive industries, where fixed costs represent a high percentage of total costs. The higher the percentage of the costs that are fixed, the greater the fear of price-cutting and the greater the desire for an agreement on price. When prices are forced down to the variable cost level in these industries, much of the costs of the individual firms are not being recouped.

Figure 3.3 compares the impact of price-war conditions on a firm in a capital-intensive industry (a) with one in an industry where more of the total costs are variable (b). Assume in each case that total costs are the same. Prices can spiral downward further in the case of the capital-intensive industry because variable costs constitute a lower percentage of

---

[21]Erickson cites periods of overcapacity in the pipe, pottery, gasoline, and electrical equipment industries as immediately preceding the formation of price-fixing agreements in those industries. "Economics of Price Fixing," p. 86.

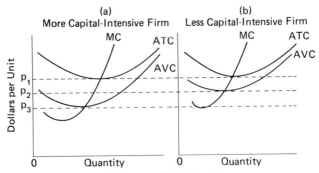

Figure 3.3 Fixed versus Variable Costs

the firm's costs. For the firm in situation (b), prices can go down no further than p_2; if they did, the firm would shut down. For the firm in industry (a), however, price can go down as low as p_3 before it would shut down operations. Thus, for the capital-intensive industries, more of the firm's total costs may go uncovered in a price war and there is more incentive to prevent a price war through a collusive agreement. It is not surprising, therefore, to find many of the price-fixing conspiracies occurring in capital-intensive industries.

Similar cost conditions within a given industry will also facilitate price-fixing agreements. If the firms that are attempting to reach an agreement on price are experiencing the same overall costs, the agreement can be more readily reached. They will be thinking in terms of the same costs which have to be covered, and no one of them will have a cost advantage in seeking a lower price.

PRICE-FIXING SYSTEMS

A price-fixing agreement among business rivals can be a relatively simple thing. A small number of sellers can all agree to charge a given price, including discounts and credit terms, in the marketplace in which they are in competition. This price can be viewed by customers and the outside world as the "going" competitive price. The end result appears to be the same as that of the model of perfect competition, which also yields a single "going" market price. The basic difference—yet a crucial difference—between these two market models is that one has only a few sellers and the other has a large number of sellers. In the real world, there are different methods of colluding with respect to price and avoiding price competition.

Alternative Methods of Bid Rigging Procurement of supplies or the letting of contracts for projects, especially by government agencies, is often accomplished through bids, frequently on a sealed-bid basis. Conspirators wishing to avoid price competition among themselves have two choices in submitting bids. First, they can all submit the same bid, in which case the buyer will have to choose among them on some basis other than price. The advantage to the sellers in this method is that the price is uniform and easily understood by all. A disadvantage is that the distribution of the business may be skewed over time in favor of one or more sellers. Indeed, if this is true, the other sellers may fear that the successful obtainer of contracts may have been engaging in some *sub rosa* means of obtaining the contracts, such as kickbacks or bribes or lavish entertaining of the buyers. This possibility may help to destroy the solidity of the price agreement. A second weakness of this method of submitting uniform bids is that it may arouse the curiosity of the buyers and possibly even the antitrust authorities. How come, they may ask, all bids are exactly alike? And grave suspicion will replace curiosity when identical bids are made down to the sixth decimal point, as when the U.S. Army Corps of Engineers opened 11 sealed bids for cement in New Mexico and found that the prices bid were all $3.286854 per barrel.[22]

Because of the suspicion uniform bid prices may arouse, conspiring contractors and suppliers seeking business through the bid method are now much more likely to allocate the business and ensure an equitable distribution among themselves by taking turns bidding low and bidding high. The now-infamous electrical equipment price-fixing conspiracies which were exposed in 1960 offer a classic example (they are examined in some detail at the end of this chapter). Nonuniform bid prices obviously offer considerably less circumstantial evidence than uniformity of bids.

Collusive Delivered Pricing   One method of collusive pricing that prevailed in several industries from the turn of the century until 1948 was a system of delivered pricing known as *basing-point pricing*. This system should now be relegated to history, but occasionally it has made a reappearance.

The member firms of an industry understand that they are expected to adhere to a certain formula so they will all arrive at quoted delivered prices which will be the same for any particular customer at the point of delivery, no matter which seller it is or from where it ships. The most elementary form of basing-point pricing is represented by the "Pittsburgh-plus" system used in the steel industry for about 20 years beginning in 1903. The formula was this: The base price in Pittsburgh plus rail freight from Pittsburgh. The Pittsburgh base price was well known to all steel sellers. Transportation charges always had to be rail freight charges. If any other form of transport cost were charged (by water, for

---

[22]*Aetna Portland Cement Co.* v. *FTC*, 157 F. 2d 533, 576 (1946).

example), the formula would not yield a uniform delivered price. All sellers had to use not only the same base price, but also the same freight charges. This single basing-point system in the steel industry was replaced by a multiple basing-point system of delivered prices as the result of an FTC order in 1924.[23] Although the FTC had intended steel sellers to price products from their actual points of shipment, the new system set up had three base points: Pittsburgh, Chicago, and Birmingham, Alabama. A new formula to achieve the quotation of uniform delivered prices now prevailed: the lowest sum of one of these three possible base prices plus rail freight from the relevant base point to the destination.

It was not until 1948 that the Supreme Court condemned as collusive the basing-point system used in the cement industry and that use of basing-point pricing became clearly recognized as violating the antitrust laws.[24] The collusiveness of prices violated Section 5 of the Federal Trade Commission Act, and the price discrimination inherent in this system violated Section 2 of the Robinson-Patman Act. Price discrimination among buyers who purchased from a given seller results whenever the transportation costs charged are not those actually incurred. Sellers of cement who shipped from locations that were not basing points could be charging nonexisting freight charges (phantom freight). And shippers of cement from base points to customers located in areas governed, for purposes of the pricing formula, by another base point could be charging less for freight than the actual freight incurred (freight absorption). Shippers of cement from nonbase points would also be absorbing freight if their shipments were to a customer located closer to a base point than to the shipper.

The Economic Costs of Price-Fixing A collusive system of basing-point pricing is an excellent vehicle through which to observe how price-fixing serves to misallocate economic resources. Transportation charges are artificial. Rail freight rates are applied even though cheaper truck or water transport is available or has been used. Customers are denied the right to go to the point of origin to pick up in their own vehicles the product they have ordered. Nor can customers set up warehouses at a base point and take delivery there instead of at the point of use. The competition among the buyers who have been paying prices not based on true cost differences is accordingly adversely affected.[25] The dominant firms in the industry, which establish the base prices, set them high enough to cover any amounts of freight that have to be absorbed. Natural economic forces that would under truly competitive conditions determine plant locations are blocked.[26]

[23]*In the Matter of United States Steel Corporation et al.,* 8 F.T.C. 1.

[24]*FTC* v. *Cement Institute,* 333 U.S. 683 (1948).

[25]See *Corn Products Refining Company* v. *FTC,* 324 U.S. 726 (1945).

[26]See George W. Stocking, *Basing Point Pricing and Regional Development* (Chapel Hill: University of North Carolina Press, 1954), for a study of the impact of basing-point pricing of steel on the economic development of the South.

Small firms whose plants are located elsewhere than at base points can be forced to adhere to the pricing system or be kept from growing and obtaining a larger share of the market by threats to declare their plant locations to be base points with base prices set at below-cost levels.[27] If a small nonbase mill suddenly finds itself a base point whose base price will not cover that firm's total costs, there is no way that firm can make a profit on any sale, since delivered prices for that firm will now be its base price plus actual freight. If the firm has to absorb freight when selling in a location governed by another base mill, its loss will be even greater. Such pricing has been referred to as *punitive pricing*. It is so punitive that just the threat that it will be applied can be enough to convince the smaller nonbase mills to adhere to the system.

Basing-points in the 1970s The FTC found what it saw as enough evidence of use of basing-point pricing in two industries to issue complaints and orders in the 1970s. In 1975 it alleged that three Portland cement manufacturers were stabilizing prices and reducing competition by collecting and exchanging price information, using a system of identical delivered prices, refusing to permit customers to pick up cement at the mill or at a terminal site, and refusing to permit the use of any hauler other than that designated by them to transport the cement. This complaint was settled by consent order in 1976.[28] In the second industry the FTC issued an order in 1978 against the system of pricing utilized by five manufacturers of softwood plywood.[29] Prior to 1963, plywood was produced entirely in the Northwest and delivered prices were a base price plus actual rail freight. But after that date, as production expanded into the South, southern manufacturers continued to use freight from the Northwest in computing delivered prices. The difference between actual freight incurred and the freight factor utilized "diverged sharply."

This was no minor matter, for by 1974, 47.5 percent of the plywood sheathing in question was being produced in the South and more than 50 percent of this southern production was accounted for by the five respondents. The FTC condemned the "extreme artificiality of the formula pricing" of this Pacific Northwest single basing-point system of pricing. In both orders it required that sellers offer to buyers the option of being quoted a point-of-origin price and the right to arrange their own transportation. Point-of-origin prices were to be delivered prices less the actual freight that would have been incurred to the destination.

The FTC's order in the plywood case was challenged, and a court of appeals ruled against the Commission.[30] One thing the court and the FTC

[27]An illustration from the cement industry can be found in *FTC v. Cement Institute, et al.*, 333 U.S. 683, 714 (1948).
[28]*In the Matter of Martin Marietta Corporation et al.*, 88 F.T.C. 989.
[29]*In the Matter of Boise Cascade Corporation et al.*, 91 F.T.C. 1.
[30]*Boise Cascade Corp., Champion International Corp., Georgia-Pacific Corp., Weyerhaeuser Co., and Williamete Industries, Inc. v. FTC.* Trade Cases para. 63,323 (1980).

agreed upon was that the above-normal or economic profits being earned in the southern portion of the industry during its early years of development as a result of prices being based upon West Coast prices plus freight from the West Coast were legitimate economic profits. They were what spurred the development of new supply capacity in the South. But once the southern portion of the industry was developed, the FTC thought the continuation of West Coast plus freight prices represented artificial pricing that caused prices to be higher than competitive prices would have been. Unfortunately for the FTC, there was inadequate evidence of collusion, and the cost and profit data available were "equivocal at best."

The court of appeals saw "certain resemblances" in this case to the classic collusive basing-point cases, but also found major differences: "Petitioners' West Coast freight is not a true basing-point pricing system." The court accepted the argument of the five plywood manufacturers that the West Coast freight factor was "merely a matter of form" that had no effect on price in the "highly competitive" plywood industry. West Coast plus freight quotations had been continued to be made, it was said, because the West Coast and southern plywoods were in competition with each other, and many customers preferred a West Coast freight price quotation as a competitive check on the delivered prices being quoted. The price comparisons being made did not represent collusive price matching. There was a range of prices, although not wide, and buyers were probing the market seeking the best possible price. There were discounts and actual bargaining over the base price. The five producers denied that they would not quote prices at the plant itself. In sum, the court of appeals took the position that the FTC had presented only a theory, and that the evidence "falls far short of the evidence presented in virtually all of the classic basing-point cases." For the court, "sophisticated economic theories" were not enough. It was looking for substantial evidence of overt collusion that actually had the effect of fixing or stabilizing prices, and no such evidence was presented. What kind of evidence is needed? We attempt to find some answers below.

PARALLEL BUSINESS CONDUCT

Agreements affecting price are, as we have seen, clearly illegal. In many oligopolistic situations, especially in oligopolies where the number of sellers is very few, outward price appearances may seem to bear the earmarks of an agreement, as when all sellers charge the same price. Yet the sellers may well hold that there is no agreement, and that they have to charge the same price as their rivals, especially where the products are highly standardized, in order to "meet the competition."

Price following with the sellers making price decisions "in the exercise of their own judgment" was found by the Supreme Court in 1927 not to constitute a suppression of competition.[31] But when are the oligopolistic firms' exercise of judgment truly their own? Oligopolistic market structures, practically by definition, present situations in which the individual sellers are aware of their interdependence. The basic questions that have to be asked are these: Is the price being charged by all sellers the same (or do the sellers' prices move in fairly close unison) because there has been an agreement? Or has there been a tacit understanding on prices—implicit collusion? Or is it a matter of the followers following because it is simply more profitable to follow than not to follow? To make one's suspicions of collusion good, one has to demonstrate some form of conspiracy, and this can involve the difficulty of inferring an agreement from the sellers' behavior.[32] To demonstrate "conscious parallelism" is not enough; parallel pricing alone does not indicate price fixing.[33]

Circumstantial Evidence Outside of obvious hard evidence, what sort of circumstances surrounding price-making are enough to convict firms of price-fixing? A 1964 court decision held that a high percentage of identical bids plus incidents of conferences held indicated understandings among conspirators.[34] A 1965 court decision held that merely showing prices had been discussed by competitors and parallel price behavior followed was sufficient to convict. According to this decision, discussion need not literally set prices; "A knowing wink can mean more than words."[35]

The Supreme Court held in 1969 that the practice of competitors supplying each other, upon request, with the most recent price quoted to a specific customer was illegal *per se*.[36] Although the exchange of such price information was informal and sporadic, there was an understanding that this type of information would be furnished on a reciprocal basis. In a similar case in 1978, the Court held illegal the systematic exchange among competitors of prices to specific customers even though the professed purpose of such price information was to establish a "meeting the competi-

[31]*U.S.* v. *International Harvester Co.*, 274 U.S. 693, 708–709.
[32]Phillip Areeda, *Antitrust Analysis*, 2nd ed. (Boston: Little, Brown, 1974), p. 293.
[33]*U.S.* v. *Chas. Pfizer & Co., Inc.*, 367 F. Supp. 91 (1973). See also *Theatre Enterprises, Inc.* v. *Paramount Film Distributing Corp. et al.*, 346 U.S. 537, 540–41 (1954).
[34]*U.S.* v. *Morton Salt and Diamond Crystal Salt Company*, Trade Cases para. 71,198 and 71,304 (1964); affirmed per curiam, Trade Cases para. 71,582 (1965).
[35]*Esco Corp.* v. *U.S.*, 340 F. 2d 1000, 1007. The court followed up the reference to the "wink" with the following words: "Let us suppose five competitors meet on several occasions, discuss their problems, and one finally states—'I won't fix prices with any of you, but here is what I am going to do—put the price of my gidget at X dollars; now you all do what you want.' He then leaves the meeting. Competitor number two says—'I don't care whether number one does what he says he's going to do or not; nor do I care what the rest of you do, but I am going to price my gidget at X dollars.' Number three makes a similar statement—'My price is X dollars.' Number four says not one word. All leave and fix 'their' prices at 'X' dollars."
[36]*U.S.* v. *Container Corporation of America et al.*, 393 U.S. 333.

tion" defense against a possible charge of price discrimination under the Robinson-Patman Act.[37] In another case, in 1977, the exchange of information among three competitors bidding for Forest Service timber combined with refusals to bid against one another was held by a court to constitute an implied agreement to eliminate competition, reduce the prices paid for timber, and allocate sales.[38]

A basic principle of conduct to which businesspeople should adhere if they are to remain free of suspicion of an implied price conspiracy is that they should avoid discussing prices with competitors in any way. A businessperson simply cannot assume that when he or she just informally discusses prices with his or her competitors that he or she will not have to pay the price of having reached an agreement. In more general terms, it can be said that, although more market knowledge is presumed to make a market more perfect, that market knowledge should not be obtained by individual oligopolistic marketers by turning directly to each other for information.

Signaling   The principal antitrust agencies have taken a step beyond the discussion of prices directly among business persons themselves in seeking evidence of price-fixing. They have launched an antitrust effort against *signaling*. This process is one in which corporate executives signal to each other about the need for or expected actions on market price increases. These signals can be in the form of *publicly* talking about the need for a price increase or of making an advance announcement in the media of a coming increase. The Antitrust Division has used its powers of civil investigative demand to try to find out just how some prices in "shared monopoly" industries where signaling has allegedly been occurring have been arrived at.[39] And in 1977 it modified the 1962 consent decrees with General Electric Company and Westinghouse Electric Corporation, the only American competitors in the steam turbine generator market, enjoining them from publishing or distributing any "price-signaling" information

---

[37]*U.S.* v. *United Gypsum Co. et al.*, 438 U.S. 422. The decision in this criminal case provided food for the legal discussion of price-fixing antitrust enforcement when it said that intent was an element to consider in a criminal antitrust offense. The Department of Justice nonetheless took the position that this decision would not alter its standards in its criminal enforcement program, since, first, it used criminal proceedings only where it considered the violations willful, and, second, it assumed that in such a *per se* violation as knowingly fixing prices the intent automatically followed. Mark Leddy, Deputy Director of Operations, Antitrust Division, "The Effects of the Gypsum Decision on Government Criminal Prosecutions," remarks before the American Bar Association 1979 Annual Meeting, August 15, 1979, mimeo.

[38]*U.S.* v. *Champion International Corp.*, Trade Cases para. 60,453 (1975); Trade Cases para. 61,442 (1977).

[39]See Gay Sands Miller, "Alcoa Omits Price-Boost Announcement, Heeds Complaints on Media 'Signaling,'" *Wall Street Journal*, September 6, 1977, p. 2.

and from using or retaining any price book, price list, or compilation of prices other than their own.[40] Such a proscription theoretically would "blind" each firm to the details of the other's pricing activities.[41] The FTC has also challenged signaling by filing a complaint in 1979 against the nation's four producers of lead-based antiknock additives for gasoline.[42] A proposed order accompanying the complaint would prohibit public announcement and any advance notice of price changes.

Attacks upon signaling have caused some reaction from industry. In the fall of 1977, for example, the aluminum industry began to notify its customers of its price increases and ignored its previous custom of informing the press and the Council on Wage and Price Stability in advance of the price increases.[43] Another reaction, however, has been to charge that an attack on signaling is an attack on the First Amendment to the Constitution guaranteeing freedom of speech.[44]

UNCOVERING PRICE CONSPIRACIES

The costs of discovery of a price-fixing conspiracy can be high: the new higher levels of possible fines and imprisonment, the threat of successful treble damage suits, the possible loss of employment for individual conspirators, and a smudge on the corporate image. It is clear, therefore, that steps are taken to cover up such a conspiracy. Communications concerning the agreement will never be in writing (or where there has been some, shredding machines will remove the evidence), travel and hotel lodging documents will be falsified if need be, price quotations will not be identical to competitors' down to the last decimal point, and even "signaling" will be minimized. How then can price-fixing conspiracies be uncovered?

The Antitrust Division announced in the fall of 1978 that it would give serious consideration to lenient treatment for corporations and their offi-

[40]Modification of 1962 consent decrees. *U.S.* v. *General Electric Co.*, Trade Cases para. 61,660; *U.S.* v. *Westinghouse Electric Corp.*, Trade Cases para. 61,661.

[41]See Timothy Schellhardt, "Antitrust Officials Plan Investigation into Pricing in Concentrated Industries," *Wall Street Journal*, May 13, 1977, p. 3.

[42]*FTC News Summary*, No. 29-1979, June 8, 1979; Docket No. 9128. The four firms challenged were Ethyl Corporation, E. I. du Pont de Nemours & Company, PPG Industries, Inc., and Nalco Chemical Company. The complaint also alleged that uniform prices were being maintained by selling only on a uniform delivered price basis. Du Pont responded by suing the Commission, charging that the complaint exceeded the Commission's authority. *E. I. du Pont de Nemours and Company* v. *FTC*, 488 F. Supp. 747 (1980).

[43]Winston Williams, "Aluminum Users Notified Quietly of Rise in Price," *New York Times*, October 14, 1977, p. D1.

[44]See editorial in *Barron's*, October 2, 1977. Du Pont's court challenge to the FTC's complaint charged that the FTC was depriving it of its First Amendment rights to free speech. Since the FTC had issued only a complaint, not an order, the court rejected this charge. 488 F. Supp. 747 (1980).

cers who voluntarily report illegal activities to the Division.[45] This policy did not mean a promise of freedom from prosecution, because violators might be willing to report the wrongdoing only because it was about to be uncovered. Of course, only the first member of a conspiracy would be given lenient treatment. This may play upon the basic fear of all conspirators that eventually the conspiracy will be uncovered as some party to the agreement weakens. On the other hand, where top management finds that an underlying level of management has been violating the antitrust laws, it may feel that the errors of its firm's ways should be admitted and reported. This announcement of leniency to the self-confessor did not bring the immediate response hoped for by the Antitrust Division.[46] The Department of Justice at one time established a price-fixing hotline (free 800 number) and accompanied this with television announcements as to its existence. This approach had a worthwhile response.[47]

Another approach is to watch price patterns that develop in an industry. Do price patterns in one area of the country for a particular good or service seem to be inexplicably higher there than in another area after different cost conditions have been allowed for? Related to this method of exposure is an experiment in constructing computer programs that can be utilized to monitor sealed-bid markets. Computerized models of certain patterns of bidding that conspirators might be anticipated to use to allocate business can be built as a possible price-fixing detection device. Thus, a program could be constructed to relate all bids to the low bid, taking into consideration the relative prices bid over different periods of time.[48]

THE ELECTRICAL EQUIPMENT CONSPIRACIES—*A CASE STUDY*[49]

The fines and prison sentences handed down by Judge Ganey in 1962 in the electrical equipment price-fixing conspiracies of the 1950s have been viewed as a turning point in American antitrust history. Never before had

[45]*Wall Street Journal*, October 5, 1978, p. 6. See also remarks of Benjamin R. Civiletti, Deputy Attorney General, at the annual meeting of the Rick-Tenn Company, Vero Beach, Florida, October 21, 1978, mimeo, pp. 7–9.

[46]*New York Times*, July 6, 1979, p. D3.

[47]Donald I. Baker, Assistant Attorney General, Antitrust Division, remarks before the Allegheny Bar Association, Pittsburgh, April 18, 1977, mimeo, p. 9.

[48]See Joseph C. Gallo, "A Computerized Approach to Detect Collusion in the Sealed-Bid Market," *Antitrust Bulletin*, 22, no. 3 (Fall 1977), 593–619.

[49]A primary source of information on the electrical equipment price-fixing conspiracies of the 1950s is *Hearings before the Antitrust and Monopoly Subcommittee of the Senate Committee on the Judiciary, Administered Prices*, 87th Cong., 1st Sess., Parts 27 and 28, "Price Fixing and Bid Rigging in the Electrical Manufacturing Industry," April, May, and June 1961. Since all the indicted corporations and individuals pleaded *nolo contendere* or guilty, there was no public trial with related evidence. *Fortune* magazine, in a two-part article by Richard Austin Smith,

fines been so large, and seldom before had top corporate executives actually been sentenced to and served prison terms for an antitrust offense. Fines imposed on individuals and corporations totaled $1,924,500. Seven individuals were given 30-day jail sentences, and an additional 24 persons received suspended sentences.

Nor had treble damage suits ever been so numerous and expensive for corporations involved in a particular set of price-fixing conspiracies. Altogether, some 1880 treble damage suits were filed in 35 different federal court districts by customers seeking redress for the excessive prices they had paid because of the price-fixing. Investor-owned public utilities had been the principal customers. They found it to their advantage, for the purpose of treble damage settlements, to cooperate in forming what was known as the Anti-Trust Investigation Group, an organization that had 164 member firms.

Indictments were returned by a Philadelphia grand jury in 1960 relating to conspiracies involving 20 different products within the electrical equipment industry. These products ranged from small items such as insulators and bushings to large-scale apparatus such as power switchgear assemblies, power transformers, and turbine generators. They were the principal equipment utilized in the generation, transmission, and distribution of electric power. Altogether some 29 electrical equipment manufacturing companies and 45 of their executives were indicted for price-fixing, bid rigging, and market division. The two largest firms were the General Electric Company and Westinghouse Electric Corporation. Both companies were involved in 19 of the 20 conspiracies.

It has been estimated that the treble damages cost General Electric $198 million, not counting the firm's own legal expenses and reimbursement of fees and expenses incurred by those who had sued.[50] It should be noted, however, that the treble damage payments were allowed as a deduction by the U.S. Treasury, so that the federal government paid approximately half. Westinghouse paid perhaps as much as $110 million in damages.[51] Smaller firms paid lesser amounts. It should also be noted that settlements by some of the smaller firms had to consider their ability to pay—otherwise, they might have been forced out of business. The gov-

---

presented further evidence beyond what was available in the slim court record through interviews with marketing men, economists, and top officers of corporations and with Justice Department attorneys, the judge, and the defendants themselves. "The Incredible Electrical Conspiracy," April and May 1961. In a similar vein is John Herling's book, *The Great Price Conspiracy* (Washington, D.C.: Robert B. Luce, Inc., 1962). A highly readable account of the conspiracy is to be found in John G. Fuller, *The Gentlemen Conspirators* (New York: Grove Press, 1962). Legal details of the treble damage suits and their settlement can be found in Charles A. Bane, *The Electrical Equipment Conspiracies: The Treble Damage Actions* (New York: Federal Legal Publications, Inc., 1973).

[50]Bane, *The Electrical Equipment Conspiracies*, p. 251.

[51]Ibid., p. 254.

ernment had foreseen the possibility of the treble damage suits and had pleaded with the judge not to accept *nolo contendere* pleas in the more serious of the 20 separate counts of conspiracy. A finding of guilt would be *prima facie* evidence in any treble damage suits brought by customers seeking redress for the monopoly overcharges. The judge agreed, and the defendants were faced in the most serious cases with the option of pleading guilty or not guilty. As the case unfolded and more individuals were willing to talk freely, all the defendants finally pleaded guilty.

After all the evidence was in, it was clear that price conspiracies had been going on throughout the 1950s. Some congressional testimony indicated that collusion on price had begun in the 1930s. Department of Justice investigations in 1949 and 1955 failed to result in any indictments; the indictments in the "big" case were confined to conspiratorial activities that occurred throughout the latter half of the 1950s.

Supply-Demand Conditions   Supply-cost conditions conducive to price-fixing were readily apparent in the electrical equipment industry. For each of the 20 different products for which indictments were handed down, the supply configuration was one of oligopoly with relatively high concentration ratios.[52] Large amounts of capital were required and certain economies of scale were present, thus creating considerable overhead or fixed costs. The technology has been complex for the larger pieces of equipment, and the construction of new capacity has taken considerable time. Entry, in general, has not been easy.

It was during the middle 1950s that supply conditions became particularly ripe for price-fixing. During the Korean conflict the suppliers had increased their capacity to product electrical equipment by more than 30 percent. This proved to be more than the industry could absorb and still sell the products at profitable prices under competitive conditions. Price competition became severe, especially in 1954–55. Price discounts amounted to as much as 45 percent off book prices: the great "white sale" was on. The principal sellers in this industry felt that something had to be done to hold up prices and profits.

Demand conditions also contributed to the urge to conspire on prices. The products were producers' goods, sold primarily to electric utility firms. Thus, the demand for these products was derived from the demand for electric power. In addition, the electric utility companies that generated and sold electric power had to plan new capacity well in advance of growing demands for power. As a result, the buyers had considerable flexibility in the timing of lumpy purchases and had a resulting bargaining leverage. On top of this, price information seemed to disseminate quite rapidly throughout the markets for electrical equipment.

[52]See Table 1-1 in Clarence C. Walton and Frederick W. Cleveland, Jr., *Corporations on Trial: The Electric Cases* (Belmont, Calif.: Wadsworth, 1964), p. 14.

How Prices Were Fixed   The price conspirators did what they could to cover up their illegal activity. They met frequently in well-known large city hotels, but they also conspired in such places as a bar or a cabin on a lake. When registering in hotels, they would not list their employers and they would not eat with other conspirators in the dining room. A special code was developed to cover meetings, and code numbers were used for firms. Communication was by letters addressed to homes and containing no return addresses. Public telephone booths were preferred to office tele-phones.

Prices were being fixed not only through the quotation of identical bids, but also through taking turns in submitting the lowest bid. A sophis-ticated technique used by the conspirators in the nonsealed bid portion of the switchgear assemblies market was the use of "phase-of-the-moon" charts, so called because of the use of two-week periods of alternation. These charts determined which of the sellers were to offer the higher prices and which was to offer the lowest price over these different periods of time. They were the starting point in the efforts to assure each seller a particular percentage of the market. Where agreed-upon distribution of the business did not result from utilization of these charts, further negotiation became necessary.[53]

Uncovering the Conspiracies   How were the conspiracies discov-ered and uncovered? The Tennessee Valley Authority (TVA) had become suspicious in 1958 when it observed that steam turbine generator prices were increasing more rapidly than normal market conditions would seem to call for. In 1959 the TVA became further suspicious when several electri-cal equipment manufacturers submitted identical bids. At the same time, the relative pricing by the bidders under the phase-of-the-moon plan at-tracted the attention of TVA officials. A Department of Justice follow-up ended with the seating of a grand jury to investigate possible antitrust law violations.

The real break in the case came when an officer in one of the small companies producing insulators who had been subpoenaed by the grand jury decided to talk. This set up a bandwagon effect. As more persons were testifying under grand jury subpoena, more persons sought to testify in an attempt to obtain immunity. So more information was uncovered about separate price conspiracies than the government had originally suspected.

The Impact of the Conspiracies   Why would a relatively small firm with a small percentage of the market wish to be part of such a conspiracy? Could it not enjoy the price umbrella established by the large firms in the industry? Perhaps not, because even the large firms were chiseling in price

[53]See John D. Kuhlman, "The 'Phase-of-the-Moon' Charts in the Electrical Industry Cases: A Curio," *Antitrust Law & Economics Review*, 1, no. 3 (Spring 1968), 93–100.

against each other. Could it not grow and increase its share of the market by price-cutting, as a smaller company often has to do? This was part of the problem. Perhaps the experience of Federal Pacific Electric Company in the sealed-bid business in circuit breakers is instructive.[54] At meetings attended by the competitors, it was implied that Federal Pacific had a certain "position" with respect to its sealed-bid business to which it should adhere. If it went beyond this position, the larger firms would retaliate: ". . . as long as we kept a fairly reasonable place in the industry, why, we might be allowed to go along normally in our business . . . if we tried to get out of place, . . . we would face more severe competition." So the smaller firm may find itself in a situation where it has little choice if it is to survive. It must go along with the conspiracy and attract no more than a given percentage of the business.

Except for the fines, and jail sentences for a few, what was the impact of the case on the principal individual conspirators? General Electric had had an official company directive against price-fixing; Westinghouse Electric had not. What then became of the division and department managers who were the actual conspirators? General Electric forced them to resign or demoted them to a position where they chose to resign—much to their bitterness, for some of them felt they had been authorized to engage in price conspiracy by their superiors. They were, however, able to find good jobs elsewhere. Westinghouse did not discipline its conspirators. It took the position that they must have thought they were acting in the best interest of the firm. It prepared a management guide which made it clear that antitrust and trade regulation laws were to be followed strictly.

It is not certain that in an oligopolistic market structure of only a few firms management directives against price conspiracy are enough. General Electric and Westinghouse were the only two domestic firms in the steam turbine generator market in 1980. And recall how in 1977 the Department of Justice found it necessary to modify the 1962 consent decrees with these two firms, enjoining them from publishing or distributing any price-signaling information and from using or retaining any price book, price list, or compilation of prices other than their own.[55]

SUMMARY

Collusive price-fixing is illegal *per se*, whether accomplished directly by determining the price to be charged or indirectly by controling the quantity of the product that gets into the marketplace. The related practices of

---

[54]See testimony of Frank Roby, Executive Vice President of Federal Pacific Electric Co., *Administered Prices*, Part 28, pp. 17526–17545.
[55]See note 40.

territorial division, customer division, and product division are likewise illegal *per se.*

The courts have refused to accept as a defense to a charge of price-fixing the prevention of ruinous or destructive competition. A series of court precedents has clearly established that the practice is *per se* illegal; a rule of reason is not to be applied to price-fixing agreements.

In spite of the fact that business should know that price-fixing is a clear-cut violation of the antitrust laws, it remains the basis for a large number of antitrust complaints. This can be explained by the character of certain markets. Principal contributing factors are a small number of sellers, trade associations as implementing devices, inelasticity of industry demand, industry over capacity, similar cost conditions for competing firms, and uniformity of product.

Different methods of fixing price are available. Bids to be made for contracts on a sealed-bid basis can be rigged, by submitting identical prices or by taking turns in offering the low bid. The use of basing-point prices and collusive delivered pricing can achieve uniformity of prices quoted by competitors. This system of pricing, although found illegal some years ago, has cropped up again in the 1970s.

Parallel business pricing is not in itself illegal; some evidence is needed to demonstrate a conspiracy. The evidence, however, can be circumstantial. Any discussion of current prices by competitors is highly suspect and is to be avoided. Even indirect "signaling" by business executives with respect to prices has been challenged. Several approaches have been used by the antitrust authorities to try to detect price-fixing conspiracies.

The electrical equipment price-fixing conspiracies of the 1950s make an excellent case study that reveals the demand and supply conditions conducive to the conspiracies, how and where the conspirators conducted their unlawful business, how the price agreements were exposed, and all the costs of the conspiracy in terms of fines, imprisonment, and treble damage suits.

Selected Readings

COMANOR, W. S., AND M. R. SCHANKERMAN, "Identical Bids and Cartel Behavior," *Bell Journal of Economics,* 7, no. 1 (Spring 1976), 281–86.

HAY, GEORGE A., AND DANIEL KELLEY, "An Empirical Survey of Price Fixing Conspiracies," *Journal of Law and Economics,* 17, no. 1 (April 1974), 13–38.

HERLING, JOHN, *The Great Conspiracy.* Washington, D.C.: Robert B. Luce, Inc., 1962.

MACHLUP, FRITZ, *The Basing-Point System: An Economic Analysis of a Controversial Pricing Practice*. Philadelphia: Blakiston, 1949.

PHILLIPS, ALMARIN, *Market Structure, Organization and Performance: An
Essay on Price Fixing and Combinations in Restraint of Trade*. Cambridge,
Mass.: Harvard University Press, 1962.

SCHERER, F. M., "Focal Point Pricing and Conscious Parallelism," *Antitrust
Bulletin*, 12 (Summer 1967), 495–503.

4 — Trade and Professional Associations

Traditionally, trade associations have gathered and compiled statistical data on various aspects of demand and supply for their industry: costs, prices, volumes of production, sales, shipments, inventories, industry plant capacity. They have also established product standards, engaged in research programs designed to develop new or to improve an industry's existing products, provided for the exchange of credit information, and engaged in advertising programs to promote the products of the industry.[1] The 1970s saw their functions expanded to enable their members to deal better with the government on such matters as health and safety, consumer affairs, environmental protection, energy, and wage and price controls.[2]

The trade association has a rather unique status with respect to antitrust regulation. Trade associations are nonprofit institutions, but their membership is usually composed of business firms that are competitors. Because of this, their activities may sometimes restrict competition and violate antitrust laws. Although firms' usual motives in joining a trade association are to cooperate in performing certain economic functions they feel to be important, their cooperative efforts may sometimes be deemed to be illegal collusion affecting price.

For many years it was only the industrial or commercial trade associations that were found on occasion to have exceeded the limits of legal behavior in their cooperation. In the 1970s, however, professional associa-

[1]See George P. Lamb and Carrington Shields, *Trade Association Law and Practice* (Boston: Little, Brown, 1971), part I.
[2]Murray L. Weidenbaum, *Business, Government, and the Public* (Englewood Cliffs, N.J.: Prentice-Hall, 1977), chap. 16.

tions were also successfully attacked by the antitrust authorities. Associations of the legal, accounting, engineering, and medical professions were found to have restrained competition through tactics that controlled price, whether by direct or indirect means.

INDUSTRIAL AND COMMERCIAL TRADE ASSOCIATIONS

The general principle justifying the existence of industrial and commercial trade associations is the dissemination of information among the members in order to increase industry and market knowledge among them. Trade associations have been characterized as clearinghouses or conduits of business information.[3] Certainly this is in keeping with the basic principle of competition that all market transactors have as much knowledge as possible with respect to the demand and supply conditions of the marketplace. The greater the amount of information available, theoretically the more effective the market mechanism will work.

The key question for antitrust policy is to differentiate trade association behavior which represents the exchange or dissemination of information in order to make producer-sellers more knowledgeable about the market from that which facilitates price collusion. When a trade association collects industry data from its members and publishes these data periodically in aggregate form, the members can get a better feel for demand and supply conditions in the marketplace. Just as farmers can do better crop planning with data published by the U.S. Department of Agriculture, so too members of industry trade associations can do better planning with data pertaining to demand and supply conditions. In both cases extremes of over- and underproduction that do not truly reflect competitive equilibrium price-cost conditions may be avoided. The problem arises when industry members use trade association data to plan future quantities of production collectively or to decide future prices collectively. The availability of recent data pertaining to costs and prices certainly can facilitate collusive price-fixing.

Trade associations, as associations of manufacturers or sellers in a given industry—whether national, regional, state, or local—provide a natural meeting place where members can talk prices. Some of these associations may be no more than a front that exists just for this purpose.[4] Clearly, such associations or those who fall prey to and use this readily

---

[3]Lamb and Shields, *Trade Association Law*, p. 4.
[4]Gerald A. Connell, "A View from the Department of Justice," 13th Annual Symposium of the Antitrust Law Committee of the Bar Association of the District of Columbia Featuring Trade Association Law and Practice, printed in *Antitrust Bulletin*, 22, no. 2 (Summer 1977), 264.

available medium for purposes of reaching price agreements or having tacit understandings have little defense when a price-fixing charge is leveled against them. When basing points were used for pricing in the cement industry, the trade association was the vehicle through which the rail freight rate schedule books were disseminated to industry members in order to ensure uniformity of delivered prices. Obviously, such behavior is illegal and was so found.[5] Even if it is not quite so obvious, as long as stabilization of price itself is the clear objective, then the price information program is to be outlawed.

The landmark so-called *Hardwood* decision in 1921 concerning a plan for exchanging information on sales, production, inventories, and prices established the principle that, even though no specific agreement to restrict trade or fix prices is shown, an information program of statistical reporting violates the antitrust laws if the business rivals have as a common purpose "to procure 'harmonious' individual action."[6] The court was convinced that the system of information exchange among the sellers represented concerted action to curtail production and increase prices. Each association member submitted to the trade association secretary reports on daily sales with customers identified, on monthly production and stocks, and monthly price lists with changes as they occurred. Various data from these reports were in turn submitted to members on a weekly or monthly basis.

Dissemination among members of a trade association of price data and other data which may be reflected in price is not in itself illegal. The line between legality and illegality is indeed obscure, and would seem to depend a good deal on particular circumstances. And it should probably remain that way, for abundant market knowledge can make a market more efficient. Certain rules of the game, however, have to be established. Court decisions and consent decrees have created these rules for the trade association.[7] There are several cautionary rules of thumb to be heeded. Competitors should not exchange intimate business details through their trade association. The identity of contributors of specific information should not be published. Nonmembers as well as members should be permitted to contribute to and to receive statistical information. No firm should be coerced into joining the program. Any membership qualifications should be uniform, nondiscriminatory, serve a legitimate purpose, and create no competitive disadvantages.[8] Distributors and customers who are an active

---

[5]*FTC* v. *Cement Institute,* 333 U.S. 683 (1948).

[6]*American Column and Lumber Co.* v. *U.S.,* 257 U.S. 377, 411 (1921).

[7]See Lamb and Shields, *Trade Association Law,* chaps. 3 and 4; and Ronald J. Dolan, "How an Association Is Investigated and What Is the Government Looking For—A Federal Trade Commission Perspective," *Antitrust Bulletin,* 22, no. 2 (Summer 1977), 273-86.

[8]See Richard J. Favretto, Deputy Director of Operations, Antitrust Division, "Access to Trade Association Membership and Information—A Competitive Analysis," remarks before the Bar Association of the District of Columbia's 15th Annual Symposium on Trade Association Law and Practice, Washington, March 1, 1979, mimeo.

part of the market should have access to the data. In general, prices conveyed should be past or current prices, but not projected future prices. And production or sales data should not be in a form from which strong inferences can be drawn as to the future of prices or desirable price-making.

A Proposed Statistical Reporting Program Trade association programs of data collection can take many forms. Each such program, therefore, has to be deciphered as to its intent or impact on price or production levels. A case in point is a statistical reporting program proposed by a trade association in the plastics industry. Concerned with the legal acceptability of the proposed program, the association submitted its plan to the Federal Trade Commission under the latter's program of advisory opinions. The FTC responded in 1979 that the proposed program was unacceptable to it under Section 5 of the Federal Trade Commission Act.[9] To illustrate the problem of interpretation of a particular statistical reporting system, the advisory opinion letter is reproduced below:

> This responds to your request for an advisory opinion on the use by the Society of the Plastics Industry (SPI) of a proposed statistical reporting program entailing the forecasting of annual sales and captive use of selected thermoplastic resins.
>
> The Commission understands that SPI is a trade association with membership open to all firms in the industry upon payment of annual dues graduated according to sales volume, and that current membership accounts for approximately 95% of the total domestic production of plastics raw materials. The Commission further understands that under the proposed program, resin suppliers would be invited to report their respective forecasts for the current year and each of the following four years to an independent accounting firm, which would compute the mean and median of the reported forecasts and publish the low forecast, the high forecast, the mean, and the median (not broken down by type or grade). There would be no exchange or disclosure whatever of individual firm data and no narrative or interpretation will be placed on the compiled figures. Non-member producers would be invited to participate in the program on the same basis as members and will receive copies of the forecasts. The report would also be available by subscription to the public after a trial period. No forecast would be reported, however, unless at least four industry members, excluding any firm with more than 65% of any reporting category, submit forecasts. Initially, the program would encompass six of the

[9]*The Society of the Plastics Industry, Inc.,* FTC Advisory Opinion, May 1, 1979. Reported in *CCH Trade Regulation Reporter,* vol. 3, para. 21,573.

major plastics materials: polyvinyl chloride (PVC); low density polyethylene (LDPE); high density polyethylene (HDPE); polypropylene; polystyrene; and acrylonitrile-butadiene-styrene (ABS).

Some types of forecast arrangements among competitors do raise serious antitrust concerns in particular market environments. On the basis of available information concerning the slowing rate of growth, the degree of concentration, the relatively small number of firms engaged in the manufacture of the individual thermoplastic resins, and the specifics of the proposed plan, the Commission is of the view that there is a significant risk that SPI's program could be used to foster an anticompetitive consensus on production levels. The Commission is therefore unable to approve use of the proposed statistical reporting program.

By direction of the Commission.

PROFESSIONAL ASSOCIATIONS AND CODES OF ETHICS

The recognized professions have codes of ethics that strongly influence the marketplace conduct of their members. The Department of Justice, the FTC, and the courts have interpreted some of the rules of these codes of ethics and attempts to ensure compliance with them as being restrictive of competition and in violation of the antitrust laws. Prices, especially, have been fixed, either directly or indirectly. The chairman of the FTC in 1979 viewed doctors, lawyers, and other professionals as having established themselves as business cartels, with resulting high fees to consumers.[10] Major antitrust actions aimed at professional groups in the 1970s, with their codes of ethics a principal target, have had an impact upon the legal, accounting, engineering, and medical professions.

The professions, in general, have argued that codes of ethics are needed to maintain high standards. Professions are not looked upon by most of their members as being ordinary business or commerce. They are not selling a commodity; they are dispensing a service. That service is considered a fairly personal one. Often the service is a confidential one. The consumer of a professional service is a client, not a customer. He or she is purchasing a service that required extensive specialized training to produce. That the quality of the service be excellent is of the utmost importance to the reputation of the profession.

The rendering of a professional service is supposed to be objective and according to the highest standards of integrity. The accountant must

[10]Michael Pertschuk, *New York Times*, February 23, 1979, p. A16.

be precise and accurate; follow basic accepted accounting principles; and attest to the validity of financial records and statements. Engineers must not approve of projects that might endanger the public health or welfare. Lawyers should not stir up or prolong litigation unnecessarily. A physician must render service to all in need first, even if the person cannot afford to pay. The professional's conduct, in short, must not be guided solely by profit. Thus, undue rivalry is considered demeaning and out of place.

The possibility of conflict between the interests of members of the profession and of the public is inherent in this environment of a felt need to maintain professional standards and ethics. If rivalry is to be controlled by self-regulation within a profession, what is to keep it from being controlled to the point where the self-interests of the individual members prevail over the interests of the public? The public policy position has been that this point has been exceeded in several instances and that professional ethics and standards have interfered excessively with the functioning of competition. Let us look at some illustrative case studies.

THE LEGAL PROFESSION—*A CASE STUDY*

Prior to the 1970s, the bar in America enjoyed limits on competition through codes of ethics that deemed fee-cutting and advertising to be unethical practices. The use of minimum fee schedules, in effect, established rigid price floors for given legal services. Advertising was considered a cardinal sin and the sign of the unethical lawyer.[11] The threat of censure, suspension, or disbarment for violating ethical codes—which could be damaging or destructive to the ability to function as a professional—effectively prevented price and advertising competition.

Fee Schedules   The Department of Justice had considered the idea of attacking lawyers' minimum fee schedules under the antitrust laws in the early 1950s.[12] When the department did file a case against the use of such a schedule, a district court ruled in 1974 that such a fee schedule was not immune from attack under the Sherman Act.[13] But it was a private class action suit (*Goldfarb*) initiated in 1971 that eventually led to a ruling by the Supreme Court against this restraint imposed upon the legal profession by that profession's system of self-regulation.[14] A husband and wife seeking to purchase a home in Fairfax County, Virginia, first had to obtain a title

[11]Benjamin R. Civiletti, Deputy Attorney General, remarks at 99th Annual Meeting of the Bar Association of Baltimore City, June 5, 1979, mimeo, p. 3.

[12]*Business Week,* December 8, 1973, p. 67.

[13]*U.S.* v. *Oregon State Bar,* 385 F. Supp. 507.

[14]*Goldfarb et ux.* v. *Virginia State Bar et al.,* 355 F. Supp. 491 (1973); 497 F. 2d 1 (1974); 421 U.S. 773 (1975).

examination in order to secure title insurance. In their efforts to obtain the best possible price for this service, they discovered that none of some 20 different lawyers would charge less than the fee suggested as the minimum by the Fairfax County Bar Association. The ensuing lawsuit vindicated their efforts as the Supreme Court, overruling various views of the lower courts, finally held that the minimum fee schedule was a violation of Section 1 of the Sherman Act.

Two principal points of issue in this case, each of which was vital to the decision, required some elaboration. First was the argument that the law is a learned profession and thus exempt from the Sherman Act. The Fairfax County Bar maintained that competition is not consistent with the practice of a profession. The profession was providing necessary community services, not trying to maximize profits. The Supreme Court, however, could not see much relationship between that argument and the effort to control the fees to be charged. Nor could it find anything in the language of the Sherman Act providing an exemption for a learned profession.

The second major argument presented to justify Sherman Act exemption was that failure to exempt represented an interference with state regulatory action, or the so-called state action exemption enunciated by the Supreme Court in *Parker* v. *Brown* in 1943.[15] It was pointed out by the defendants in *Goldfarb* that the Virginia legislature had given the Virginia Supreme Court (the Supreme Court of Appeals) the power to regulate the practice of law in that state by prescribing rules and regulations which would include a code of ethics and procedures for disciplining, suspending, and disbarring attorneys. The Virginia Supreme Court, in establishing rules for the Virginia State Bar, did include a rule that a lawyer could consider a schedule of minimum fees adopted by a bar association. The wording of the rule, however, was crucial. It stated that "... *no lawyer should permit himself to be controlled* thereby or to follow it as his sole guide in determining the amount of his fee."[16] Thus, said the Supreme Court, since the minimum fee schedule was advisory and not directed, it could not fall under the state action exemption. It followed that the state bar, by providing that not following the minimum fee schedule might lead to disciplinary action, had become a party to private anticompetitive action.

Advertising   A second restriction on competition in the legal profession, the ethical ban on advertising, was altered by the U.S. Supreme

[15]317 U.S. 341. In this case the State of California had regulated the state's raisin industry, requiring each producer to deliver two-thirds of its annual production to a state marketing committee to be sold collectively by that agency as it saw fit. Although this state regulation may have affected interstate commerce, it was deemed to be a legitimate exercise of state power to solve a local problem.
[16]Cited in 421 U.S. 773, n. 19. Emphasis was added by the U.S. Supreme Court in this footnote.

Court in its 1977 *Bates* decision.[17] This landmark case was also the result of a private suit.[18] Two attorneys had opened a "legal clinic" and placed advertisements in newspapers offering legal services "at very reasonable fees." The advertisements listed the fees for certain routine legal services, such as uncontested divorces, uncontested adoptions, simple personal bankruptcies, and changes in name. Such advertisements clearly violated a "disciplinary rule" established by the Arizona Supreme Court in its regulation of that state's legal profession. The state bar recommended a one-week suspension for the two lawyers. The latter appealed to the Supreme Court of Arizona, arguing that the disciplinary rule violated Sections 1 and 2 of the Sherman Act and the First Amendment to the Constitution, which guarantees the freedom of speech. The Arizona Supreme Court upheld the state bar but reduced the sanction to censure.

The U.S. Supreme Court, in its decision in *Bates*, held that the Sherman Act was not being violated by the disciplinary rule against the advertising of legal services. The *Parker* v. *Brown* state action exemption was held to be valid because the disciplinary rule established by the Arizona Supreme Court for members of the bar in that state concerning advertising had specifically *directed* that a lawyer not publicize himself through any of the commercial media. But, although reliance on the Sherman Act was of no help to the two young attorneys, they did win their case on the basis of the First Amendment. The particular professional advertising of these lawyers, the pricing of certain routine services, was protected by the freedom of commercial speech. Such advertising was not viewed by the Supreme Court as substituting commercialism for professionalism. The advertising in question was not inherently misleading, because only routine services were involved. Furthermore, advertising makes the consumer that much better informed. Advertising, rather than create a cost barrier to entry, should facilitate the entry of new attorneys into the marketplace. As for the argument that advertising will lead to efforts by members of the profession to mislead and distort, the Court found this incongruous in the face of the profession's extolling of its own altruism and virtues.

But what about the advertising of legal services that are of a non-routine character? These were not at issue in *Bates*. The Court did not address the issue of the advertising of the quality of legal services or the more direct solicitation of clients. Indeed, the Court stated that some regulation of advertising by lawyers might be necessary to prevent false, deceptive, or misleading advertising and that reasonable restrictions on the time, place, and manner of advertising were not out of order. In-person solicitation of clients—which can be defined as an extreme form of advertising—

---

[17]*Bates* v. *State Bar of Arizona*, 433 U.S. 350.

[18]A Justice Department 1976 complaint against the American Bar Association alleging that it unreasonably restricted advertising in violation of Section 1 of the Sherman Act was dropped after the Supreme Court decision in the *Bates* case. Civil Action No. 76-1182.

was cited by the Court as being an area in which restrictions might be justified. Does, for example, the "advertising" of one's services under ambulance-chasing conditions, such as in the hospital or at the accident site, constitute harassment? There are many forms of advertising, and what kinds can be subjected to the profession's self-regulation through ethical rules remains to be determined. The decision, in effect, sent the bar associations back to the drawing boards to fashion new rules on advertising by attorneys. But even when new rules are framed, they may still find themselves, or their interpretation in the light of given factual circumstances, being tested in the courts.

Will the removal of certain restraints on advertising in the legal profession raise or lower prices and quality? Advocates of the rules against advertising argued that advertising would increase overhead costs and prices and that the quality of service would decline as the spirit of true professionalism was replaced by commercialization. The Supreme Court, on the other hand, thought it was entirely possible that advertising would reduce the price of legal services. A barrier to entry facing the new attorney would be removed as the information flow was facilitated. Consumers would be able to identify the lower-cost sources of legal service and would create a competitive force that could force prices lower. As to the effect on quality, the Court felt that the attorney who engages in shoddy work would continue to do so. Legal clinics would even improve service by reducing the probability of mistakes. Only time and empirical studies will provide the true answer to these questions.[19]

THE ACCOUNTING PROFESSION—*A CASE STUDY*

The accounting profession was one of the earliest professions to be the target of antitrust action by an enforcement agency. In 1972 the Department of Justice filed an antitrust complaint against the American Institute of Certified Public Accountants (AICPA). The particular object of attack was the rule in the association's code of professional ethics that prohibited a member from making a competitive bid for public accounting services. The rule said that competitive bidding was not in the public interest, was a form of solicitation, and was unprofessional. The profession had been taking the position that clients should select accountants on the basis of

[19]The American Bar Association in its first national review of the issue three years after the *Bates* decision concluded that advertising by lawyers was cutting the cost of routine legal services and had not increased frivolous litigation. Reported in *Wall Street Journal*, October 10, 1980, p. 1. For some early observations, see Carol H. Falk, "Legal Upheaval: Lawyers Are Facing Surge in Competition as Courts Drop Curbs," *Wall Street Journal,* October 18, 1978, pp. 1, 21; "Where Consumers Buy Legal Advice at Retail," *Business Week*, July 2, 1979, p. 44; and Barbara Slavin, "It's Legal, but Few Lawyers Are Prepared to Advertise," *New York Times,* April 23, 1979, p. A12.

their quality, and that this was to be judged by professional attainment, not by price. Negotiated fees were to be preferred over open price competition.

Competitive Bidding AICPA had been aware of the possibility of the illegality of the rule banning competitive bidding. It had formally indicated in 1966 that it would not enforce this rule because of the antitrust ramifications.[20] Failure to enforce a rule, however, is not quite the same thing as removing a rule from a code of ethics. If it is still there to be read, members might still be likely to adhere to it. When faced with the federal government's official complaint, the association signed a consent order under which it agreed to remove the rule from its code of professional ethics. The order required not only the deletion of the particular rule from the code, but also the deletion of any bylaws, resolutions, or policy statements that would prohibit or limit the submission of price quotations to anyone seeking accounting services or state or imply that price quotations were unethical or unprofessional or contrary to the association's policy.[21]

Obtaining a consent order from the national association of accountants does not automatically mean winning the concurrent consent of various state associations as to restrictive rules in their codes. Most state associations did alter their rules to comply with the precedent of the consent order.[22] The Texas State Board of Accountancy, however, resisted a federal civil investigative demand all the way to the Supreme Court.[23] Climaxing this action was a suit filed in 1976 against this state board by the Department of Justice charging that its rule against competitive bidding was a violation of Section 1 of the Sherman Act.[24] The Texas State Board of Accountancy was composed of nine practicing accountants appointed by the governor of Texas. It issued licenses and permits to practice accountancy in Texas, and promulgated, policed, and enforced the rules of professional conduct. The rules became effective after referendum approval by a majority of the permit holders. The rule against competitive bidding could thus be viewed as an agreement not to compete in price among the accountants practicing in the state.

A district court accepted this view and found a *per se* violation of the Sherman Act.[25] The State of Texas in creating the board had given it the authority to adopt rules that would help to maintain high standards of professional integrity, but Texas had in no way mandated the anticompetitive conduct required by this rule. The court ordered the board to cancel

[20]*Business Week*, June 10, 1972, p. 20.
[21]*U.S.* v. *American Institute of Certified Public Accountants, Inc.*, Trade Cases para. 74,007 (1972).
[22]*Wall Street Journal*, October 30, 1979, p. 4.
[23]*Texas State Board of Accountancy* v. *U.S.*, Trade Cases para. 60,021 (1975).
[24]*U.S.* v. *Texas State Board of Accountancy*, Civil No. A-76-CA-219 (1976).
[25]464 F. Supp. 400 (1978).

whatever provisions of its rules which had as their purpose or effect the suppression or elimination of price competition. On appeal a circuit court agreed that the contested rule banning competitive bidding was an antitrust violation.[26] Although one circuit court judge dissented on the grounds that price competition can adversely affect the type and quality of accounting service that clients and the public ultimately receive, the Supreme Court refused to review the appeals court decision.

Advertising and Solicitation   With pressure from the Department of Justice, other changes in the AICPA's rules of conduct for accountants have been made. In 1978 advertising became permitted, providing it was not false, misleading, or deceptive. In 1979 accountants could, for the first time, directly solicit prospective clients without waiting to be invited to make a direct approach. Such changes in rules of professional conduct can effect changes in the market behavior of accountants. But how much change will actually occur is subject to dispute.[27] Some believe indirect methods of solicitation have been occurring all along in an effective manner. Country club memberships are one such device. Others feel that top corporate executives react negatively to the knocking-on-the-door approach. In any case, the market for accountants has been freed from the anticompetitive restrictions of self-regulation by the profession.

THE ENGINEERING PROFESSION—*A CASE STUDY*

Antitrust action in the 1970s against professional engineers began in 1972 when the Department of Justice obtained a consent order against the American Society of Civil Engineers.[28] This decree prohibited the traditional practices of this professional association of not only frowning on the submission of price quotations by members, but also disciplining such members by expelling them for violation of this pricing provision of the association's code of ethics. The decree did not prohibit advising customers that they ought to select an engineer on a basis other than price, but submission of price quotations could no longer be held against an engineer and injure his or her professional reputation. The society's guides to professional practice, code of ethics, manuals, rules, bylaws, resolutions, and any other policy statements were to be amended to eliminate any provision

[26]592 F. 2d 921 (1979).
[27]See Tom Herman, "Accountant Group Votes Change in Code to Allow Direct Solicitation of Clients," *Wall Street Journal*, April 30, 1979, p. 12.
[28]*U.S.* v. *American Society of Civil Engineers*, Trade Cases para. 73,950 (1972). A similar consent order was obtained against professional architects at about the same time, *U.S.* v. *American Institute of Architects*, Trade Cases para. 73,981 (1972).

that prohibited or restrained any member from submitting price quotations for his or her services.

The *National Society of Professional Engineers* Case   The engineering profession as a whole, through the National Society of Professional Engineers (NSPE), had operated since 1964 under a code of ethics that prohibited competitive bidding by its members. More specifically, engineers had been prohibited from discussing or negotiating the fee for their services with a prospective client until *after* the client had chosen the engineer for the project.[29] If a prospective client were to insist on a price quotation, the engineer would be obliged to withdraw from consideration. This system obviously prevented the purchaser of engineering services from making any price comparisons. An engineer therefore had to be selected on the basis of background and reputation.

This pricing behavior was effectively policed by various means of communication among members of the association and prospective clients. The NSPE utilized educational campaigns and personal admonitions to members and clients who were suspected of engaging in the banned behavior. Although the NSPE had no authority to expell members who were not abiding by the rule, there was no evidence of any significant defections from this system. As the Department of Justice pointed out, the NSPE's ethical restrictions have been of great importance to professional engineers. They have been treated as a binding standard of professional conduct and are aggressively enforced by the NSPE and its state societies; censure for unethical conduct can have a damaging effect on a member's standing as a professional.[30] The Department of Justice challenged this self-regulatory ban on competitive bidding in the engineering profession as being price-fixing in violation of Section 1 of the Sherman Act. A district court, a court of appeals, and the Supreme Court all supported this position.[31] Although the ethical rule did not call for a direct setting of price, its anticompetitive nature was seen as a classic example of price-fixing.

Several defenses were provided to try to justify what was recognized even by the NSPE as being a restriction on competition. A purely *legal* defense was that statutes in 16 states prohibited fee bidding by engineers. The ethical rule therefore coincided with state law, and the *Parker* doctrine of state action immunity should protect from Sherman Act liability. This thinking was not accepted by the courts because the anticompetitive ban

[29]Fees may be calculated in different ways: a percentage of a project's cost, actual cost plus some overhead plus some profit, rates per hour, a specific sum, or some combination thereof.
    [30]*U.S.* v. *National Society of Professional Engineers*, Civil No. 2412-72, Plaintiff's Memorandum on Remand, October 15, 1975, pp. 9–12.
    [31]389 F. Supp. 1193 (1974); on remand, 404 F. Supp. 457 (1975); 555 F. 2d 978 (1977); 435 U.S. 679 (1978).

on bidding was a private conspiracy and not mandated by any state legislature or enforced by any state agency. Furthermore, the activities of the engineers were clearly interstate in their character.

A *sociological* defense was that professional engineering was a "learned profession," and as such was not in trade or commerce. If not in trade, then there could not be a restraint of trade. This argument was written off by the lowest court and was never pressed further in the higher courts. First, the idea had no precedent to support it in any Supreme Court decision. Second, the court found the concept fraught with difficulties. Just what constitutes a learned profession? How would one define it? If one were to use the educational level required in order to practice a profession as a criterion, then that would be "a dangerous form of elitism."[32] Furthermore, the court saw engineering as being clearly an industry, and one directly involved in construction and manufacture: "It is a driving force of seminal character which continues to forge the very foundation from which our commercial trade emanates."[33]

An *economic* defense was that price competition among engineers was contrary to the public interest. If engineers had to submit bids to obtain particular project work, they would tend to submit designs that were cheaper and easier to prepare. That kind of design would tend to specify inefficient and unnecessarily expensive structures and methods of construction. To design and test for the most economical and efficient structures and methods of production was "complex, difficult and expensive." The higher-cost, higher-quality professional engineering services were the most economical, lowering overall costs and resulting in the increased efficiency of the final structures. Low-cost, low-bid engineering services would thus lead to an inferior product—one that would be dangerous to the public health, safety, and welfare.

According to another scenario, it was not possible to formulate precise specifications for many engineering tasks without extensive consultation and planning with the buyer. If forced to submit a bid on the buyer's general requirements, the price quoted would be only a guesstimate. The resulting bid would be unreasonably low, include mistakes, and foster optimism in the buyer. In the long run, renegotiation of contract would be required, or the engineer would cut corners to the disadvantage of the client and probably the general public. Therefore, according to either scenario, the restraint should be considered a reasonable restraint under the rule of reason.

The courts did not hesitate to decline to accept this rule of reason defense of the association's ban on competitive bidding. According to the Supreme Court:

[32]389 F. Supp. 1193, 1198 (1974).
[33]Ibid., p. 1199.

> Contrary to its name, the Rule [of Reason] does not open the
> field of antitrust inquiry to any argument in favor of a chal-
> lenged restraint that may fall within the realm of reason. In-
> stead, it focuses directly on the challenged restraint's impact on
> competitive conditions.[34]

The question to be answered under the rule of reason is whether the
restraint promotes or suppresses competition. There is no room to debate
the question of whether a monopolistic arrangement would promote trade
and commerce better than competition. There is no room for any cost-
benefit analysis. Although refusing to discuss price with a potential client
is not an overt price-fixing agreement among competing engineers with
respect to particular prices, a ban on competitive bidding has the same
effect. Since price-fixing has been determined to be illegal *per se*, the engineering society's ethical rule is illegal under the antitrust laws.

But suppose price competition among engineers actually does lead to
injury to the purchaser and/or the public. Suppose safety hazards do result.
Suppose the intensity of the competition leads to unethical behavior by
engineers selling their services and some purchasers of these services are
misled by deceptively low bids. How can such results of competition be
prevented? The Supreme Court agreed that professional deception itself is
"a proper subject of an ethical canon."[35] But the answer does not lie in
throwing out the baby with the bath water, as the NSPE tried to do by
avoiding competition itself.

Other Cases   Tradition, by definition, is hard to change. The American Society of Civil Engineers was found in 1977 to be in contempt of the
decree it consented to in 1972.[36] Two engineers were found by the society
to have violated the society's code of ethics by attempting to "supplant"
another engineer in a particular engagement after initial steps had already
been taken by the client to utilize the services of the latter. They were
accordingly disciplined by being expelled from the society. The "attempt to
supplant" took the form of submitting price quotations about which they
had actually been approached and which they were encouraged to submit.
The society held that the particular professional ethic against an attempt to
supplant was legitimate and that it was not covered by the 1972 consent
decree. The government held that the attempt to supplant was nothing
more than price competition, which the 1972 consent order was aimed to
permit.

In 1980 the Department of Justice found it in accord with recent court
precedent to file a Sherman Act suit against the American Consulting

[34]435 U.S. 679, 688.
[35]Ibid., p. 696.
[36]*U.S.* v. *American Society of Civil Engineers,* Trade Cases para. 61,574.

Engineers Council (ACEC), an association of some 3550 consulting engineering and land surveying firms.[37] The complaint charged suppression of price and other forms of competition since 1974 through adoption of and required member adherence to a code of ethics and professional conduct guidelines that prohibited members from entering design competitions without reasonable compensation, from providing engineering services on a free basis (except for civic, charitable, or religious organizations), and from providing professional services on a contingent basis. The suit sought the cancellation of any ethical rules that suppressed competition among the council's members.

Resistance to price competition after the Supreme Court's decision against the National Society of Professional Engineers has been evidenced by pressure on state legislatures and regulatory boards. Members of the NSPE have worked to urge these state bodies to adopt as their own official position that which the Supreme Court has condemned.[38] Rather than seek new modes of combatting what they have argued have been the evil side effects of competition, an immediate reaction of a portion of the profession has been to continue to seek to avoid the competition itself.

THE MEDICAL PROFESSION—*A CASE STUDY*

Costs in the health care industry rose faster than costs in most other industries in the United States during the decade of the 1970s. Perhaps not coincidentally, therefore, the FTC and the Department of Justice leveled strong antitrust attacks against medical professional associations in the second half of that decade. Objects of the attack were codes of ethics and effective professional discipline that banned or restricted advertising and solicitation and the means of determining the prices of physicians' services.

Advertising and Solicitation   The FTC issued a complaint against the American Medical Association (AMA) and two of its constituent and component associations in late 1975.[39] The complaint charged the associations with having agreed to prevent or hinder members from soliciting business, by advertising or otherwise, from engaging in price competition,

[37]*U.S.* v. *American Consulting Engineers Council,* Civil No. 80-2067.

[38]Charles S. Stark, Assistant Chief, Special Litigation Section, Antitrust Division, "Professionalism on Trial," remarks before the Florida Engineering Society, 1979 Annual Meeting, September 24, 1979, mimeo, p. 15.

[39]*In the Matter of The American Medical Association et al.,* 94 F.T.C. 701 (1979). The AMA is a federation of its state associations (constituent societies). County and district component societies are chartered by the state associations. Generally, a physician must be a member of all three levels of association if he or she is to be a member of any one. The two related associations that were respondents in this case were the Connecticut State Medical Society and The New Haven County Medical Association, Inc.

and from otherwise engaging in competitive practices—all in violation of Section 5 of the Federal Trade Commission Act. The result, it was charged, was that prices of physicians' services had been fixed or stabilized, that competition between physicians had been restrained or foreclosed, and that the consumer had been denied the kind of information in selecting a doctor that competition would ordinarily provide. Outside of a physician's street address and specialty, available in the Yellow Pages of the telephone directory, the consumer has been able to learn in advance little or nothing about the price, credit terms, service, facilities and equipment, training, current schooling, number of years of practice, and so on, of a physician except what he or she can pick up by neighborly word-of-mouth. The initial decision of the administrative law judge was unfavorable to the AMA, and the FTC issued a cease-and-desist order that affected not only the American Medical Association, but also the American Dental Association.[40] The FTC's order was upheld by a court of appeals,[41] and the Supreme Court agreed to review the order.

The restraints on competition were made possible by the publication, distribution, and enforcement of the AMA's code of ethics, the Principles of Medical Ethics. The administrative law judge held that the threat of disciplinary action for violating the code of ethics was "extremely effective."[42] The ultimate penalty for violation was expulsion from the associations. And this could be costly, for the physician might lose certain valuable rights as well as professional reputation and status. He or she might lose malpractice insurance, suffer withholding of claims reimbursement by health insurance carriers, lose referrals and hospital staff privileges, be unable to deliver papers and display exhibits at professional meetings, and incur legal expenses.

The AMA's position on advertising had been that solicitation of business by that method was unethical because "the refraining from or the employment of advertising is the clearly defined difference between a reputable physician and a quack...."[43] Self-advertising, according to the AMA, indicated selfish purposes and subjected the profession to commercialization. Advertising that cited dollar figures was deemed a business practice rather than a professional one and was to be avoided as being

[40]Ibid., Initial Decision, November 13, 1978; Opinion and Order, October 12, 1979. The FTC order omitted the two affiliated associations from the requirements of the order. Instead, it ordered the AMA to disaffiliate itself from any state or local medical society that engaged in any conduct prohibited by the order. Conditioned upon a final order of the FTC in this action was a consent order agreed to by the American Dental Association and four state and local dental associations that would bind them to the same cease-and-desist order. *In the Matter of American Dental Association et al.*, 94 F.T.C. 403 (1979), 94 F.T.C. 701 (1979).
[41]*American Medical Association* v. *FTC*, 638 F. 2d 443 (1980). A principal issue in the appeals process has been whether the FTC has jurisdiction over the AMA because it is a nonprofit corporation.
[42]94 F.T.C. 701, 806.
[43]AMA's 1971 *Judicial Council Opinions and Report*, Opinion 4 of Section 10. Cited in ibid., p. 813.

beneath a professional's dignity. In short, the trappings of business and competition were to be shunned. Indeed, the associations' first response to the charges was that neither they nor their members were engaged in business and thus they were not subject to the jurisdiction of the FTC. But this position was denied by both the administrative law judge and the FTC. The AMA and the two lower-level associations had certainly and admittedly engaged in numerous practices that had pecuniary benefit for their members, such as effective legislative lobbying, insurance programs, and providing professional management information and guides to increase a practice's profitability. According to the judge's decision: "The record evidence in this proceeding is overwhelming in establishing the anticompetitive effects of respondents' ethical restrictions, their economic motivations and their consequent harm to the public interest."[44] In short, ethical considerations had spilled over into the economic.

Quacks, by definition, should be excluded from the marketplace, for a quack is "an untrained person who practices medicine fraudulently."[45] But it does not follow that any physician who solicits business by advertising his or her services or the prices thereof is engaging in fraud. First, a physician who has received recognized medical training and has earned a license to practice cannot be said to be untrained. Second, although advertising or solicitation of business by a physician may be a necessary condition for intentionally trying to deceive a prospective patient as to what or who the physician pretends to be, it is certainly not a sufficient condition; this is not proof that the physician is trying to deceive anyone. On the other hand, it is possible that a physician who does not solicit patients or advertise may deceive some patients as to his or her capabilities and particular expertise even though he or she does have the necessary pedigree.

The administrative law judge and the Commission recognized this distinction. They made it clear that an association and its members can report to appropriate governmental authorities any advertising, solicitation, or representations made by a physician which they believed to be false or deceptive, together with the evidence. Likewise, they can report to governmental authorities any case of uninvited in-person solicitations by physicians of potential or actual patients who "because of their special circumstances are vulnerable to harassment or duress."[46]

It should be noted that in 1975, at the time of the complaint in this case, several states had statutes regulating advertising or solicitation by physicians.[47] Ten states declared illegal any form of physician advertising. Eight states outlawed any advertising in an "unethical" manner. And four states prohibited all advertising by physicians except for notices of openings or closings of a practice or listing in a directory. Since only a bit more

[44] 94 F.T.C. 701, 955.
[45] *Webster's New World Dictionary of the American Language* (New York: World, 1958).
[46] 94 F.T.C. 701, 976.
[47] See ibid., pp. 979–80.

than half of all licensed physicians in the United States were members of the AMA at that time, some of these state laws carried AMA-like prohibitions to nonmember physicians as well. But 16 states prohibited only misleading or deceptive advertising by physicians. And false or deceptive advertising in general was prohibited by statutes in every state and the District of Columbia.[48] These latter should, by themselves, provide the necessary statutory cover for the problem the AMA has professed to see.

The FTC's order permitted the AMA to adopt and enforce rules of ethical conduct in the matters of false and deceptive advertising and oppressive forms of solicitation. It saw the medical context of false and deceptive advertising as being different from that of selling goods or other types of services. Although no waiting period or Commission approval would be required, the AMA would have to make annual reports to the FTC on these self-regulatory activities for a period of five years. The rules, of course, would have to be "reasonable" rules. Price advertising would have to remain "as unfettered as possible." And the guidelines would have to be "within the meaning of Section 5." This approach represents the delegation of an important responsibility to the AMA. In view of the FTC's feeling that the AMA had previously taken a distinctly negative attitude toward physician advertising and given the AMA's lack of experience with the body of precedential law embodied in Section 5, the FTC, in its order, reminded the AMA that its advice would be available on request.

Relative Value Scales   Bans on advertising are a way to dampen price competition. But other ways may be even more effective in controlling competition. One is the adoption of suggested minimum fee schedules. A consent order was obtained in 1977 to prohibit use of such a schedule by veterinarians.[49] An alternative to suggested minimum fee schedules and one that has stirred up more litigation has been the use of relative value scales by medical associations. A relative value scale lists in nonmonetary units comparative numerical values for various surgical and medical procedures and other services. Each value can be converted into a monetary fee by the application of a dollar conversion factor to the basic unit. Circulation by professional associations of such scales has been viewed by the FTC as a device by which medical fees have become fixed. Consent orders were obtained in 1976, 1977, and 1979 against their use by obstetricians and gynecologists, orthopedic surgeons, radiologists, and two state medical associations.[50] These consent orders not only prohibit

[48]Ibid., pp. 952–53, citing *Opthalmic Rule*, 43 Fed. Reg. 23997, n. 89.

[49]*U.S.* v. *Alameda County Veterinary Medical Assn.*, Trade Cases para. 61,738.

[50]*In the Matter of The American College of Obstetricians and Gynecologists*, 88 F.T.C. 955 (1976); *In the Matter of The American Academy of Orthopaedic Surgeons*, 88 F.T.C. 968 (1976); *In the Matter of The American College of Radiology*, 89 F.T.C. 144 (1977); *In the Matter of Minnesota State Medical Association et al.*, 90 F.T.C. 337 (1977); and *In the Matter of the California Medical Association*, 93 F.T.C. 519 (1979).

the use of relative value scales, but also require that all existing scales be abrogated, withdrawn, and returned by all parties receiving them to the issuing association. Recipients included certain third-party payers such as Blue Cross and Blue Shield organizations.

A 1975 complaint by the Antitrust Division of the Department of Justice likewise sought to prevent the use of relative value scales by members of The American Society of Anesthesiologists.[51] It charged the society with a violation of Section 1 of the Sherman Act by agreeing to adopt, publish, and circulate relative value guides or schedules among its members, with the result that fees for anesthesia services by members of the association had been raised, fixed, and maintained at noncompetitive levels. The government's position was that the society's issuance of these guides was a *per se* violation of Section 1. As such, no evidence of effect would be required.

A district court viewed the matter in a different light.[52] It held that there had not been even a suggestion by the society that its members adhere to a pricing formula. It could see no agreement, express or implied; the guides were only guides. To be sure, at one time or another most anesthesiologists had used these guides. But there was a need being met, a need "... for a cohesive, internally consistent, logical and appropriate method for arriving at their fees...."[53] Indeed, evidence existed that the guides helped to define medical procedures and were useful in dealings between anesthesiologists and third-party payers such as insurance carriers. Some evidence even suggested that the guides tended to save these third parties money. In sum, the court held there was no evidence of agreement or of an anticompetitive effect. The Department of Justice did not appeal this decision, but the FTC had meanwhile signed a consent decree with the association that restricted certain of the latter's efforts which had the effect of fixing prices.[54]

The argument that relative value guides may tend to reduce costs has a parallel in a program of the AMA to assist physicians in calculating increases in costs and fees. This Physician's Fee and Cost Index Program was cleared by the Antitrust Division of the Department of Justice in 1979 through its business review procedure as not presenting any substantial antitrust issues.[55] The program was designed to teach the association's members how to compute fee and cost indices. The cost index would enable a physician to calculate the approximate rate of increase in costs. And the fee index would provide a method of keeping track of the rate of increase in the physician's fees. These were understood by the Department

[51]*U.S.* v. *The American Society of Anesthesiologists, Inc.*, Civil No. 75-4640.
[52]473 F. Supp. 147 (1979).
[53]Ibid., p. 158.
[54]*In the Matter of The American Society of Anesthesiologists, Inc.*, 93 F.T.C. 101 (1979).
[55]U.S. Department of Justice release, March 9, 1979.

of Justice to be a managerial aid to try to keep health care costs down. No collection or circulation of data from physicians was planned. If such a program were to prove to be more than a managerial aid, then the Department of Justice could change its position, for its approval indicates only "no present intention" to challenge.

Contractual Relationships   Medical associations' efforts to preserve through ethical rules a fee-for-service manner of payment to physicians was another FTC target in its complaint against the AMA and affiliated associations. The cease-and-desist order prohibited any association interference with the commercial terms under which a physician contracts to sell professional services. Contract practice, as contrasted with a fee-for-service system of payments, has been anathema to the association. A prepaid health delivery system such as Health Maintenance Organization (HMO), under which the doctors work for a salary and under which patients pay a fixed sum on a regular basis, is illustrative of the type of arrangement the AMA has been opposed to and has boycotted. Even as early as 1943, the Department of Justice had won a criminal suit against the AMA and its ethical rules against salaried practice and prepaid medical care.[56]

That the effort to maintain freedom for individual physicians to compete as they desire has necessarily been a continuing one is illustrated by consent orders obtained by the FTC and the Department of Justice with groups of physicians and medical centers providing that the latter not boycott HMOs, physicians providing services under HMOs, or physicians providing services on an other than fee-for-service basis.[57] The boycotting actions have allegedly taken the form of hindering access of physicians working for HMOs to a hospital's medical staff and facilities and to contractual relationships with prepaid medical plans. In similar vein, a dental association settled by consent order the complaint that it was campaigning among its members not to compete in dealing with insurance plans.[58] It was alleged that, by getting the insurance companies to eliminate provisions that were unacceptable to the dental association, competition among dentists was being restricted and the cost-control efforts of the insurance companies were being undermined.

The Commission order in the *AMA* case also prohibited any further interference by the AMA with physicians' partnerships with nonphysicians. The AMA had previously declared it unethical for physicians to form a professional association or corporation unless ownership and management were solely in the hands of licensed physicians. A psychiatrist, for

---

[56]*American Medical Assn.* v. *U.S.*, 130 F. 2d 233 (1942), affirmed, 317 U.S. 519 (1943).

[57]*In the Matter of Medical Service Corporation of Spokane et al.*, 88 F.T.C. 906 (1976). *In the Matter of Forbes Health System Medical Staff*, 94 F.T.C. 1042 (1979). *U.S.* v. *Halifax Hospital Medical Center and Volusia County Medical Society, Inc.*, Trade Cases para. 50,782 (1981).

[58]*In the Matter of Indiana Dental Association et al.*, 93 F.T.C. 392 (1979).

example, could not be in partnership with a psychologist. Nor could a physician be in partnership with a physician's assistant or physical therapist. The theory was that a person without a physician's license might be in a position to make decisions that only a physician should be making. Or the public might perceive that the unlicensed person had skills or training that he or she did not have. Or the public might believe that the physician was supervising the partner's work when he or she was not. The FTC rejected this theory in favor of the benefits that could be obtained from these business relationships and working conditions, since the productivity of a physician could be increased by working with nonphysician health personnel. A ban on such joint enterprises could also rule out the participation of a physician in an HMO. Accordingly, the Commission ordered an end to such restrictions as being unfair methods of competition.

Remaining Issues   Other forms of conduct by and through medical associations have been noted as being possible unfair methods of competition or unreasonable restraints of trade. This leaves us with some final questions. Do Blue Shield type medical plans give physicians' organizations an excessive amount of control over decisions with respect to payments to themselves so that these costs are higher than they otherwise would be? This relationship is believed by some to have helped account for the inflation of medical costs.[59] Have medical prepayment plans provided for the unreasonable exclusion from participation in service to the consumer of health care providers who are not physicians? Has the system of occupational licensing tended to make all health care providers excessively physician-dependent?[60] Perhaps these questions will have some answers in the future.

SUMMARY

Industry trade associations perform a variety of functions for the members of an industry. Because they represent a central gathering place for the

---

[59]See *Medical Participation in Control of Blue Shield and Certain Other Open-Panel Medical Prepayment Plans,* Staff Report of the Bureau of Competition to the Federal Trade Commission and Proposed Trade Regulation Rule, April 1979; and David I. Kass and Paul A. Pautler, *Physician Control of Blue Shield Plans,* Staff Report, Bureau of Economics, Federal Trade Commission (Washington, D.C.: U.S. Government Printing Office, November 1979). For an opposing view, see William J. Lynk, "Regulatory Control of the Membership of Corporate Boards of Directors: The Blue Shield Case," *Journal of Law and Economics,* 24, no. 1 (April 1981), 159–73. The Federal Trade Commission decided to treat the issue of physician control of medical prepayment plans on a case-by-case basis rather than promulgate an industrywide trade regulation rule. *FTC News Summary,* vol. 30–81, May 1, 1981.

[60]For discussion of licensure obstructions in health care, see Andrew K. Dolan, "Occupational Licensure and Obstruction of Change in the Health Care Delivery System: Some Recent Developments," in Roger D. Blair and Stephen Rubin, eds., *Regulating the Professions: A Public-Policy Symposium* (Lexington, Mass.: D. C. Heath, 1980), pp. 223–44.

members of an industry or for the collection of industry data, they have not infrequently become the subject of antitrust investigation or complaint. The dissemination of market knowledge is important in making markets less imperfect than they otherwise would be. But members' knowledge of economic data about their industry is sometimes used (and thus abused) to fix prices or production. The problem is to ferret out the abuses.

Professional associations, such as those of the legal, accounting, engineering, and medical professions, operate under codes of ethics. These codes are viewed by the members of these professions as necessary to maintain high standards of performance. Having a special personal relationship with clients, the members of these professions believe their conduct should be above that of ordinary commercial transactions. Codes of ethics should assure conduct that will maintain the reputation of the professions. But this self-regulation can conflict with the competitive norms established by antitrust policy.

Associations of lawyers have established minimum fee schedules and banned advertising as being unethical. The Supreme Court has ruled that both restrictions on competition are illegal under the antitrust laws. The debate continues as to the ultimate effect of these decisions on the price and quality of legal services.

The accounting profession has long held in its code of professional ethics that competitive bidding for public accounting services is unprofessional. Accountants should be selected on the basis of quality, not price. Antitrust pressure and action have changed this to permit price competition.

The engineering profession has traditionally frowned upon the submission of price quotations by its members as a means of obtaining business. Members of the engineering profession have found it important to abide by their particular association's code of ethics if they are to maintain their standing in the profession. The argument that the prohibition of the submission of price bids is a reasonable restraint of trade was rejected by the Supreme Court. So too has been the position that professional engineering is a "learned profession" and thus not subject to the antitrust laws because it is not trade or commerce.

Restrictions in the medical profession's codes of ethics have been viewed as contributing to the rising costs of medical care and have been successfully attacked under the antitrust laws. Although medical associations are nonprofit organizations, some of their activities have been economic in nature, and have not therefore been exempt from antitrust attack. The FTC has been upheld by a court of appeals in its insistence that restrictions on physician advertising be removed from medical codes of ethics. Devices to fix prices such as use of minimum fee schedules and relative value scales have also been successfully attacked. Finally, the FTC cease-and-desist order has provided for maintenance of the right of physicians to charge for their services in any way they wish in addition to the fee-for-service system. A physician may now also go into partnership with a nonphysician if he or she so wishes.

Selected Readings

BLAIR, ROGER D., AND STEPHEN RUBIN, eds., *Regulating the Professions: A Public Policy Symposium.* Lexington, Mass.: D. C. Heath, 1980.

GILB, CORINNE L., *Hidden Hierarchies: The Professions and Government.* New York: Harper & Row, 1966.

GRAD, FRANK P., "The Antitrust Laws and Professional Discipline in Medicine," *Duke Law Journal,* 1978, no. 2 (May 1978), 443–86.

KISSAM, PHILIP C., "Health Maintenance Organizations and the Role of Antitrust Law," *Duke Law Journal,* 1978, no. 2 (May 1978), 487–541.

LAMB, GEORGE P., AND CARRINGTON SHIELDS, *Trade Association Law and Practice.* Boston: Little, Brown, 1971.

RAYACK, ELTON, "The Physicians' Service Industry," In *The Structure of American Industry,* 5th ed., ed. Walter Adams. New York: Macmillan, 1977, pp. 401–41.

5 — Firm Size, Mergers, and Monopoly

The large corporation is recurringly the object of public policy scrutiny. The populist attitude distrusts bigness and equates bigness with monopoly. The big corporation cannot escape being in the public eye because it stands out in the business population. It is the proverbial goldfish in the goldfish bowl. It can be the object of criticisms small business can escape. Its size is viewed as giving it a market strength or power not enjoyed by the small firm. The large firm is perceived as being large in several respects especially: sales, assets, dollars for advertising, size of purchases, and financial strength. In general, it projects an image of economic power in the marketplace.

ABSOLUTE AND RELATIVE SIZE

Absolute Size *Fortune* magazine in its Fortune 500 series lists annually the first and second 500 largest industrial corporations in the country by sales and assets, ranking them primarily by sales. Table 5.1 lists the top 12 largest industrial corporations in 1980. They are clearly multibillion-dollar corporations, whether measured by sales or assets, and they are within the 12 largest industrials by whichever of these two ways they are measured. The industrial corporation closest to the $1 billion sales point on the list was the 301st corporation.[1] The 500th largest corporation had $488 million of sales, and the 1000th corporation had sales of $125 million.[2]

---

[1] *Fortune*, May 4, 1981, p. 336.
[2] Ibid., p. 342; June 15, 1981, p. 216.

Table 5.1 Twelve Largest U.S. Industrial Corporations Sales, Assets, and Rank Positions, 1980 (Dollar figures rounded)

Rank by Sales	Corporation	$ Sales (billions)	$ Assets (billions)	Rank by Assets
1	Exxon	$103.1	$56.6	1
2	Mobil	59.5	32.7	3
3	General Motors	57.7	34.6	2
4	Texaco	51.2	26.4	5
5	Standard Oil of California	40.5	22.2	7
6	Ford Motor	37.1	24.3	6
7	Gulf Oil	26.5	18.6	9
8	International Business Machines	26.2	26.7	4
9	Standard Oil (Indiana)	26.1	20.2	8
10	General Electric	25.0	18.5	10
11	Atlantic Richfield	23.7	16.6	12
12	Shell Oil	19.8	17.6	11

Source: Fortune, May 4, 1981, p. 324. © Time, Inc. Dollar figures have been rounded. Data are also provided annually by *Fortune* on the 50 largest companies in the following additional sectors: commercial banking, life insurance, diversified-financial, retailing, transportation, and utilities.

The large corporation has a basic advantage over the small firm in its ability to grow to an even larger absolute size because profits are a source of funds for capital expenditures.[3] Assume that firm A has assets of $1 billion and that firm B has assets of $100 million. Assume further that each firm earns profits on its assets at a rate of 10 percent. Firm A has profits of $100 million. Firm B has profits of $10 million. Even if the larger firm uses only half of its profits toward new capital formation and the smaller firm puts all its profits to that use, the larger firm will have added $50 million to its assets and the smaller firm $10 million.[4]

Related to the existence of very large individual firms of absolute size is aggregate concentration. In 1976 the 50 largest firms in manufacturing accounted for 24 percent of the value added in manufacturing, and the 200 largest accounted for 44 percent.[5] These 50 largest manufacturing firms accounted for 18 percent of employment in manufacturing, and the 200

[3]Large corporations openly argue and advertise the proposition that a basic function of profits is to provide a source of funds for capital investment. See, for example, Exxon Corporation, *Profits and Investments,* summarizing a series of advertisements appearing in newspapers in 141 American cities during December 1979.

[4]The average payout of dividends on the Dow Jones 30 industrial stocks between 1929 and 1980 has been 53.26 percent, according to Edson Gould Reports, *Findings and Forecasts* (New York: Anametrics, Inc., March 26, 1980), p. 42. Sergei Dobrovolsky, using selected years between 1922 and 1943, found that the proportion of net income retained by manufacturing corporations tended to be somewhat below 50 percent. *Corporate Income Retention, 1915–1943* (New York: National Bureau of Economic Research, 1951), table I, p. 15.

[5]Value added is factor income generated, or sales minus purchases of inputs from other firms.

101

largest accounted for 34 percent. With respect to the value of shipments, these 50 firms accounted for 25 percent, and these 200 firms accounted for 46 percent.[6]

The existence of corporations of such large absolute size has raised concern over the existence of "discretionary corporate power." This concern is nothing new; an important factor in the passage of the Sherman Antitrust Act of 1890 was fear of the power of the large industrial corporation. Economic power in the hands of a few has always gone against the grain of the populist tradition. Bills in Congress in the late 1970s, certain of them supported by the Federal Trade Commission and the Department of Justice, would have prohibited mergers wherever the result would represent a combination of large firms.[7] Some of the fear of firm size has been that it might culminate in excessive political power. Antitrust in action, however, has been primarily concerned with the impact of size on competition and with the goal of efficiency.[8] In this context of competition as a goal, the very large firm may be found to be a dominant monopolistic firm in its market. On the other hand, it may not, since several large firms may be faced against one another in direct competition.

Relative Size   Whereas the absolute size of the large industrial corporation is successful in attracting public attention and in generating a certain fear of bigness in business, it is knowledge of the relative size of the competitors in a market that can help throw some light on the degree of competition, monopoly control, or oligopolistic interdependence occurring in that market. Concentration ratios that express the share of a particular market accounted for by the largest few firms in that market have been used as a measure of the degree of imperfection of market structures. The percentages of a market held by the top four or top eight firms have been the principal concentration ratios used. In antitrust cases, market shares are usually taken as percentage shares of total market sales.[9]

The Bureau of the Census has provided data on concentration ratios

[6]Bureau of the Census, *Statistical Abstract of the United States: 1980* (Washington, D.C.: U.S. Government Printing Office, 1981), table 1454, p. 821.

[7]See *Mergers and Industrial Concentration, Hearings before the Subcommittee on Antitrust and Monopoly of the Senate Committee on the Judiciary*, 95th Cong., 2nd Sess., July 27 and 28, 1978, prepared statements of Michael Pertschuk, Chairman of the Federal Trade Commission, and John H. Shenefield, Assistant Attorney General, Antitrust Division, Department of Justice, at pp. 154–58 and 202–16, respectively. See also Federal Trade Commission, *Briefing Book for Mergers Policy Session*, 1979, pp. 17–20.

[8]The impact of large firm size on goals other than that of efficiency has attracted the attention of economists. See the proceedings of a conference sponsored by the Bureau of Economics of the Federal Trade Commission in 1980, *The Economics of Firm Size, Market Structure and Social Performance*, John J. Siegfried, ed. (Washington, D.C.: U.S. Government Printing Office). The four nonefficiency social objectives examined were the distribution of income and wealth, local community welfare, business political power, and worker satisfaction.

[9]The size variable selected could also be assets representing productive capacity, value added, or employment. Sales represent the variable in which firms are directly competing.

Table 5.2 Concentration Ratios in Selected Manufacturing Industries (4-digit SIC Code) and Classes of Products (5-digit SIC Code) Value of Shipments, 1977

SIC Code	Industry or Class of Products	% by Four Largest Companies	% by Eight Largest Companies
2043	Cereal breakfast foods	89	98
20471	Dog and cat food	58	76
2086	Bottled and canned soft drinks	15	22
27111	Daily and Sunday newspapers*	24	38
29111	Gasoline	30	53
32210	Glass containers	54	75
3273	Ready-mixed concrete	5	8
3334	Primary aluminum	76	93
33513	Copper and copper-base alloy rods, bars, and shapes	52	70
33531	Aluminum plate	87	†
3411	Metal cans	59	74
34114	Aluminum cans	55	79
37111	Passenger cars	99+	99+

*Receipts from subscriptions and sales.
†Withheld to avoid disclosing operations of individual companies.

Source: U.S. Bureau of the Census, *1977 Census of Manufacturers,* "Concentration Ratios in Manufacturing," MC77-SR-9 (Washington, D.C.: U.S. Government Printing Office, 1981), Tables 7 and 9. Concentration ratios for the top 20 and top 50 firms are also provided.

in SIC (Standard Industrial Classification) four-digit manufacturing industries and five-digit product groups.[10] We have selected and included in Table 5.2 certain Census industries and classes of products that are discussed in one connection or another within this book or that illustrate a weakness of these ratios. A principal weakness of these data for antitrust purposes is that the figures represent data for the nation as a whole, not for the *markets* most directly relevant to competition. As we pointed out in Chapter 1, an industry is represented by those firms producing a particular product or line of products within the United States. Markets, on the other hand, are composed of those sellers who are competing for the business of a common group of buyers.

Census concentration ratios can understate or overstate the true concentration ratio among competitors in a market. For ready-mixed concrete, market concentration is understated. The actual competitive markets are small and local or regional, because the product is both heavy and costly to transport and "perishable," since it is mixed on the way to the construction

[10]Starting with basic 2-digit industry groups, the industries and products become more narrowly defined with successive addition of numerical digits. There are 20 major groups (2-digit), 150 groups (3-digit), 450 industries (4-digit), 1,500 classes of products (5-digit), and 13,000 products (7-digit).

project where it is to be used. The concentration ratio of passenger automobiles overstates concentration in terms of its impact on market competition because imports of foreign autos are excluded. If the latter were included, they would account for around 25 percent of the automobile market.

Census concentration ratios will understate the true state of concentration where industries or product classes are defined so broadly as to include nonsubstitutable products. This can be so because product groupings from which industry classifications are derived are based on considerations of the similarity of manufacturing processes and types of input materials used, as well as on types of customers. The sellers of copper and copper-base alloy rods, bars, and shapes are not always competing for the business of the same group of buyers. Likewise, Census concentration ratios will overstate the degree of true concentration where definitions of industries are too narrow. Metal cans and glass containers can be in competition, yet they are placed in separate industry and product group classifications by the Census.

What this means is that in each antitrust case where concentration ratios can be of some significance, as in merger and in monopoly cases, ratios will most likely have to be calculated afresh from the particular market data found to be relevant. When it comes to actual cases, individual firm market percentages can be just as important to know—as, for example, in a merger case where it should be determined how much the market share of a newly merged firm will be, or in a monopoly case where the market percentage accounted for by the largest, dominant firm will want to be known. The total number of competing firms can also contribute to the analysis of the nature of the competition in a particular market.[11]

Measures of the number and size distribution of the competing sellers in a market are of interest because they are believed to be of some help in predicting market behavior and consequently understanding the degree of competition present in a market. A highly concentrated industry can suggest the interdependence of decision-making of an oligopoly or market dominance by a single firm. But an index itself is not proof of lack of competition, and other factors need to be known. How many close substitutes are there? How many potential competitors are there? What has been the rate of new entry and exit? How stable have been the relative market shares of firms over time? Is the market expanding or contracting? How

[11]Indexes representing the concentration of the full distribution of firms in an industry have been devised. Such a summary index is the Herfindahl index, which is the sum of the squares of individual firm market shares. If all firms have equal shares, then the index is equal to $1/n$ where n is the number of firms. For example, if there are 10 firms in the market, each with the same market share, the index would have a value of .10. A maximum value of 1 is reached where there is only one firm in the market. For a discussion of several different measures of concentration, see Douglas Needham, *The Economics of Industrial Structure Conduct and Performance* (London: Holt, Rinehart and Winston, 1978), pp. 122-32.

rapid has been the rate of introduction of new products? A concentration ratio is a starting point, not an ending point, of an investigation into the monopolistic or competitive nature of a market.

FIRM GROWTH BY MERGER

As we have seen, a firm can grow in size by plowing profits back into the formation of new capital. A firm can also grow by going to the money markets to procure funds for new capital growth by selling new issues of securities, either stocks or bonds. Such forms of capital growth are usually strongly favored by public policy, since capital expenditures are considered vital to full employment, economic growth, and control of inflation. Provisions in the corporate profits tax structure for accelerated depreciation of plant and equipment are evidence of this view.[12]

Another form of growth for a corporation is for it to acquire the assets or a majority of the stock of another corporation. This merger process may cause the acquired firm to disappear as a separate business entity as its assets become fully integrated with those of the acquiring firm, both nominally and in operation. The acquired firm may, however, retain its corporate identity and become a subsidiary of the acquiring firm. In either case, however, there is centralization of decision-making.[13] The average consumer-citizen often will not know what firm really controls the company from which he or she is buying goods or services. The rent-a-car industry provides such an illustration. The Hertz Corporation is a subsidiary of the RCA Corporation. Avis is a subsidiary of Norton Simon. National Car Rental is a subsidiary of Household International. And Budget Rent-A-Car is a subsidiary of the Transamerica Corporation.

The merger as a means of growth for a firm has not received the same general favorable acceptance as has new capital formation. A merger does not represent economic growth. It represents, in the last analysis, an exchange of pieces of paper representing ownership rights over existing assets. Furthermore, a merger represents "instant" growth of the acquiring firm. An already large firm can double its size in a short time through the

---

[12]Increasing the rate of depreciation of plant and equipment for corporate income tax purposes has the effect of having an interest-free government loan. The higher depreciation charges per year that result from using a smaller number of years keep costs higher and profits and corporate profits taxes lower for those years.

[13]Sometimes corporations are organized as a "group" of corporations, whether through merger or through self-growth. The very large petroleum firm is more likely than not to be organized as a "group" of corporations, with a top holding company holding controlling interest in a large number of subsidiary corporations. Some of its subsidiaries may be in the form of joint ventures with more than one other petroleum company, in which case the subsidiaries with less than 50 percent stock ownership are known as affiliates. Such a "group" may be constituted of as many as 500 corporate subsidiaries, as is the case with the Royal Dutch Shell group.

consummation of a merger with another firm of equal size. Sometimes, too, a smaller firm, perhaps with the help of borrowed money, can grow rapidly by acquiring a firm larger than itself.[14]

Growth through merger has not been as important for the large firm as publicity would sometimes suggest. According to the FTC data, in the 31 years from 1948 through 1978, the number of large acquisitions (where the acquired company had assets of $10 million or more) of mining and manufacturing companies totaled 1923.[15] Of these acquisitions, 728, or about 38 percent, were made by firms among the top 200. The assets acquired in these mergers by the largest 200 firms accounted for a little more than 54 percent of the acquired assets. Yet the acquired assets in large mergers as a percentage of total new investment by mining and manufacturing firms has been relatively small, averaging an annual 23.6 percent in the 1960s and 12.7 percent in the first nine years of the 1970s.[16]

Such findings are consistent with those of J. Fred Weston, whose study of 74 oligopolistic firms from roughly the turn of the century through 1948 showed that growth by merger was a relatively small fraction of the total growth of most of the firms, and that mergers after those of the merger movement of 1898–1903 had relatively little effect on industry concentration.[17] Using assets of the initial year as a base from which subsequent growth was measured, 30 of the 74 corporations studied showed growth by acquisition of less than 10 percent. Overall, growth by acquisition accounted for approximately one-fourth of the growth of the firms studied. But it is true that for some firms, the merger route has been a principal means of increasing size.

Types and Motives for Mergers   Mergers can be of three basic types: horizontal, vertical, or conglomerate. The horizontal merger involves firms directly competing in the sale of similar goods or services. Vertical mergers represent the combining together of firms operating in different stages of the same industry that have been in an actual or potential buyer-seller relationship. A conglomerate merger is neither horizontal nor vertical in nature. One form of conglomerate merger occurs when one firm acquires another producing a product not being produced by the acquiring firm but

[14]Not all mergers are "friendly." One corporation can "take over" another corporation by acquiring a majority of the stock of the acquired firm in spite of the wishes of the management of the acquired corporation.

[15]Federal Trade Commission, *Statistical Report on Mergers and Acquisitions, 1978* (Washington, D.C.: U.S. Government Printing Office, 1980), table 14, p. 110. Data for 1978 are preliminary. This report does not include data on mergers for which data were not publicly available, but it does include the corporate names and asset values of each and every merger summarized in the aggregate data.

[16]Ibid., derived from table 24, p. 121. New investment is defined as total expenditures for new plant and equipment.

[17]J. Fred Weston, *The Role of Mergers in the Growth of Large Firms* (Berkeley: University of California Press, 1953), pp. 13–20.

functionally related to the production and/or distribution efforts of the acquiring firm. This is known as a product-extension merger. Another form of conglomerate merger is market extension, in which the acquiring firm simply extends the geographic limits of its competition by acquiring a firm producing like product(s) in an area into which the acquiring firm had not yet penetrated. A third form of conglomerate merger is that referred to as "other," or "pure." This represents the combination of firms producing entirely unrelated products or services, such as insurance, auto parts, cigars, motion pictures, and pulp and paper (Gulf and Western Industries). As can be seen from Table 5.3, the conglomerate merger has accounted for about three-quarters of all large mergers in the post-World War II period.

Several motives for merger exist. Some are applicable to all types of merger; others apply only to a certain type. First, mergers are a faster means of growth for a firm than new construction. This can be satisfying to growth-oriented firms and to corporate leaders seeking corporate size for its own sake.[18] Second, growth through merger can be cheaper than growth through new construction if the market value of the acquired firm's assets is not fully reflected in the price of that firm's securities. Third, a merger may be the best, or perhaps the only, route through which a firm may be able to obtain a scarce resource, such as rights to a patent or to some important engineering knowhow. Even the cash of a firm may be the object of acquisition.

Fourth, real economies of scale may be envisioned as resulting from a merger. A horizontal merger may permit the centralization of certain functions represented by various administrative overhead costs, with a resulting reduction in unit costs. Or such a merger, by adding another plant(s), may allow for greater flexibility in production runs. The same may be true of the conglomerate merger, but the "synergy" supposedly result-ing from such a merger (where $2 + 2 = 5$) is probably much overstated. In the case of the vertical merger, there may be some cost savings in better coordination between the different stages of production in terms of admin-istration and the elimination of certain transactions costs. Perhaps better coordination in a physical or technological sense may result as well, but new well-planned construction, designed for a specific purpose, would seem to be a better route than merger for the better handling of materials as they move from one stage of the production process to another. Envisioned real economies do not necessarily actually result from mergers, as many a

[18]The 1980 chairman of the Securities and Exchange Commission has referred to corpo-rate "Napoleons" who make corporate acquisitions for "ego satisfaction, prestige, and re-muneration associated with size and the appearance of growth." Reported by Robert Metz in "Market Place: The Unfriendly Tender Studied," *New York Times*, February 6, 1980, p. D8. Another observer has noted that the chief executive officer of a firm may "enjoy(s) spotting and adding new companies to his fold." Agis Salpukas, "Parker-Hannifin Buys Growth," *New York Times*, December 28, 1979, p. D1.

voluntary divestment of acquired firms or acquired firms' assets attests. Some of the economies achieved may be pecuniary in nature, achieved through bargaining power that can sometimes come from size, such as lower unit advertising rates or lower unit costs of capital.

A motive peculiar to a horizontal merger is the elimination of a competitor. Market share can be increased in the process. A motive peculiar to a vertical merger is the security of supply or security of sales outlets. Owning its own raw materials can insulate a firm against possible monopolistic control of supply. Owning its own sales outlets can insulate a firm against the insecurities of competition, as represented, for example, by the loss of the volume business of a chain outlet. Purchase of such "security," however, means incurring the costs of trying to operate the purchased assets on a profitable basis on their own merits. A motive peculiar to a conglomerate merger is diversification in order to reduce the risks present in any one market. Operating in several markets can spread the risks and perhaps provide greater stability in earnings performance. The management of a firm may even arrange a merger with a more profitable firm in order to make its own profits appear to be better than they have been.

Conglomerates and Diversification   A distinction must be made between a genuine conglomerate that has fairly equal large divisions or subsidiary corporations, each of which is operating in distinctly separate spheres of economic production, and a firm that is intensifying its efforts toward diversification. In the latter case, the firm maintains a position fairly clearly based on one industry, but begins to apply resources in one or more new economic directions. Some oil industry spokesmen, for example, have argued that the world will eventually run out of crude oil and that, if diversification efforts are not pursued by oil firms, these firms will be faced with liquidation.[19]

This conflict between the alleged absolute limits of certain resources and the immortality of the corporation can be resolved only by investment in other resources, by new search or by acquisition. In any case, oil companies have been diversifying not only into other energy sources, such as coal, uranium, geothermal, and solar, but also into clearly separate types of industries. Mobil Oil acquired Montgomery Ward and Container Corporation of America. Gulf Oil has become involved in real estate. Exxon has entered the office and electric equipment businesses. Cities Service and Standard Oil (Indiana) have entered the copper business. And Sun Company has diversified into trucking and convenience stores. It can even be argued that constant efforts to diversify are a necessary corollary to a firm's

---

[19]Winston Williams, "Oil Giants Work Related Fields," *New York Times*, September 25, 1979, p. D15.

long-run survival or viability. Changing technologies and demands, with resulting changes in market opportunities, require constant adaptation. Entry into a new industry can perhaps occur with the least amount of error by gaining a "foothold" through acquiring a small firm that already has operating experience in that industry.

MERGERS AND PUBLIC POLICY

Growth of a firm through merger falls directly within the jurisdiction of the FTC and the Department of Justice. Each of these agencies can file complaints under Section 7 of the amended Clayton Act, which states that mergers involving the acquisition of stock or assets of another corporation are illegal "where in any line of commerce in any section of the country, the effect of such acquisition may be substantially to lessen competition, or tend to create a monopoly." The Department of Justice can also utilize the Sherman Act, and the FTC can use Section 5 of the Federal Trade Commission Act, to prosecute merger cases. Although achieving economies of scale might be claimed as a reasonable justification for a merger, there is no statutory provision for such a defense. The statute does, however, specifically permit the purchasing of stock solely for investment, providing that does not bring about a substantial lessening of competition.

Prior to 1976, the FTC and the Department of Justice were forced to rely for knowledge of mergers and pending mergers on the culling of business and financial journals and newspapers. The Hart-Scott-Rodino Antitrust Improvements Act of 1976, however, requires that proposed mergers involving corporations of certain size must be reported in advance to the enforcement agencies. A firm having net sales or total assets of $100 million desiring to merge with another with net sales or total assets of $10 million is subject to this reporting requirement.[20] The statute provides that the rules governing the reporting procedures and the establishment of any exemptions because of the unlikeliness of violating the antitrust laws were to be drawn up by the FTC. Provisions were also made in this statute to expedite the seeking of a preliminary injunction to forestall a merger that otherwise might later have to be carefully unraveled.

As is clear from Table 5.3, the majority of mergers involving the acquisition of large firms (assets of $10 million or more) have been conglomerate mergers. But the horizontal merger, accounting for somewhat less than 17 percent of the total, has been the type of merger most subject to antitrust attack. Between 1951 and 1966, more than half of all large mergers of mining and manufacturing companies challenged by the De-

---

[20]The act provided for a 30-day waiting period that could be extended for another 20 days and, in the case of cash tender offers, a 15-day waiting period that could be extended 10 days.

Table 5.3 Large Mergers* in Manufacturing and Mining: Numbers, Types, and Percentages by Type Selected Years

Type of Merger	Percent 1948–1978	Numbers 1948–1978	1975	1976	1977	1978
Horizontal	16.8	323	4	12	26	21
Vertical	10.2	196	3	4	4	13
Conglomerate	73.0	1400	52	61	70	76
Product extension	59.1	828	25	26	38	37
Market extension	5.4	76	1	8	0	0
Other	35.5	496	26	27	32	39
Total	100.0	1919	59	77	100	110

*Large mergers involve an acquired company with assets of $10 million or more.

Source: Federal Trade Commission, *Statistical Report on Mergers and Acquisitions,* Bureau of Economics, November 1977, Table 18, p. 105. Federal Trade Commission, *Statistical Report on Mergers and Acquisitions, 1978* (Washington, D.C.: U.S. Government Printing Office, 1980), Table 18, p. 115.

partment of Justice and the FTC were horizontal in nature.[21] That figure is clearly more than proportionate to the percentage of large mergers represented by the horizontal merger. Of the 18 merger cases filed by the Department of Justice in the years 1974 through 1976, 16 were horizontal.[22]

The success rate in merger prosecutions by the federal enforcement agencies was phenomenal until 1972. From 1950 to 1972, these agencies won all merger cases not involving regulated industries upon which the Supreme Court ruled.[23] After 1974, however, the success rate of government merger cases in the courts fell significantly. Attacks against conglomerate mergers were particularly unsuccessful. A noticeable trend favoring defendants in conglomerate merger cases was apparent at all levels of the federal courts after that date.[24]

HORIZONTAL MERGERS

The possible adverse impact on competition is most obvious in the case of the horizontal merger. When two competing firms are merged, one compe-

[21]Willard F. Mueller, "The Celler-Kefauver Act: Sixteen Years of Enforcement," mimeo, 1967, p. 17.

[22]Donald L. Baker, Assistant Attorney General, Antitrust Division, "Government Litigation under Section 7: The Old Merger Guidelines and the New Antitrust Majority," remarks before the Southwestern Legal Foundation, Dallas, mimeo, February 24, 1977, p. 18.

[23]Joseph P. Bauer, "Challenging Conglomerate Mergers under Section 7 of the Clayton Act: Today's Law and Tomorrow's Legislation," *Boston University Law Review,* 58, no. 2 (March 1978), 199.

[24]Ibid., p. 200.

titor disappears. It could be argued that, if all price-fixing is illegal *per se*, then any horizontal merger ought to be illegal *per se* since the effect is the same as if the merging firms were getting together to fix prices. What better way is there to make a price-fixing agreement that will stick than by combining the two decision-making bodies into one? On the other hand, the merger of two small, weak competitors may make for one stronger competitor.

The courts have almost always supported the enforcement agencies in their attacks on horizontal mergers, whether the concentration ratios are quite high or relatively low. Bethlehem Steel, the second largest steel producer, and Youngstown Sheet and Tube, the sixth largest steel producer at the time, were prevented from merging in 1958 in the first test case under Section 7 of the Clayton Act as amended by the 1950 Celler-Kefauver Act. The steel industry was fairly heavily concentrated, with the largest four firms accounting for almost 60 percent of basic ingot capacity, and the court saw this merger as offering the threat of creating a chain reaction of further mergers. Since the two companies had argued that they needed to merge to be better able to compete with U.S. Steel, the number one firm in the industry, what would there be to stop other large firms in the industry from also merging to compete better? The court envisioned the possibility of an eventual triopoly in the industry under this rationale.[25]

The Failing Company Doctrine   A major exception to the restrictions against a large firm acquiring another large competing firm is the so-called failing company doctrine. A large firm that has no reasonable prospect of survival can be merged with another large firm even if it otherwise would be challenged. The automobile industry has provided a classic illustration of this principle. In 1954 Studebaker merged with Packard to form Studebaker-Packard and Hudson Motor Car merged with Nash-Kelvinator to form American Motors. Both mergers, although reducing the number of passenger car manufacturers from seven to five, were approved by the Department of Justice and the FTC as the only means of survival for these firms.[26]

A "failing company" merger of two very large firms approved in 1978 by the Department of Justice was that involving Jones & Laughlin Steel Corporation, number seven in the steel industry, with Youngstown Sheet & Tube Company, number eight in the industry. Jones & Laughlin Steel Corporation was a subsidiary of the LTV Corporation and Youngstown Sheet & Tube Company was a subsidiary of the Lykes Corporation. Both parent companies were conglomerate firms with operations in several dif-

[25]*U.S.* v. *Bethlehem Steel Corp.*, 168 F. Supp. 576 (1958).

[26]Studebaker-Packard finally shut down its auto manufacturing in the United States in 1963 and discontinued Canadian operations in 1966. American Motors, although financially shaky at times, has survived by successfully specializing in certain types of vehicles.

ferent industries. The Justice Department at first challenged the merger but later reversed that position on the basis of the failing company doctrine. The surviving firm, going under the Jones & Laughlin name, became the third largest producer of basic steel. A significant question here, and in all such cases, is just what constitutes a failing company. In this steel merger the parent companies were not on the verge of bankruptcy. On the other hand, the subsidiaries were showing a series of annual deficits or minimal profits over a period of years.

The logic of the failing company doctrine is that it is better to have the assets managed by the new owner who has acquired them by merger and thus keep them in the competition. An alternative is to let the firm be thrown into bankruptcy and let the investors (stockholders, bondholders) pay the economic price for the failure. In the steel merger the attorney general saw a disadvantage in bankruptcy in that the firm's assets might have to be sold on a "distress basis."[27] But the reduced prices of the assets sold on a distress basis could well perhaps bring those assets down to a value at which they could be operated and return a normal profit to the new owners. One problem, of course, can be to find a new owner at any price. If an industry is in a declining stage or suffering a severe cyclical recession, and if the assets are not convertible to other uses, it may be next to impossible to find any buyer at all.

Forestalling Concentration   The logic of the *Bethlehem Steel* case was pursued in *Brown Shoe,* but in the latter case the industry was a fragmented one, not an oligopoly.[28] Brown Shoe Company, a retailer as well as a manufacturer of shoes, acquired the largest single group of independent retail stores (Kinney). Brown and Kinney together controlled more than 20 percent of sales of women's and children's shoes in several cities. Combined market shares of women's, children's, or men's shoes exceeded 5 percent in 118 cities. The Court saw a tendency in this fragmented industry toward concentration and wanted to "call a halt" to it:

> If a merger achieving 5 percent control were now approved, we might be required to approve future merger efforts by Brown's competitors seeking similar market shares. The oligopoly Congress sought to avoid would then be furthered, and it would be difficult to dissolve the combinations previously approved. Furthermore, in this fragmented industry, even if the combination controls but a small share of a particular market, the fact that this share is held by a large national chain can adversely affect competition. . . .[29]

---

[27]*Business Week,* July 3, 1978, p. 30.
[28]*Brown Shoe Co.* v. *U.S.,* 370 U.S. 294 (1962). Vertical aspects of the merger were also ruled upon.
[29]Ibid., pp. 343–44.

The logic of declining numbers was applied by the Supreme Court to a relatively unconcentrated industry in its *Von Grocery* decision.[30] Two retail food chains in the Los Angeles market, representing the third and sixth largest firms in that relevant market, were found by the Supreme Court to have violated the Clayton Act by merging. After the merger in 1961, these two combined chains represented only 7.5 percent of the market; and there were a total of 3818 food companies in the market. The Court's position was that the number of food companies in the market had been declining, from 5365 in 1950, and that concentration was increasing. It viewed as being a mandate of the law "to prevent concentration in the American economy by keeping a large number of small competitors in business."[31]

Dissenting opinion took the position that a decline in the number of firms in the market was insufficient evidence of a substantial lessening of competition and failed to recognize the "dynamism and vitality" of the competition in the retail grocery business in the Los Angeles area at the time. There was ease of entry and exit. In the previous ten-year period, 173 new chains had entered the market and 119 had gone out of existence. The new chains usually resulted from successful one-store operations. The market share of the leading chain had declined from 14 to 8 percent. There was also substantial turnover among the firms that made up the top 20 firms. The dissenters, in short, objected to the majority's position that, in effect, followed a *per se* rule based on a declining number of firms in a market.

A Structural Approach   The merger guidelines established by the Department of Justice in 1968 utilized a structural approach with respect to horizontal mergers, setting maximum market percentages for acquiring and acquired firms which it felt were legitimate.[32] For example, in a highly concentrated market (which was defined as the four largest firms accounting for 75 percent or more of the market), an acquiring firm with 4 percent of the market would have gone beyond the bounds of acceptability if it were to acquire a firm with 4 percent or more of the market. Or an acquiring firm with 15 percent or more of the market should not attempt to merge with a firm with 1 percent or more of the market. Even smaller market percentage mergers were viewed suspiciously by the guidelines if a small firm was a particularly "disturbing" or "disruptive" factor in a market or had an "unusual competitive potential." The guidelines took the position that, barring exceptional circumstances, achieving economies of scale was an unacceptable defense. The incoming Reagan administration in 1981 viewed these guidelines as being too severe and planned to modify them.

---

[30]*U.S.* v. *Von's Grocery Co.,* 384 U.S. 270 (1966).
[31]Ibid., p. 275.
[32]U.S. Department of Justice, *Merger Guidelines,* May 30, 1968.

The guidelines on horizontal mergers in the food distribution industry issued by the FTC in 1967 were also based on a structural approach. A nationwide merger movement among large supermarket chains had been found alarming, so absolute size volumes of business were cited in these guidelines. Mergers by retail food chains involving annual food store sales in excess of $500 million annually would "warrant attention." And mergers by voluntary and cooperative groups of food retailers creating a wholesale volume of sales comparable to those food chains with sales exceeding $500 million annually likewise would require attention.

The Supreme Court's position in its 1974 *General Dynamics* decision has been offered as evidence that market shares (in this case, production) will not always serve to condemn a horizontal merger.[33] The merger of two competing coal producers raised their combined market shares from 33.1 to 37.9 percent. But the Court held that it was not current production of coal (much of which was already committed under long-term contracts) which was the relevant measure, but rather coal reserves. In terms of uncommitted reserves, the Court felt that the merged firm had limited ability to compete in the future and therefore the merger would not substantially lessen competition. This meant that exclusive reliance on market shares and concentration ratios would not always be sufficient.[34]

VERTICAL MERGERS

Vertical mergers can have two basic properties under which they can be condemned under Section 7 of the Clayton Act. First, when a supplier merges its assets with or controls through stock holdings a buyer, other suppliers can be foreclosed from that part of the market represented by that buyer. Second, any market power a supplier may have may be transferred to the market of that controlled buyer.

Market Foreclosure   The first variety of vertical merger case is illustrated by the Department of Justice's 1949 suit against Du Pont, resolved by the Supreme Court in 1957.[35] The suit was brought under the original Section 7 of the Clayton Act (prior to the 1950 Celler-Kefauver amendment which made Section 7 applicable to the acquisition of assets). The FTC had held the view that Section 7 of the Clayton Act did not apply to vertical acquisitions.[36] The Supreme Court in this case put the idea to rest.

---

[33]*U.S.* v. *General Dynamics Corp.*, 415 U.S. 486. This was a 5 to 4 decision.

[34]William F. Baxter, Assistant Attorney General, Antitrust Division, *Concerning Merger Policy, Hearings before the Subcommittee on Monopolies and Commercial Law of the House Committee on the Judiciary*, August 26, 1981, mimeo, p. 2.

[35]*U.S.* v. *E. I. du Pont de Nemours & Co.*, 353 U.S. 586.

[36]Ibid., p. 590.

Du Pont had acquired 23 percent of the voting common stock of General Motors. The question before the Court was whether Du Pont's "commanding position" as a supplier of automotive fabrics and finishes to General Motors had been the result of competition or its large holdings of General Motors stock. Because the record showed that the bulk of Du Pont's production of these goods went to General Motors, the Court found the inference overwhelming that the latter was the true explanation. The stockholdings gave Du Pont a competitive advantage, said the Court.

The outcome of the decision rested largely on the determination of the relevant product market—that of automotive finishes and fabrics. General Motors, representing approximately half of the automobile industry's sales, purchased 67 percent of its finishes and about 45 percent of its fabrics from Du Pont. In total, annual sales of these products to General Motors by Du Pont amounted to over $26 million. This was deemed to be a substantial foreclosure of the market to other sellers. Suppose, however, that the relevant product market had been industrial finishes and fabrics, representing all uses of these finishes and fabrics. If the relevant product market had been so defined, paint sales foreclosed to other sellers represented by these General Motors' purchases would have represented only 3.5 percent of the market and the equivalent percentage represented by the General Motors–Du Pont fabric purchases would have been only 1.6 percent.

These latter market percentages are not small compared to those in a second major precedent-setting decision pertaining to a vertical merger, this time involving the acquisition of assets under the 1950 amended Clayton Act, that of *Brown Shoe* in 1962.[37] Brown Shoe was the fourth largest shoe manufacturer in the country, although accounting for only about 4 percent of shoe output. It merged with the G. R. Kinney Corporation, which owned and operated more than 350 retail outlets, the largest independent chain of family shoe stores in the country, accounting for 1.2 percent of national shoe sales by dollar volume. According to the Court: "Thus, in this industry, no merger between a manufacturer and an independent retailer could involve a larger potential market foreclosure."[38] This would be especially true since the avowed purpose of the acquisition by the manufacturer was to use the acquired retailer as an outlet for its shoes.

The market percentages were not the only deciding factor in the *Brown Shoe* decision. Brown and other shoe manufacturers had been acquiring retailers. The Court envisioned a trend in such vertical acquisitions that would mean increased concentration and the change of a fragmented industry to an oligopoly. This trend should be caught in its incipiency, to prevent further market foreclosure to other manufacturers. In addition,

[37]*Brown Shoe Co.* v. *U.S.*, 370 U.S. 294.
[38]Ibid., pp. 331–32.

Congress had expressed the desire to protect "viable, small, locally owned businesses."[39] Thus, something other than efficiency had become part of the basis of the decision.[40]

The FTC noted another dimension to this phenomenon of market foreclosure through vertical merger in the guidelines it announced in 1967 with respect to vertical mergers in the cement industry.[41] Between 1960 and 1966, cement producers had acquired 72 users of cement.[42] The Commission viewed this trend toward vertical integration through merger as possibly triggering off a chain reaction of acquisitions. As some cement manufacturers acquired ready-mixed concrete companies (the principal users of cement), other cement producers, in turn, would acquire some of their customers. This could be viewed as a defensive move designed to avoid further market foreclosure. At the same time, several large ready-mixed concrete companies were integrating backward into the manufacture of cement, presumably in order to preserve source of supply. As vertical integration became more general, there would be less open market supplies and fewer customers available to any nonintegrated firms remaining. In addition, the Commission envisioned as a major barrier to entry the higher capital requirements dictated by the necessity of entering into the production of cement and ready-mixed concrete on an integrated basis.

In spelling out its enforcement guidelines for the cement industry in absolute terms, the Commission stated that the acquisition by a cement company of any ready-mixed concrete firm among the top four in any given market, or the acquisition of any ready-mixed concrete firm regularly purchasing 50,000 or more barrels of cement in a year, would be subject to challenge. The acquisition of several smaller ready-mixed concrete firms whose cumulative annual purchases were 50,000 barrels would likewise be offensive to the Commission's enforcement policy.

Does such an announced policy against vertical mergers in the cement-concrete industry represent valid public policy? Would vertical mergers that lead to foreclosure occur if there were not economies and greater profitability in them? Bruce Allen's research suggested to him that such "captive marketing" strategy by the cement industry had not been

[39]Ibid., p. 344.
[40]See John L. Peterman, "The Brown Shoe Case," *Journal of Law and Economics*, 18, no. 1 (April 1975), 81–146, for a discussion of the abuse of efficiency as a standard in this landmark decision.
[41]Federal Trade Commission, *Enforcement Policy with respect to Vertical Mergers in the Cement Industry*, January 3, 1967. See also Federal Trade Commission Staff Report, *Economic Report on Mergers and Vertical Integration in the Cement Industry*, 1966.
[42]William I. Boyd, Jr., Chief, Division of Mergers, Federal Trade Commission, "Vertical Integration in the Cement and Concrete Industries: The Decline of the Direct Acquisition; The Emergence of Indirect Leverage," remarks before the Annual Convention of the National Sand and Gravel Association and the National Ready Mix Concrete Association, Chicago, January 28, 1970, mimeo, p. 10.

profitable.[43] Why then engage in it? Allen had several answers to this question. The industry had not tried it before. The industry had been bound by tradition. It was no longer protected by the collusive basing-point system. Its members were seeking stable market shares, and forward integration in a period of excess capacity (when much of the merger integration took place) was seen as a method of obtaining them. If all that is true, then, as Allen pointed out, the FTC through its cement industry merger guidelines would have been protecting the cement firms from their own mistakes by protecting the market competition from foreclosure.

Extension of Market Power   The second major complaint leveled against the vertical merger is that a large firm with the financial resources bigness can often provide can confer that power on a smaller subsidiary it has acquired at a forward stage of integration. Reynolds Metals, one of the "Big 3" producers of basic aluminum and in the late 1950s the world's largest producer of aluminum foil, purchased Arrow Brands, a firm that converted aluminum foil into florist foil. The latter was found to be the relevant market for antitrust purposes.[44] The florist foil market contained only eight relatively small producers, but Arrow Brands held about 33 percent of that market.

A district court held that Reynolds' resources gave it the power of the "rich parent" with the "deep pocket." That, said the court, was enough to condemn the merger under the doctrine of incipiency. It "opened the possibility and power to sell at prices approximating cost or below and thus to undercut and ravage the less affluent competition."[45] In actuality, prices were cut by Reynolds' new subsidiary below total cost and retroactively. The result was a substantial drop in business for five of the other seven sellers, ranging from 14 to 47 percent, in the following year. Arrow Brands sales increased over the same period by 18.9 percent.

CONGLOMERATE MERGERS

The impact of conglomerate mergers on market competition is more subtle than the impact of a horizontal or vertical merger. Four issues applicable to the problem of the conglomerate merger have been given attention by enforcement agencies, courts, and critics: potential competition, entrenchment, business reciprocity, and competitive forebearance.

[43]Bruce T. Allen, "Vertical Integration and Market Foreclosure: The Case of Cement and Concrete," *Journal of Law and Economics*, 14, no. 1 (April 1971), 251–74.
[44]*Reynolds Metals Co.* v. *FTC*, 309 2d 223 (1962). Florist foil is aluminum foil which is embossed and often colored and is used by florists to wrap flowers and flower pots.
[45]Ibid., pp. 229–30.

Potential Competition   Potential competition is a concept that has been used as a criterion to test the legality of conglomerate mergers under Section 7 of the Clayton Act. This concept has actually appeared in two forms. One is that of the significantly large firm entering a new market through merger with a firm of considerable market share already in that market when it could have and was likely to have entered that market through construction of the necessary new facilities on its own—entry *de novo*. If the firm had taken the latter route, rather than acquiring an existing firm, the number of competitors would have been increased by one. That, according to this theory, would increase the competition by increasing the number of active competitors and reducing the degree of concentration in the market. This has been called the theory of *actual potential competition*.

This form of potential competition is illustrated by the case of Procter & Gamble, a very large diversified manufacturer of low-price, high-turnover household products sold through grocery, drug, and department stores, acquiring Clorox Chemical, a manufacturer of liquid bleach, a product that fit into P&G's line of products and distribution but that P&G did not produce. Clorox, although much smaller than P&G in absolute size, held close to 50 percent of national liquid bleach sales. The FTC and the Supreme Court both found this product-extension merger to be illegal because P&G was found to be a potential entrant into the industry.[46] That is, if P&G had not taken the merger route to enter this market, it would have entered on its own.

Potential entry by a large firm into a new market through merger can be viewed as beneficial to competition when the acquired firm is one with a small market position in a highly concentrated industry. With the power of a large firm now behind a small yet viable firm, such a firm can add a potent competitive force to the industry. Such entry by a large firm has become known as a "toehold" or "foothold" acquisition. This type of entry has been considered an acceptable alternative to *de novo* entry under actual potential competition theory because in the long run it should help to deconcentrate a market.

The second form of potential competition has been called the *perceived potential entrant* theory. The question here is not just whether the large firm would have entered the market *de novo* or through foothold acquisition, but rather whether it was *perceived* by those firms already in the market as being one which, being on the fringe of the market, might well enter if prices and profits looked enticing enough. To be so perceived, it would have to be one of a limited number of firms "standing in the wings." If it were so perceived, the firms in the market would take this into account in their pricing policies and would be more careful about charging prices that

---

[46]*FTC* v. *The Procter & Gamble Co.*, 63 F.T.C. 1465 (1963), 386 U.S. 568 (1967). A court of appeals had ruled against the FTC's position. 358 F. 2d 74 (1966).

might attract the potential entrant into the market. If this firm on the fringe of the markt were to merge with a firm already in the marketplace, this force conducive to the firms limiting their prices to reasonable levels would be lost.

This form of potential competition is illustrated by the Department of Justice's case against the Falstaff Brewing Corporation.[47] In 1965 Falstaff, the fourth largest producer of beer in the United States, desiring to enter the New England beer market for the first time, acquired the Narrangansett Brewing Company, the largest seller of beer in New England with 20 percent of that market. The Supreme Court in this market-extension merger case held that the lower court should have found out whether Falstaff, being positioned on the edge of the market, was being perceived as a potential entrant by firms already in the market. When remanded, the district court found no evidence to that effect and ruled in favor of Falstaff.[48]

Both versions of potential competition suffer certain drawbacks in application. How can one decide whether a firm was likely to have entered a particular market on its own if it had not actually entered the market in that way? How can one truly determine whether a large firm on the edge of the market has been really perceived as a potential entrant?[49] Although some documents may exist to help answer these questions, testimony can be self-serving. Yet until 1974 the doctrine of potential competition was viewed as a principal vehicle through which to attack the problem of the large conglomerate merger.

Attempts by the government to apply the doctrine of potential competition to conglomerate mergers have been set back by the courts sufficiently to question seriously the ability of enforcement agencies to prevent conglomerate mergers through the use of potential competition theory. The Supreme Court in its 1974 *Marine Bancorporation* decision set difficult standards that would have to be met to demonstrate the necessary illegal anticompetitive effects under the doctrine of potential competition.[50] First, it must be shown that the target market is sufficiently concentrated so that the "dominant participants" are behaving in an interdependent or parallel manner and have the capacity to determine price and total output. If, instead, the market were effectively competitive, then the firms in it would

---

[47]*U.S.* v. *Falstaff Brewing Corp.*, 410 U.S. 526 (1973).

[48]383 F. Supp. 1020 (1974).

[49]The probability of entry of a potential competitor can depend not only on the number of potential competitors, but also on how they view each other. For a discussion of this problem, see Lionel Kadish, Henry J. Cassidy, and Jerry Hartzog, "Potential Competition: The Probability of Entry with Mutually Aware Potential Entrants," *Southern Economic Journal,* 44, no. 3 (January 1978), 542–55.

[50]*U.S.* v. *Marine Bancorporation*, 418 U.S. 602. This case involved a bank merger, and federal and state regulations pertaining to entry played a significant part. But basic principles applicable to all mergers were enunciated.

not be concerned with any potential entrant. Second, it must be shown that the acquiring firm has available feasible means of alternative entry, either *de novo* or through a foothold acquisition. The likelihood of *de novo* entry should also be considered. Third, entry by one of these alternative means must "offer a substantial likelihood of ultimately producing decon-centration of that market or other significant procompetitive effects."[51] This last requirement demands it be shown that there will be a long-run improvement in competition resulting from an alternative means of entry before the merger is to be denied. The difficulty in meeting these standards stems basically from the fact that a number of speculative possibilities or subjective elements have to be examined and certain of these points have to be convincingly shown.

The difficulty in meeting such standards for applying potential com-petition theory and difficulties in securing the cooperation of the courts have steered the FTC's conglomerate merger efforts to those in which there are horizontal or vertical overlaps.[52] It also has contributed to support by the enforcement agencies of legislation limiting mergers by absolute size.

Entrenchment   Entrenchment is a theory the Office of Policy Plan-ning and Evaluation of the FTC has held may help to fill the gap created by the difficulties in applying the theory of potential competition to the control of conglomerate mergers.[53] It is illustrated by the *Procter & Gamble* decision discussed above. A firm dominant in its market is acquired by an even larger firm which had not been in that market. P&G, with assets of $500 million, acquired Clorox Chemical, which had 50 percent of the liquid bleach market but also had only $12 million of assets. The smaller acquired firm now has the support of the "deep pocket" of the acquiring firm and becomes thoroughly "entrenched" in its market. The result can be a rise in barriers to entry.

The *Procter & Gamble* decision pointed out that P&G's size and vol-ume discounts in advertising would discourage new entrants and active competition from firms already in the market for fear of retaliation. Clorox might now obtain the preferred retailer shelf space that P&G enjoyed. P&G might also subsidize liquid bleach price wars, subsidizing the underpricing with revenue from its other operations (cross-product subsidization). Two basic weaknesses are present in this theory of entrenchment. One, it is only a theory. Can it be supported in fact by actual market behavior?[54] Two, it would seem to apply only to the limited case of the acquisition of a dominant firm.

[51]Ibid., pp. 630–33.
[52]Federal Trade Commission, *Mergers Policy Session,* pp. 19–20.
[53]Ibid., p. 19.
[54]See comment and references to differing opinions in Bauer, "Challenging Conglom-erate Mergers," pp. 226–29.

The concept of cross-product subsidization as applied to the conglomerate multiproduct firm hypothesizes that such a firm subsidizes its more competitive operations from the revenues of its less competitive operations.[55] A conglomerate merger, adding to a firm the business of selling a new product or line of products, provides the conglomerate firm with one more possible operation which may at some time be useful in this fashion. At one extreme, cross-product subsidization can be viewed as "deep pocket" predation. A less extreme view is that this represents unplanned or even unconscious subsidization.[56] On the other hand, it can be argued that a profit-maximizing firm will not subsidize operations which in the long run cannot be made to yield a normal profit, and where there are no serious barriers to entry the elimination of a competitor will only lead eventually to another competitor arising. In any case, there is no documentary evidence to support the general existence of cross-product subsidization.[57]

Business Reciprocity A third concern with respect to the conglomerate merger has been that such a merger enhances the possibility of business reciprocity. This practice is illustrated by the situation in which two firms buy and sell to and from each other. The classic case often used to illustrate the circumstances where this practice has been found to be illegal is that of the Consolidated Foods Corporation, which sold dehydrated onion and garlic to food processors from whom it purchased their final products. Consolidated Foods had acquired its dehydrated onion and garlic production capability by acquiring Gentry, Inc. The Supreme Court backed the position of the FTC in condemning this product-extension merger because it had given Consolidated, a very large firm, an unfair advantage in dealing with its suppliers.[58]

> Reciprocal trading may ensue not from bludgeoning or coercion but from more subtle arrangements. A threatened withdrawal of orders if products of an affiliate cease being bought, as well as a conditioning of future purchases on the receipt of orders for products of that affiliate, is an anti-competitive practice. Section

---

[55]We examine the case of the single-product firm selling in different geographic areas at different prices in Chapter 7.

[56]Corwin D. Edwards, "The Changing Dimensions of Business Power," *St. John's Law Review*, 44, Special Edition (Spring 1970), "Conglomerate Mergers and Acquisitions: Opinion & Analysis," 432.

[57]Jesse W. Markham's empirical study of firm structure and decision-making has indicated that pricing and advertising decisions in the highly diversified firm have almost always been left in the hands of division or operating unit managers. Such divisional autonomy might suggest a lack of cross-product subsidization. *Conglomerate Enterprise and Public Policy* (Boston: Graduate School of Business Administration, Harvard University, 1973), chap. 4.

[58]*FTC v. Consolidated Foods Corp.*, 380 U.S. 592 (1965).

7 of the Clayton Act is concerned "with probabilities, not certainties."[59]

The 1968 merger guidelines of the Department of Justice stated that reciprocal buying is an "unjustified business practice" and that a conglomerate merger will ordinarily be challenged where it creates a significant danger of reciprocal buying or is accomplished in order to create a reciprocal buying arrangement.[60] Under the guidelines, therefore, any coercion or attempted coercion by a large seller-buyer need not be shown. The FTC announced in 1970, in a similar vein, that it considered any reciprocal dealing practices which were prevalent and systematized and which involved a not insubstantial amount of commerce to be a violation of Section 5 of the Federal Trade Commission Act. It would not accept any assurances of voluntary compliance from firms it believed were using their purchasing-selling power to secure business.[61] On the other hand, it was noted in a staff report to the FTC in 1972 that ". . . it is difficult to regard reciprocity as a generalized, pernicious consequence of conglomerate mergers."[62]

Business reciprocity has also been opposed simply because it means poor managerial control over buying and selling.[63] Any firm tying itself into a reciprocal dealing relationship with another firm or firms is not likely to be keeping its eyes open for alternative better buys. The supplier too, knowing that sales are assured under this relationship, may feel it can survive even with poor product quality and delivery performance. This view also holds that reciprocity tends to weaken price competition from third parties who see reciprocal business as being already tied up and not worth trying to get.

From a contrary point of view, the Stigler Report expressed lack of concern over reciprocity, holding that its threat to economic competition is small or nonexistent.[64] The argument presented is that monopoly power in

[59]Ibid., pp. 594–95.
[60]U.S. Department of Justice, *Merger Guidelines*, pp. 23–25.
[61]*Federal Trade Commission News*, September 1, 1970; and *FTC News Summary*, No. 25, October 1, 1970, p. 3.
[62]Stanley E. Boyle and Philip W. Jaynes, *Staff Report to the Federal Trade Commission, Conglomerate Merger Performance: An Empirical Analysis of Nine Corporations* (Washington, D.C.: U.S. Government Printing Office, 1972), p. 128, n. 3. This report examined nine large conglomerate firms actively engaged in mergers of unrelated lines of business. The nine firms, all ranked among the 200 largest manufacturing corporations in 1969, were Litton Industries, Inc.; Ling-Temco-Vought, Inc.; Gulf & Western Industries, Inc.; International Telephone & Telegraph Corporation; Textron, Inc.; Rapid-American Corporation; White Consolidated Industries, Inc.; FMC Corporation; and Norton Simon, Inc.
[63]See Dean S. Ammer, "Realistic Reciprocity," *Harvard Business Review*, 40, no. 1 (January–February 1962), 116–24.
[64]*1969 Presidential Task Force Report on Productivity and Competition*, 115 *Cong. Rec.* 6472 (June 16, 1969). Reproduced in *Journal of Reprints for Antitrust Law and Economics*, 1, part I (Winter 1969), 851.

one product cannot be used to affect the price of another, unrelated product. If a buyer is being charged more than a competitive price available
elsewhere, he or she will switch to the alternative. This position assumes
away the bargaining power of the large buyer.

Competitive Forebearance   A fourth conglomerate merger issue is
that of conglomerate interdependence and forebearance, or *competitive
forebearance*. Oligopoly theory tells us that large oligopolistic firms facing
each other in a market find it in their best interest not to compete actively
through price. Large conglomerate multiproduct firms may find themselves exposed to competition with one another in several different markets. This contact of oligopolists in several different markets may cause
each to be wary of active price competition with the others in any one of
these markets. As Areeda and Turner point out, the feared retaliatory
moves may well be made in product or geographic markets different from
those in which an initial price cut was made.[65]

MONOPOLY AND THE LARGE FIRM

In 1911 a Sherman Act antitrust suit was filed by the government against
the U.S. Steel Corporation charging that it was engaged in illegal restraint
of trade and the exercise of monopoly. The complaint asked that the firm
be dissolved. The Supreme Court held in 1920 that, although the firm had
tried to achieve monopoly, it had not succeeded. In its decision the Court
clearly pointed out that bigness is not in itself an offense against the Sherman Act, which outlaws monopolizing and attempts to monopolize.[66] U.S.
Steel clearly represented bigness, being the largest corporation of its kind
in the United States when it was formed through a series of mergers in
1901. At the time of the antitrust suit, it controlled approximately 44 percent of the industry's steel ingot capacity and 66 percent of its output.[67]
The Court's position, however, was that, even though bigness might have
some market power, it cannot be condemned for simply having that power:
". . . the law does not make mere size an offense or the existence of unexerted
power an offense."[68]

The Court reasoned that the firm had not succeeded in achieving a
monopoly primarily because it did not have the power to impose its prices

---

[65]Phillip Areeda and Donald Turner, "Conglomerate Mergers: Extended Interdependence and Effects of Interindustry Competition as Grounds of Condemnation," *University of
Pennsylvania Law Review*, 127, no. 4 (April 1979), 1092.

[66]*U.S. v. United States Steel Corp.*, 251 U.S. 417 (1920).

[67]Leonard W. Weiss, *Case Studies in American Industry* (New York: Wiley, 1971), pp.
155–58.

[68]251 U.S. 417, 451.

on the rest of the industry. Of special importance, it argued that U.S. Steel had "... resorted to none of the brutalities or tyrannies that the cases illustrate of other combinations."[69] In so speaking, it had in mind what it viewed as the oppressive market tactics utilized by the Standard Oil Company of New Jersey and the American Tobacco Company, which had led to their dissolution under antitrust decrees.[70] The "bigness is no offense" position of the Court in the *U.S. Steel* decision reiterated the 1916 position of a lower court in the *American Can Co.* case, where it was said: "It [Congress] has not accepted the suggestions of some influential men that the control of certain percentage of industry should be penalized."[71]

New precedent was created in 1945 by the decision in the *Alcoa* case.[72] The government suit charged that Alcoa had monopolized the manufacture of virgin aluminum and the sale of certain aluminum products. This decision, in effect, reversed the "bigness is no offense" defense. For the Aluminum Company of America was found to violate Section 2 of the Sherman Act simply because it held 90 percent of the aluminum reduction (ingot) market. If a firm controls that percentage of a market, it must by its very position be behaving as a monopolist: "... no monopolist monopolizes unconscious of what he is doing."[73] The court said however, that "it is doubtful whether 60 or 64 percent would be enough; and certainly 33 percent is not." Since then, courts in most cases have made a finding of monopoly power where market share is greater than 70 percent and no monopoly power where market share is less than 50 percent.[74] In between these figures, more evidence beyond market percentages is required.

But in how many markets does the largest firm have more than 70 percent of the market? The number is unquestionably higher than one would suspect by examining national industry concentration ratios. In some regional or local markets, a firm may well have a dominant position represented by its share of the market. Take the case of the high-purity industrial water service markets in which the suppliers provide water purification service for commercial and industrial applications. An industry of such a specialized nature, in which customer service is a key element of

[69]Ibid., pp. 440–41.

[70]*Standard Oil Co. of New Jersey v. U.S.*, 221 U.S. 1 (1911). *U.S. v. American Tobacco Co.*, 221 U.S. 106 (1911).

[71]*U.S. v. American Can Co.*, 230 Fed. 859, 902 (1916), appeal dismissed, 256 U.S. 706 (1921).

[72]*U.S. v. Aluminum Company of America*, 148 F. 2d 416 (1945). The Supreme Court—unable to meet the required quorum of six justices since four disqualified themselves—was replaced by the three senior judges of the appeals court which had territorial jurisdiction. An Act of Congress was required to resolve the problem in this fashion.

[73]Ibid., p. 432.

[74]John J. Flynn, "Monopolization under the Sherman Act: The Third Wave and Beyond," *Antitrust Bulletin*, 26, no. 1 (Spring 1981), 51.

sales, can easily provide an illustration of market dominance by a single firm in a particular region. Thus, the Department of Justice successfully resolved by consent order a merger suit against firms in this industry where one of the firms controlled 85 percent of the high-purity industrial water service market of Northern California.[75] Then too, if the relevant product is narrowed down enough, a monopoly percentage can be found for the nation. For example, the Grinnell Corporation was found to have 87 percent of the nation's accredited central station hazard-detecting service business.[76]

Tests for Monopolizing and Attempts to Monopolize   Section 2 of the Sherman Act condemns both monopolizing and attempts to monopolize. The traditional test for *monopolizing* has come to be recognized as proof of monopoly power *plus* deliberate conduct to achieve or maintain that power.[77] In 1979 the National Commission for the Review of Antitrust Laws and Procedures (Antitrust Commission) held for a stronger view, believing "that persistent monopoly power, in all but the most exceptional instance, can only result from culpable conduct."[78] In short, according to this thinking, culpable behavior to achieve monopoly must have occurred if persisting monopoly power is present. In either case, it is evident that a significant market share would be necessary in order to violate Section 2. For if a firm is to be able to engage in any deliberate censurable conduct, it must have some leverage in the marketplace, and to have that leverage it would be expected to have some advantage such as that provided by its relative size.

The traditional test for an *attempt to monopolize* under Section 2 has been simply conduct deliberately undertaken to obtain monopoly power. This has required proof of two elements: specific intent to monopolize and a dangerous probability of success.[79] It is obvious that "intent" and "dangerous probability" do not provide standards of precision. This can help to explain the current state of the law. As the Antitrust Commission report stated:

> The current state of the Section 2 attempt offense poses serious problems for effective antitrust enforcement. The development of the law of attempted monopolization has been uneven; the

[75]*U.S.* v. *Coca-Cola Bottling Company of Los Angeles, Arrowhead Puritas Waters, Inc., Aqua Media, Ltd., and A. M. Liquidating Co.,* Civil No. 76-3988-LTL, Consent order, Competitive Impact Statement, 1978, p. 3.

[76]*U.S.* v. *Grinnell Corporation,* 384 U.S. 563 (1966).

[77]*Report to the President and the Attorney General of the National Commission for the Review of the Antitrust Laws and Procedures* (Washington, D.C.: U.S. Government Printing Office, 1979), vol. I, p. 151. Hereinafter cited as *Antitrust Commission Report.*

[78]Ibid., p. 156.

[79]Ibid., pp. 145–49.

scope of the offense is much disputed and remains unclear. Even within a circuit, courts often apply different standards. The Supreme Court has unfortunately declined to resolve the conflicts that have arisen by establishing controlling principles for the attempt provision.[80]

Some of the members of the Antitrust Commission were in favor of applying a "No-Conduct" standard to Sherman Act Section 2 cases. Under such a standard, where persistent monopoly power was present, proof of bad conduct would not be required. This position assumes that monopoly power arises from objectionable conduct. The great advantage in this assumption is that it would speed up what would otherwise be protracted litigation over the conduct issue. Opposing opinion is to the effect that persistent monopoly power is more likely to be the result of efficiencies and better performance than of predatory conduct. Thus, Robert Bork has argued that a "No-Conduct" standard would not be in the public interest. To strike down this power would be to strike down efficiencies.[81]

The economic efficiencies argument has not been ignored by the courts and in judicial procedures. In the *Grinnell* case, the lower court noted that the defendants had not sought to show "that their share is attributable primarily to their skill, efficiency, and foresight, or to like factors of obvious social utility," implying that the outcome might have been different if they had.[82] The high court in this same case said that, given the possession of monopoly power, the problem was to distinguish between "the willful acquisition or maintenance of that power" and "growth or development as a consequence of a superior product, business acumen, or historic accident."[83] Even the *Alcoa* decision pointed out that "The successful competitor, having been urged to compete, must not be turned upon when he wins."[84] Perhaps the *Alcoa* decision would have been different if Alcoa's conduct had been good and it had not engaged in the vertical price squeeze (see Chapter 6).

An appeals court judge overruled an $87 million antitrust award in favor of Berkey Photo against Eastman Kodak in 1979 on the grounds that a large company does not violate the Sherman Act "simply by reaping the competitive rewards attributable to its efficient size."[85] In 1980 the FTC

[80]Ibid., p. 144.
[81]Ibid., p. 155. See also Robert H. Bork, *The Antitrust Paradox: A Policy at War with Itself* (New York: Basic Books, 1978), pp. 192–95.
[82]*U.S.* v. *Grinnell Corporation,* 236 F. Supp. 244, 254 (1964). The defendants were plural because Grinnell controlled three subsidiary corporations in the field.
[83]384 U.S. 563, 570–71 (1966).
[84]148 F. 2d 416, 430 (1945).
[85]*Berkey Photo* v. *Eastman Kodak,* 603 F. 2d 263, 276 (1979). The smaller firm had argued that the larger firm had taken advantage of its dominant position in the market by simultaneously introducing its pocket instamatic camera and cartridge film for it without giving advance notice of the new products to its competitors.

dismissed its complaint against Du Pont in which it had charged the company with overwhelming small competitors in the titanium dioxide market, where its market share had risen from 30 to 42 percent between 1972 and 1977. The Commission supported the position of the administrative law judge who had held that Du Pont's success was the result of intelligent planning and business foresight. It emphasized that Du Pont's conduct was consistent with its technological capability and market opportunities.[86]

In sum, a firm can be suspected of monopoly when it holds a very large market share. Any behavior that might be characterized as in any way predatory must clearly be avoided. If a firm does not do this, its efficiencies may be ignored in favor of the abuse of its market power.

THE BIG ANTITRUST CASE—*A CASE STUDY*

The monopoly antitrust attacks against large firms that started in 1969 and dragged on into the 1980s were attacks on oligopolies as well as against very large single firms.[87] The complaints emphasized alleged misconduct rather than market shares, but it is clear from the complaints that the charged conduct was also related to the market percentages. The alleged offensive conduct was of a much less obvious nature than the gross "brutalities or tyrannies" or the classic trade restraints of an earlier era. A feature of those big monopoly and so-called shared monopoly oligopoly cases has been that they sought to alter the structure of the firms and therefore of the industries involved.[88] The structure to be altered in one case would consist of intangible as well as tangible assets.

International Business Machines   The Antitrust Division of the Department of Justice filed a Sherman Act Section 2 complaint against the International Business Machines Corporation in 1969.[89] The suit, publicized as the largest antitrust case in history, charged the company with monopolizing the general-purpose digital computer systems market. Although this firm accounted for approximately 67 percent of the installed general-purpose digital computers in 1967, it was certain exclusionary market tactics that were under attack.

[86]*FTC News Summary*, vol. 5–81, October 31, 1980.

[87]Of all the 965 cases filed by the Federal Trade Commission and the Antitrust Division of the Department of Justice during the decade of the 1970s, only 26 were directed at monopolization. Don E. Waldman, "Economic Benefits in the *IBM*, *AT&T*, and *Xerox* Cases: Government Antitrust Policy in the '70's," *Antitrust Law & Economics Review*, 12, no. 2 (1980), 87. Waldman holds that most of these monopolization cases involved small defendants or relatively unimportant economic markets.

[88]"Shared monopoly" is the phrase applied to the situation in which the behavior of oligopolists in highly concentrated markets yields the same market result as if there had been one monopolist.

[89]*U.S. v. International Business Machines Corporation*, Civil Action No. 69 Civ. 200.

The complaint condemned the firm's combining of the price of hardware, software, and related support services; this foreclosed the market to firms supplying only parts of this market. It charged that IBM was pricing new computer models at unusually low profit levels to choke off sales of competitors' new models. It alleged that the company announced new computer models when it knew it was unlikely to be able to deliver them within the announced time in order to forestall sales by competitors coming out with new models. It accused the company of using discriminatory discounts, especially favoring educational institutions whose experience with new equipment was believed to have considerable impact on purchasing decisions in the commercial market. It also alleged that IBM engaged in other various pricing and marketing practices with respect to various pieces of equipment in order to raise barriers to entry. The result of all this was said to be a monopolizing of the general-purpose digital computer systems market in the United States. The complaint was following the principle, as stated by a federal court, that "... the essence of monopoly is exclusion."[90]

In addition to requesting that IBM be enjoined from these various marketing tactics, the complaint asked for relief by way of divorcement, divestiture, and reorganization. As the case finally went to trial in 1975, the Justice Department asked that IBM be broken up into "several discrete, separate, independent and competitively balanced entities."[91]

Ready-to-Eat Cereal Oligopoly   In 1972 the FTC filed a complaint against the four largest firms in the ready-to-eat (RTE) cereal industry charging them with monopolizing that industry through the use of unfair methods of competition in violation of Section 5 of the Federal Trade Commission Act.[92] The basis of the case was the shared monopoly theory of anticompetitive business behavior. The four firms were Kellogg Company (45 percent market share), General Mills, Inc. (21 percent), General Foods Corporation (16 percent), and The Quaker Oats Company (9 percent). (Quaker Oats was later dropped as a defendant.)

The general charge was that the cereal companies had maintained a highly concentrated, oligopolistic, noncompetitive market structure in the marketing of breakfast cereals and had used oligopolistic market power to exclude new entrants. More specifically, they had built and shared monopoly power for over 30 years through brand proliferation (150 brands), product differentiation, and trademark promotion—all of which concealed basic product similarities. Control of shelf space by these major cereal companies had interfered with smaller and regional cereal producers

[90]*U.S.* v. *Associated Press, et al.,* 52 F. Supp. 362, 374–75 (1943).
[91]*New York Times,* May 20, 1975, p. C53.
[92]*In re Kellogg Co., et al.,* FTC Docket No. 8883.

obtaining their share of shelf space.[93] Acquisition of competitors eliminated strong private label companies. It was further alleged that advertising and product promotion had been misleading, especially as to the contribution to the physical capabilities of children and to weight-reducing properties. All of this, it was alleged, led to artificially high prices, excessive profits (more than double the average for all manufacturing firms), the supplanting of product innovation with product imitation, and a significant barrier to entry (almost no new entry since World War II). It had allegedly cost the consumer over $1 billion between 1958 and 1972.[94]

The FTC's proposed solution included divestiture of plant and other facilities to form five new corporate entities.[95] Transfer of knowhow would be required where necessary. Royalty-free licensing of all but a few existing brand names for a period of 20 years would be required. Any mergers with the newly formed entities would also be prohibited for 20 years. Finally, any unfair selling practices, including shelf space control, would be prohibited. In short, reorganization was designed to restructure the industry and therefore, hopefully, alter market behavior to make it more competitive.

Big 8 of the Petroleum Industry   A third major deconcentration antitrust effort during the 1970s was that aimed at the "Big 8" of the petroleum industry by the FTC. The complaint, filed in 1973, charged the nation's eight largest petroleum companies with combining or agreeing to monopolize refining and maintaining monopoly power over refining in the Eastern and Gulf Coast states and in parts of the midcontinent area.[96] All these major oil companies are vertically integrated, operating at all the several stages of the industry: exploration and extraction, crude oil trans-

[93]See David M. Elsner, "Bran X: A Small Cereal-Maker Has a Tough Struggle in a Big Guy's World," *Wall Street Journal*, April 26, 1977. Shelf space is usually allocated by retailers according to a product's rate of turnover. The position and amount of shelf space are significant in facilitating turnover. So unless a product has already obtained choice shelf space, it is difficult to obtain it. Even Quaker Oats, the fourth largest in the industry, found it a difficult and losing battle for shelf space. *Business Week*, February 25, 1980, p. 153.

[94]Summation of FTC's case-in-chief, reported in *CCH Trade Regulation Reports*, no. 461, October 27, 1980, p. 4.

[95]The proposed dissolution order as prepared by the FTC's staff attorneys is available in *Antitrust Law & Economics Review*, 12, no. 3 (1980), 19–40. According to *Consumer Reports* (February 1981, p. 80), the cereal companies had called for the assistance in 1977 of a major labor union representing workers in that industry after a study commissioned by the cereal makers indicated that the creation of eight firms out of three might lead to the loss of 2000 jobs. The union took the case to Congress, where bills were introduced to prevent the FTC from dividing up firms found guilty of the antitrust laws. City officials in Battle Creek, Michigan, a principal cereal manufacturing town, sued the FTC to cease prosecuting the case until an environmental study on the effects of dissolution on air and water pollution could be completed. The city also asserted that dissolution would lead to an increase in child abuse, alcohol abuse, divorce, and juvenile delinquency.

[96]*In re Exxon Corp., et al.*, FTC Docket 8934. The eight firms cited were Exxon Corporation, Texaco, Gulf Oil Corporation, Mobil Oil Corporation, Standard Oil Company of California, Standard Oil Company (Indiana), Shell Oil Corporation, and the Atlantic Richfield Company.

portation, refining, and distribution and marketing. The FTC complaint stated that other petroleum companies had engaged in some of the same alleged practices but were not being named as respondents in the suit.

It was not the concentration ratios themselves in the petroleum industry that the suit directly attacked. After all, there are other industries in the economy with much higher concentration ratios. What the FTC objected to were the acts and practices being engaged in which these concentration ratios permitted. The complaint urged that these companies had maintained and reinforced a noncompetitive market structure by pursuing a common course of action at several stages of the industry. They were charged with exchanging crude oil among themselves in a restrictive and exclusionary manner. They used a system of posting crude oil prices that led to artificially high crude oil prices. Their crude oil processing agreements with independent refiners created barriers to the entry of new, independent firms in marketing. By keeping crude oil prices high and profits at the refining level relatively low, they were able to create barriers to entry into refining. They exploited their controlling position in the transportation of refined products. They had refused to sell gasoline and other refined products to independent marketers. They had made exchanges and sales among themselves of refined products to the exclusion of others. They were charged with pursuing a common course of action in avoiding price competition in the marketing stage of the industry.

The statement of contemplated relief of the FTC took the position that the only real solution to the problem was to create a structural change in the relevant markets. Structural surgery would alter the market behavior. Just as John D. Rockefeller had figured (successfully) in the nineteenth century that he could monopolize the petroleum industry by controlling the refining stage, the FTC would alter the concentration ratio at the refining stage. This would induce changes in certain practices of refiners and in so doing reduce barriers to entry into refining and promote open market transactions.

According to one plan, the FTC would divest the Big 8 companies of from 40 to 60 percent of their refining capacity and from these divested plants create 10 to 13 new companies. Petroleum companies are multiplant firms, and it is feasible to delineate the particular plants to be designated for divestment. Mergers of these new refinery companies would be banned. Also to be divested would be the crude and product pipelines that were connected to the refineries, and fractional ownership shares of connecting joint-venture pipelines would be eliminated. Limits would be put on any joint ventures, processing agreements, and crude oil and product exchanges.

A final feature of the FTC's contemplated relief would be to carve out the divested refinery assets in such a manner as to create eight major oil company refiners whose crude oil production would exceed their refinery capacity, and eight major oil company refiners that would have retail capacity exceeding their refinery capacity. The resulting vertical imbalances, combined with limits on crude oil and product exchanges, would theoretically create buyers and sellers of substantial proportions who would need to engage in open market transactions—thus contributing to the creation of an open market, the existence of which has been lacking to a substantial degree in the past in the domestic petroleum industry.

The danger inherent in attempting to spell out the details of a proposed divestiture plan too far in advance is well illustrated by this proposal to create imbalances in the vertical integration of major oil companies. Since 1973, when the complaint against the eight companies was filed, changes in the petroleum industry have come about rapidly and unexpectedly as political upheavals in some of the principal oil exporting nations have drastically altered the security and sources of crude oil supplies. Some major oil companies that in 1973 were rich in crude oil supplies (with quantities beyond their own needs) found themselves having to turn to world spot markets in 1980 to meet their own needs.[97]

American Telephone and Telegraph Company   In 1974 the Department of Justice filed a Section 2 Sherman Act suit against the American Telephone and Telegraph Company (AT&T) charging it with monopolizing the telecommunications business.[98] AT&T is essentially a holding company that owns or controls 23 domestic telephone operating companies (the Bell System), Western Electric Company (equipment manufacturing), and the Bell Telephone Laboratories (research and development). AT&T as a telephone company has been treated as a public utility and has, accordingly, not been included in the usual listings of the top 500 industrial firms. But it is the largest corporation in the world. At the time of the filing of the suit, AT&T assets totaled $67 billion, and at the end of 1980 they were valued at more than $125 billion.[99] Its public utility status, being subject to direct regulations by the Federal Communications Commission and various state regulatory bodies, did not, however, immunize it from Sherman Act liability.[100]

The suit charged that AT&T had used illegal methods to prevent other companies in the telecommunications business from interconnecting with its so-called Bell System. It alleged that it had excluded competitors mainly in the area of services provided to businesses. For example, attempts to restrict or eliminate the competition coming from private communications systems, primarily microwave systems, were cited in the complaint. But the number of specific issues was so large that one of the

---

[97]See Bro Uttal, "Life Is Getting Scary in the Oil Markets," *Fortune,* January 28, 1980.
[98]*U.S.* v. *American Telephone and Telegraph Co., et al.,* Civil Action No. 74-1698.
[99]*New York Times,* November 21, 1974, p. 1; *Fortune,* July 13, 1981, p. 126.
[100]*U.S.* v. *American Telephone and Telegraph Co.,* 427 F. Supp. 57 (1976).

problems that had to be resolved as the case proceeded was to narrow the issues down. As the Justice Department's principal attorney in the suit in 1978 put it: "There are a lot of bad acts. We could spend all our lives describing things that are at issue. We have to cut things out—cut, and cut, and cut—but intelligently."[101]

A principal objective of the government was the divestiture of AT&T's manufacturing subsidiary, Western Electric Company—ranked twelfth in sales in the nation in 1973. The latter firm was, in effect, the captive supplier of telephonic equipment to AT&T, thus excluding other such equipment suppliers from that market. The market was a very substantial one, since 82 percent of the nation's telephone business and 90 percent of the long-distance business were done by the Bell System. An earlier attempt of the Department of Justice to force the divestiture of Western Electric had ended in a consent decree in 1956, under circumstances that appeared to have political overtones. Now, not only divestiture was being sought, but also the dissolution of Western Electric into two or more companies. Divestment of Bell Laboratories, the country's largest industrial laboratory, might also be sought, depending upon interfirm relationships to be brought out in the trial. The suit would also seek some kind of loosening of the controls of AT&T over some parts of the Bell telephone subsidiaries or of the long-distance business.

The Big Case Is a Lengthy Case   The big civil antitrust suit tends to be complex and of considerable duration. Such suits are lengthy partly because of their economic complexity; the substantive economic issues and the character of particular markets vary from industry to industry. Additional causative factors are the nature of legal procedures and the fact that the stakes can be high. The government may be seeking dissolution. A competitor may be seeking treble damages. The defendants will apply all possible legal efforts to defend against such results.

A principal time-consuming factor in the big antitrust case is pretrial discovery, in which the parties to the litigation seek information or documents from the adversary so that they may better pursue the case or defend themselves. The Antitrust Commission held that discovery "too often" was used purposely to drag out the proceedings.[102] Procedural maneuvers during the trial as well as during pretrial discovery can also contribute to the delay. And incentives to delay are clearly present: to be able to continue the challenged practice, to fend off dissolution or divestment, or to obtain a relatively advantageous out-of-court settlement without further costs of litigation.

[101]Kenneth C. Anderson, quoted in *Business Week*, September 11, 1978, p. 105.
[102] *Antitrust Commission Report*, I, 13.

Whatever the ultimate motives, the big case can involve much time, energy, and paperwork. Discovery in the 1969 IBM antitrust suit has been described as "mammoth."[103] Millions of pages of documents were produced. Hundreds of depositions (statement of a witness under oath and recorded in pretrial discovery) were taken. The actual trial began in 1975. In 1979 IBM formally accused the judge of being prejudiced and asked him to withdraw from the case.[104] An appeals court rejected the request to remove the judge in early 1980.[105] By that time the case had already covered 612 trial days, more than 90,000 transcript pages and had been recorded, 8,400 exhibits had been introduced, and testimony had been received from 71 witnesses and depositions from several hundred others.[106] In addition, 79 written motions had been filed and more than 7,000 objections to testimony and documents had been lodged.[107] Some persons on both sides of this case saw the possibility of the suit not being concluded until 1989.[108]

The Antitrust Procedural Improvements Act of 1980—an outgrowth of the 1979 Antitrust Commission Report—included several provisions to expedite any big antitrust case. The Department of Justice can require an analysis and an index of documents that it requests in its investigations. Attorneys who engage in dilatory litigation practices can be required by the judge to pay for some of the excess costs incurred as a result. The court may award interest on any single damages awarded if the progress of an antitrust suit experiences "undue delay" because of the action of parties to the litigation. It remains to be seen whether such procedural changes can actually speed up an antitrust suit.

Three forces can bring a "big" antitrust government case to its conclusion earlier than it would through completion of all the usual judicial processes (including the appeals procedures). One is the realization that the parties are becoming so bogged down in the litigation that some form of settlement may appear to be a more desirable path to follow than exhausting resources in the prolonged litigation. A second is changing market circumstances surrounding the defendants. Perhaps after 10 years of litigation, defendant firms may no longer appear to be as monopolistic as they did at the time of the initial investigation. A third is the ebb and flow of economic ideologies and related changes in government administrations and Congress, which can affect the decisions being made as to whether to

---

[103]Ibid., II, 22.

[104] *Wall Street Journal,* July 20, 1979, p. 6.

[105]*Wall Street Journal,* February 26, 1980, p. 5.

[106]Arnold H. Lubasch, "Judge Won't Step Down in I.B.M. Antitrust Case," *New York Times,* September 12, 1979, p. D6.

[107]David Bird, "I.B.M. Brief Disputed by U.S. as Distorted," *New York Times,* August 28, 1979, p. D4.

[108]Frank J. Prial, "Clark's I.B.M. Suit a Decade Old," *New York Times,* January 18, 1979, p. D2.

prosecute, continue to prosecute, or end a prosecution effort. If a big anti-trust case is settled out of court or dropped, we may not be able to deter-mine which of these forces played the most prominent part.

In the big cases we have briefly summarized, one or more of these forces have been at work. The judge in the IBM case, after six years of the trial, urged the litigants in 1981 to settle out of court; the government, in-stead, dismissed the suit in 1982, citing litigation costs, the unlikelihood of success, and questionable benefits.[109] Congress threatened to cut the FTC's 1982 budget to prohibit it from spending any monies to issue an initial decision in the ready-to-eat cereal case three months before the administra-tive law judge was to issue that decision in 1981. These threats turned out to be unnecessary, as the administrative law judge ultimately did rec-ommend dismissal of the charges as being groundless and the FTC decided to pursue the issue no further.[110] The staff of the FTC engaged in the eight-year-old Big 8 petroleum case withdrew its divestiture proposals in early 1981 and then shortly thereafter advised the FTC to drop the case, which it did, pointing to limited progress and a possible five to eight more years of litigation.[111] As for the AT&T case, the government and the corporation reached a proposed settlement in 1982 under which AT&T would divest itself only of its local Bell telephone operating companies.[112]

The fact that the big antitrust case can go on seemingly interminably or can be ended with a settlement that provides for only a partial remedy as originally viewed (or end with no settlement at all) raises some serious questions. Can it be that when the defendant is exceedingly large or is composed of several large oligopolists the antitrust suit is not the appro-priate vehicle to create changes in market behavior through changes in market structures? Is the antitrust suit too unwieldy a process? By the time anything is accomplished, if anything indeed is, are the original objectives still sound? These are some of the questions that have to be asked in considering the big antitrust case.

PROPOSALS TO RESTRUCTURE INDUSTRIES

Proposals to restructure concentrated industries come and go. The fact that they reappear evidences considerable concern over the impact of industrial concentration on the proper functioning of markets.

[109]*Wall Street Journal,* April 20, 1981, p. 12. U.S. Department of Justice release, January 8, 1982.
[110]*Wall Street Journal,* June 26, 1981, p. 7; September 11, 1981, p. 7. January 18, 1982, p. 6.
[111]Edward Cowan, "F.T.C. Staff Eases View in Oil Case," *New York Times,* February 3, 1981, p. D1; *Wall Street Journal,* June 24, 1981, p. 2; and Stan Crock, "FTC Ends Oil Trust Case Against 8 Firms in Another Move Away from Activist Era," *Wall Street Journal,* September 17, 1981, p. 2.
[112]U.S. Department of Justice release, January 8, 1982.

Recommendations to limit the size of business units have come from several quarters. In 1959 Professors Kaysen and Turner of Harvard presented a program aimed to eliminate the possession of "unreasonable market power."[113] The Sherman Act would be amended and an Industrial Reorganization Commission established to institute proceedings in equity where necessary. Market power would be represented by the persistent ability of a firm or group of firms to restrict output or set price without loss of a substantial share of the market or without suffering any substantial loss of profits due to the increased output or lower prices of competitors. Market power would be conclusively presumed where one company accounted for 50 percent of annual market sales or four or fewer companies accounted for 80 percent of market sales over a five-year period. Under such a plan, the structural reorganization of firms by creating new firms would be the expected and standard remedy for the problem of unreasonable market power. Market power, where it existed, would be considered unreasonable unless shown to be based upon economies, patents, or low prices or superior products due to innovations of products, processes, or marketing methods.[114]

In 1968 the White House Task Force on Antitrust Policy (Neal Report) recommended the passage by Congress of a Concentrated Industries Act that would reduce industrial concentration.[115] A "Concentrated Industries Act" based on the Neal Report was introduced as a bill in Congress in 1971. It would require the dissolution of oligopoly industries so that no one firm in an industry would have a market share exceeding 12 percent. It defined an oligopoly industry as a market in which four or fewer firms had an aggregate market share of 70 percent or more during at least seven of the ten and four of the most recent five base years and aggregate sales in the market exceeded $500 million during each of at least four out of the five most recent base years. The Department of Justice and the FTC would make the necessary investigations. The Department of Justice would have the enforcement authority. Proceedings would be conducted by a Special Antitrust Court. A restructuring decree would not be issued where the result would be a substantial loss of economies of scale, but the proof of such loss would rest with the firm.

In 1972 (and later years) Senator Philip Hart introduced in Congress a bill entitled the "Industrial Reorganization Act." Designed to eliminate the possession of monopoly power, it would have restructured an oligopolistic market where the four or fewer largest firms had 50 percent or more of sales. Such legislation would have created an Industrial Reorganization Commission. It would have had a life span of 15 years, at the end of which

---

[113]Carl Kaysen and Donald F. Turner, *Antitrust Policy: An Economic and Legal Analysis* (Cambridge, Mass.: Harvard University Press, 1959).

[114]Ibid. See pp. 266–72 for the proposed statute.

[115]Submitted to the president, July 5, 1968. Reproduced in *The Journal of Reprints for Antitrust Law and Economics*, 1, part I (Winter 1969).

period its powers and duties would be transferred to the FTC. The Reorganization Commission would be required specifically to study the structure, conduct, and performance of each of the following seven industries: chemicals and drugs; electrical machinery and equipment; electronic computing and communication equipment; energy; iron and steel; motor vehicles; and nonferrous metals. These industries were held to account for 40 percent of total U.S. manufacturing.[116] Divestment would not be required if the monopoly power were due to the rightful ownership of valid patents or if the result would be a loss of substantial economies. The Industrial Reorganization Commission would develop a plan for each relevant industry that would indicate the maximum feasible number of competitors and the minimum feasible degree of vertical integration possible without loss of substantial economies. The maximum feasible degree of ease of entry would also be determined.

All three proposals involving the possible dissolution of large firms provide for one escape hatch: the loss of economies. This would require elaborate studies. The firm to suffer structural reorganization would have to demonstrate that unit costs of production and distribution would rise if the firm were to lose its existing identity. It would have to be demonstrated that the firm targeted for restructuring would produce and distribute more output with a given amount of resources than the proposed alternative new firms. Obviously there are some indivisibilities of resource units which affect the concatenation of process, and there are economies in the specialization of labor and machinery.[117] Exactly what these economies are will vary from one industry to another. Economies of scale for a given plant should also be distinguished from those of the firm. It is the firm that would be broken up, not the plant. Where a large firm is producing out of one plant, restructuring into several separate firms is not possible. By the same token, a firm operating as a holding company would be the easiest to dissolve.

A serious question raised by any restructuring proposal that cuts across all industry lines is the possible effect upon the entrepreneurial spirit or the nature of competition itself. Why would managers or investors seek growth or an increase in sales against competitors if it would take the firm beyond the forbidden market percentages? Would the larger firms encourage smaller (and perhaps weaker) firms to increase the latter's share of the market by easing up on the intensity of their competitive efforts?[118]

---

[116]Philip A. Hart, "Restructuring the Oligopoly Sector: The Case for a New 'Industrial Reorganization Act,'" *Antitrust Law & Economics Review*, 5, no. 4 (Summer 1972), 40. S. 3832, Industrial Reorganization Act, is presented as an appendix to this article.

[117]For a concise statement on the issue of economies of scale, see Douglas F. Greer, *Industrial Organization and Public Policy* (New York: Macmillan, 1980), pp. 178–87.

[118]See Simon N. Whitney, "The Economic Impact of Antitrust: An Overview," *Antitrust Bulletin*, 9, no. 4 (July–August 1964), 510–43.

Perhaps, however, these are only short-run worries, since the increased number of competitors may initiate a new kind of competition in some industries in which the firms previously had experienced only oligopolistic relationships.

Proposals to restructure an industry by means other than an antitrust decree carry with them special problems of their own related to the private property nature of the free enterprise system. Equity must be an inherent part of any industry restructuring. All vested rights must be fully taken into consideration. Thus, these proposals would permit subject corporations to file appeals or be given the opportunity to file an alternative plan of reorganization.

What is involved in a dissolution under an antitrust decree and some of the particular problems inherent in dissolution by legislation can be seen by examining, respectively, the dissolution of the Standard Oil Company of New Jersey in 1911 and the dissolution of the holding company structures in the electric power industry as per the legislative mandate of the Public Utility Holding Company Act of 1935. It should be emphasized that restructuring or reorganization is, first of all, a matter of redistributing contractual rights in order to alter the locus of decision-making. The plants and equipment themselves would have to be assigned to those holding these new rights.

STANDARD OIL: DISSOLUTION BY ANTITRUST DECREE—*A CASE STUDY*

The first major antitrust decree under the Sherman Act ordering dissolution of a large industrial corporation was that against Standard Oil Company of New Jersey in 1911.[119] In the 10 years prior to the filing of the complaint in the suit in 1906, Standard accounted for more than 80 percent of the crude transportation, refining, and marketing of refined oil products in the nation. Dominant in these phases of the industry, it was thus able to exert influence over its crude oil supplies. This dominance of Standard within the industry plus public criticism of it had given the company an unfavorable public image. As put by Hidy and Hidy: "Public policy toward Big Business was crystallizing, and the Standard Oil dissolution suit was a part of that process."[120]

---

[119]*Standard Oil Co. of New Jersey* v. *U.S.*, 221 U.S. 1. A companion case against the American Tobacco Company also ended in a dissolution order. *U.S.* v. *American Tobacco Co.*, 221 U.S. 106 (1911). An earlier court decree had mandated the dissolution of the holding company that controlled the Great Northern and Northern Pacific railroads. *Northern Securities Co.* v. *U.S.*, 193 U.S. 197 (1904).

[120]Ralph W. and Muriel E. Hidy, *Pioneering in Big Business, 1882–1911: History of Standard Oil Company (New Jersey)* (New York: Harper, 1955), p. 714.

The Court Decisions   Standard had achieved dominance in these stages of the petroleum industry through mergers, some of which were held to have been coerced, and through what were observed to be oppressive market tactics. The principal practices of which Standard was accused were engaging in local price-cutting to eliminate competitors, the use of bogus independent companies through which to compete, obtaining information on sales of competitors through competitors' employees, the granting of secret rebates to favored customers, and the receipt of preferential rates from railroads. The district court found in 1909 that Standard, 7 individuals, and 37 subsidiary corporations had engaged in an illegal conspiracy in restraint of trade and had achieved an illegal monopoly of a substantial portion of interstate and international commerce in petroleum.[121] The Supreme Court upheld the lower court decision in 1911 and, in introducing the rule of reason, held that Standard had intended to and had achieved a monopoly position in the industry; its purpose had clearly been to drive out and exclude others.[122]

The dissolution order of the lower court was based on the idea that the cause of the problem lay in the control Standard held over its various subsidiary corporations through the holding of their stock. It was a holding company as well as an operating company. Standard Oil represented the Standard "group" of companies. Indeed, some of Standard's subsidiaries had some of their own subsidiaries; in total, Standard controlled some 114 companies.[123] It was the centralized control over its subsidiaries that gave Standard control over such a large segment of petroleum markets throughout the country. The stocks of some 33 subsidiaries were therefore ordered to be removed from the asset portfolio of Standard.

The Redistribution   Who was to get these stocks? The easy way and, as the court saw it, the rightful way, to redistribute the ownership shares in these subsidiary petroleum corporations was to distribute them to their ultimate owners, the owners of the Standard Oil Company of New Jersey. The shares of these subsidiary corporations were assets of Standard, and if Standard was to be forced to remove those assets from its holdings, who was more legally rightful of receiving them than the owners of the Standard Oil Company itself? Thus, the stocks of these subsidiaries were distributed on a pro rata basis to the holders of the stock of Standard.

Certain advantages pertain to this kind of dissolution. There is full knowledge of just who the owners of Standard Oil are. To determine their share of these assets is easy. There is little likelihood of legal challenge as to

---

[121]173 Fed 177.
[122]221 U.S. 1, 75–77.
[123]George W. Stocking, *The Oil Industry and the Competitive System* (Boston: Houghton Mifflin, 1925), p. 52.

the rightful ownership of these shares. Knowing clearly who those rightful corporate stockowners are permits rapid completion of the dissolution process. In the Standard Oil case, Standard was given six months to complete the redistribution.[124]

The previously existing centralized control of the Standard Oil "group" was now eliminated in theory as the shareholders in Standard now became shareholders in the subsidiary corporations. They now owned directly what they had previously owned indirectly. Standard as an intermediary stockholder had been removed from the corporate structure. If the stock ownership of Standard had been widely diffused with no dominant groups of shareowners, the centralization of control would have been effectively eliminated. But Rockefeller family interests held sizable percentages of Standard stock. As late as 1922, Rockefeller interests were the largest group of stockholders in 28 of the Standard group of companies.[125] John D. Rockefeller, Jr., was the largest single stockholder in nine of the companies, with holdings varying from 11 to 24.9 percent. The Rockefeller Foundation was the largest single stockholder in 17 of the companies, with holdings of more than 20 percent of the stock in 14 of the companies. These holdings, combined with holdings of more than 1 percent of the stock of several companies by several other individuals or trust funds, gave this "more or less common group of stockholders" a range from 25 to 45 percent ownership in each of 28 of the companies.[126] A community of interests could thus well persist. On the other hand, the dissolution decree enjoined the new owners of the stock of what had been the subsidiary corporations from in any way conspiring or combining in violation of the Sherman Act.

The Aftermath   Differences in the functions of the subsidiary corporations served to delay somewhat the transformation of a monopolistic group into a group of intensely competing companies through this particular dissolution process. In the first place, only one of the subsidiary corporations, Standard of California, was integrated throughout all stages of crude production, crude transportation, refining, and marketing. Only six of the companies engaged in the production of crude. Only nine engaged in refining. Only twelve engaged in domestic marketing. Ten were purely crude oil pipeline companies.[127] For one of the same principal reasons that

---

[124]The lower court's decree at first would have provided that the stock redistribution take place in 30 days, but the Supreme Court raised this period to six months.

[125]See Stocking, *The Oil Industry*, pp. 57-58, for a summary of some of the principal Standard Oil group stockholders as drawn from hearings of the Senate Committee on Manufacturers.

[126]Ibid., p. 58.

[127]For a table of functional organization of the Standard Oil Company (New Jersey) and its previously affiliated companies immediately after dissolution, see Harold F. Williamson and others, *The American Petroleum Industry: The Age of Energy, 1899-1959* (Evanston, Ill.: Northwestern University Press, 1963), p. 13.

the Standard group had been formed (to achieve some degree of vertical integration), the now-severed parts found it advantageous to stick together and do business with one another.

Second, the subsidiary corporations and their operations were scattered throughout the nation geographically, and many of them were thus in no position to compete among themselves directly in a given local or regional geographic market.[128] With much of the transportation of the product being by rail, transport costs were too high relative to the cost of the product to make it commercially feasible to distribute the product physically over long inland distances. For example, Standard itself operated refineries in New Jersey, West Virginia, Maryland, and Ontario, Canada. The Atlantic Refining Company had refineries in Pennsylvania. The Solar Refining Company had one refinery in Lima, Ohio. Standard Oil Company (California) had three refineries in California. Standard Oil Company (Indiana) operated refineries in Indiana, Illinois, Missouri, and Wyoming. Standard Oil Company (Kansas) owned one small refinery in Kansas. Standard Oil Company of New York operated four refineries in New York State. Standard Oil Company of Ohio had two refineries in Cleveland. The Vacuum Oil Company operated a refinery in Olean, New York. Finally, the Waters-Pierce Company refined and sold products in Mexico. Being cut loose from the control of Standard Oil Company of New Jersey left most of them more or less to operate as regional monopolies. It is true that in 1904 the Standard group was competing with 75 independent refineries, but its refineries were processing more than 84 percent of the total crude oil being refined in the country.[129]

In spite of the weaknesses in the dissolution of the Standard Oil group, it undoubtedly accelerated the economic market forces already at work to create more competition in the expanding American petroleum industry. Williamson, Andreano, Daum, and Klose provide data which show that Standard's percentage control over refining and the share of major products sold, such as kerosene, fuel oil, and gasoline, had been declining from the turn of the century to 1911.[130] New competitors were entering the industry, some of considerable size and strength, such as Gulf, the Texas Company, Union Oil of California, and the Sun Oil Company.

The expanding and dynamic nature of the petroleum industry continued after the dissolution. Great new demands, especially for gasoline for the rapidly growing automobile industry, induced new entry. New sources of crude created demand for new pipelines and new refineries at

---

[128]Raymond F. Bacon and William A. Hamor, *The American Petroleum Industry* (New York: McGraw-Hill, 1916), present a table of the operating functions and geographic locations of the corporations of the Standard Oil Group at I, 262–65.

[129]Stocking, *The Oil Industry*, p. 51, drawn from Bureau of Corporations, *Report of the Commissioner of Corporations on the Petroleum Industry*, part I, pp. 14–16.

[130]Williamson, *The American Petroleum Industry*, p. 7.

new locations. The previous Standard subsidiaries engaged in their own expansion and did not rely entirely on their previously affiliated companies. As for the stockholdings in the Standard subsidiaries, time brought change in these holdings. Holders of stock died and the stock was sold or passed on to children. The stock was bought and sold on the stock exchanges and distributed through employee stock-ownership plans. In short, over time the stock ownership became more diffused.[131]

Dissolution Recommendations of the 1970s Sixty and 70 years after the dissolution of the Standard group, proponents of further dissolutions in the American petroleum industry have surfaced. They have been unhappy with the large, oligopolistic, and vertically integrated structure of the some 20 major petroleum firms in the country. These major firms are basically groups of firms interrelated by stockholdings, just like the Standard Oil Company of New Jersey group at the turn of the century. But recommended dissolutions have taken different forms from that of the 1911 dissolution of Standard Oil.

As we saw in the previous section, the FTC at one time wanted to create more firms out of the largest firms. As the Commission saw it, there were just not enough of these refining firms. Bills in Congress in the 1970s and into the 1980s sought to break up the vertical structure of the petroleum industry by permitting one firm to operate at only one level, or stage, of the industry—in crude production, transportation, or refining and marketing. The underlying fear of the proponents of such legislation has been the bigness and vertical character of these petroleum firms and the power and vested interests seen to reside in this bigness and firm structure. Proponents of yet another method have been represented by bills in Congress calling for horizontal divestiture, whereby petroleum firms would be forced to limit their efforts in the energy field to that of petroleum. Participation in the coal and uranium industries, for example, would not be allowed. Here the fear has been that the concentration in the petroleum industry represented by the Big 8 or the 20 major oil companies would be duplicated in the field of energy as a whole.

THE ELECTRIC POWER INDUSTRY: DISSOLUTION BY LEGISLATION—*A CASE STUDY*

The electric power industry had become heavily concentrated during the 1920s. Electric power companies at the operating company level were generally regulated as public utility companies by state public utility regulatory

---

[131]For a detailed discussion of these changes, see Stocking, *The Oil Industry*, pp. 49–114; and Henry R. Seager and Charles A. Gulick, Jr., *Trust and Corporation Problems* (New York: Harper, 1929), pp. 125–36.

commissions. The ownership of these operating companies, however, had become the object of competition by systems of holding companies, as the latter vied for control over these assets.

The financial incentives underlying this competition contributed heavily to this concentration. Ownership of operating companies by holding companies provided captive customers for equipment, construction, service, and engineering and managerial consulting firms affiliated with the holding companies. The pyramiding of holding companies built upon other holding companies (in some major systems as many as six tiers) enabled the holders of the voting stock of the super holding company not only to control a system in which their own holdings represented a very small percentage of the total investment of the entire system, but also to reap very great profits.[132] As a result, some firms became overcapitalized through promotion deals, write-ups accompanying consolidations of controlled properties, and failure to write off obsolete units.

The financial advantages to the incorporators and owners of such holding company systems were of such dimensions that by 1935 fifty-seven principal systems controlled the operations of 90 percent of the industry. Four electric utility systems (Electric Bond and Share Company, Consolidated Gas Company of New York, The Commonwealth and Southern Corporation, and The North American Company) controlled almost one-third of the industry.[133] The operating companies controlled by any one system were often scattered all over the nation, and in many cases nonaffiliated holding companies controlled adjoining properties in crazy-quilt fashion.

The resulting concentration of control and financial abuses related to that concentration ultimately led to the passage of the Public Utility Holding Company Act of 1935. Unfortunately, although these corporate financial structures thrived in good times, they could not withstand the adverse conditions of depression. In the 1930s many of the securities of the holding companies became almost worthless when operating companies could not pump any income upward through the holding companies above them. Pursuant to a Senate Resolution, the Federal Trade Commission undertook an in-depth investigation lasting from 1928 through 1934. This study resulted in 101 volumes of reports.[134]

---

[132]If the capital structure of an operating company were to consist of one-half 4 percent bonds, one-quarter 5 percent preferred stock, and one-quarter common stock, and if the overall fair return permitted by the state regulatory commission were, say 6 percent, then the common stock might well yield more than 6 percent. This return, distributed in turn among the bonds and preferred stock and common stock of a holding company of similar capital structure immediately above this operating company, would yield a still higher percentage return to the common stock of the holding company. Magnify this "leverage" through several tiers of holding companies and the common stock of a super holding company could be made to yield well over 100 percent per annum return.

[133] Federal Power Commission, *Principal Electric Utility Systems in the United States, 1935,* Power Series No. 2, 1936, pp. 9–10.

[134]Federal Trade Commission, *Utility Corporations,* Senate Document No. 92, 70th Cong., 1st Sess., 1935.

The Public Utility Holding Company Act of 1935 contained the famous Section 11(b)(1), known as the "death sentence" clause. It called for the elimination of the top-heavy corporate system of holding companies in the industry in order to create a more rational industry structure. The dissolutions that were mandated were not designed to create a competitive structure. Rather, they were designed to create single-integrated, electric power public utility systems wherever these would be economically advantageous. As public utilities, they would be rationally ordered and structured to provide a given electric power service with a minimum of plant capacity at the lowest possible average cost of production and distribution. The legislative plan was to achieve, where it would be economical, integrated systems that would not be so small as to prevent realization of engineering progress and not so large as to lose their local character.[135] Although a "father" holding company could be utilized as a coordinating device for several operating companies, the multitier systems of holding companies were to be dismantled.

The corporate reorganizations required by the act of 1935 are illustrative of two basic problems to be resolved in any industry restructuring. First, decisions have to be made as to which assets will be allocated to each new separate corporate entity. In the case of the Public Utility Holding Company Act of 1935, this meant identifying the operating companies that could stand alone or best serve under the controlling ownership guidance of one particular holding company. Second, new securities would have to be issued to replace those being eliminated. Under the act of 1935 this meant providing the holders of the securities of the holding companies that were to be eliminated with new securities of the new single holding company or an independent operating company.

Because of the necessary recapitalizations, the reorganization of the electric power industry was turned over to the Securities and Exchange Commission (SEC). The existing holding companies were given until January 1, 1938, to register with the SEC and to take voluntary steps to comply with the integration and simplification requirements. Rather than come forth with reorganization proposals, some 58 legal actions had been brought by holding company interests by the end of 1935 to enjoin enforcement of the act and for declaratory judgments holding all its provisions unconstitutional.[136] In a test case the Supreme Court ruled in early 1938 that the registration provisions of the act were constitutional.[137]

---

[135]Section 2(a)(29) defines an integrated public utility system as "a system . . . whose utility assets . . . are physically interconnected or capable of physical interconnection and which under normal conditions may be economically operated as a single interconnected and coordinated system confined in its operation to a single area or region, in one or more states, not so large as to impair (considering the state of the art and the area or region affected) the advantages of localized management, efficient operation, and the effectiveness of regulation."

[136]Securities and Exchange Commission, *10th Annual Report*, p. 114.

[137]*Electric Bond & Share Co.* v. *S.E.C.*, 303 U.S. 419 (1938).

The plans for reorganization then presented to the SEC by the holding companies were not generally satisfactory in meeting the integration requirements of the act.[138] Finally, in 1940 the SEC instituted integration proceedings against nine major holding company systems, of which The Commonwealth and Southern Corporation was one. Ordered, as a first step, to reduce its outstanding preferred and common stock to a single class of common stock, it appealed. Losing the appeal, it then filed its own plan. A year later it amended its plan. It was not until 1946 that the final plan was completed. For the electric power industry as a whole, the required reorganizations were not completed until 1952. Although the process took a considerable amount of time, the reorganization of this industry removed the potential for financial abuses and provided solvency and more stable values for an industry that had been the victim of competitive chaos.

SUMMARY

The large corporation has drawn particular attention to itself just because it is big. It is important to differentiate between the absolute size of a firm and its size relative to its competitors. In terms of measuring the impact of a firm's size on competition, it is more important to consider relative size and factors contributing to the concentration of sellers in a market.

A firm can grow larger through spending on new capital or through purchasing existing capital through merger. Growth of a firm through merger does not represent economic growth. Mergers can take three forms: horizontal, vertical, and conglomerate. Antitrust policy must necessarily vary as to these three types of merger. A horizontal merger eliminates that part of the market competition which had existed between the two merging firms. A vertical merger may lead to market forclosure for competitors or cause any market power that might exist at one stage of an industry to be transferred to and used at another stage of that industry. Conglomerate merger policy can revolve around issues of potential competition, entrenchment, business reciprocity, and oligopolistic competitive forebearance.

The Sherman Act condemns monopolizing and attempts to monopolize. Antitrust policy with respect to each of these concepts has been established through court precedent. Monopolizing requires proof of monopoly power plus deliberate conduct to achieve or maintain that power. An attempt to monopolize is conduct deliberately undertaken to

[138]See comments of William O. Douglas, then Chairman of the SEC, "Scatteration v. Integrations of Public Utility Systems," *American Bar Association Journal*, 24, no. 10 (October 1938), 800.

obtain monopoly power. Opposing opinion exists as to possible changes in these standards.

The large firm with a substantial share of its market and the "shared monopoly" of a highly concentrated oligopoly have been the targets of antimonopoly action in the 1970s. Their market behavior, even more than their market shares, have been the object of antitrust attack. The antitrust cases against IBM, the three large ready-to-eat cereal manufacturers, the Big 8 of the petroleum industry, and AT&T are illustrative of the long-drawn-out "big" case of the 1970s.

Concern with firm size and market concentration has led from time to time to proposals to restructure highly concentrated industries. Such proposals would achieve by legislation what antitrust enforcement has not generally been able to achieve in attempting to solve the problem of monopoly or quasi-monopolistic oligopolies. Two case studies illustrate the different ways in which two different industries have been subjected to reorganization and restructuring. The antitrust decree against Standard Oil Company of New Jersey illustrates the importance of proper fashioning of an antitrust dissolution decree. The reorganization of the electric power industry under the Public Utility Holding Company Act of 1935 illustrates how one industry can be restructured according to legislative mandate.

Selected Readings

BAUER, JOSEPH P., "Challenging Conglomerate Mergers under Section 7 of the Clayton Act: Today's Law and Tomorrow's Legislation." *Boston University Law Review,* 58, no. 2 (March 1978), 199–245.

DE CHAZEAU, M. G., AND A. E. KAHN, *Integration and Competition in the Petroleum Industry.* New Haven, Conn.: Yale University Press, 1959.

GOLDSCHMID, HARVEY J., H. MICHAEL MANN, AND J. FRED WESTON, eds., *Industrial Concentration: The New Learning.* Boston: Little, Brown, 1974.

GOULDEN, JOSEPH C., *Monopoly* [American Telephone and Telegraph Company], rev. ed. New York: Pocket Books, 1970.

MEEHAN, JAMES W., JR., "Rules vs. Discretion: A Reevaluation of the Merger Guidelines for Horizontal Mergers," *Antitrust Bulletin,* 23, no. 4 (Winter 1978), 769–95.

STEINER, PETER O., *Mergers: Motives, Effects, Policies.* Ann Arbor: University of Michigan Press, 1975.

6 — Vertical Interfirm Relations

In many industries production and distribution are carried out by an assortment of firms representing varying degrees of vertical integration. A firm is said to be vertically integrated when it operates at more than one stage of production or distribution within a given industry. In the petroleum industry, for example, a major oil company refiner is fully vertically integrated if it performs all the functions of crude oil production, transportation of crude, refining, wholesaling, and retailing. Looking forward toward the consumer, some refiners may be partially integrated, performing the refining and wholesaling functions, but not the retailing. Some retailers may be integrated backward into wholesaling (or, with the same result, some wholesalers may be integrated forward into retailing). Some refiners may engage in dual distribution, competing with independent distributors for whom they are the source of refined products. In this chapter we will concern ourselves with the problems that arise from the varying degrees of vertical integration which exist forward from manufacturing toward the consumer.

There are advantages to a manufacturer being vertically integrated all the way forward to the consumer. Such a firm will have full control of its product from factory to retail outlet and can set the price on the final product it thinks will maximize its profits, given the nature of the competition for its product. It can save the transactions costs of searching out and contracting with processors and distributors. It can bypass any monopoly elements that might be present in the path to the ultimate consumer. On the other hand, search and transactions costs are replaced by internal costs of resources and their coordination and movement. A manufacturer will have to balance these costs in making the decision to perform these functions for itself or to rely upon outside parties to perform them. It is the same question as that of deciding to "make or buy": Which is the least costly?

A limiting factor for a firm in the decision as to how far to carry vertical integration is the availability of funds. There are limits to the funds available for capital expenditures or working capital for any firm, even the largest, and a firm has to consider the relative profitability of different uses of those funds available to it. Vertical integration may not be one of the most profitable uses for the funds available. Relying upon independent firms to perform some of the functions of further processing of goods or distributing final products to the ultimate consumer may be the most economical solution.

If, for whatever reason, a manufacturing firm is not fully integrated through retailing, it will still desire to be able to control the resale market in such a way as to maximize its own overall profits. If it uses independent distributors, it will want to use the most efficient ones possible to give it the best possible representation, but will also want to keep their profits as low as possible, consistent with their continuing to perform their economic function—they should be earning a normal profit but no more.

A host of possible interfirm relationships is thus found to exist among manufacturers and the firms forward from manufacturing. Some of these firms are larger than others. Some are more vertically integrated than others. This mix of firms and their vertical relationships can create market structure relationships, particularly with respect to their impact upon small firms, which have led to both private and public antitrust suits. It is not always immediately clear whether any alleged restrictions on competition are reasonable or unreasonable, and if unreasonable, what the best cure is. In any case, there are differences of opinion not only between the antagonists attempting to protect their vested interests, but also between the antitrust enforcement agencies and the courts.

RESALE PRICE MAINTENANCE

Price is an important variable in the profit equation, and manufacturers who sell through independent distributors are anxious to control that price wherever possible, especially if the goods are branded or covered by trademarks. They may try to force prices down, as in the case of petroleum refiners who in periods of market glut may pester independent retail dealers to lower price and sell a larger volume of product in order to relieve the pressure on inventory storage. Or they may try to keep prices up, for a variety of reasons.

Too much price competition in the sale of branded products could be injurious to a manufacturer's interest because it may be reflected back to an oligopolistic market structure at the producer level. This may create pressures on the oligopolists' prices and cause a break in their otherwise sticky character. Manufacturers may try to prevent price competition at retail to preserve the product image of large-ticket quality items. Manufacturers may want to prevent too much price competition at the retail level in order to assure the retailers a margin of profit high enough so that the retailers will stay loyal to the manufacturer and continue to carry its products. Or the manufacturer may want to provide a high enough markup for the retailer so that the latter can provide special services in conjunction with the sale of the product in order to increase sales.[1] Another argument has been to keep in business a large enough number of retail outlets to keep up the volume of sales, even though this means keeping margins high enough to support some inefficient outlets. High enough margins for retailers can also provide them with enough funds to engage in forms of nonprice competition.

Independent retailers have favored manufacturers' programs of resale price maintenance because it provides a shield against price-cutting competition. Small retailers have favored control of resale prices in order to prevent loss-leader selling by the larger retailers, who may heavily discount the price of a well-known brand item in order to attract customers into the store, where the losses can be made up through the sale of other products with high markups. This policy may succeed for the large store with many items to sell but can be hard on the smaller store. A basic problem here, of course, is distinguishing between "unfair" loss-leader selling and the garden variety of price-cutting competition.

Fair Trade   The interest of the retailer in having manufacturers conduct resale price maintenance programs is well illustrated in the successful efforts of retailers in the 1930s, through the boycotting of manufacturers if necessary, to force the latter to use fair trade programs. These were made legal in the states under state fair trade statutes. The statutes simply legalized resale price maintenance of branded goods within a state. The Supreme Court approved of the principle of state fair trade in a 1936 decision, including the nonsigner clause under which all resellers were bound to the stipulated minimum resale price when even just one reseller signed such an agreement.[2] The justification was that the goodwill residing in a branded good was an intangible asset still belonging to the producer, and thus the producer had the right to control the resale price of the product. By 1941, 45 of the 48 states had passed fair trade laws. Federal statutes in 1937 and 1951 exempted fair trade resale price maintenance from the Sherman and Federal Trade Commission acts.

[1]See Lester G. Telser, "Why Should Manufacturers Want Fair Trade?" *Journal of Law and Economics,* 3 (October 1960), 86–105.
[2]*Old Dearborn Distributing Co.* v. *Seagram Distillers Corp.,* 299 U.S. 183.

The forces of competition turned out to be so strong that they overcame some of the best of manufacturers' fair trade programs. Manufacturers could not ignore the growing use of the discount house as a method of merchandising. Discontented resellers found ways to evade the fair trade requirements foisted upon them by manufacturers. The giving of indirect rebates, the use of overvalued trade-ins, the giving of trading stamps in excessivly large ratios to the value of the goods—all these devices were utilized to evade fair trade. The necessity of private enforcement of fair trade programs could be costly and burdensome, because manufacturers had to sue the reseller who failed to confirm to fair trade contracts. The manufacturer had, in fact, to sue all nonconforming resellers; otherwise, it could be charged with discrimination.

Beginning in the 1950s, one by one the courts of particular states were finding the fair trade laws of those states unconstitutional—or if not the whole law, then the heart of that law, the nonsigner provision. Some state legislatures repealed their fair trade laws. The economic rationale for such repeals was that, in general, they were discouraging to price competition. These laws may have seemed appropriate for the years of the Great Depression of the 1930s, but they were not appropriate for the inflationary years of the post-World War II period. The fading away of fair trade finally culminated in its death when the Consumer Goods Pricing Act of 1975 removed the federal exemptions of fair trade from the antitrust laws. That was the coup de grâce for fair trade.

Suggested Retail Prices   Whereas whatever remnants of fair trade laws remaining on the books are, in effect, dead, attempted resale price maintenance by some manufacturers is not. Suggested retail prices are still utilized by many manufacturers. A retailer need not abide by the suggested prices, but in some cases the manufacturer may then refuse to sell that retailer its products. The manufacturer can still refuse to deal with such a reseller, provided that the decision is made strictly on a unilateral basis.

The legal ability of a manufacturer to maintain control over the price of its products after they have left its hands was initially delivered a blow by a 1911 decision of the Supreme Court.[3] The reasoning of the court was simple: Resale price maintenance agreements between manufacturers and distributors prevented price competition among the distributors. The result was the same as if the distributors had combined together in a price-fixing conspiracy.

That legal blow was eased, however, in 1919 in the Supreme Court's *Colgate* decision.[4] To refuse to sell to any distributor who would not maintain resale prices at the level desired by the producer was found to be legal.

---

[3]*Dr. Miles Medical Co.* v. *John D. Park & Sons Co.*, 220 U.S. 373.
[4]*U.S.* v. *Colgate & Co.*, 250 U.S. 300.

On the other hand, no agreement between the producer and the distributor, either express or implied, was to be allowed. Furthermore, discussion between the producer and competing retailers or attempts to induce wholesalers not to do business with retailers who would not abide by stipulated prices could be found to be a combination in restraint of trade violating the Sherman Act.[5]

The risks in attempting resale price maintenance are great. To follow a strictly unilateral policy of price maintenance can be well nigh impossible. How can a manufacturer refuse to deal with a distributor who refuses to abide by suggested resale prices without that refusal to sell being taken as a threat? Or where the distributor does adopt such a policy, how can that not be taken as an agreement, either express or implied? To cap this off, a Supreme Court decision in 1980 emphasized the illegality of vertical price-fixing: "This Court has ruled consistently that resale price maintenance illegally restrains trade."[6]

In 1980 the Department of Justice viewed resale price maintenance not only as a violation of the antitrust laws, but also as a criminal violation of those laws. In that year it obtained a grand jury indictment against vertical price-fixing, and the case was settled by a consent order, with a fine of $250,000 being assessed.[7] Among the charges were that the seller was not only establishing suggested retail prices, but also monitoring and investigating instances of price-cutting of its product; obtaining resale price maintenance agreements from retailers; and threatening to reduce, suspend, or terminate shipments to retail stores that did not maintain the suggested retail prices.

Resale price maintenance may be achieved by means other than threats and refusals to deal. A consumer paint manufacturer, for example, was alleged to have conditioned cooperative advertising payments on the promise that suggested retail prices be followed.[8] It would seem that, in fact, by 1980 vertical price-fixing was truly a *per se* violation of the antitrust laws. Between 1970 and 1979, the number of resale price maintenance suits filed by the Department of Justice was 11 and by the Federal Trade Commission, 38.[9] One might be tempted to conclude, since it had become clearly found to be a *per se* violation of the antitrust laws, that future cases would be more numerous. A new administration in Washington in 1981 altered some such expectations as the new assistant attorney general in charge of the Antitrust Division of the Department of Justice, testifying before a congressional committee, stated: "In my view, there is no such

[5]See *U.S.* v. *Parke, Davis & Co.*, 362 U.S. 29 (1960).
[6]*California Retail Liquor Dealers* v. *Midcal Aluminum*, 445 U.S. 97, 102.
[7]*U.S.* v. *Cuisinarts, Inc.*, Criminal No. H-80-49 (1980). Civil Action No. H80-559 (1981).
[8]*U.S.* v. *E. I. du Pont de Nemours*, Civil No. C-76-566, Consent Order (1980).
[9]Don E. Waldman, "Economic Benefits in the *IBM*, *AT&T*, and *Xerox* Cases: Government Antitrust Policy in the 1970s," *Antitrust Law & Economics Review*, 12, no. 2 (1980), 87.

thing as a vertical 'problem.' . . . The only possible adverse competitive consequences of vertical arrangements inhere in their horizontal effects. Only where vertical arrangements facilitate restricted output and raised prices—horizontal impacts—should they be inhibited."[10] It has been the FTC, however, which has been the most active in opposing resale price maintenance efforts by suppliers.

THE VERTICAL PRICE SQUEEZE

A vertical price squeeze occurs when a vertically integrated monopolist which is competing with its own customers controls the profit margin of those customers through the price it sets to customers and the price it sets in the next stage of the industry. A manufacturer, for example, may be the source of supply to fabricators who compete with it in the fabricated goods market. The manufacturer, by setting the price of its product to the fabricators and the price of the fabricated good, can control the margin of profit of the fabricators. If the profit margin of the fabricators is reduced through such price action, the fabricators will accuse their monopolistic supplier of applying a vertical price squeeze. If the profit margin that results represents a normal level of profit, they do not have much of a case against the monopolist except that the monopolist has the power to control their profit level. If the level of profit resulting from the price squeeze is below normal, they can accuse the monopolistic supplier of attempting to drive them out of business.

For this phenomenon to occur, it is obvious that an imperfect market structure must exist. The basic supplier must have a significant enough market share at both levels, or stages, of the industry to control prices at both levels. If it does not, it cannot maintain the margin spread of the resellers at the level it desires. If it does not have large enough market shares to control prices, competition will dictate one or both of two possible courses of action. The resellers being threatened by a squeeze will seek new and lower-priced sources of supply. Or the vertically integrated firm will have to raise its own resale price to make at least a normal profit for itself. Where squeeze conditions do exist, the large integrated firm as a whole can still be making a normal profit; what it is losing at the second stage of the industry it is making up at the first stage.

Antitrust Litigation   Allegations of vertical price squeezes have been made with respect to several industries. The 1973 complaint of the FTC

[10]William F. Baxter, Statement before the House Subcommittee on Monopolies and Commercial Law of the Committee on the Judiciary, "Concerning Department of Justice Authorization Fiscal Year 1982," April 29, 1981, mimeo, p. 4.

against the eight largest oil companies in the nation charged that they pursued a common course of action in using their vertical integration to keep profits artificially high at the crude oil level of the industry and artificially low at the refinery level to raise entry barriers into refining.[11] Walter Adams has pointed to vertical price squeezes on nonintegrated steel fabricators by the large integrated steel companies.[12] A case alleging that a private electric power company had applied a price squeeze to municipal power systems has been before the Federal Energy Regulatory Commission.[13] The private company was charging such a high price to the municipal systems that it was cheaper for the customers of the municipal systems to purchase directly from the private company.

A similar situation is represented by a suit by municipalities.[14] Several cities in Indiana and Michigan sued a private electric utility that served several municipal electric power distribution companies. The latter were paying a higher wholesale price than consumers were paying at retail. The court said that intent had to be shown, but intent was inferred from the disparity between the wholesale and retail rates. The court also relied on threats made to the municipal distribution companies' supplies, the private utility's policy of acquisition of municipal systems, and the desire of the private utility to preserve and expand its existing monopoly.

Alcoa, in the famous monopoly court decision of 1945, was found to have abused its monopoly power in practicing the vertical price squeeze against independent aluminum sheet producers.[15] It had set the price of aluminum ingot too high relative to the price it had set for aluminum sheet. With Alcoa accounting for 90 percent of the supply of virgin aluminum ingot (with the remaining 10 percent coming from imports) and 33 percent of the aluminum sheet market, it was able to control both prices. At least this charge was never successfully rebutted by Alcoa. The key question, of course, is this: If the prices charged were not "fair," what prices would be? How is one to determine exactly what a "fair" price is when the market structure is imperfect? The difficulties in providing a remedy for the vertical price squeeze are illustrated by the decree of the district court against Alcoa:

> The defendants are enjoined and restrained from selling aluminum ingot for the fabrication of aluminum sheet or aluminum alloy sheet at higher than fair prices, if the fabricator of such sheet is thereby prevented from fabricating and selling

[11]*In re Exxon Corp., et al.*, FTC Docket 8934 (1973).

[12]Walter Adams, "Vertical Power, Dual Distribution, and the Squeeze: A Case Study in Steel," *Antitrust Bulletin*, 9, nos. 3 and 4 (June and August 1964), 493–508.

[13]Federal Energy Regulatory Commission, Docket No. E-7738 (1977).

[14]*City of Mishawaka, Indiana , v. American Electric Power Co., Inc. et al.*, 616 F. 2d 976 (1980).

[15]*U.S.* v. *Aluminum Company of America*, 148 F. 2d 416.

aluminum sheet or aluminum alloy sheet at a reasonable profit, provided that such fabricator is efficient, well equipped, and otherwise able to fabricate and sell such sheet on a fully competitive basis; and further enjoined and restrained from selling aluminum sheet and aluminum alloy sheet . . . at prices below its selling prices for aluminum ingot, plus the cost of manufacturing and selling such sheet.[16]

The price of the independent fabricators' basic raw material, ingot, is mandated to be a "fair" price that will yield a "reasonable" profit to the independent fabricators. But a reasonable profit is to be ordained only for the efficient and well-equipped fabricator, and only for that fabricator functioning on a fully competitive basis. When one speaks of "fair" prices, one is substituting personal judgment for competition. It is competition that is supposed to determine which fabricators of sheet are efficient and sufficiently well equipped to be operating on a fully competitive basis.

The mandate further specifies that the price of aluminum sheet as set by Alcoa is to be high enough to cover its ingot selling price plus its cost of manufacturing and selling that sheet. What about Alcoa's normal profit from sheet production? Unless some profit can be assumed to be treated as a cost in the decree, then no provision is made for it. On the other hand, if Alcoa were the lowest-cost sheet producer, and assuming it to be allowed only a reasonable profit on sheet production, no room for the survival of the independent sheet rollers is provided for. Since this is obviously not the intent of the decree, and is contradictory to the first requisite of the decree, it would be guaranteeing more than a normal profit to Alcoa.

Some Broader Solutions   A more complete solution to the vertical squeeze problem would be to make the market itself less monopolistic. Removal of market power is a more direct attack upon that power. Such a remedy would require structural change. If there is enough monopoly power in the 90 percent of the ingot market or in the 33 percent of the sheet market to control price, then dissolution applied to those stages of Alcoa's facilities could remove those sources of power.[17]

Another, but less complete, solution would be to divorce the fabricating assets from the rest of Alcoa's corporate body. This would at the very least create independence of profit-seeking on the part of the dismembered parts of the corporate body. No longer would there be a vertically inte-

---

[16]*U.S.* v. *Aluminum Company of America, et al.,* Judgement on Mandate against Aluminum Company of America, et al., Equity 85-73 (April 23, 1946) (D. Ct. So. N.Y.).

[17]The court considered the possibility of breaking up the ingot phase of Alcoa's operations, but wished to await the outcome of the disposal of government World War II-built aluminum plants. By 1950 Alcoa held 50 percent, Reynolds Metals 30 percent, and Kaiser Aluminum 20 percent of aluminum reduction capacity; and the court declined to resort to any dissolution of Alcoa. *U.S.* v. *Aluminum Co. of America,* 91 F. Supp. 333 (1950).

grated firm viewing the maximization of profits as a goal for the firm as a fully and vertically integrated whole.

TIE-INS

A tie-in sale occurs when a seller sells one product, product A, on the condition that the buyer also purchase along with it another product, product B. Product A is referred to as the "tying" product, and product B as the "tied" product. Where the seller ties in a full line of products, it is known as "full-line forcing."

If the seller is to be able to tie in a tied product, the tying product must have some unique quality that has created for it a particular demand and thus a certain amount of market power. Otherwise, buyers who did not wish to purchase the tied product would seek an alternative source of supply for the tying product. A patent on a useful product or a product with some particular uniqueness can provide the necessary leverage for the tying product.

The tying and tied products must also be distinct products. A tie-in can exist only where there is a tying and a tied product. An automobile, for example, is one product; the tires on it are not a separate product from the car itself. Distinctions between products are not, however, always crystal clear. In one long drawn-out private suit, both the point of uniqueness of a product and whether a product is a distinct product were argued.[18] The case involved a developer purchasing prefabricated housing from the U.S. Steel Corporation. The latter loaned the developer money at a low rate of interest. The developer, after defaulting on the loan, claimed that the loan was a tying product tying in the housing, which he claimed was of poor quality. The final decision of the Supreme Court held that the low-interest loan was not a distinct product; it was a reduction in the price of the housing. It also held that uniqueness, to contribute to an illegal tie-in, must be a kind of uniqueness from which one can draw an inference of market power—the power to raise price or require a buyer to accept "burdensome terms." In this case U.S. Steel was held not to hold any power over the credit market.

Motives for Tie-Ins   A seller may utilize the tie-in sale for a variety of economic motives. One, it may believe it can achieve cost savings by selling and physically distributing its full line of related goods together, rather than selling and distributing the several parts of the line separately. Two, it may want to tie in the sale of service with the sale of machines to assure the buyer of proper service of the machines and thus retain the

[18]*United States Steel Corp.* v. *Fortner Enterprises, Inc.*, 429 U.S. 610 (1977).

goodwill of the customer. Three, selling a tied and tying product as a package at a single-package price can conceal the price that either might sell for separately. Government-established ceiling prices could be evaded if a price-controlled item was packaged with an uncontrolled item. Oligopolistic price-cutting could be hidden, thus avoiding any dreaded retaliatory price-cutting. Four, goods that are not in strong demand can be packaged and sold with goods for which there is a strong demand. Some liquor wholesalers in World War II forced customers who wanted to purchase scotch, bourbon, or rye (scarce) to purchase X cases of rum or dry wines (abundant) along with it. This practice was replaced after the war with "incentive tie-ins." The scarce item of liquor was priced high; it could be purchased more cheaply as part of a package with abundant items.

Finally, the seller who has some degree of monopoly in the tying product can use tie-in sales to achieve additional monopoly returns through selling the tied product at higher than competitive prices. Because this seller has been able to obtain a monopoly price for the quantity of the tied product it does sell, it can be said that it has been able to achieve a partial monopoly in the market of the tied good. But it is unlikely that it can achieve a monopoly of the total market for the tied good. It would, for example, be practically impossible for a seller of a unique salt-dispensing machine to obtain a monopoly of the salt market or a seller of a unique tabulating machine to obtain a monopoly of the paper products industry.

The more intensively a customer uses the tied product in conjunction with the tying product—for example, tabulating cards with tabulating machines—the more the seller might be induced to sell the tying product at a lower price, perhaps at cost, calculating that the lost profit on the tying good will be made up by the added profits on the tied goods. In the same way, the differences in intensity of use by different customers of the tied product in conjunction with the tying product represent discrimination. The more intensive users will, in effect, be paying higher prices for the tying product than will the less intensive users.[19]

Antitrust Activity   There is nothing objectionable to a tie-in unless it may substantially lessen competition. Buyers may be forced to give up substitutes for the tied product, and sellers of the tied product are being excluded from a particular market.[20] Section 3 of the Clayton Act specifically addresses the issue of the tie-in. Sections 1 and 2 of the Sherman Act can also be relied upon, charging a restraint of trade or monopolization. It is more difficult to convict under the Sherman Act. The Supreme Court laid down a basic rule in its 1953 *Times-Picayune* decision with respect to the

[19]See Meyer L. Burstein, "A Theory of Full-line Forcing," *Northwestern University Law Review*, 55, no. 1 (March–April 1960), 62–95, for a full treatment of this subject.
[20]*U.S.* v. *Loew's, Inc.*, 371 U.S. 38 (1962).

evidence necessary under these statutes.[21] Under the Clayton Act and the application of the doctrine of incipiency, the seller must be shown to have "sufficient economic power" in the tying product *or* that a substantial amount of commerce in the tied product is affected.[22] If the suit is filed under the Sherman Act, *both* conditions must be met. The Supreme Court in its Sherman Act Section 1 *Northern Pacific Railway* decision (1958) laid down another rule.[23] *If* the necessary sufficient economic power is found to be present and *if* a not insubstantial amount of commerce in the tied good is affected, then the tie-in is illegal *per se*. That is, no further economic analysis of the effect of the tie-in is necessary.

Tying clauses have been utilized where the market power of the tying product has been created by a patent grant. Where the tying product is patented or copyrighted, the Supreme Court has presumed the required economic power to be present.[24] International Business Machines at one time required the lessees of its patented automatic punch card tabulating machines (for which there was only one competitor as well) to purchase their tabulating cards from it. In this way it was able to use the monopoly power of the patented machines to tie in the unpatented cards. It was found guilty of violating Section 3 of the Clayton Act.[25] It had argued, unsuccessfully, that cards produced by others would not perform as well on its machines and this would injure the machines and the firm's reputation.[26]

International Salt Company was forced to cease tying in the sale of salt with the leasing of its patented salt-dissolving and dispensing machines.[27] It had argued that its salt was of higher quality than that of competitors and that this reduced maintenance costs on the machines. And American Can Company had illegally required lessees of its patented can-closing machines to buy their tin cans from it.[28] American Can had leased the machines very cheaply and tied this in with five-year tin can supply contracts. Not only was American Can ordered to cease the tie-in, but it was also required to limit tin can supply contracts to one year.[29] Note that in each of these cases the owner of the patented machines was leasing rather than selling the machines. In this way a secondhand market for the

---

[21]*Times-Picayune Publishing Co.* v. *U.S.*, 345 U.S. 594, 608–609.
[22]The Clayton Act applies only to goods. Where services are at issue, the Sherman Act would have to be used.
[23]*Northern Pacific Railway Co.* v. *U.S.*, 356 U.S. 1.
[24]*U.S.* v. *Loew's, Inc.*, 371 U.S. 38 (1962).
[25]*International Business Machines Corp.* v. *U.S.*, 298 U.S. 131 (1936).
[26]One way to demonstrate that a competitor's substitutes for tied products can injure a machine is to sabotage a machine which is using just such a competitor's substitute. See John Emshwiller, "Image Problems?: If Your Copy Machine Doesn't Work, Maybe It Has Been Sabotaged," *Wall Street Journal*, September 11, 1973.
[27]*International Salt Co.* v. *U.S.*, 332 U.S. 392 (1947).
[28]*U.S.* v. *American Can Co.*, 87 F. Supp. 18 (1949).
[29]1950–1951 Trade Cases para. 62,679.

machines cannot develop and thus cut into the ability of the original machine owners to tie in another product.

One industry where tie-ins have been frequently used—and repeatedly and successfully attacked under the Sherman Act—has been the motion picture industry. Tie-in sales of copyrighted films in this industry have been referred to as *block booking*. The exhibitor would have to take a package of films—one or more films would be tied in with the sale of the preferred film. The basic purpose of the use of tie-ins in film distribution has been to unload an inferior film under the umbrella of a high-quality film. In 1940 the five major companies in the industry signed consent decrees which provided that a block of films contain no more than five.[30] In 1948 the Supreme Court ruled against the practice of block booking altogether.[31] In 1951 and 1952 consent decrees were signed by six major companies agreeing not to tie in one picture with another.[32] In 1962 six major distributors were found in violation of the Sherman Act for the use of block booking in sales of films to television stations.[33] Finally, in 1978 20th Century-Fox Film Corporation was fined $25,000 and court costs after pleading *nolo contendere* for being in criminal contempt of its 1951 consent decree. It was charged with demanding that theater chains take *The Other Side of Midnight* in order to be able to get *Star Wars*.[34]

Exception to the Per Se Rule   The per se rule with respect to tie-ins can have an exception. The courts have upheld the position that an infant industry could be exempt from this rule.[35] In the early 1950s community antenna systems (cable television) were new. Jerrold Electronics was a leader in the field, designing and producing certain specialized equipment that had no equal. This equipment was, therefore, much in demand. Jerrold sold a system as a whole and only on the condition that Jerrold install and service it. An obvious tie-in existed. To get key equipment, the buyer had to purchase all the equipment, its installation, and its servicing.

Yet the court concluded that the tie-in restraint had been reasonable for a time. The industry was young and its future uncertain. The equipment was sensitive and unstable. Modifications were still being made. Most of the others who considered installing community antenna systems lacked the necessary technical background. If Jerrold were to ensure suc-

[30] *U.S.* v. *Paramount Pictures, Inc.*, 1940–1943 Trade Cases para. 56,072.

[31] *U.S.* v. *Paramount Pictures, Inc.*, 334 U.S. 131.

[32] Simon N. Whitney, *Antitrust Policies: American Experience in Twenty Industries* (New York: The Twentieth Century Fund, 1958), II, p. 160. These decrees involved divorcement of production-distribution from exhibition as well. For a full story of the antitrust experience of the motion picture industry through 1956, see chap. 15.

[33] *U.S.* v. *Loew's, Inc.*, 371 U.S. 38.

[34] *U.S.* v. *Twentieth Century-Fox Film Corporation*, 78 CR 641 (ELP), September 12, 1978.

[35] *U.S.* v. *Jerrold Electronics Corp.*, 187 F. Supp. 545 (1960), affirmed per curiam, 365 U.S. 567 (1961).

cess of its own investment, it should be allowed to install and service its own equipment. The successful growth of the whole industry might depend upon the early success of the Jerrold system. And, said the court, a situation such as this could not have been envisioned by the Supreme Court when it handed down its *per se* illegal rule with respect to tie-ins in its *Northern Pacific Railway* decision. So Jerrold's *early* use of a package tie-in was cleared by the court. But continued use of the tie-in in the face of development of the industry was no longer justified and violated Section 1 of the Sherman Act and Section 3 of the Clayton Act.

EXCLUSIVE DEALING

Exclusive dealing occurs when a producer of a particular product or line of products has its distributors, whether wholesalers or retailers, handle all of its brand of that product or line of products. Perhaps the distributor will carry only that one producer's goods, in which case it is selling as well as buying exclusively. Perhaps the arrangement will permit the distributor to carry other producers' goods if the producer does not carry the full line of goods appropriate to the particular distributor's setup.

Exclusive dealing can carry with it economies derived from larger shipments to particular locations, from reduced inventory requirements for the buyer, and from the buyer's concentrating promotion efforts on one brand. On the other hand, the producer may have more bargaining power than the distributor and may coerce the distributor into going exclusive. Not only may the distributors be coerced into making purchases they would not ordinarily make, but other suppliers to these distributors are being excluded from this market. Thus the antitrust laws have been brought into play to examine whether alleged coercions are reasonable or unreasonable restrictions on trade.

Section 3 of the Clayton Act is the principal antitrust statute that addresses the issues of exclusive buying and selling of goods. Stripped to its essentials, it says:

> That it shall be unlawful for any person... to lease or make a sale or contract for sale of goods... on the condition,... that the lessee or purchaser thereof shall not use or deal in the goods... of a competitor... where the effect of such lease, sale, or contract for sale... may be to substantially lessen competition or tend to create a monopoly in any line of commerce.[36]

As we saw with tie-ins, Sections 1 and 2 of the Sherman Act can also be utilized. The FTC can also apply Section 5 of the Federal Trade Commis-

---

[36]For the full wording of Section 3, see the Appendix to this chapter.

sion Act, unfair methods of competition, to exclusive dealing arrangements.

Dominant Firm Exclusive Dealing Where one firm clearly dominates the market in which it sells, an exclusive dealing agreement is not too difficult to arrange. The dominance can create an absence of satisfactory substitutes, usually because the consumer demands the branded products of the well-known highly prominent producer.

Take the case of the manufacturer of patterns for women's and children's garments which had exclusive contracts with 40 percent of the sales outlets for that type of pattern in the United States. The Supreme Court felt that such a market position could only become greater over time if these contracts were allowed to continue.[37] Because of the dominance of this manufacturer's patterns and brand, they were in special demand, thus forcing retail outlets to handle them if they wanted to maximize sales of patterns and to have in the store a product that induced customers to come to the store. The exclusion of other manufacturers' patterns would become cumulative. As the percentage of the total market covered by this particular manufacturer's patterns increased because of the greater market exposure, the more necessary it would become for retail stores to handle them. All this meant the exclusion of more and more patterns of other manufacturers.

The FTC's decision against the Harley-Davidson Motor Company in 1954 is another illustration of a dominant firm requiring exclusive dealing from its dealers, in this case of its motorcycles, motorcycle equipment, parts, accessories, and oil.[38] The largest manufacturer of motorcycles in the United States at the time, it was one of only a few motorcycle manufacturers in the country. Its relative size plus the unique nature of motorcycle sales outlets in the country gave it the power to demand exclusive dealing. The motorcycle dealer had not only to run a motorcycle shop, but also organize motorcycle clubs and promote races. Motorcycle enthusiasts would hang around the shop. It was the major outlet for motorcycles, parts, and accessories. So when Harley-Davidson made efforts to go exclusive, other manufacturers lost their one real source of distribution and Harley-Davidson prevailed.

Franchising A franchise relationship is a contractual relationship between two business parties whereby the franchisor either licenses a trademark or brand name to the franchisee to do business under that mark or name, and/or sells branded goods to the franchisee for resale under certain conditions. The term "franchise" has been applied to enough different business arrangements that a consistent definition is difficult to

---

[37]*Standard Fashion Co.* v. *Magrane-Houston Co.,* 258 U.S. 346 (1922).
[38]*In the Matter of Harley-Davidson Motor Co.,* 50 F.T.C. 1047. A violation of Section 5 of the Federal Trade Commission Act, as well as of Section 3 of the Clayton Act, was found.

come by.[39] The industries most widely known for franchising are fast foods, soft drinks, gasoline, automobiles, restaurants, and hotels. Exclusive dealing takes place within this framework in varying degrees.

Advantages exist for both franchisor and franchisee in the franchising arrangement. For the producer of branded goods, a franchising arrangement provides an outlet for those goods. For the licensor of branded goods or services, the franchisee can provide a producer as well as a sales outlet. All or some of the capital for the manufacturing or retailing functions can be obtained from smaller independent businesspeople and reduce the capital outlay requirements of the franchisor. The latter can thus achieve greater market coverage with a minimum of investment.

To the small independent businessperson, a franchise provides an opportunity to sell branded goods or services whose quality is vouched for by regional or national advertising. The franchisee may also benefit from training provided by the franchisor which can give him or her necessary technical and marketing knowhow. Thus entry into the market is facilitated for small businesses.

Franchisors enjoy an inherent position of economic power over franchisees. They are the source of the goods and/or the brand names. They can select those persons or firms they believe will best perform the required functions for them. Initially they can refuse to deal with any party they wish to, provided this is not part of a conspiracy or group boycott.

The franchisee, in general, has to take the conditions laid down in the franchise, or not get the franchise at all. The holder of a franchise may have to comply, for example, with certain restrictions as to quality, exclusive buying, exclusive selling, or customer and territorial limits of operations. Such restrictions are potentially within the proscription of the antitrust laws. Some of these restrictions may have reasonable business justification; others, however, may not. Collusive price-fixing is clearly *per se* illegal. This includes vertical price control by the franchisor over the franchisee and horizontal price-fixing agreements that might occur among franchisees of the same product. The legality of some other restraints is not so clear. According to a staff report of the FTC, "... all restraints on franchisees should be viewed with a sharply critical eye."[40]

The maintenance of quality control is a clearly legitimate restriction. The advertising proclaims quality; it is up to the purveyor of the goods or services to provide the quality claimed. The reputation of all the sellers of the branded good or service rides with adherence to that quality by each and every one. An image of quality can also be generated by the cleanliness, smartness, and appropriateness of the marketing outlets. Control

---

[39]Federal Trade Commission, *Report of Ad Hoc Committee on Franchising*, mimeo, 1969, p. 5.

[40]Ibid., p. 34.

over all these merchandising elements is therefore deemed to be essential by the franchisor. The party to whom the franchise has been granted must thus agree to certain limitations on decision-making. To minimize misunderstandings between franchisor and franchisee, the FTC promulgated a trade regulation rule effective in 1979 regarding disclosures the franchisor must make to the prospective franchisee. The full facts about the franchisor and the various restrictions under which the franchisee must operate must be revealed in advance.[41]

The franchisor's right to assume some control over the franchisee's decision-making in order to maintain quality control can be abused. Franchisors have sometimes attempted to tie in with their trademarked product a non-trademarked product. In this way the monopoly of the brand name can be extended to cover a good over which the franchisor does not enjoy a monopoly. In this fashion a fast-food franchisor attempted to tie in the sale of various packaging items, cooking equipment, and certain food-mix preparations with the sale of the branded item. A court found this to be a violation of Section 1 of the Sherman Act.[42] The franchisor may argue that quality is adversely affected when the franchisee purchases related goods from another source. Yet the franchisee may find that it can purchase the related goods from another source at a lower price. A solution to this dilemma is, where feasible, to have the franchisor lay out the required specifications for the related goods and then be forced to compete with other suppliers of these related goods.

THE LESSEE GASOLINE DEALER—*A CASE STUDY*

The major oil company refiners, the some 20 large corporations which have been the principal sources of gasoline in the United States, controlling more than 85 percent of the refinery capacity, have shown over the years a distinct preference for marketing their branded gasoline through independent small business dealers. Such retailers can be described as falling into one of two categories. They may own and operate their own service station and have supply contracts with a refiner or a wholesaler (jobber) who has received supplies from a refiner. Or they may lease a refiner-owned, or in some cases wholesaler-owned, station, almost always on a short-term, one-year basis.[43] This last category accounts for well over half of the service stations selling gasoline in the United States. The Petroleum Marketing

[41]16 C.F.R. 436. The FTC found it advisable to issue a lengthy set of guides to facilitate the interpretation of this rule.
[42]*Siegal* v. *Chicken Delight, Inc.*, 448 F. 2d 43 (1971), certiorari denied, 405 U.S. 955 (1972).
[43]Sometimes the supplier controls the property through a long-term lease of the property from a third party.

Practices Act of 1978 defines this contractual relationship as a franchise. A court of appeals emphasized in 1980 that it was more than simply a landlord-tenant relationship.[44] Major oil company owned and operated service stations represent a very small percentage of the total number of retail outlets through which gasoline is dispensed to the consuming public.[45]

The Lessee Dealer System   Large-scale use of the lessee dealer began in 1935 when the State of Iowa enacted a heavy chain-store tax. Other states followed Iowa's example. Some of these taxes were quite severe, as they were progressive with the number of retail outlets in the chain. Such taxes could be avoided by having the service stations removed from company operation.

This adoption by gasoline suppliers of the so-called Iowa Plan was only one of several economic factors leading to the use of the short-term lease and the lessee dealer. Major oil company spokespeople have argued that the profit-seeking independent dealer has more incentive to operate efficiently than the salaried company employee. Then, too, overtime wages need not be paid to the service station dealer, who frequently works long hours.

Other costs can be avoided by use of a lessee dealer. No social security tax contributions need to be paid on the dealer. Local taxes or license fees fall directly on the dealer, as does public liability with respect to accidents. The necessity of dealing with labor unions at the retail level is averted. A lessee dealer does not go on strike against a supplier. If there is any "strike" at all, it is more likely to take the form of blockading another price-cutting dealer. Finally, with service station dealers establishing the retail price, the large oligopolistic refiner is essentially free from possible accusations of fixing the retail price. One danger in utilizing company-operated stations is that a price set too low brings charges of attempting to control the dealers' margin of profit and a price set too high may not be competitive.

This desire of the major oil companies to use lessee dealers rather than operate their own stations makes for relatively easy entry into gasoline retailing. The capital investment in plant has already been made by the large corporation. The lessor may provide some training and/or advice drawn from years of experience, ranging from the best means of

---

[44]*George Arnott* v. *The American Oil Co.,* 609 F. 2d 873 (1979), certiorari denied, 100 S. Ct. 1852 (1980).

[45]In 1948 the typical major oil company operated only 1 percent of the service stations through which its products were sold. Marshall C. Howard, "Interfirm Relations in Oil Products Markets," *Journal of Marketing,* 20, no. 4 (April 1956), 360. Perusal of 1978 major oil company annual reports indicates that some major refiners operate as much as 10 percent of their owned stations.

conducting operations to accounting procedures. A set of tools and inventory are the principal investments required of the dealer.

The biggest "cost" to the lessee dealer is operating on a short-term lease. Goodwill and good relations must exist between lessor and lessee. Otherwise the lessor can take advantage of the dealer and not renew the lease. The lessor is looking for responsible and successful dealers who will maximize sales of the suppliers' products. A conflict can easily arise if the two parties do not agree on how the retail business should be run. Unfortunately for the dealer, the supplier has more bargaining power in the ownership of the station property and the lever of the short-term lease.

The complaints of dealers under this franchise arrangement have been numerous. They have charged that there have been pressures from the supplier to deal exclusively, to raise price,[46] to lower price, to sell more, to keep the station open longer hours, or to be a party to give-away promotion deals (give a drinking glass to a customer with the purchase of so many gallons of gasoline).[47] Dealers have complained that when they do well their rent on the service station property gets increased so that their profits are passed back to the supplier. They have accused suppliers of price discrimination that has triggered price wars at retail. The final blow to their independence, if they do not show a spirit of mutual cooperation with the supplier's suggestions, is loss of the lease.

With the investment in the service station property, the major oil company obviously wants to see that investment used to the maximum as a vehicle for the sale of as much product as possible. The flow of gasoline "gallonage" is a prime measure of the success of a lessee dealer in the eyes of the refiner-supplier. The flow of other products through this distribution outlet can also bring the supplier profits. The latter has, therefore, often urged the dealer to go exclusive and handle all the products it either produces or sponsors. In addition to gasoline and motor oil, the refiner has been interested in seeing a variety of TBA (tires, batteries, and accessories) sold through its service stations. Those it does not produce itself it can still make some profit on, perhaps through a commission, by having them sold through the stations over which it has some control.

Litigation over the System   The issue of exclusive dealing at the retail level of the oil industry was bound to reach the courts. In 1949 the

---

[46]Some major oil refiners have at one time attempted to set the price of gasoline at service stations operated by lessee dealers by selling the gasoline to the dealer on consignment. The refiner was to own the gasoline and be able to price it until it was sold to the consumer. The Supreme Court struck down this "clever draftmanship" as an illegal means of resale price maintenance. *Simpson* v. *Union Oil Co.*, 377 U.S. 13, 24 (1964).

[47]Even in conservation-oriented years, whenever supply exceeds demand, even for a short period of time, the pressures from suppliers to sell more continue. See Bill Paul, "Are Oil Giants Twisting Arms to Push Gasoline," *Wall Street Journal*, September 16, 1980, p. 41.

Supreme Court ruled against the written exclusive dealing requirements contracts utilized by the Standard Oil Company of California.[48] These contractual efforts of Standard to force dealers to buy not only all their petroleum product needs but also their tires, tubes, and batteries were found to violate Section 3 of the Clayton Act. Some 8000 exclusive supply contracts and several millions of dollars of sales were involved, and this represented a substantial volume of business. Furthermore, this was a widespread practice among Standard's competitors. The result was a foreclosure of the market to other suppliers and manufacturers who might wish to make sales in this market, and this represented "a potential clog on competition."[49]

Justice William O. Douglas dissented in the *Standard Oil* decision; he saw competition among the oil companies as being "vigorous." If exclusive dealing were to be judged illegal, then the oil companies would turn to operating the retail service stations themselves. This would mean a loss to the economy as the independent small businessperson would be replaced by corporate employees. His prediction, of course, proved to be wrong.

Justice Robert H. Jackson also dissented. His reasoning was different from that of Douglas. True, the dealers' freedom in selecting sources of supply was restricted and this did prevent other companies from selling to them, but the supply contracts were a basic and important means through which the oil company suppliers competed: ". . . we cannot in fairness also apply the lash whenever they hit upon a successful method of competing."[50]

Not long after *Standard Oil* came the *Richfield Oil* case (1951).[51] Here the exclusive dealing contracts were oral, not written. They were found to be equally violative of the antitrust laws. A few years later, in 1959, a lower court found illegal Sun Oil Company's tactics, which induced exclusive dealing by its lessee dealers.[52] Sun did not have contracts requiring exclusive dealing. Its sales representatives, however, "recommended" to its dealers that they go exclusive. In the case at hand, the dealer did not follow this advice, and he was given a 60-day notice of lease cancellation.

Litigation involving exclusive dealing demands by major oil company suppliers continued into the 1960s. In three companion suits, the FTC successfully attacked agreements between oil companies and tire manufacturers that called for the tire companies to distribute their tires directly to the oil companies' service stations and to pay the oil companies an "over-

[48] *Standard Oil of California and Standard Stations, Inc.* v. *U.S.*, 337 U.S. 293.
[49] Ibid., p. 314.
[50] Ibid., p. 324.
[51] *U.S.* v. *Richfield Oil Corp.*, 99 F. Supp. 280 (1951), affirmed per curiam, 343 U.S. 922 (1952).
[52] *U.S.* v. *Sun Oil Company*, 176 F. Supp. 715.

ride" commission on the volume of tires thus sold. The charge was a violation of Section 5 of the Federal Trade Commission Act, an unfair method of competition. The Commission noted pressure on the service station dealer now from two sources: the oil company lessor and the tire manufacturer. "Double teaming" solicitation by representatives of both companies proved to be very effective. Advising the dealers that their status as dealers for the oil companies was at stake was all that was required.[53] Some noncooperating dealers did lose their leases.

In the first of these cases the Supreme Court in 1965 found "abundant evidence" that The Atlantic Refining Company "not only exerted the persuasion that is a natural incident of its economic power, but coupled with it direct and overt threats of reprisal . . . so that the Commission could properly have concluded that it was for this bundle of persuasion that Goodyear paid Atlantic its commission."[54] The Court noted that competition had been restrained in that other manufacturers and wholesalers of tires found The Atlantic Refining market foreclosed and in that the Atlantic dealers were at a disadvantage compared with other dealers, who were free to stock several brands of tires.[55]

In a second decision, by the Court of Appeals of the 5th Circuit in 1966, an override agreement involving tires between the Shell Oil Company and the Firestone Tire and Rubber Company was found illegal because the oil company's "persuasion" was found to be objectionable.[56] Evidence of overt coercion was lacking. But with the oil company as the dealer's supplier, banker, and landlord, "the velvet glove of request has within it the mailed fist of command."[57] In a third, Supreme Court, decision in 1968, a sales commission plan between Texaco and The B. F. Goodrich Company was also found to be in violation of Section 5. In this case the Court saw the large refiner's economic power over its dealers as being "inherent in the structure and economics of the petroleum distribution system."[58] Because of this, no overt pressure tactics needed to be shown to prove illegality.

[53]Pressure applied to those service station dealers who owned their own stations but who were operating with some equipment on a loan contract basis from the oil companies was also effective. Supplies of gasoline itself were also a concern to dealers.

[54]*The Atlantic Refining Co.* v. *FTC. The Goodyear Tire & Rubber Company* v. *FTC*, 381 U.S. 357, 368.

[55]The Court noted a further restraint on competition in that Firestone Tire & Rubber Company and Goodyear Tire & Rubber Company had agreed not to sell to Atlantic Refining Company dealers in each other's territory. Firestone had a similar override agreement with Atlantic Refining covering a separate territory.

[56]*Shell Oil Company* v. *FTC. The Firestone Tire & Rubber Company* v. *FTC*, 360 F. 2d 470, certiorari denied, 385 U.S. 1002 (1967).

[57]360 F. 2d 470, 487.

[58]*FTC* v. *Texaco, Inc.*, 393 U.S. 223, 226. Here the Supreme Court quoted from CA-5 in the *Shell Oil Company* case, 360 F. 2d 470, 481.

Legislative Remedy In spite of these court decisions in favor of the lessee gasoline dealer, these small businesspeople continued to complain against their suppliers and landlords. Finally, Congress passed the Petroleum Marketing Practices Act of 1978, Title I of which was designed to protect the franchised retailer against unfair termination or nonrenewal of the franchise. This act gives the lessee dealer a statutory right to go to a federal court to seek relief. The franchisor must then successfully defend its action as being permissible within the conditions laid down in the act.

Under this statute, the franchisor can show as a legitimate cause for termination of the franchise fraud or criminal misconduct, insolvency or failure to pay the franchisor in a timely manner, severe physical or mental incapacitation, failure to operate the marketing premises for seven consecutive days, willful adulteration or misbranding of products, failure to comply with government regulations, or conviction of any felony involving moral turpitude. Positive grounds for nonrenewal are receipt of numerous *bona fide* customer complaints or failure to operate the premises in a clean, safe, and healthful manner.

From the franchisor's point of view, there are two key provisions in the statute. One ground specifically cited as reasonable cause for nonrenewal is the inability of franchisor and franchisee to agree on any changes in the provisions of the franchise. The proposed changes do have to be in good faith and in the normal course of business, not a subterfuge to permit nonrenewal. The second ground is where renewal is likely to be uneconomical to the franchisor despite any reasonable changes that would be acceptable to the franchisee. Determination of the state of being uneconomic is to be made by the franchisor, again in good faith and in the normal course of business. The oil company supplier will always be seeking thoroughly adequate representation of its interests by the lessee dealer. Such adequate representation can be assumed to be synonymous with the most economic operation of the service station as viewed by the franchisor. What remains to be seen, therefore, is how the courts will interpret the application of these "good faith" clauses as nonrenewals are challenged in the courts by franchisees.

THE AUTOMOBILE DEALERS FRANCHISE ACT—*A CASE STUDY*

"Good faith" is an important provision in the Automobile Dealer Franchise Act of 1956. This act was designed to balance the bargaining power between the auto manufacturer and the auto dealer. It may be fruitful to take a brief look at the experience under that act.

The Automobile Dealers Franchise Act of 1956, otherwise known as the Automobile Dealers' Day in Court Act, was passed as a result of automobile dealers' complaints that manufacturers were unfairly terminating or refusing to renew dealer franchises when the dealers were not fully complying with all the wishes of the manufacturer with respect to how the dealer was conducting the business. Just before the passage of this legislation by Congress, the auto manufacturers began to use five-year rather than one-year franchises, presumably to forestall passage of the legislation.

The act was designed "To supplement the antitrust laws . . . in order to balance the power now heavily weighted in favor of automobile manufacturers" by enabling a dealer to sue a manufacturer for damages incurred as a result of the manufacturer's failure to act in good faith in complying with the terms of the franchise or terminating or not renewing the franchise.[59] Good faith was defined in such a way as to free the dealer from any "coercion, intimidation, or threats of intimidation." However, the act specifically stated "That recommendation, endorsement, exposition, persuasion, urging or argument shall not be deemed to constitute lack of good faith."[60]

The dealer is of the utmost importance to the manufacturer. There is not much point in producing cars if they cannot be sold. Thus manufacturer-dealer contracts have established standards of dealer performance and have called for the dealer to promote sales aggressively. They have dealt in some detail with the dealer's business with respect to service, parts, personnel, and adequacy of premises and investment in the business. Failure to live up to some of these requirements can mean nonrenewal of the franchise agreement.

The experience of the first few years after the passage of the act gave clear indication that it would not be effective in establishing the countervailing power Congress hoped to create. Of some 90 suits filed by dealers under the act in its first nine years, only one resulted in a final judgment in favor of the dealer.[61] Some dealers received some damages in out-of-court settlements, but most received nothing for their legal effort. Although some situations undoubtedly represented incompetence on the part of the dealer, it proved almost impossible for a dealer to demonstrate coercion. As neatly put by a court in 1964: "Threats and coercion may be subtle. But the cases clearly establish that the burden of proving bad faith is a high one under the Act."[62]

The manufacturer has continued to hold the upper hand in the bar-

---

[59]70 Stat. 1125.

[60]An appeals court has stated: "The legislative history and other cases use slightly different language, but with the same meaning, stating that 'good faith' must be determined in the 'context' of coercion or intimidation or threats thereof." *Kotula* v. *Ford Motor Co.*, 338 F. 2d 732, 734 (1964), certiorari denied, 380 U.S. 979 (1965).

[61]Stewart Macaulay, "Changing a Continuing Relationship between a Large Corporation and Those Who Deal with It: Automobile Manufacturers, Their Dealers, and the Legal System–Part II," *Wisconsin Law Review*, 1965, no. 4 (Fall 1965), 742–51.

[62]*Zarbock* v. *Chrysler*, 235 F. Supp. 130, 133.

gaining. In 1975 General Motors came out with new five-year franchise agreements. Although a number of dealers complained that it gave the manufacturer too much control over the operations of their businesses, they had little choice but to sign.[63] Warranty-claim settlements were a primary issue. Dealers have claimed that they have been burdensome. Manufacturers have claimed that they have been padded. Other issues of dealer discontent have been the manufacturers' sales quotas and push to increase or improve plant investment. Dealers have also charged that the manufacturers have made fleet sales at below the dealers' costs.

The media have continued to report dealer displeasure. As long as the bargaining power of the manufacturer is greater and as long as both manufacturer and dealer each desire to maximize its own profits first, this state of discontent will likely continue indefinitely. Probably the only way in which the franchise friction can be eliminated is to eliminate the franchise! It could be required of all auto manufacturers, for example, that they sell to all prospective purchasers on nondiscriminatory and nonexclusive terms.[64] Such a radical proposal to interfere with private business choices has not received serious attention.

EXCLUSIVE TERRITORIES

One form of arrangement between manufacturer and distributor which has been in use has been that of exclusive territories for distributors. Under such a plan a distributor is granted a geographic territory within which that distributor will be the sole and exclusive sales representative for the particular manufacturer's products. That territory will be the distributor's exclusively; no other distributor of that same producer's products can make any sales in that territory. Likewise, the distributor cannot make any sales outside that territory; any market beyond the territory will be the exclusive territory of another distributor of the same producer. Some arrangements will even prohibit a distributor from selling to a customer who comes from outside that distributor's own territory. In some cases there will be customer restrictions even within these territories; for example, sales to institutions will be reserved for the supplier.

Certainly such an arrangement is restrictive of the competition between distributors of the same brand products. The effect is also the same as if these distributors had conspired to divide up the territories among themselves. Such market allocations could, therefore, easily be viewed as being

[63]Terry P. Brown, "GM's Relations with Dealers Are Roiled as Some Dealers Call New Pact Unfair," *Wall Street Journal*, October 30, 1975, p. 40.
[64]See Stanley E. Boyle, "Restructuring the Automobile Industry: 'Exclusive Dealing' as an Unfair Method of Competition under the FTC Act," *Antitrust Law & Economics Review*, 5, no. 1 (Fall 1971), 19–42.

illegal *per se*. The usual rationale of manufacturers, however, has been that the restraint on *intrabrand* competition certainly does not weaken the *interbrand* competition. The argument is that, if a particular distributor has an area all to himself or herself in which to sell without having to compete with other distributors of the same brand products, then he or she will pay closer attention to building, developing, and promoting that territory. From the manufacturer's point of view, this greater sales effort on the part of the distributor should increase the overall interbrand competition.

The First Court Cases   The first case on exclusive territories to reach the Supreme Court was that of the *White Motor Company* in 1963.[65] The lower court had held that the use of exclusive territories by a manufacturer was illegal *per se* and granted a summary judgment.[66] The Supreme Court, however, noted that a vertical arrangement was at issue and wanted to know exactly what was involved: "We do not know enough of the economic and business stuff out of which these arrangements emerge to be certain."[67] If, for example, such a vertical restriction were unilaterally determined by the manufacturer and this was the only way in which a small business could survive against aggressive competitors, then such an arrangement could well be considered reasonable. Thus there was a need to apply the rule of reason. The Supreme Court, therefore, remanded the case back to the lower court to find out just what "the economic and business stuff" was in the case. In this particular instance the public was never to find out, for White Motor, expressing no desire to be tied up in litigation for another few years, no longer contested the suit.

Some of these vertical arrangements contain within them structural relationships that brand them as horizontal restraints, in which case they *are* found to be illegal *per se*. Such was the situation in the *Sealy* case.[68] Sealy licensed mattress manufacturers to produce and sell under its trademark. Territories were allocated to individual manufacturers so that they were not competing directly with each other. The licensees, however, had to be stockholders of Sealy. And each member of Sealy's board of directors had to be a stockholder or a stockholder-licensee's nominee. The executive committee, too, was composed of licensee-stockholders. The vertical arrangement was not, therefore, strictly determined unilaterally from above, for the licensors were also the licensees. Different, yet bearing the same horizontal restraint earmarks, was the *Topco* case.[69] Here a cooperative purchasing association of 25 small- and medium-sized regional

---

[65]*White Motor Co.* v. *U.S.* 372 U.S. 253.

[66]194 F. Supp. 562 (1961). The case was decided without a trial and only on the basis of the pleadings, White Motor's answers to interrogatories, the deposition of White Motor's secretary, copies of the contracts, and a White Motor distributor organization chart.

[67]372 U.S. 253, 263.

[68]*U.S.* v. *Sealy, Inc.*, 388 U.S. 350 (1967).

[69]*U.S.* v. *Topco Associates, Inc.*, 405 U.S. 596 (1972).

supermarket chains operating in 33 states were granted exclusive territories. Because new memberships were subject to voting approval by existing members, the arrangement was found to be *per se* illegal by the Supreme Court.

Another variation on this theme is represented by the case involving Chevrolet dealers in the Los Angeles area.[70] Each had a basic market territory to work. When one of them began to cut prices and draw customers from other Chevrolet dealers' territories, the other dealers went to General Motors to enlist its aid to see that this price-cutting dealer got no more deliveries. (The dealer had set up referral agents throughout the total Los Angeles megalopolis promising Chevrolets at so much above wholesale cost.) Because these dealers had cooperated among themselves and with General Motors in an effort to put a stop to this price-cutting, they were found to be guilty of a horizontal price-fixing conspiracy.

Except for situations such as the above where the distributors are themselves combining to prevent price competition, the courts, after *White Motor*, applied a rule of reason to territorial restriction cases. In the 1964 *Sandura* case, a court of appeals overturned an FTC order against the arrangement because it felt that the use of exclusive territorial distributorships was important to the survival of the relatively small (less than 5 percent of industry sales) manufacturer.[71] Producing hardfloor covering (linoleum), Sandura had experienced some quality-control failure with a resulting almost 50 percent fall in sales. It found the use of closed sales territories important to induce distributors to handle the product and advertise and promote it and bring the company back to a healthy condition. The court rejected the FTC's position that the closed territories represented a plan conceived by the distributors and enforced by the manufacturer.

Another court of appeals overruled the FTC in another decision because it simply felt that interbrand competition in the industry was very effective.[72] Snap-on Tools Corporation had assigned exclusive territories to dealers with mobile walk-in trucks. The court could not see the assignment of territories as a conspiratorial device among supplier and dealers to limit competition horizontally; it viewed the arrangement as promoting interbrand competition. Indeed, with some 80 competing concerns in the hand-tool industry, the competition was referred to as being "bitter and bloody."

Landmark Decisions   In its landmark *Schwinn* decision, the Supreme Court in 1967 ruled that it was *per se* illegal for a supplier to establish exclusive territories for distributors when the title to the goods had passed to the distributors.[73] If the supplier retained title to the goods, however,

[70]*U.S.* v. *General Motors Corp.*, 384 U.S. 127 (1966).
[71]*Sandura Co.* v. *FTC*, 339 F. 2d 847.
[72]*Snap-on Tools Corporation* v. *FTC*, 321 F. 2d 825 (1963).
[73]*U.S.* v. *Arnold, Schwinn & Co.*, 388 U.S. 365.

the exclusive territory issue was to be decided under the rule of reason. This decision was a departure from the principle laid down in *White Motor* and succeeded in producing more confusion than light. Even the academics got into the fray through the scholarly journals, most of them highly critical of the decision. As noted by Robert W. Knapp:

> Certainly, few if any marketing cases produced more confusion, debate, and judicial gymnastics. . . .

> This has been the usual pattern in these cases for a decade: one day, one court—the rule of reason; next day, different court—the per se doctrine. The following day, all courts switch doctrines. Then all the conflicting cases and doctrines are thrown back in the pot, mixed, and some combination randomly extracted and served up for the next case.[74]

Finally, ten years later, in *GTE Sylvania*, the Supreme Court reviewed its holding in *Schwinn* and found that it had not been correct when it had applied the *per se* illegal rule in those situations where title had passed to the distributor.[75] It now said that the rule of reason should apply both when the supplier retains title and when the supplier does not. To make it illegal *per se* just when the supplier does not is to make a distinction based upon "formalistic line drawing," not upon economic effect.[76] It noted that the *Schwinn* decision had failed to differentiate between the *interbrand* competition among all the competitors of a product and the *intrabrand* competition among the sellers of that product as produced by a given manufacturer.

The Court observed, noting the weight of scholarly opinion, that although vertical restrictions placed upon its distributors by a given manufacturer represented putting limitations on intrabrand competition, these restrictions might enable manufacturers to compete more effectively with other manufacturers.[77] New manufacturers might be induced to enter if they could find competent distributors willing to make the necessary investment, and that willingness would more likely be found if distributors were to be partially insulated from intrabrand competition. Likewise, established

[74]Robert W. Knapp, "Legal Developments in Marketing," *Journal of Marketing*, 42, no. 1 (January 1978), 106–107.

[75]*Continental T.V., Inc. v. GTE Sylvania, Inc.*, 433 U.S. 36 (1977).

[76]The Supreme Court did not rule out entirely the application of *per se* illegality to vertical restrictions. Such restraints which were "pernicious" or without "any redeeming virtue" could still be found to be illegal *per se*. Ibid., pp. 58–59.

[77]See, for example, Lee E. Preston, "Restrictive Distribution Arrangements: Economic Analysis and Public Policy Standards," *Law and Contemporary Problems*, 30, no. 3 (Summer 1965), 506–29; and Richard A. Posner, "Antitrust Policy and the Supreme Court: An Analysis of the Restricted Distribution, Horizontal Merger and Potential Competition Decisions," *Columbia Law Review*, 75, no. 2 (March 1975), 282–99. But also see William S. Comanor, "Vertical Territorial and Customer Restrictions: White Motor and Its Aftermath," *Harvard Law Review*, 81, no. 7 (May 1968), 1419–38.

manufacturers might encourage distributors to promote their territories more intensively. That investment would have to be not only in sales but also in service facilities, modern technology being what it is. One of the problem areas seen by a distributor, whether a new entrant or one well established, is that of the "free rider," the distributor who sits by without much investment in promotion and development work and gains from that effort by other distributors of the same branded products. The free rider problem could be at least partially resolved by providing distributors with exclusive territories. This solution would more closely relate an individual distributor's promotional input effort to output result.

With the rule of reason to be applied to territorial restrictions, more of the "economic and business stuff" of these arrangements will have to be analyzed in particular market situations. The history of an industry and the particular characteristics of products should be understood before an appropriate decision can be made.

SOFT DRINK DISTRIBUTION: EXCLUSIVE
TERRITORIES—*A CASE STUDY*

In 1971 and 1972 the Federal Trade Commission filed complaints against eight large soft-drink manufacturers charging that the use of geographically restricted sales territories by bottling companies licensed by soft-drink syrup manufacturers were in violation of Section 5 of the Federal Trade Commission Act.[78] One indirect industry response was obtaining the filing of bills in Congress that would confer special antitrust excemption for the use of exclusive territorial agreements between soft-drink manufacturers and bottlers. The pressure to get such a bill passed became even greater when the FTC issued cease-and-desist orders against The Coca-Cola Company and PepsiCo in 1978.[79] (The *Coca-Cola* and *PepsiCo* cases were treated as companion cases and the findings and conclusions in the *Coca-Cola* case were adopted as the findings and conclusions in the *PepsiCo* case.) Coca-Cola appealed.

While the appeal of the decision was pending, Congress passed the Soft Drink Interbrand Competition Act of 1980.[80] Except for one proviso, it exempted from the antitrust laws the use of exclusive geographic areas by the soft-drink industry for bottling and distribution. That one proviso states: "That such product is in substantial and effective competition with

---

[78]The complaints were against Crush International Ltd., Dr. Pepper Co., The Coca-Cola Co., PepsiCo., Inc., The Seven-Up Co., Royal Crown Cola Co., Cott Corp. (FTC Docket Nos. 8853–59), and Canada Dry Corp. (FTC Docket No. 8877.)

[79]*In the Matter of The Coca-Cola Company*, 91 F.T.C. 517; and *In the Matter of PepsiCo., Inc.*, 91 F.T.C. 680.

[80]94 Stat. 939.

other products of the same general class in the relevant market or markets." As a result of the passage of this act, the FTC withdrew its contest of the appeal by Coca-Cola, and the court remanded the case back to the FTC for dismissal. The FTC dismissed the pending complaints against the other soft-drink bottlers as well. The legal standards for enforcement of the antitrust laws against the use of exclusive territories in this industry had now been changed. If the FTC were to renew its efforts against Coca-Cola's use of exclusive territories, it would have to do so under the new standards.[81]

The views of The Coca-Cola Company (representing the soft-drink industry) and the FTC differed quite sharply. We present a summary of both below, as expressed in the lengthy FTC decision presented by Commissioner Elizabeth Dole. The reader may find interesting economic points made in each. They have to be balanced and a choice made. The Coca-Cola approach is presented first, since this permits using the status quo as a takeoff point.

Background First, some background information. The relevant product market was that of take-home finished soft drinks packaged in tins and bottles. These were the products whose sales were restricted to exclusive market territories throughout the United States. The sale of post-mix syrup, which was mixed with carbonated water in restaurants and stadiums, was not at issue, because the syrup jobbers operating in this market were free to compete in any geographic area. Coca-Cola as a syrup manufacturer maintained two other restrictions over bottlers in addition to that of the exclusive territories. It kept the secret Coca-Cola syrup formula to itself. And it retained the right to establish quality standards.

The licensing of Coca-Cola bottling rights and the assignment of exclusive territories to bottlers first took place around the turn of the century. Although The Coca-Cola Company did not initially do any bottling itself, at the time of the litigation it operated 27 bottling plants, each with its own exclusive territory, and representing coverage of 14 percent of the population of the United States. It acquired these businesses by reacquiring the bottling rights it had previously granted to independents, together with the same exclusive territories. Of the total of 726 licensed bottlers of Coca-Cola in 1971, most were small independents.[82] These exclusive territories represented, except for some mergers, essentially the same territories parceled out originally. Mergers, and there had been 107 of them, served to combine territories, enabling one bottling plant to serve a larger territory. In some cases certain bottlers would bottle the requirements of certain other Coca-Cola bottlers who were distributing but not bottling. A Coca-Cola bottler might also handle not only the Coca-Cola allied products of

[81]*CCH Trade Regulation Reports*, No. 477, February 16, 1981, p. 2.
[82]91 F.T.C. 517, 539, 543.

TAB, Sprite, Fresca, Fanta, and Mr. PiBB, but also "piggybacked" trademarked soft drinks of other manufacturers, although again within exclusive territories.

The Coca-Cola View   The bottlers, using the same method of physical distribution which had been used for years, delivered to the retail store directly from the bottling plant. Some bottlers had testified they preferred this system because it gave them closer control over the way the retailer merchandised the product. The manufacturer also expected the bottlers to expand their sales within their territories intensively. Deep penetration of a given market and product availability were felt to be necessary to the successful selling of soft drinks in bottles and cans. Some of this market penetration, such as serving vending machines and small outlets, was believed to be unprofitable in itself but was necessary to achieve product awareness and overall success. What was being said, in effect, was that such "unprofitable" sales were really a part of necessary advertising and promotion to cement the product's value in the consumer's mind. As for more explicit forms of advertising, it was felt that exclusive territories were necessary to solve the problem of the "free rider."

Coca-Cola contended that better product quality was achieved by use of the territorial restrictions. If quality was not maintained, the bottler would lose sales to other brands. Exclusive territories enabled the manufacturer to monitor the quality in a tighter fashion. Both manufacturers and bottlers felt that the exclusive territories provided a favorable climate for capital investment in a capital-intensive industry, and this would provide the profits necessary to provide superior products and service. In addition, it was claimed that removal of territorial restrictions would see small bottlers driven out of business by the larger bottlers of the same brand.

The FTC View   The FTC's emphasis in its examination of these exclusive territories was considerably different. It concluded that the practice was an unreasonable vertical restraint of trade not because the bottlers exercised any control over the manufacturer or because there was any horizontal agreement among the bottlers, but because the impact of the use of the restrictive sales territories fell primarily on *price* competition among the bottlers. Its decision did not rely on a full and detailed statistical analysis of concentration and market shares, barriers to entry, product differentiation, and profits of manufacturers and bottlers. Rather, it represented a weighing of the impact of the use of exclusive sales territories on intrabrand and interbrand competition. Further, it limited its proof of competitive impact to the "corridor area" extending from southern Virginia to upstate New York.

The FTC saw the territorial restrictions as being a serious impediment to the working of free market forces. Without these restrictions, the geographic boundaries served by bottlers would undoubtedly have evolved in a different configuration and created natural market boundaries different from those dictated by the manufacturer. The territories had been carved out years ago under different and much cruder bottling technology and transport conditions. In spite of this changing context, the bottlers had continued to use the traditional store-door route-delivery system to serve each retail outlet within much the same territories. Without the territorial restrictions, new ways of doing business would have developed and expansion into new territories would have occurred—and this fluid process would have increased *price* competition.

The FTC envisioned automated production lines as encouraging expansion by a bottler into a larger geographic area in order to take advantage of potential economies of scale. It pictured widespread possible use of warehouse facilities and central warehouse delivery and plant pickup by certain types of customers. Such possibilities should be available to those who might want to attempt them. But under the required territorial restrictions, a bottler was not permitted such marketing exploitations whenever they were not consistent with such restrictions.

As for attracting capital, the FTC's position was that competitive markets would direct the appropriate amount of capital to the appropriate investments. Free competition should be the judge as to whether and where more capital investments should be made. As for generating profits that could be plowed back into this industry, what is to guarantee that profits earned here will be spent here? Would not an unfettered competition ensure the best quality products and the best possible innovations in product and service?

As for "piggybacking," which the industry used as a good illustration of interbrand competition, the FTC felt it was unlikely that the same bottler carrying more than one manufacturer's brand would try to compete with itself in *price*. If the price of one brand were taking sales away from a bottler's second brand, that bottler would be unlikely to lower the price of the second brand to meet the price competition of the first. The greater probability would be that the price of the first brand would be raised.

Finally, the FTC noted that, because of the industrywide use of exclusive territories, a Coca-Cola bottler was prevented, in effect, not only from competing with other Coca-Cola bottlers, but also with any bottlers in other territories. Exclusive territories thus limit interbrand price competition as well as preventing intrabrand competition. Price cannot be used to expand into other territories. Evidence existed that the bottlers of different manufacturers in different territories used different pricing strategies. Yet the territorial restrictions prevented different pricing strategies from "clash[ing] head-on."[83]

[83]91 F.T.C. 517, 641–42.

The FTC contention that the use of restricted territories prevented price competition at the wholesale level was reflected in the testimony of almost all the bottlers who testified. The president of Coca-Cola expressed the view that without restraint on intrabrand competition, Coca-Cola's price would fall. And if Coca-Cola were more price competitive, this would have an effect throughout the whole industry, since other brands were sensitive to the price of Coca-Cola, the principal product of the largest firm in the soft-drink industry.

What about the small bottler in the industry? Would it be driven out of business without an exclusive territory? The FTC thought not, unless it was too small to be efficient. Indeed, the smaller bottler could have a better chance to survive, seizing parts of the markets of larger bottlers, using either price or innovative marketing methods to accomplish its objective. In this way concentration among bottlers could decrease.

The Views Compared   In comparing the approaches of the soft-drink industry to that of the FTC, it is apparent that the former has emphasized nonprice competition and the latter price competition. The industry approach embodies the concept that the industry must exert some control over its own fate in an imperfect market situation. The FTC's approach relies on the natural market forces of price competition and market change. It is not concerned with the free rider problem, for that is a problem related primarily to nonprice competition. And it is not concerned with quality, capital investment, or individual firm survival, for those are matters to be handled by the impersonal market forces of competition.

SUMMARY

Between a manufacturer and the ultimate consumer, there may be several stages of further processing and distribution through which goods must pass before the final products reach the consumer. In many industries, the manufacturer may perform some of these functions itself, but it may also rely on independent firms to perform some of them in whole or in part. It may find itself, therefore, in competition with those to whom it is a supplier. It also, in any case, will want to control these independents to maximize its own profits from the ultimate sale of its own final products. Because of these two factors, antitrust problems can arise.

Manufacturers have various reasons for wishing to maintain the resale price of their products. Retailers have enjoyed resale price control by manufacturers in order to prevent price-cutting at retail. Depression-born enactment of state fair trade laws provided the necessary legal support to resale price maintenance for a number of years in many states, but for both economic and legal reasons these were not thoroughly effective, and these state policies were eventually abandoned. Manufacturers can still use suggested list prices in dealing with distributors, but vertical price-fixing has become, as the result of court decisions, illegal *per se*. Whether such an antitrust offense will be tolerated by the enforcement authorities is another matter.

When a monopolistic supplier competes with further processors or distributors of its products, it may sometimes be in a position to squeeze the margin of profit of those with whom it is competing. This has been found to have occurred in some industries and alleged to have occurred in others. Solutions to the problem of the vertical price squeeze are requiring a conduct change or ordering some form of dissolution or divestiture.

A seller at one stage of production or distribution can require a buyer at the next stage to purchase more than one product—it may tie in the sale of product B with the sale of product A. In doing this, the seller may be forcing the tie-in in violation of the antitrust laws. A more complete form of tie-in is represented by exclusive dealing. A buyer may be forced not only to buy all the given products of a manufacturer, but may be coerced into reselling only those products. The antitrust laws have been the principal agent through which it is determined which of such arrangements may substantially lessen competition or tend to create a monopoly. Franchising is an operation in which exclusive dealing often becomes part of the arrangements. The complications such arrangements have for the lessee gasoline dealer were presented as a case study. The experience of automobile dealers under the Automobile Dealers Franchise Act of 1956 would not forecast much success for the lessee gasoline dealer in balancing more favorably its bargaining power with that of the refiner-supplier under the Petroleum Marketing Practices Act of 1978.

The use by manufacturers of exclusive territories for their distributors has raised the question of whether the market restrictions involved can be justified if competition is the basic goal of public policy. There are pros and cons to this issue, and the case of soft-drink distribution is an excellent example of the many factors that can be taken into consideration.

APPENDIX

Section 3 of the Clayton Act. 15 U.S. Code, Sec. 14:

That it shall be unlawful for any person engaged in commerce, in the course of such commerce, to lease or make a sale or contract for sale of goods, wares, merchandise, machinery, supplies or other commodities, whether patented or unpatented, for use, consumption, or resale within the United States or any Territory thereof or the District of Columbia or any insular possession or other place under the jurisdiction of the United States, or fix a price charged therefor, or discount from, or rebate upon, such price, on the condition, agreement or understanding that the lessee or purchaser thereof shall not use or deal in the goods, wares, merchandise, machinery, supplies, or other commodities of a competitor or competitors of the lessor or seller, where the effect of such lease, sale, or contract for sale or such condition, agreement or understanding may be to substantially lessen competition or tend to create a monopoly in any line of commerce.

Selected Readings

BOYLE, STANLEY E., "Restructuring the Automobile Industry: 'Exclusive Dealing' as an Unfair Method of Competition under the FTC Act," *Antitrust Law & Economics Review*, 5, no. 1 (Fall 1971), 19–42.

COMANOR, WILLIAM S., "Vertical Territorial and Customer Restrictions: White Motor and Its Aftermath," *Harvard Law Review*, 81, no. 7 (May 1968), 1419–38.

McKIE, J. W., *Tin Can and Tin Plates*. Cambridge, Mass.: Harvard University Press, 1959.

THOMPSON, DONALD N., *Franchise Operations and Antitrust*. Lexington, Mass.: D. C. Heath, 1971.

U.S. Senate, Subcommittee on Antitrust and Monopoly of the Committee on the Judiciary, *Hearings. Exclusive Territorial Allocation Legislation* (Bottling), 92nd Cong., 2nd Sess., Aug. 8, 9, 10, Sept. 12 and 14, 1972. Washington, D.C.: U.S. Government Printing Office, 1973, part 1, pp. 1–575.

YAMEY, B. S., ed., *Resale Price Maintenance*. Chicago: Aldine, 1966

7 — Price Discrimination

The federal antitrust statute most relevant to price discrimination is the Robinson-Patman Act of 1936.[1] This statute amends Section 2 of the Clayton Antitrust Act of 1914. In legally attacking price discrimination, Section 2 of the Sherman Act (attempt to monopolize) and Section 5 of the Federal Trade Commission Act (unfair methods of competition) can also be used.

THE LEGISLATIVE BASE

The Clayton Act (1914)—Objective Section 2 of the Clayton Act made it unlawful to discriminate in price between different purchasers "where the effect of such discrimination may be to substantially lessen competition or tend to create a monopoly in any line of commerce." The principal intent behind that section of law was to be able to reach geographic territorial price discriminations, which were viewed as a serious anticompetitive practice of the time.[2] Large, financially powerful firms

---

[1]In-depth insight into the Robinson-Patman Act can be obtained through the following book-length studies, limitations being set by their date of publication: Corwin D. Edwards (economist), *The Price Discrimination Law: A Review of Experience* (Washington, D.C.: The Brookings Institution, 1959); Frederick M. Rowe (attorney), *Price Discrimination under the Robinson-Patman Act* (Boston: Little, Brown, 1962, with 1964 supplement); Wright Patman (U.S. Senator and co-sponsor of the act), *Complete Guide to the Robinson-Patman Act* (Englewood Cliffs, N.J.: Prentice-Hall, 1963); Earl W. Kintner (attorney and former FTC Commissioner), *A Robinson-Patman Primer: A Businessman's Guide to the Law against Price Discrimination* (New York: Macmillan, 1970).

[2]*FTC v. Anheuser-Busch, Inc.*, 363 U.S. 536, 543 (1960).

could cut prices in selected localities, damaging the ability of other sellers to compete. In more general terms, it was aimed at *primary line* injuries to competition, whereby a seller engaging in price discrimination can impair competition at the seller's level.

Two major weaknesses were found in the language of the Clayton Act. One privoso stated that a discrimination in price "on account of differences in the grade, quantity or quality of the commodity sold" was permissible. The reference to differences in quantity made possible large price differences based on quantity discounts; a small difference in quantity could allow a large difference in price.[3]

A second proviso that proved, as written, to be a weakness was one which stated that a discrimination in price in the same or different communities could be "made in good faith to meet competition." Under this wording retaliatory pricing became legitimate. Only the party initiating a price cut was at fault; those who followed with price cuts were immune. A seller need only show that a competitor was also cutting price.[4]

The Clayton Act proved to suffer from another weakness. In 1923 it was held by a court of appeals not to apply to injury at the *secondary line* of competition, competition among buyers.[5] Although this position was rejected by the Supreme Court in 1929,[6] some doubt had been cast on the ability of the Clayton Act to reach the growing problems of the big buyer demanding and receiving large discounts that gave it an advantage over other buyers who did not receive discounts.[7] It was during this period of 1914 to 1936 that the large chain stores were becoming a growing and challenging institution. The growth of chain stores was "a revolution in distribution."[8] The Robinson-Patman Act was passed largely at the behest of small business groups that were feeling the pressure of this new element and were concerned about injury to competition at the secondary line.

The Robinson-Patman Act (1936)—Objective The Robinson-Patman Act is a much more complex statute than the old Section 2 of the Clayton Act, being divided into six separate sections, Sections 2(a) through 2(f), with Section 2(a) having within it four separate provisos.[9] It tried to specify the particular market practices involving price differentials that were to be ruled out of the marketplace. This attempted codification of

[3]Rowe, *Price Discrimination*, p. 7.
[4]Kintner, *A Robinson-Patman Primer*, p. 8.
[5]*Mennen Co.* v. *FTC*, 288 Fed. 774.
[6]*George Van Camp & Sons Co.* v. *American Can Co., et al.*, 278 U.S. 245.
[7]Patman, *Complete Guide*, p. 8.
[8]U.S. Department of Justice, *Report on the Robinson-Patman Act* (Washington, D.C.: U.S. Government Printing Office, 1977), p. 102.
[9]For the full language of the amended Section 2 of the Clayton Act, see the Appendix to this chapter.

antitrust law provided more fodder for litigation as to exactly what was meant by its several sections and provisos and how they related to one another. Hardly a phrase or clause of the Robinson-Patman Act has gone without litigation as to its proper interpretation.

A brief survey of the several sections of the Robinson-Patman Act is in order. Section 2(a) starts out by stating: "That it shall be unlawful for any person . . . either directly or indirectly, to discriminate in price between different purchasers of commodities of like grade and quality. . . ." Just what is a commodity of "like grade and quality"? Is the same product in different cans with different labels of like grade and quality? The Supreme Court has ruled that it is the physical sameness of the product which provides the basic criterion. The Borden Company was found to be discriminating in price by selling the same canned evaporated milk at two prices, one under its own label and another to which private companies attached their own labels.[10] An appeals court ruled on remand, however, that no injury resulted where the price differential between the two represented no more than consumer preferences between the two.[11]

Next, in addition to including "where the effect of such discrimination may be substantially to lessen competition or tend to create a monopoly in any line of commerce," it adds "or to injure, destroy, or prevent competition with any *person* who either grants or knowingly receives the benefit of such discrimination, or with customers of either of them" [emphasis added]. What has been introduced here is the distinction between an injury to *competition* and injury to a *competitor*. An efficient competitor can be injured by a larger rival that can survive deep price-cutting over a longer period of time or can demand and receive discounts because of its size and bargaining power. An inefficient competitor can be injured where there is effective competition. With the statute specifically referring to injury to an individual competitor, the antitrust enforcement agencies and the courts are put to the task of differentiating between these two possible types of "injury."

The first proviso of Section 2(a) allows price differentials based on "differences in the cost of manufacture, sale, or delivery resulting from the differing methods or quantities in which such commodities are to such purchasers sold or delivered." Although the word "manufacture" is in this proviso, it is relevant only when it affects differing methods of sale or delivery. The burden of showing cost differences falls on the seller.[12] Cost differences have been expected to be based on full costs, not marginal cost, and no carefully defined rules have been established for allocating such

[10]*FTC* v. *Borden Co.*, 383 U.S. 637 (1966).
[11]*Borden Co.* v. *FTC*, 381 F. 2d (1967).
[12]*FTC* v. *Morton Salt Co.*, 334 U.S. 37 (1948).

costs. The Federal Trade Commission, the principal agency handling price discrimination cases, has set such high cost-study standards that few firms have been able to justify their price differentials on this basis.[13]

The second proviso of Section 2(a) permits the FTC to establish quantity limits to discounts "where it finds that available purchasers in greater quantities are so few as to render differentials on account thereof unjustly discriminatory or promotive of monopoly." In other words, even though cost savings may support large quantity discounts, the Commission may prevent them from playing their part in the marketplace if it sees a monopolistic market structure evolving. It has tried to apply this principle only once, in the case of replacement automobile tires, setting a quantity limit at one carload (20,000 pounds).[14] It lost a challenge to this rule in the courts on a legal technicality; it never specified how many is "few."[15]

The third proviso of Section 2(a) is a repeat of the original Clayton Act's statement that sellers can select their own customers so long as it is not in restraint of trade.

The fourth proviso of Section 2(a) permits price changes "from time to time" which result from changes in the marketability of goods, including perishability, obsolescence of seasonal goods, distress sales under court order, or discontinuance of the sale of certain goods. This proviso thus permits price differences over time and does not freeze the price of goods as far as charges of price discrimination are concerned.

Section 2(b) allows a firm in a price discrimination case to rebut the charge on the grounds that the "lower price . . . was made in good faith to meet an equally low price of a competitor, or the services or facilities furnished by a competitor." This is a substantive, not just a procedural, defense; that is, such a good-faith price difference is legal even though there is a substantial lessening of competition.[16] But what constitutes a good-faith meeting of competition and what constitutes a bad-faith meeting of competition? We examine this question in a separate section below.

To sum up, Sections 2(a) and 2(b) provide four possible defenses to a charge of price discrimination: that there was not a likely injury to competition (the doctrine of incipiency would have to be considered); that there were legitimate cost differences justifying a price differential; that the price discrimination was made in good faith to meet the equally low price of a competitor; and that there were changes in the marketability of the goods.

Sections 2(c), 2(d), and 2(e) deal with those marketing practices that were seen to be indirect price discriminations which injured competition at

---

[13]A case-by-case analysis of cost defenses attempted under the Robinson-Patman Act can be found in Herbert F. Taggart, *Cost Justification* (Ann Arbor: Bureau of Business Research, University of Michigan, 1959).

[14]Federal Trade Commission Quantity Limit Rule 203-1, January 4, 1952.

[15]*B. F. Goodrich Co.* v. *FTC*, 134 F. Supp. 39 (1955), affirmed, 242 F. 2d 31 (1957).

[16]*Standard Oil Co.* v. *FTC*, 340 U.S. 231 (1951).

the secondary line. They are concerned with brokerage payments, promotional allowances, and the furnishing of services and facilities to buyers. Section 2(f) makes a buyer equally as liable as the seller. We examine these sections below when we discuss the problem of injury to competition at the secondary line.

The Robinson-Patman Act includes a criminal section (Section 3) which states that it is illegal to discriminate against competitors of a purchaser, or to sell at lower prices in one part of the country than those elsewhere in the country "for the purpose of destroying competition, or eliminating a competitor in such part of the United States," or to sell goods "at unreasonably low prices for the purpose of destroying competition or eliminating a competitor." As a criminal statute, it provides for up to $5000 in fines and one year imprisonment. But it is outside the jurisdiction of the FTC, and it cannot be used as the basis for private treble damage suits because it is technically not a part of the antitrust laws.[17] As a result, it has lain largely dormant.

INJURY TO PRIMARY LINE COMPETITION

Injury to competition at the primary line is represented by injury being inflicted by a discriminating seller against another seller. This event is captured well by the phrase "predatory competition." Geographic price discrimination can provide a classic illustration of predatory competition. In its simplest form, a financially powerful firm that sells in more than one part of the nation will single out a particular area in which there is a smaller seller and selectively cut price in that market. The large firm has staying power; the small firm does not. If the selective price cuts are deep enough, the small firm will be driven out of business or forced to come to some terms with the predator. History books continually cite this type of predatory price-cutting as one of the principal means used by John D. Rockefeller in the latter part of the nineteenth century to create the Standard Oil monopoly.[18]

Geographic price discrimination is not the only kind of discriminatory pricing behavior through which one seller can injure another. A large multiproduct firm can deliberately price one product at a level that does not represent a full allocation of joint costs to it. Aimed at an independent firm which produces only that one product, this discriminatory pricing can

[17]*Nashville Milk Co.* v. *Carnation Co.*, 355 U.S. 373; and *Safeway Stores, Inc.* v. *Vance*, 355 U.S. 389 (1958). The constitutionality of Section 3 was upheld in *U.S.* v. *National Dairy Products Corp.*, 372 U.S. 29 (1963).

[18]For an attempt to disprove this thesis on the basis of the full record in the Standard Oil antitrust case, see John S. McGee, "Predatory Price Cutting: The Standard Oil (N.J.) Case," *Journal of Law and Economics*, 1 (October 1958), 137-86.

drive the independent from the marketplace. Such pricing can be very difficult to detect. A large firm can argue that it merely enjoys economies of scale. Finally, a large firm can practice price discrimination within the same market by more than meeting a rival's price to individual customers.

How Prevalent Is Predatory Price Discrimination? How common is predatory price discrimination? It has been argued that predatory price-cutting is irrational, because once a competitor is driven from the market and price is raised to a higher level, a new competitor (or the same old one) will enter the market, leaving the would-be monopolist in the same position as before, and suffering the losses of the attempt. Such thinking assumes that there are no real barriers to entry. Certainly, when the real assets of the firm that has been driven from the market remain, reentry should be relatively easy. Perhaps even easier, for the price of these assets may be reduced through resale. When there are barriers, however, the monopolistic firm may well be able to earn profits over a period of time which, when discounted, will more than offset the losses, or lower profits, sustained during the period of price-cutting. This is assumed to be the aim of predatory price-cutting. Nevertheless, the record of successful instances of predatory price-cutting is slim.[19]

Predatory pricing need not have as its immediate objective the elimination of a competitor. The purpose may be, rather, to persuade a competitor to merge. Or it may be to induce the competitor to cooperate in some monopolistic plan, such as collusive price-fixing or agreed-upon market shares. The would-be predatee may receive advance warning of the proposed predatory action in the form of a threat. In such an instance, overt predatory behavior may never actually take place. Instead, a merger may occur or a collusive scheme may become more effectively activated.[20] This may help account for why there are relatively few proved cases of predatory competition, even though collusive schemes and some mergers are themselves illegal.

Evidence of Predatory Pricing What economic evidence will support a charge of predatory price-cutting by a large firm? Cutting price below cost is frequently cited as the necessary evidence to be procured. But what cost? Marginal cost? Variable cost? Total cost? Short-run cost? Long-run cost?

Areeda and Turner recommended in a 1975 *Harvard Law Review* article that a price below reasonably anticipated short-run average variable cost be

---

[19]Roland H. Koller II, "The Myth of Predatory Pricing: An Empirical Study," *Antitrust Law & Economics Review*, 4, no. 4 (Summer 1971), 105–23.

[20]See, for example, the illustration of the Federal Pacific Electric Company, as presented in the case study of the electrical equipment conspiracies in Chapter 3.

used as a standard for predatory pricing.[21] They would have preferred to utilize short-run marginal cost because marginal cost pricing is supposed to yield the socially optimal competitive allocation of resources. But since accounting determination of marginal cost is difficult to come by, they decided to utilize average variable cost as a surrogate.[22] A price below average variable cost would be conclusively presumed to be illegal predation, and this principle would apply to price discrimination, whether the discrimination were between different geographic markets or in the same market. Promotional pricing would be available as a defense, but it would be considered predatory when timed to coincide with entry or promotion by a rival.

Assuming that pricing below average variable cost represents predatory behavior is according to analytical expectations. A competitive firm will ordinarily shut down if it cannot cover its variable costs of operation. If it is selling below average total cost but above average variable cost, it can minimize its losses by continuing to operate. But to continue to operate when not covering variable costs would cause losses to be greater than if the firm were to shut down and not operate at all. Thus pricing below average variable cost in itself can provide the basis for necessary intent of predatory pricing.

Areeda and Turner go one step further and say that a price at or above reasonably anticipated short-run average variable cost should be conclusively presumed to be lawful. Such a price would be deemed lawful whether or not it were a profit-maximizing or a loss-minimizing price. A firm selling at a price below average total cost, even though it could be maximizing profits at a higher price above average total cost, would not be found guilty of predatory pricing. Their logic is based on the impact of such pricing on resource allocation. A price equal to marginal cost that is below average total cost would represent less wasted excess capacity than that accompanying a higher price above average cost. An equally efficient firm with less staying power would thus be sacrificed to the better resource allocation.[23]

In Figure 7.1 a monopolist intent solely on maximizing short-run profits would set its price at p_1 (determined by the equating of MC to MR). This price would yield an economic profit, since that price is greater than the firm's average total cost. Such a price could very well attract new entry, however, since above normal profits would be being earned; it would depend on the height of any barriers to entry. At the threat of any possible new entry, the monopolist might decide to try to dissuade such an attempt

---

[21]Phillip Areeda and Donald F. Turner, "Predatory Pricing and Related Practices under Section 2 of the Sherman Act," *Harvard Law Review*, 88, no. 4 (February 1975), 697–733.

[22]Ibid., pp. 716–18.

[23]Ibid., p. 710.

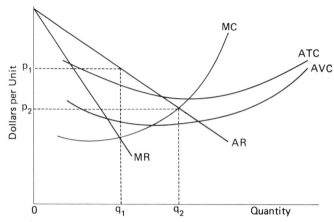

Figure 7.1 Alternative Monopoly Pricing

by pricing where price equals marginal cost. As we show in Figure 7.1, this price, p_2, no longer covers average total cost (a normal profit is not being earned), but is above average variable cost. Areeda and Turner would condone such pricing because the monopolist, although now utilizing its resources more fully, still has some excess capacity (is still producing on the declining portion of the average total cost curve). Any new entry would, according to them, only contribute to a further waste of resources.

Selling below average total cost but above average variable cost could, under some circumstances, be considered to be predatory and unacceptable even from a resource allocation point of view. A financially weaker yet more efficient firm might be excluded. The firm being excluded might be one whose long-run average costs (including depreciation, interest, cost of equity capital, overhead expenses, and any other costs treated as fixed costs in the short run) are less than those of the firm whose pricing is forcing it out of business or inducing it not to attempt entry.[24] But intent to exclude a financially weaker, although even more efficient, firm could not be conclusively presumed from such pricing. Demand, for example, could be temporarily, or over a longer period, inadequate to support a price equal to or greater than short-run average total cost. It would be necessary to analyze all the demand-supply conditions of the market, especially the existence or nonexistence of any excess industry capacity.

Difficult as it may be to identify intent, it should be helpful to understand the intent in arriving at the truth with respect to some pricing actions by large firms. F. M. Scherer views the problem as one of *long-run* allocative efficiency, and holds that it is important to try to understand the intent

[24]See Richard Posner, *Antitrust Law: An Economic Perspective* (Chicago: The University of Chicago Press, 1976), pp. 189–93.

of the alleged predators just as it is important to understand all the circumstances surrounding the alleged predatory behavior.[25] Greer, too, sees it as important to try to understand intent.[26] Intent may be difficult to determine, since business firms and their legal staffs can develop procedures and communications which are successful in covering up any evidence of predatory intent. But that is no reason for failing to make the attempt. If direct evidence cannot be obtained, then an inference can be drawn from circumstantial evidence.

A key issue in analyzing complaints of predatory pricing is to distinguish between, on the one hand, efficient firms that have been intentionally driven out of business in order to remove them as competitors and, on the other hand, firms that have gone or are going out of business because they have not been efficient enough to survive the competition. Predatory pricing can be defined as pricing designed to exclude from the market an equally or more efficient competitor.[27] An antitrust effort that mistakes the inability of a firm to survive the competition because of inefficiency for victimization of predatory pricing can itself be contributing to a misallocation of resources.

GEOGRAPHIC PRICE DISCRIMINATION—*A CASE STUDY*

The theory of geographic price discrimination is easily stated, as we have seen. An examination of individual cases involving that concept reveals that the facts of alleged discriminatory pricing can vary considerably from case to case. So can the fundamental reasoning of court decisions. Each case seems to have its own peculiarities. Questions to be kept in mind in reviewing the cases are these: How was predation measured? Was predatory intent identifiable? If so, was the evidence of intent direct, or was intent inferred from circumstances? Did the final resolution of the case by the courts succeed in protecting competition? Or did it protect individual competitors from competition?

We will draw on certain older court cases which the FTC has called leading cases on the subject,[28] the Supreme Court's controversial decision in the *Utah Pie* case,[29] and certain decisions postdating Areeda and Turner's groundbreaking article on the subject, which attempts to make decision-making as to guilt follow a standard formula.

[25]F. M. Scherer, "Predatory Pricing and the Sherman Act: A Comment," *Harvard Law Review*, 89, no. 5 (March 1976), 869–90.

[26]Douglas F. Greer, "A Critique of Areeda and Turner's Standards for Predatory Practices," *Antitrust Bulletin*, 24, no. 2 (Summer 1979), 233–61.

[27]Posner, *Antitrust Law*, p. 188.

[28]*Anheuser-Busch, Inc.* v. *FTC*, 289 F. 2d 835, 841–42 (1961).

[29]*Utah Pie Co.* v. *Continental Baking Co. et al.*, 386 U.S. 685 (1967).

Case 1. *E. B. Muller & Co.* **v.** *FTC (1944)*[30]   In this case the FTC charged two sellers with unfair methods of competition in violation of Section 5 of the Federal Trade Commission Act and with unlawful discrimination in price in violation of the Robinson-Patman Act. The relevant industry was that of granulated chicory, a product sometimes mixed with coffee as blend or as filler. The time was the middle 1930s. The firms in this industry were only three in number. The two largest were interlocked by family and stockholdings and in effect were one enterprise with "unitary domination and control." Further, one (Franck) sold primarily in bulk, the other (Muller) primarily as packaged goods. Franck sold through brokers, Muller through traveling salesmen. The net worth of the two largest firms together was about 30 times as great as that of the third and smallest firm (Schanzer).

Schanzer was located in New Orleans and sold only in the New Orleans, or southern, trade area (Florida, Alabama, Mississippi, Louisiana, Texas, and Tennessee). Seventy-five percent of Franck's sales and 40 percent of Muller's sales were in the southern trade area, where 75 percent of all domestic chicory sold in the United States was consumed. Imports were insignificant.

Franck and Muller initiated price cuts in the southern trade area, leaving prices elsewhere unchanged. The FTC charged deliberate intent to destroy their only competitor. What was the evidence of the intent? Franck and Muller sold "below cost" in the New Orleans trade area, and these losses were recouped by sales in other parts of the nation. The price cuts were not greatly below cost, but Schanzer did suffer a loss. The court held, however, that losses to the victim of the predation need not be shown; a purpose of the Federal Trade Commission Act was to stop unfair methods of competition in their incipiency. It upheld the FTC.

Evidence before the FTC and the court as to intent was more complete and compelling than just the geographic price discrimination. Correspondence between Franck and Muller spoke of "putting a crimp into him wherever possible" and "hope we can, as you expect, eliminate him entirely, by making prices that he cannot meet without losing money." In addition, Franck and Muller not only made disparaging and false statements about Schanzer to the trade, but also were making false statements about their own products. Their hands were unclean, too, in that they were admittedly practicing personal discrimination among firms and were obtaining illegal freight rate rebates and making falsified billings on freight shipments.

Case 2. *Moore* **v.** *Mead's Fine Bread Co. (1954)*[31]   A local baker (Moore) in a small town in New Mexico (Santa Rosa) sued a corporation in

---

[30]33 F.T.C. 24 (1941); 142 F. 2d 54.
[31]348 U.S. 115.

the baking business in a nearby city in New Mexico for treble damages. The latter corporation was one of several having interlocking ownership and management and operating in several towns and cities in Texas and New Mexico (the Mead companies). The charge was a violation of both Sections 2(a) and 3 of the Robinson-Patman Act.

The small-town baker had threatened to relocate in another town, but the local merchants agreed to purchase his products exclusively to keep him from moving. The larger corporation considered this action to be a boycott and reduced the wholesale price of its bread in Santa Rosa from 14 to 7 cents for its pound loaf and from 21 to 11 cents for its pound-and-a-half loaf. The Mead companies did not cut price in any other locality.

The price war in Santa Rosa lasted seven months. The local baker was finally forced to close down. The court held that the destruction of a competitor had been clearly established as required by Section 2(a), and the evidence was clear that the purpose of the discriminatory price-cutting was to eliminate a competitor, as required by Section 3.

Case 3. *The Maryland Baking Company* **v.** *FTC (1957)* [32]   In this case the FTC charged one of the largest ice cream cone manufacturers in the nation, Maryland Baking, with lowering price in one geographic area where there was only one small competitor, Sandler, while maintaining higher prices elsewhere, with the purpose of eliminating Sandler from the market. The product in question was rolled sugar cones. Sandler was operating in the Washington-Baltimore market and was the sole competitor of Maryland Baking in that market. At the time of the initial discriminatory price cut, Sandler, which had been selling only rolled sugar cones, had begun to enter the cake cone business. Maryland Baking was selling not only rolled sugar cones but also three other types of ice cream cones: chocolate-coated rolled sugar cones, cake cones, and cake cups.

Maryland Baking lowered its price for rolled sugar cones in the Washington-Baltimore area in 1951 from $6.66 per thousand to $5.00, leaving its price at $7.16 in the Philadelphia-Maryland-New Jersey area. This price decrease was apparently triggered off in retaliation for Sandler's entry into the cake cone business. Sandler responded by lowering its price of rolled sugar cones from $6.80 to $6.00. But by 1954 Sandler had lost much of its rolled sugar cone jobber-distributor business to Maryland Baking. On the other hand, its total business had increased substantially as Sandler shifted its selling efforts to selling direct to drugstores and other customers of those distributors and expanded its chocolate-coated rolled sugar cone business (sales to ice cream manufacturers who prefilled them and then sold them to retail outlets).

The FTC and the appeals court held that Maryland Baking had violated Section 2(a) of the Robinson-Patman Act. Testimony before the FTC

[32]52 F.T.C. 1679 (1956); 243 F. 2d 716.

elicited the information that a "declared purpose" of the price cuts was to drive this competitor out of business. In fact, Sandler's share of the rolled sugar cone market of the Washington-Baltimore area declined from 91.3 percent to 58.2 percent. The Commission emphasized that, although Sandler had a major share of this business prior to the discriminatory price-cutting, his was still a small business relative to his large competitor's. According to the FTC, the declared purpose to eliminate a competitor was not essential to a finding of illegality. The appeals court relied, however, on both the purpose of the price cuts and the fact that the small firm had lost about half of that part of its business to the large competitor.

Case 4. *Utah Pie Co.* v. *Continental Baking Co., et al. (1967)*[33] In this case before the Supreme Court a relatively small family-run local producer of frozen pies (Utah Pie) sued three nationwide multiplant producers of food products (Continental Baking, Pet Milk, and Carnation Company) for treble damages. A jury awarded Utah Pie damages under Section 2 (a) of the Robinson-Patman Act but denied any awards for charges of conspiracy in violation of Sections 1 and 2 of the Sherman Act. An appeals court reversed the Robinson-Patman Act decision, but the Supreme Court in turn reversed and sided with the jury.

The scene was the Salt Lake City frozen fruit pie (apple, cherry, boysenberry, peach, pumpkin, and mince) market. The time was the years 1958 through most of 1961. The three large baking companies were already in this market, bringing product from some distance away, principally from California, when Utah Pie entered in late 1957. Utah Pie had been producing and selling fresh pies for 30 years in its Salt Lake City plant, but entered the frozen pie market with a new plant at that time.

Utah Pie, with a natural location advantage, entered the frozen pie market at a price below the going prices of the three large bakeries. The three larger companies reacted by lowering their prices and met, or on occasion more than met, the prices of the smaller company. Utah Pie's reaction was to lower its prices even more. Over the four-year period, frozen pie prices tended downward. The Supreme Court viewed this as a "deteriorating price structure." Between 1958 and 1961 Utah Pie's price went from $4.15 per dozen when it entered the market to $2.75 when it filed the suit. Pet's price, $4.92 at the start, dropped to $3.46 in 1961. Carnation's price went from $4.82 to $3.46. And Continental's price went from $5.00 to a low of $2.85.

The discrimination existed in the difference between the prices the three large bakeries were receiving in Salt Lake City and those they received elsewhere closer to their own plants. For several months of the period, Pet and Carnation were selling at prices lower than those received in California, Carnation's being 20 cents to 50 cents lower. The transport

---

[33]386 U.S. 685.

cost from California to Salt Lake City was 30 to 35 cents. Continental and Carnation were selling below cost, this being defined in the case of Continental as being a price less than direct cost plus an allocation for overhead, which could be interpreted as meaning below average total cost. Pet's losses were described as being greater than those it was suffering elsewhere.

What was the impact on Utah Pie's profibability? Curiously enough, it showed a fairly steady dollar profit throughout the four-year period. It did lose a certain share of the market, however. Utah Pie's market share dropped from 66.5 percent in 1958 to 34.3 percent in 1959, but recovered in 1960 and 1961 to 45.5 percent and 45.3 percent, respectively. One can say that its dominant and successful market share when it entered the market for the first time had been trimmed a bit. Furthermore, the market was a rapidly expanding one, from total frozen pie sales of 57,060 dozen in 1958 to 266,908 dozen in 1961.

What convinced the Supreme Court of there being a probable eventual injury to competition in this case was the economic philosophy that the Robinson-Patman Act was designed to reach price discrimination which "erodes" competition as much as that which has an "immediate destructive impact." In short, the Court was applying the doctrine of incipiency without evidence of any real actual injury. It did, however, see what it viewed as predatory intent in the use by Pet on one occasion of an industrial spy and reference by Pet's management to Utah Pie as an "unfavorable factor" which "dug holes in our operation" and posed a constant "check" on performance.

This singular Supreme Court decision has been viewed by some observers as having had an adverse impact on competition because it protected a competitor at the expense of competition.[34] Two Supreme Court Justices strongly dissented for this same reason. Yet such protection for the small firm cannot ensure survival. Utah Pie went out of business in 1972, but not without first experiencing management and product quality problems as one generation of a family replaced another. The firm was sold shortly before going bankrupt.[35]

Case 5. *International Air Industries, Inc. and Vebco, Inc. v. American Excelsior Company (1975)*[36]   The bigger of the two antagonists in this case was American Excelsior Company (AMXCO), the world's largest producer of cooler pads used in evaporative air conditioners, with its principal place of business in Arlington, Texas. It sold this product throughout the Southwest and Far West through distributors, except for direct sales to

[34]See especially Ward S. Bowman, "Restraint of Trade by the Supreme Court: The Utah Pie Case," *Yale Law Journal*, 77, no. 1 (November 1967), 70–85.
[35]Kenneth G. Elzinga and Thomas F. Hogarty, "Utah Pie and the Consequences of Robinson-Patman," *Journal of Law and Economics*, 21, no. 2 (October 1978), 427–34.
[36]517 F. 2d 714; certiorari denied, 424 U.S. 943 (1976).

"national accounts." The smaller firm was Vebco, primarily a distributor of heating and air-conditioning equipment. Vebco sold only AMXCO cooling pads from 1953 to 1969, but in the latter year developed a production capability of its own for cooling pads and began to compete with AMXCO. AMXCO then terminated the distributor relationship with Vebco. Vebco's principal place of business was El Paso, Texas, and it sold primarily in Arizona, New Mexico, and West Texas.

The cooling pad competition in this Southwest market was composed of AMXCO, Vebco, Southwest Industries, and numerous small-scale producers. AMXCO and Southwest Industries produced a machine-made cooling pad. Vebco and the other manufacturers produced a handmade product. Hand- and machine-made were interchangeable in use; but the machine-made could be produced, transported, and stored more cheaply. The existence of numerous small-scale producers produced evidence of ease of entry.

The two competitors met head-on in competing for the business of discount houses, and discounts granted to buyers went as high as 39.25 percent. Vebco sued, claiming discriminatory pricing in violation of Section 2(a) of the Robinson-Patman Act and Section 2 of the Sherman Act. Vebco charged, and AMXCO admitted, that AMXCO's prices were lower in the El Paso area than in other areas in which it sold. It was not that Vebco was being driven out of business; actually, its sales had been expanding until the year it sued. But it did claim lost profits.

The court, with credits to Areeda and Turner's contemporary article in the *Harvard Law Review* and to Paul Samuelson's eighth edition of *Economics*, decided that AMXCO's cost-price relationships in the El Paso market area were to be the crucial standard. As long as AMXCO's price in that geographic area was above average variable cost and there were no significant barriers to entry, it did not matter whether AMXCO's price was higher in other areas. More completely put, the court said that a case would be made for predation in the particular local market if (1) price was below average variable cost or (2) it was below a short-run profit-maximizing price where barriers to entry were such as to enable the discriminating seller to recover the lost profits before new entry could come about. In studying the price and cost data available to it, the court found that the price in question was actually above average total cost, even though barriers to entry were "virtually nonexistent." Thus, there was no predation. The appeals court upheld the lower court's (jury) decision in favor of AMXCO.

Case 6. *Janich Bros., Inc.* v. *The American Distilling Co.* (1977)[37] This case was a treble damage suit by a California rectifier of

[37]570 F. 2d 848; certiorari denied, 439 U.S. 829 (1978).

alcoholic beverages (Janich) against a nationwide distiller (American Distilling). Janich charged American Distilling with violating Section 2 of the Sherman Act and Section 2(a) of the Robinson-Patman Act. More specifically, it charged that American Distilling was engaging in predatory conduct in attempting to monopolize the California market by maintaining lower prices for certain liquors in California than it did in the rest of the nation.

A jury in a district court ruled against Janich. The appeals court agreed with the lower court. Three issues became part of the appeal. The first was that of selling below cost in California. The court held that, if American Distilling's price in California were to be an illegal discriminatory price, it would have to be shown to be below average variable cost. Ideally, said the court, prices below marginal cost would be the best measure of illegal prices for antitrust purposes. But since marginal cost data are not readily available from conventional accounting records, the judge accepted Areeda and Turner's suggestion that average variable cost be used instead.

Evidence was submitted showing that the relevant prices were below "cost of merchandise sold." That cost figure turned out to include some fixed as well as variable costs; namely, plant depreciation, real estate and personal property taxes, and business licenses. A price below "cost of merchandise sold" was thus not necessarily a price below average variable cost. This evidence therefore failed to support Janich's position.

A second issue was that of the relevant product. American Distilling had been selling half-gallons of gin below cost (as defined above) from 1963 to 1968 and half-gallons of vodka below cost from 1964 to 1968 in California. The court viewed the relevant product as being a full line of liquors. Pricing only a certain size bottle of certain liquors at a predatory level would not be enough to drive rivals out of business.

The third issue was that of direct evidence of predatory intent. Janich had wanted to present a witness who would have testified that he had been told by an American Distilling salesman that the latter had had conversations with an executive of the company to the effect that American Distilling was going to lower gin and vodka prices in California in order to put the rectifiers there out of business and then increase prices. Far from providing good direct evidence of intent, that would-be witness would have provided "incurable hearsay." This offer of evidence was therefore rejected.

Case 7. *O. Hommel Co.* v. *Ferro Corp. (1979)* [38]   In this case a manufacturer of frit (an ingredient in porcelain enamel and ceramic finishings) charged a competitor with geographic price discrimination under Section 2 of the Sherman Act and Section 2(a) of the Robinson-Patman Act. The

[38]472 F. Supp. 793.

competitor, it was alleged, was subsidizing below-cost prices in the United States from profits obtained in foreign markets in which the complaining competitor was not operating.

In this decision a motion for summary judgment by the defendant was denied by a district court. Certain principles were enunciated, however. First, the Robinson-Patman Act does not apply to price discrimination between domestic and foreign markets. Second, if the case were to be pursued under the Sherman Act, it would have to be shown that the alleged predator had a specific intent to monopolize and the requisite power "to create a dangerous probability of success." Third, that intent could be inferred from a showing of predatory intent which, in turn, could be determined by showing predatory pricing. What then was the test of predatory pricing?

The court pointed out that the recent trend in the circuit courts was to utilize Areeda and Turner's basic rule that prices below marginal or average variable cost were the appropriate test of predatory pricing.[39] It went on to say, however, that these courts seemed to be ignoring the test of the *Utah Pie* decision of the Supreme Court, which had utilized pricing below fully allocated costs (average total cost). If the Supreme Court had established that test, why should the circuit courts rely instead on an article in the *Harvard Law Review*?

The general principle adopted by this court was that, whereas the marginal or average variable cost test "may be a more accurate economic indicator of predatory intent in some cases," such intent could also be inferred in some circumstances (not specified) by prices below average total cost. The plaintiff could therefore submit evidence of that latter cost-price relationship in a trial.[40] A basic reason for not fully accepting the marginal or average variable cost rule was that "Areeda and Turner's analysis . . . has not survived unscathed." That is to say, it had been subjected to considerable criticism by scholars who had offered alternative views on predatory pricing.[41] Through their writings, especially in law journals, scholars can have considerable influence on public policy as made by the courts. Disagreements among the scholars, however, may also contribute to disagreements among the judges.

[39]Citing *Janich Bros., Inc.* v. *American Distilling Co.*, 570 F. 2d 848 (9th Cir. 1977); *Pacific Engineering* v. *Kerr-McGee*, 551 F. 2d 790 (10th Cir. 1977); *Hanson* v. *Shell Oil Co.*, 541 F. 2d 1352 (9th Cir. 1976); *International Air Industries, Inc.* v. *American Excelsior Co.*, 517 F. 2d 714 (5th Cir. 1975).

[40]A jury trial resulted in an award of $1.5 million damages trebled plus attorney fees, a total of approximately $5 million. The third circuit court of appeals reversed, however, in September of 1981, finding no evidence of a lessening of competition in what it considered to be non-geographic selective price discrimination. It held that evidence of below-average cost pricing is not enough in itself to condemn. Trade Cases para. 64,264 (1981).

[41]For a full panoply of the academic debate on the tests for predatory pricing, see the array of scholarly articles in *The Journal of Reprints for Antitrust Law and Economics*, 10, no. 1 (1980).

MEETING THE COMPETITION

Section 2(b) of the Robinson-Patman Act provides a defense against a charge of price discrimination. A seller can rebut a *prima facie* case against him "by showing that his lower price or the furnishing of services or facilities to any purchaser or purchasers was made in good faith to meet an equally low price of a competitor, or the services or facilities furnished by a competitor." This is an absolute defense. Even if competition may be substantially lessened, it is still a defense.[42]

The "Erosion" Theory of Oligopoly Pricing   On the face of it, it seems unfair that a large seller could be legitimately charging one customer a lower price than it is charging other customers when all those customers are competitors. A theory of oligopolistic competition does exist to justify this pricing, however. Sometimes referred to as the "erosion" theory, it holds that such price discrimination provides the initial break in what would otherwise be rigid and stable oligopolistic prices. It may be the only real catalyst for price competition, since an oligopolistic seller may be willing to cut price to hold a customer or even to obtain a new customer if this is done on a sporadic basis and the seller is not forced to lower price to all customers in the market. But sporadic price cuts to meet an equally low price of a competitor are likely, over time, to become known to other buyers. The seller is then forced to grant the same lower price to others, and prices break and decline to a new lower level. Professor Adelman has described this process as being a highly dynamic force: "*Sporadic, unsystematic* discrimination is one of the most powerful forces of competition in modern industrial markets. Like a high wind, it seizes on small openings and crevices in an orderly price structure and tears it apart."[43]

Critics of this theory point to two possible weaknesses in this theory. First, it is said that there is no real empirical evidence to support the theory.[44] Second, some small businesses may be seriously injured during the time required before the process can be completed, if it is completed at all.[45]

Defensive v. Offensive Meeting of Competition   The law of Section 2(b) clearly allows the meeting of competition defense when it is used defensively to retain an old customer. Does it also apply to offensive or

[42]*Standard Oil Co. v. FTC*, 340 U.S. 231 (1951).

[43]M. Adelman, "Effective Competition and the Antitrust Laws," *Harvard Law Review*, 61, no. 3 (September 1948), 1331–32. © (1948) by the Harvard Law Review Association.

[44]See Vernon A. Mund, *Recent Efforts to Amend or Repeal the Robinson-Patman Act, Hearings before the Ad Hoc Subcommittee on Antitrust, the Robinson-Patman Act, and Related Matters of the House Committee on Small Business*, 94th Cong., 2nd Sess., 1976, Part 3, p. 56.

[45]See Ronald H. Wolf and Vernon A. Mund, *Business and Government* (n.p.: Advocate Publishing Group, 1980), p. 187.

"aggressive" discriminatory pricing designed to win new customers? The FTC had taken the position that the Section 2(b) defense is applicable only to the retention of old customers, and it had been upheld in that position by a court of appeals.[46] Three later courts of appeal decisions have, however, rejected that position, and one of them overturned an FTC order.[47]

One problem in limiting the defense to the retention of old customers is the difficulty in distinguishing between old and new customers. In a highly competitive market, the same buyer could be a particular seller's customer one day, not the next, but then again the following day. Certainly, the "erosion" theory would be more likely to function better where sellers would be allowed to discriminate in price offensively as well as defensively. The 1955 *Report of the Attorney General's National Committee to Study the Antitrust Laws* stated that limiting the meeting of competition defense to holding existing customers "would not be in keeping with elementary principles of competition, and would in fact foster tight and rigid commercial relationships by insulating them from market forces."[48]

Sporadic v. Systematic Meeting of Competition   In applying Section 2(b) to the marketplace, several questions have had to be answered. First, when is the meeting of a competitor's equally low price done in "good faith"? Are there circumstances when the meeting of a competitor's price is not in good faith? The distinction that has to be made is between sporadic and systematic price discrimination. *Sporadic* price discrimination occurs when a seller from time to time meets, as required by competitive market conditions, competitors' lower prices. It includes the holding of old customers and the aggressive seeking out of new customers. In contrast, *systematic* discrimination involves a collusive system of pricing or even some long-standing oligopolistic discriminatory pricing pattern. What appears to be sporadic price discrimination may have to be examined closely to see whether it really represents competitive forces at work. Clearly, systematic price discrimination can be assumed to be illegal under the antitrust laws.

Basing-point pricing is clearly illegal under Section 2(b). The meeting of competitors' prices under such a system of pricing by absorbing freight is all part of a collusive system of uniform delivered prices. The FTC's successful suit against this delivered pricing system involving the whole cement industry used Sections 2(a) and 2(b) of the Robinson-Patman Act, as well as Section 5 of the Federal Trade Commission Act, to break up the

---

[46]*Standard Motor Products, Inc.* v. *FTC*, 265 F. 2d 674 (1959, 2nd Circuit), certiorari denied, 361 U.S. 826 (1959).

[47]*Sunshine Biscuits, Inc.* v. *FTC*, 306 F. 2d 48 (1962, 7th Circuit); *Hanson* v. *Pittsburgh Plate Glass Indus., Inc.*, 482 F. 2d 220 (1973, 5th Circuit); *Cadigan* v. *Texaco, Inc.*, 492 F. 2d 383 (1974, 9th Circuit).

[48]Washington, D.C.: U.S. Government Printing Office, p. 184.

system in that industry.[49] The courts nevertheless have said that absorbing freight truly to meet the competition is not illegal. So the problem remains: how to distinguish between freight absorption done on a sporadic basis and that done on a systematic (collusive) basis.

Likewise, an individual seller cannot follow an unlawful system of pricing practiced by a competitor. The A. E. Staley Manufacturing Company, a seller of corn syrup, was found to be in violation of Section 2(b) when it followed the pricing system of the Corn Products Refining Company.[50] Corn Products was basing its prices to customers using Chicago as the base point from which freight charges were added in calculating the delivered price to a customer, no matter where the shipments originated. Staley, located in Decatur in central Illinois, adopted Corn Products' pricing system. It claimed it was meeting the competition. Staley's charging customers higher prices the closer the customer was located to Decatur vis-à-vis Chicago does not make logical sense, and the court found the practice to be a violation of Section 2(b) as well as of 2(a).

The so-called *Standard-Detroit* case well illustrates how the same facts can be interpreted differently by different viewers of those facts.[51] Standard Oil (Indiana) was charging four "jobbers" (jobber-retailers) gasoline tankcar prices 1.5 cents less than the tankwagon prices it was charging its own retail customers in the Detroit area. Standard said it was meeting the competitive price of other major and local suppliers in order to keep its jobber customers. These customers were threatening to change suppliers if they were not given the discount. The FTC held that the lower prices to the jobbers were part of a system of pricing. But it did not make it very clear just what that system was. It referred to Standard Oil's jobber prices as being similar to the jobber prices of Gulf Oil, the Texas Company, and Shell Oil; yet it had dismissed similar pending cases against those three major oil company suppliers. It objected to Standard's continued use of this "pricing standard," which seemed to be described as the granting of tankcar prices to those resellers who had bulk plant facilities that could accept tankcar-size deliveries, purchased more than one million gallons annually, and had distribution equipment and a satisfactory credit rating.

Both the court of appeals and the Supreme Court failed to find anything systematic about this pricing. They saw the price differences as being the result of competition. After all, there had been considerable haggling over price, Standard had previously lost three jobber customers by not meeting "pirating" offers, and the pricing was within the context of a

[49]FTC v. *Cement Institute*, 333 U.S. 683 (1948). Earlier cases involving individual companies are *Corn Products Refining Company* v. FTC, 324 U.S. 726 (1945), and *FTC v. A. E. Staley Manufacturing Co.*, 324 U.S. 746 (1945).
[50]Ibid.
[51]*FTC v. Standard Oil Co.*, 49 F.T.C. 923 (1953); 233 F. 2d 649 (1956); 355 U.S. 396 (1958).

major gasoline price war in the Detroit area. Standard was therefore cleared of the charge of pricing according to a discriminatory system.

INJURY TO SECONDARY LINE COMPETITION

Sections 2(c), 2(d), and 2(e) of the Robinson-Patman Act were designed to eliminate injury at the secondary level of competition—that is, among buyers. These three sections of law spotlighted three particular marketing practices thought to be vehicles for price discrimination: brokerage allowances to buyers, payments to buyers for services or facilities provided by the buyers, and the furnishing of services or facilities to the buyers. These price discriminations were indirect, and as such were often difficult to identify, because they did not represent a direct discount or rebate on the price of the goods.

Section 2(f) attempts to place legal responsibility on the buyer. Since a prime objective of the Robinson-Patman Act was to reach the problem of the big buyer, it was felt appropriate to make the buyer, as the recipient of a discriminatory allowance or service, equally as liable as the seller.

Section 2(c). Brokerage Allowances   Brokerage is the fee or commission paid by a seller (or in some situations by a buyer) to an agent, the broker, for bringing the seller in contact with a buyer and consummating a sale. The broker does not take title to the goods; its function is to contact a buyer for the seller and make the sale.

Some large buyers, with wide market contacts and knowledge, were buying direct from sellers, bypassing brokers. They would then request a "brokerage allowance," presumably representing the saving to the seller by bypassing the use of a broker. Depending upon the bargaining power of the buyer, the allowance could be equal to, or more or less than, the brokerage the seller otherwise would have to pay an independent broker.

The purpose of Section 2(c) of the Robinson-Patman Act was to prevent the use of brokerage fees by large buyers, especially chain stores, to cover up discriminatory price reductions. This was often accomplished through the use of dummy brokers. The Great Atlantic & Pacific Tea Company (A&P) was a favorite target for these allegations. Indeed, the Robinson-Patman Act has also been known as the A&P Price Discrimination Act. Yet at least one authority has claimed, after a thorough study of all of the facts, that A&P was receiving less compensation than was justified by its performance of the brokerage function.[52]

Section 2(c) was written to make it illegal for any firm "to pay or

---

[52]M. A. Adelman, *A&P: A Study in Price-Cost Behavior and Public Policy* (Cambridge, Mass.: Harvard University Press, 1959).

grant, or to receive or accept, anything of value as a commission, broker-age, or other compensation, or any allowance or discount in lieu thereof" to or from the other party to the transaction or any agent of the other party if that agent were affiliated in any way with that other party. In short, no brokerage allowance could be paid to any other party except an indepen-dent broker. This prohibition is absolute.[53] The act thus created a protected and preferred position in the marketplace for the independent broker. Such protection can be evaded by buyers who can get sellers to agree to sell to them direct without using brokers in any other sales. Yet it is considered bad law from an economic standpoint, and there are few economists who do not think that this section should be repealed.

Section 2(d). Promotional Allowances   One evil seen as demanding a remedy by statute was the granting of promotional allowances by sellers to some of the larger retailers. Payments would be made to some retailers to help them pay for certain services they were rendering that promoted not only the business of the retailer, but also the product(s) of the supplier. The services rendered toward which suppliers made contributions were primarily advertising in newspapers or on radio or television, but could also be special store displays or demonstrations arranged by the retailer. We will examine below in a case study the various problems to be resolved in attempting to apply controls to cooperative advertising (co-op ads).

Promotional allowances to buyers could mean discrimination not only because just certain buyers received them. Some buyers received larger allowances than others. This was seen to be an indirect price discrimination because the overall result was the same as if a buyer had paid a lower price for the goods.

Assume buyer A and buyer B are competing retailers who are pur-chasing the same amount of product from the same supplier. If retailer A paid $5000 for an advertisement in the local newspapers and received a co-op payment of $2500 from its supplier while retailer B paid $5000 for an advertisement and received a co-op payment of a full $5000 from the same supplier, then retailer A was being discriminated against and the products it was purchasing were, in effect, more expensive than they were to retailer B. The cost of goods sold for retailer B was lower and retailer B thus had a competitive advantage over retailer A. More specifically, such discrimina-tion is an indirect price discrimination in that the granting of these allowances is not directly related to the price of the supplies purchased in the accounting records of the buyer. They are not shown as discounts or rebates from the price of the goods purchased.

This illustration is simpler than situations ordinarily encountered in

[53]*Great Atlantic & Pacific Tea Co.* v. *FTC*, 106 F. 2d 667, 674 (1939); *FTC* v. *Simplicity Pattern Co., Inc.*, 360 U.S. 55, 65 (1959).

the real world. Purchasing retailers are of different sizes doing business with given suppliers in varied proportions. The problem has been to keep all the relevant variables in proper proportion. Section 2(d), therefore, was written to read that all payments made for services or facilities furnished by the customer should be made "available on proportionally equal terms to all other customers competing in the distribution of such products or commodities." But the proportions relative to what were not specified. Nor was reference made to any possible injury to competition, nor to the relative real benefits received by competing retailers. A failure to grant allowances on proportionally equal terms was written to be a *per se* violation. No actual or possible injury to competition need be shown.

Section 2(e). Furnishing Services and Facilities   The furnishing of services or facilities to customers toward the promotion and resale of the supplier's goods was also thought to be the source of competitive problems. If, for example, a supplier provided demonstration or display facilities to one retailer and not to others, theoretically that retailer would have a net real cost advantage over other retailers who had to provide their own demonstration facilities or do without. The result might be similar if some retailers received more in the way of services and facilities than others.

Section 2(e) of the Robinson-Patman Act sought to cure this competitive problem by declaring that the furnishing of any services or facilities must be "accorded to all purchasers on proportionally equal terms." But no allowance was made in the statute for differences in the costs of providing services or facilities to different customers. Nor did it take into account relative benefits, or the effect on competition itself. It may be noted that there is no mention made in Section 2(e) of competing customers; it refers to "all purchasers." The Supreme Court has determined that this was meant to cover competing purchasers.[54] In short, as with the case of Section 2(d), a failure to grant services or facilities on proportionally equal terms is a *per se* violation of the act.

Section 2(f). Buyer Liability   That Congress aimed to meet the problem of the big buyer in its passage of the Robinson-Patman Act is attested to by its inclusion of Section 2(f): "That it shall be unlawful for any person engaged in commerce, in the course of such commerce, knowingly to induce or receive a discrimination in price which is prohibited by this section."

The main thrust of this antidiscrimination statute is directed toward the seller engaging in the discrimination. The buyer, however, may have been the party largely responsible for the seller's discrimination. Indeed,

[54]Ibid.

that is the assumption underlying the complaints of small businesspeople who lobbied for a more detailed antidiscrimination law prior to the passage of the Robinson-Patman Act. The large chain stores especially were demanding and receiving discounts from prices paid by the smaller buyers.

How is a buyer to know whether it is getting a lower price, adjusted for any cost differences, than competitors are getting? One firm may think it has successfully demanded a lower price than other purchasers but may actually be paying a higher price, since some others have been more successful in their demands.

The Supreme Court has said that a buyer must be reasonably aware of or have knowledge of the illegality of the lower price it has demanded and received.[55] It may be difficult for the buyer to know the seller's costs, but the buyer should be alert to what might be appropriate cost differences. In any case, a buyer cannot be liable if the seller has not first been found to violate the price provisions of the antidiscrimination law.

Section 2(f) refers to *price* discrimination. But the FTC, in applying buyer liability to Section 2(d) and 2(e) indirect price discriminations, has successfully used Section 5 of the Federal Trade Commission Act. Finding it almost impossible to show that a buyer had known it was receiving discriminatory promotional allowances compared with competitors, the Commission found it could successfully attack them as unfair methods of competition.[56] According to its guides on advertising allowances and other merchandising payments and services, it will use Section 5 wherever necessary to attack the buyer as a guilty party.

COOPERATIVE ADVERTISING—*A CASE STUDY*

The cooperative advertising (co-op ads) the Robinson-Patman Act was designed to control through Section 2(d) concerns the joint contributions by both a manufacturer-supplier and a distributor, usually a retailer, toward the cost of the advertising of the manufacturer's branded goods available at the retailer's location. The ads in question can include newspaper and television advertising, outdoor signs, in-store displays, taped in-store commercial messages, and whatever other media are used to promote and advertise a particular store's merchandise. Joint arrangements to meet such advertising costs seem in themselves to be innocuous enough. It is situations in which some retailers benefit more from such arrangements than other competing retailers that Section 2(d) was designed to prevent. When discrepancies of considerable dimensions in the contributions re-

---

[55] *Automatic Canteen Co. of America* v. *FTC*, 346 U.S. 61 (1953).
[56] See Kintner, *A Robinson-Patman Primer*, pp. 263-65.

ceived by some retailers as compared with others arise, the resulting indirect price discrimination can theoretically put the unfavored retailers at a market disadvantage as they have, in effect, to pay more for the goods they are selling than the favored do.

The Buyer-Seller Relationship   That there was a problem requiring some kind of solution was evidenced by the facts that sometimes not all of a supplier's contributions toward promotional allowances were actually being used for such, that services presumably being rendered were sometimes not rendered at all, and that payments on some occasions were grossly in excess of value received. Some promotional allowances have been simply flat dollar monthly allowances granted by a manufacturer to selected retailers and have had the earmarks of unfair discrimination.[57] As might be expected, it was the larger retailers (often chains) with more bargaining power that received the most benefit from promotional allowances provided by manufacturers. A way was sought through legislation to assist the smaller retailer-buyer in receiving benefits proportionally equivalent to those being received by the larger retailer-buyer.

Examination of the manufacturer-retailer seller-buyer relationship shows that negotiating pressures over the matter of how much is to be contributed by the manufacturer toward the retailer's promotion and advertising exist on both sides of the bargaining table. The manufacturer is under no legal requirement to contribute toward retailers' advertising in general. But pressure from the retailer to do so may be strong. The retailer may threaten to switch to another supplier. If the buyer is a large one, this pressure can be hard to resist. Some department stores have simply required suppliers to contribute to co-op ads.[58]

Manufacturers can have reasons originating from their own needs for wanting to contribute to retailers' advertising programs. Through this method they can ensure that advertising of their branded products at the retail level takes place in sufficient volume. The more generous the promotional allowance offered to the retailer, the greater will be the retailer's cooperation. In addition, the local advertising may be less expensive than national advertising. Manufacturers can also attach strings to their contributions and perhaps achieve a second purpose. Such a string may be an agreement on the part of the retailer not to advertise the goods at discount prices or below certain stipulated minimum prices.[59]

[57]Patman, *Complete Guide,* pp. 128–29.
[58]Jeffrey H. Birnbaum, "Major Department Stores Are the Focus of an FTC Probe over Buying Practices," *Wall Street Journal,* November 20, 1980, p. 4.
[59]See, for example, the consent orders of 1980 signed with the FTC by manufacturers of rainwear and rubber footwear, and consent order signed with the Department of Justice by a manufacturer of consumer paints. *Tingley Rubber Corp.,* FTC Docket C-3041; *totes, inc.,* FTC Docket C-3040; and *U.S.* v. *E. I. du Pont de Nemours & Co., Inc.,* Civil No. C-76-566.

Types of Co-op Plans   R. Allen Moran surveyed the data available in all the FTC's complaint dockets and advisory opinions falling under Section 2(d) between the inception of the Robinson-Patman Act and June 1970, and found that co-op advertising plans fell generally into two basic types.[60] One type relates the size of the contribution (perhaps given as a rebate) to the size of the retailer's purchases from the manufacturer. The allowance is calculated by multiplying the number of units purchased by a given dollar amount. Or a certain percentage of total purchases may determine the size of the rebate. Such co-op allowances would seem to have more of the earmarks of an outright discount or rebate than they do of a spur to increasing advertising expenditures.

The second type of co-op ad plan calculates the rebate as a certain percentage of the dollars expended by a retailer in advertising the manufacturer's products. This plan is directly related to the retailer's advertising costs, and has the effect of reducing the cost of the advertising to the retailer. All other things being the same, this plan would tend to stimulate retailer expenditures on advertising.

Moran also shows periodic lump-sum payments as a method by which suppliers contribute to co-op advertising. In fact, this method of payment shows a larger number than the other two types together. The relationship between such payments and a retailer's purchases or advertising expenditures is not too clear, although they seem to be related to the volume of purchases from the manufacturer.[61] In-depth analysis of a retailer's accounting records would be required to unlock that secret. Unfortunately, the details of most co-op ad allowances have been "shrouded in vagueness and confusion."[62]

The use of co-op plans has varied from industry to industry and from company to company. The relative contributions of the two parties to a plan have also varied. In some cases the retailer has paid for most of the advertising, but in others the retailer has been able to recover twice the cost of the advertising. The degree of use has also seemed to vary according to the condition of the economy, with greater use in the depressed periods of a buyers' market.[63] This would seem to indicate that buyer pressure is a prime determinant of the use of co-op ad plans.

Enforcement Efforts   The FTC, which has assumed the responsibility of enforcing Section 2(d) of the Robinson-Patman Act, does not have to

---

[60]"Cooperative Advertising: An Alternative Interpretation of Price Discrimination," *California Management Review*, 15, no. 4 (Summer 1973), 61-63.
[61]Ibid., p. 62.
[62]Roland L. Hicks, "Excerpts from an Analysis of Prevailing Cooperative Practices," in *Advertising Allowances, Hearings before the Senate Select Committee on Small Business*, 88th Cong., 1st Sess., September 11, 1963, p. 57.
[63]Ibid., p. 59.

show any substantial lessening of competition or tendency to create a monopoly when bringing a case against a co-op arrangement. All that need be shown is that co-op payments are not available on proportionally equal terms to all customers competing in the distribution of the products in question. A lack of proportionality constitutes a *per se* violation. For those critics who believe that the enforcers are most interested in improving their batting average in the number of cases won, this section of law gives them an argument that too many Section 2(d) cases have been brought because they are easy to win. Admittedly, if one is to go out looking for a case to win, this area might well provide, given the necessary investigative power, a fruitful field. If the law were to require a finding of injury to competition instead of a lack of proportionally equal terms, a stop would automatically have been put to any possible application of a numbers game.

Orders issued by the FTC under Section 2(d) exhibit a curious chronological pattern. Between 1936 and 1957, only 41 violations were found, of which 19 were in 1956 and 1957.[64] Between 1960 and 1966, 478 orders were issued, of which 225 were in 1963.[65] Then, in the nine-year period 1967 through 1975, only 22 were issued.[66] It is highly unlikely that violations were occurring in reality at the same tempo as that in which orders were being issued. It is more likely that the differences in the number of cases selected were determined by whether attention was being paid to a strict interpretation of the wording of the law or whether a more liberal approach was being taken.

A strict interpretation of the law of Section 2(d) ignores the benefits that may be received by all the competitors. Take an extreme case. Suppose one large "prestige" retailer is receiving a co-op ad allowance equal to the amount of the actual cost of the ads and suppose one small retailer is receiving no ad allowance at all. Both retailers may be better off than if both had received proportionally equal allowances. This is because the advertising expenditures of the "prestige" retailer may be more productive than that of the small retailer and create a "spillover" effect that increases the sales of the branded good by the small retailer more than any increase in sales the small retailer's advertising would have achieved.[67]

Section 2(d) of the statute is only one sentence long. The FTC has found it necessary, however, to issue a set of guides several pages in length so that business can comply with the terms of that section of the law.[68] Of the greatest importance has been the necessity to provide some guide to the meaning of "available on proportionally equal terms." The statute does

[64]Edwards, *The Price Discrimination Law*, table 4, p. 679.
[65]*Recent Efforts to Amend or Repeal the Robinson-Patman Act, Hearings*, Part 2, p. 189.
[66]Ibid.
[67]See R. Allen Moran, "Price Discrimination, Competition and Market Shares: A Note," *Industrial Organization Review*, 3, no. 2 (1975), 95–97.
[68]16 C.F.R. 240, effective 1969 and amended in 1972.

not state what the proportionality is to be related to. The Commission does not specify any particular method, but it does suggest relating the co-op ad payments to dollar volume or the quantity of goods purchased. It provides as one illustration a plan that would have the supplier pay 50 percent of the cost up to an amount equal to 5 percent of the dollar volume of purchases during a specified period of time. Whatever method is selected, it must be "fair" to all competing customers.

Another of these guides is concerned with the availability of a co-op ad plan. It must be available to all competing customers—and the FTC advises that it be in writing so all competing customers can have full knowledge of it and understand it. Where a manufacturer distributes a product not only directly to retailers but also indirectly to competing retailers through wholesalers, that manufacturer is still responsible for seeing that the latter competing retailers are receiving the required proportionally equal treatment.[69] The manufacturer may turn over the funds to the wholesaler to be passed on to the retailer, but it is the manufacturer's responsibility to see to it that the wholesaler carries out that responsibility.

If all competing customers cannot partake of a plan because it is not functionally available to them, an alternative has to be provided. A large buyer, for example, may advertise in the local newspapers regularly, whereas this form of advertising may not be useful to the very small customer. To maintain the proportional treatment, the guide states that sufficient alternatives must be provided so that all buyers can benefit.

Another guide provides suggestions for how all competing customers are to be notified. The manufacturers are supposed to take reasonable action in good faith to see that all competing customers are notified of the plan and all the possible alternatives available to them. Three basic means of notification are suggested: by contract, by announcements within or on the outside of product containers, or by publication of notice in a publication that receives general distribution throughout the particular trade.

Another guide discusses the issue of competing customers. Which customers are actually competing with one another? The FTC here cautions that the trade area selected for determining the competing firms should be a "natural" one. The manufacturer is alerted not to ignore competing customers located on the fringes of a trading area.

A final guide to manufacturers is also reflected throughout the guides as a theme: Be sure the buyers are using the co-op payments for the purpose for which they were granted. Be sure these services are actually performed. An ideal co-op ad plan would require certification of performance by the buyer. If buyers are to be prevented from receiving indirect price discrimination under the cloak of a co-op ad plan, performance must be ensured.

[69] *FTC* v. *Fred Meyer, Inc.*, 390 U.S. 341 (1968).

Although it is true that Section 2(d) applies to manufacturers (sellers) and not to customers (buyers), one guide warns that the FTC can still issue a complaint against a customer under Section 5 of the Federal Trade Commission Act if a customer engages in certain unfair methods of competition related to co-op ad allowances. If a customer knowingly receives payments not available to competitors, that is unfair. And last, but not least, a retailer who makes unauthorized deductions from purchase invoices for an alleged advertising allowance is clearly violating Section 5.

Finally, a guide points out that a seller may grant discriminatory co-op ad allowances to a particular customer to meet the equally high payments of a competitor. The granting of such a discriminatory allowance must be made to meet the competition of a particular competing seller, however. The granting of an allowance "to be competitive," to meet the competition in general, is not a satisfactory reply to a charge of discrimination.

SUMMARY

Price discrimination was deemed to be such a prevalent antitrust problem that antitrust legislation in the form of Section 2 of the Clayton Act was passed in 1914 to provide specific enforcement capability against it. The original danger seen to reside in price discrimination was that of one seller discriminating among buyers in order to injure a competing seller. With changing market conditions, particularly the development of the chain store and the buying power that accompanied its size, Section 2 of the Clayton Act was amended in 1936 by the Robinson-Patman Act to make the law against price discrimination not only more specific, but also more directly applicable to the discrimination resulting from the buying power of large buyers. Because the law became more specific in its wording, there was now more statutory language that had to be interpreted as efforts were made to enforce it.

Injury to primary line competition—that where one seller attempts to injure another competing seller—has been classically illustrated by geographic price discrimination in which a large seller selling in more than one market selects a particular market and lowers price in that market in order to drive out of business a smaller seller that is selling only in that market. The basic question to be resolved in any actual cases of geographic price differentials is whether this represents predatory competition or just plain price competition. Is there any single easy formula that can be applied to these cases so appropriate economic justice can be done? Two Harvard professors think there is, and they have influenced the courts. Acceptance of the formula, both by other scholars and by judges, has been far from complete. A series of court decisions on geographic price discrimination illustrates the principles that have been applied to this phenomenon by the courts.

Section 2(b) of the Robinson-Patman Act provides a "good faith" meeting of competition defense against a charge of price discrimination. Allowing an oligopolistic seller to cut prices selectively where necessary to hold onto a customer or to attain the business of a new customer may be a form of price competition that represents the beginning of the erosion of an otherwise rigid oligopolistic price structure. On the other hand, one has to distinguish between sporadic meeting of the competition and outright collusive systems of pricing that give the appearance of meeting the competition in good faith.

To prevent injury to secondary line competition, that among buyers, was a primary purpose of the Robinson-Patman 1936 amendment to the Clayton Act. Brokerage allowances, promotional allowances, and the furnishing of services and facilities to customers by suppliers were all singled out in the statute as representing indirect forms of price discrimination that should be brought under control. The payment of brokerage commissions to anyone other than an independent broker was made a *per se* violation. Promotional allowances and the furnishing of services and facilities must now be made available to all competing customers on proportionally equal terms. And buyers receiving discriminatory prices were made equally as liable as the sellers granting the discriminations.

Cooperative advertising as a form of indirect price discrimination illustrates the different forms these plans may take, the economic results they may produce, and how a problem that might appear to have a relatively simple solution actually requires a complicated set of guides.

APPENDIX

Robinson-Patman Act (1936), amending Section 2 of the Clayton Act (1914). 15 U.S. Code, Sec. 13:

Sec. 2(a). That it shall be unlawful for any person engaged in commerce, in the course of such commerce, either directly or indirectly, to discriminate in price between different purchasers of commodities of like grade and quality, where either or any of the purchases involved in such discrimination are in commerce, where such commodities are sold for use, consumption, or resale within the United States or any Territory thereof or the District of Columbia or any insular possession or other place under the jurisdiction of the United States, and where the effect of such discrimination may be substantially to lessen competition or tend to create a monopoly in any line of commerce, or to injure, destroy, or prevent competition with any person who either grants or knowingly receives the benefit of such discrimination, or with customers of either of them: *Provided,*

That nothing herein contained shall prevent differentials which make only due allowance for differences in the cost of manufacture, sale, or delivery resulting from the differing methods or quantities in which such commodities are to such purchasers sold or delivered: *Provided, however,* That the Federal Trade Commission may, after due investigation and hearing to all interested parties, fix and establish quantity limits, and revise the same as it finds necessary, as to particular commodities or classes of commodities, where it finds that available purchasers in greater quantities are so few as to render differentials on account thereof unjustly discriminatory or promotive of monopoly in any line of commerce; and the foregoing shall then not be construed to permit differentials based on differences in quantities greater than those so fixed and established: *And provided further,* That nothing herein contained shall prevent persons engaged in selling goods, wares, or merchandise in commerce from selecting their own customers in bona fide transactions and not in restraint of trade: *And provided further,* That nothing herein contained shall prevent price changes from time to time where in response to changing conditions affecting the market for or the marketability of the goods concerned, such as but not limited to actual or imminent deterioration of perishable goods, obsolescence of seasonal goods, distress sales under court process, or sales in good faith in discontinuance of business in the goods concerned.

Sec. 2(b). Upon proof being made, at any hearing on a complaint under this section, that there has been discrimination in price or services of facilities furnished, the burden of rebutting the prima-facie case thus made by showing justification shall be upon the person charged with a violation of this section, and unless justification shall be affirmatively shown, the Commission is authorized to issue an order terminating the discrimination: *Provided, however,* That nothing herein contained shall prevent a seller rebutting the prima-facie case thus made by showing that his lower price or the furnishing of services or facilities to any purchaser or purchasers was made in good faith to meet an equally low price of a competitor, or the services or facilities furnished by a competitor.

Sec. 2(c). That it shall be unlawful for any person engaged in commerce, in the course of such commerce, to pay or grant, or to receive or accept, anything of value as a commission, brokerage, or other compensation, or any allowance or discount in lieu thereof, except for services rendered in connection with the sale or purchase of goods, wares, or merchandise, either to the other party to such transaction or to an agent, representative, or other intermediary therein where such intermediary is acting in fact for or in behalf, or is subject to the direct or indirect control, of any party to such transaction other than the person by whom such compensation is so granted or paid.

Sec. 2(d). That it shall be unlawful for any person engaged in commerce to pay or contract for the payment of anything of value to or for the benefit of a customer of such person in the course of such commerce as compensation or in consideration for any services or facilities furnished by or through such customer in connection with the processing, handling, sale, or offering for sale of any products or commodities manufactured, sold, or offered for sale by such person, unless such payment or consideration is available on proportionally equal terms to all other customers competing in the distribution of such products or commodities.

Sec. 2(e). That it shall be unlawful for any person to discriminate in favor of one purchaser against another purchaser or purchasers of a commodity bought for resale, with or without processing, by contracting to furnish or furnishing, or by contributing to the furnishing of, any services or facilities connected with the processing, handling, sale, or offering for sale of such commodity so purchased upon terms not accorded to all purchasers on proportionally equal terms.

Sec. 2(f). That it shall be unlawful for any person engaged in commerce, in the course of such commerce, knowingly to induce or receive a discrimination in price which is prohibited by this section.

Selected Readings

AREEDA, PHILLIP, AND DONALD F. TURNER, "Predatory Pricing and Related Practices under Section 2 of the Sherman Act," *Harvard Law Review,* 88, no. 4 (February 1975), 697–733.

GREER, DOUGLAS F., "A Critique of Areeda and Turner's Standard for Predatory Practices," *Antitrust Bulletin,* 24, no. 2 (Summer 1979), 233–61.

KINTNER, EARL W., *A Robinson-Patman Primer: A Businessman's Guide to the Law against Price Discrimination.* New York: Macmillan, 1970.

McGEE, JOHN S., "Predatory Pricing Revisited," *Journal of Law and Economics,* 23, no. 2 (October 1980), 289–330.

POSNER, RICHARD A., *The Robinson-Patman Act.* Washington, D.C.: American Enterprise Institute, 1976.

SCHERER, F. M., "Predatory Pricing and the Sherman Act: A Comment," *Harvard Law Review,* 89, no. 5 (March 1976), 869–90.

8 — Direct Consumer Protection

This chapter is concerned with the ways in which the government intervenes with buyer-seller relationships in order to protect the buyer directly. Sales and merchandising strategies of sellers and the intricacies of technically sophisticated modern products may make it difficult for buyers to distinguish clearly those goods and services they most wish to purchase in order to maximize the utility of their demands. This problem relates not just to the competition between directly competing products, but also to all sellers competing for all buyers' dollars. The problem may be one of omission, of not telling the consumer all the characteristics of a product. Or it may be one of commission, of making statements that are not well founded. Government intervention in this area comes under the heading of trade regulation because it pertains directly to trading relationships.

Consumers are protected by other forms of government intervention, but these usually occur at an earlier stage of producer-seller planning. Government activity here is related to such things as the establishment and maintenance of consumer credit card ratings, product safety, or quality of the environment. Consumers have been given legal rights to protect themselves against any unfairly adverse consumer credit rating. Consumers are protected against unwholesome foods by required government inspection of foods. Consumers are protected against unsafe and ineffective drugs and therapeutic devices and harmful cosmetics by Food and Drug Administration controls. Flammable fabrics have been banned. Automobiles have been compelled to meet certain specific safety standards. The National Commission on Product Safety develops and enforces standards of safety for consumer products. And manufacturers can be compelled to control and limit their contributions to air, water, and noise pollution. Consumers benefit from these government regulations, which do not, however, affect the actual trading relationships.

Our main concern here is with unfair or deceptive acts or practices as they impinge upon the consumer as a buyer. Because they can also affect competition, such acts or practices can also constitute unfair methods of competition. We are concerned as well with those efforts by government to help the consumer become a more knowledgeable buyer.

MARKET IMPERFECTIONS AS BASIS FOR INTERVENTION

Economic theory postulates that, if a business environment of effective competition is maintained, no further social controls need be applied to the economy to ensure that consumers are faced with the best possible set of alternatives of different quality products at the lowest possible set of market prices. Effective use of the antitrust laws will eliminate any serious restraints of trade, monopoly, and monopolistic behavior that generates clogs to the competition. The resulting free and open competition permits the consumer to be sovereign and, in the last analysis, to dictate to the producer what the producer will produce. The marketplace will then coordinate the simultaneous achievement of maximum profits to producers and maximum satisfaction of wants for consumers.

Such a theoretical marketplace functions quite simply. It assumes that the nature and functioning of all products and differences among products are fully grasped and understood by buyers before they make a purchase. It also assumes that the dissemination of market knowledge has been accomplished in a manner lacking in any serious distortion.

A more than cursory examination of many a marketplace provides ready illustrations of the weaknesses of this theory. Perhaps these weaknesses are not too serious; a buyer may have to try out any particular product or service once before he or she really knows whether that choice satisfied the want according to expectations. If the buyer decides after an initial purchase that a particular product is not as expected, that buyer need not purchase another unit of it. And if enough customers behave in that fashion, the seller will be forced out of business or into a new line of production. Indeed, this may be the way the market is really supposed to work to allocate resources appropriately, with various consumer tests occurring before an equilibrium is reached. On the other hand, there can be real costs in this process in the form of expenditures wasted because they do not provide utility as anticipated. The greater the price of a good, the greater can be that cost. The need for some direct interference with the marketplace to protect the consumer against these imperfections has been generally recognized. It is a matter of the degree of interference. How serious are these imperfections in particular markets?

Producer Distortion   Puffery is a marketplace phenomenon that may cause the otherwise rational decision-making of a consumer to go somewhat askew. This exaggerated or undue praise of a product by the seller is natural; it has been said repeatedly that a salesperson cannot be good at his or her calling unless he or she believes in the product he or she is selling. There is little that can or should be done about such circumstances. The enthusiasm of a salesperson should be recognized by a purchaser for what it is.

One degree beyond puffery lies misrepresentation. A sales or service effort can lead to a representation that is misleading or not satisfactorily accurate. This is not a matter of enthusiasm; it is an effort to distort the value of a product favorably. It might take a good deal of research on the part of the purchaser to disprove the claims of a promotional sales effort or a service job. The intervention of an outside party to eliminate erroneous impressions left with a consumer through gross misrepresentations has been deemed by most people to be in order. Thus, the Federal Trade Commission has found itself, as the principal consumer protection agency at the federal level, devoting a considerable part of its resources to the elimination in promotion and advertising of half-truths that can be effective in channeling consumer expenditures in directions which do not yield the expected or desired utility.

Beyond misrepresentation is outright fraud, the deliberate intent of the seller to deceive. False advertising comes under this heading. No serious question exists that government should use its enforcement power to rid the economy of deliberately fraudulent selling.

Consumer Demand Fallibilities   Consumers can be victims in varying degrees of misrepresentation and fraud for a variety of reasons. Some consumers are simply more gullible than others. They believe everything anyone tells them. Barnum would put such consumers in the class of "suckers," one of whom is born every minute. Perhaps a gullible consumer can be considered a stupid consumer. On the other hand, it has been argued that the advances of modern technology have inclined people toward being exploited by phony assertions of fact.

It is certainly true that consumers can lack full knowledge of a product and its workings or of a technical service because they do not have the necessary access to the required information. The world of modern technology may put the required information beyond the ken of even the most well informed or learned. Most consumers have no way of checking on the repair claims of television and auto repair personnel—two areas in which it is believed serious distortions to truth often occur. Similarly, many products are simply too complex for the average consumer to understand.

Finally, some consumers, especially the elderly, are desperate for relief from distressing chronic illness and physical ailments. Terminally ill patients become the victims of quacks who peddle sure remedies. Patients who are victims of chronic illness may turn to highly touted but ineffective drugs or devices in the hope of alleviating their suffering. The Arthritis Foundation, for example, estimated that sufferers of that disease would spend $915 million in 1981 on quack devices, unproven remedies, and "miracle cures."[1] The age of snake oil is not dead.

CONSUMER PROTECTION AGENCIES

A host of agencies participate in the overall effort to protect consumers against the excesses or distortions that competition may permit or even induce. The chief burden has fallen upon the FTC. Where the nation's health is at stake, the Food and Drug Administration (FDA, within the Department of Health and Human Services) assumes consumer protection responsibilities. Various independent agencies such as the Civil Aeronautics Board, the Interstate Commerce Commission, and the United States Department of Agriculture engage in their own consumer protection activities to combat unfair, false, or deceptive practices within their jurisdictions. The United States Postal Service is instructed to prevent the use of the mails to deceive or defraud.[2] And most states and some cities have passed consumer protection laws.

We will examine the principal federal regulatory unit, the FTC, and explore briefly those of the state and local levels here.

The Federal Trade Commission As we saw in Chapter 2, the 1938 Wheeler-Lea amendment to Section 5 of the Federal Trade Commission Act declared *unfair or deceptive acts or practices,* as well as unfair methods of competition, to be unlawful. The purpose of adding these new words to Section 5 was to reach that business conduct which had a direct adverse impact upon the consumer. It thus covered more than injury to a competitor arising from an unfair method of competition.

The basic enforcement tool of the FTC has been the cease-and-desist order. These orders can be issued after a finding by the FTC that there has been a violation of Section 5 or one of the more specific trade regulation rules officially promulgated by the Commission, after full public hearings,

---

[1]Reported by Martin J. Shannon, "Business Bulletin," *Wall Street Journal,* February 5, 1981, p. 1.

[2]The Postal Service said that consumers lost more than a half billion dollars through mail fraud in 1976. *New York Times,* February 20, 1977, p. 29.

to supplement Section 5. The FTC also has the responsibility of enforcing Sections 12 through 15 of the Federal Trade Commission Act (as added by the Wheeler-Lea Act of 1938), which condemn the false advertising of food, drugs, therapeutic devices, and cosmetics. This advertising is false when it is "misleading in a material respect."

Because proceedings before the FTC can be time-consuming, a temporary injunction or restraining order can be obtained from a district court by the FTC in the case of the false advertising of foods, drugs, devices, and cosmetics. If a violation shows that the use of the commodity advertised may be injurious to health or the advertising had been with intent to defraud or mislead, the manufacturer or distributor may be fined up to $5000 or imprisoned up to six months, or both. For a second offense, fines or term of imprisonment can be doubled.

The 1975 amendments to the Federal Trade Commission Act (Magnuson-Moss Warranty—Federal Trade Commission Improvement Act) strengthened the rule-making procedure of the Commission. Interpretive rules could be prescribed with respect to "unfair or deceptive acts or practices in or affecting commerce." And rules could "define with specificity" unfair or deceptive acts or practices in order to make Section 5 more explicit. Procedures for the conduct of the hearings prior to the final formulation of such a rule were prescribed by the statute. Whereas the FTC, since 1963, had issued rules that had been referred to as "trade regulation rules," rules since the 1975 statute have sometimes also been referred to as Magnuson-Moss rules.

The FTC was given authority by the 1975 legislation to undertake civil actions in district courts against violators of trade regulation rules, with liability being not more than $10,000 for each violation, but with each day of failure to comply with a rule being treated as a separate violation. Furthermore, where there is a violation of such a rule or where the FTC has issued a final cease-and-desist order in a Section 5 case, it can go to court (either federal or state) to seek redress for consumers. The redress can take the form of rescission of contracts, refund of money, return of property, or payment of damages.

The FTC was given added responsibilities in its consumer protection work when the wool products (1939), fur products (1951), and textile fiber products (1958) labeling statutes gave it the duty of drawing up rules to enforce those acts. Similarly, the FTC was given the responsibility by Congress of issuing regulations for the enforcement of the Fair Packaging and Labeling Act of 1966 with respect to all consumer products except foods, drugs, devices, and cosmetics (which were to be covered by regulations issued by the FDA). The FTC has been instructed to help supervise the Consumer Credit Protection Act of 1968 (Truth in Lending), which imposes full disclosure requirements on creditors with respect to the terms and overall cost of consumer credit.[3] And finally, the Magnuson-Moss Warranty—Federal Trade Commission Improvement Act of 1975 required the FTC to draw up rules concerning the issue of written warranties by manufacturers.

The FTC's consumer protection efforts have been highly controversial. At one time it has been charged with not being effective enough. At another time it has been charged with going too far. It was accused, for example, by a study commission of the American Bar Association in 1969 of having "fallen far short" of what it could have accomplished.[4] Its efforts, it was complained, had been piecemeal and not backed by thorough planning with respect to identifying and attempting to solve the most important consumer problems.

On the other side of the coin, when the FTC prepared to issue a trade regulation rule in 1964 requiring strong health warning statements on packages of cigarettes and in cigarette advertising, Congress passed a law specifically denying the FTC the power to do so and itself did the honors and passed a statute that required the use of a much weaker statement. Likewise, in 1980, after the FTC had proposed controversial trade regulation rules to govern advertising aimed at children and to control certain practices in the funeral industry, Congress, under strong pressure from certain business lobbies, curbed its powers to some extent in the Federal Trade Commission Improvements Act of 1980. Under the provisions of that act, an FTC rule will become effective within 90 calendar days of continuous session of Congress after its being submitted to Congress unless both Houses of Congress disapprove it within that time period. The 1980 act also stated that, for a period of three years, any new advertising rule would have to be based on *deception* rather than on *unfairness*, the latter being considered to be a much wider net which the FTC had been given with respect to its rule-making by the Magnuson-Moss Act of 1975. In addition, the 1980 legislation stated that the FTC could not study the insurance industry unless the Senate and House commerce committees asked it to do so. In short, it has sometimes been difficult for it to follow a line that does not annoy those who think it is not doing enough or those who think it is doing too much to protect the consumer.

State and Local Consumer Protection Statutes   One category of state consumer protection statute is aimed at untrue, deceptive, or misleading

[3]The Truth in Lending Act is supervised in one way or another by nine different federal agencies: The FTC, the Federal Reserve Board, the Agriculture Department, the Federal Deposit Insurance Corporation, the Federal Home Loan Bank Board, the Bureau of Federal Credit Unions, the Comptroller of the Currency, the Interstate Commerce Commission, and the Civil Aeronautics Board.

[4]*Report of the ABA Commission to Study the Federal Trade Commission*, September 15, 1969, p. 37.

advertising. This category is the so-called Printer's Ink legislation, the state truth-in-advertising laws.[5] Most of the states have passed some form of such legislation. In making advertisers liable for their representations, most such statutes do not require proof that the advertiser was aware of the falsity of an advertisement or that there was an intent to deceive.[6] "Puffing" is exempted by these statutes.[7]

The second category of state consumer protection law is that prohibiting unfair or deceptive acts or practices, the so-called UDAP statutes. In 1978, 48 states had comprehensive UDAP statutes and all states have enacted legislation against particular consumer fraud practices.[8] Many of these statutes are based on the Federal Trade Commission Act, with its prohibition of unfair or deceptive acts or practices and, with state case law being very limited, state courts have looked to decisions by the FTC for direction.[9] This is an important reason for us to concentrate on the enforcement actions of this federal commission in examining consumer protection in action.

Certain practices that may be injurious to consumers and are not covered by Printer's Ink or UDAP state statutes have been covered by separate legislation in some states. One of the oldest is weights and measures legislation (passed by all states), designed to eliminate inaccuracy in weighing and measuring devices. It is still difficult, however, to keep that generic "thumb" off the scales.[10] Of later vintage have been the unit-pricing laws passed by some states in the 1970s, which require food stores to indicate on the store shelves the prices of products according to a given standard unit of measure, such as per ounce or per pound. A great variety of box, bottle, or can sizes, involving various fractional sizes, makes it difficult for the consumer to make the calculations necessary in order to determine the lowest unit-cost package. Sometimes an "economy" size can cost more per ounce of product than a small size.

For the most part, local governments rely on the state's efforts to enact and enforce consumer protection legislation. Some do, however, play a part in the enforcement of the state legislation, and some local district attorneys are beginning to set up special consumer fraud units.[11]

---

[5]*Printer's Ink*, a national weekly covering advertising problems, first prepared a model law providing desirable language for a truth-in-advertising law in 1911, and in 1945 provided the format that was followed by several states in legislation enacted soon thereafter.

[6]Jonathan A. Sheldon and George J. Zweibel, *Survey of Consumer Fraud Law* (Washington, D.C.: U.S. Government Printing Office, 1978), p. 28.

[7]Ibid.

[8]Ibid., p. 127.

[9]Ibid., pp. 29–30.

[10]See James MacGregor, "Heavy Thumbs," *Wall Street Journal*, July 2, 1971, p. 1. A different but similar problem is the short-counted package. See Michael L. Geczi, "Short Counts Mean That the Consumer Pays More for Less," *Wall Street Journal*, November 4, 1974, p. 1.

[11]Sheldon and Zweibel, *Survey*, pp. 127–33.

Coordination between state and local authorities in the enforcement of state consumer laws is more general than passage and enforcement of strong local laws. Exceptions are the local licensing of business activities to prevent consumer fraud and provide controls over local door-to-door selling. This is not to say that some cities do not have strong and relatively effective consumer fraud protection. New York City has a fairly comprehensive set of consumer protection ordinances that includes controls over billing and repair procedures for the repair of autos, watches, and household appliances. But in general, the work of the FTC has set the pace, standards, and precedents for consumer protection. We will examine its work in what follows.

PREVENTING DECEPTIVE PRICING PRACTICES

The uses of deception in price advertising can be numerous. The FTC's first guides involving pricing, effective in 1959, were against bait advertising. Its revision of its guides against deceptive pricing, effective in 1964, discussed the problems of comparing current prices with former prices, of comparing one's prices with others' prices, of utilizing retail prices established or suggested by manufacturers, and of bargain prices based on the purchase of other merchandise. A guide concerning the use of the word "free" in advertising was issued by the FTC in 1971.

FTC guides do not have the full force and effect of law. They are, rather, the expression of the FTC's views, which could be valuable aids to businesspersons who honestly want to avoid making misrepresentations. In effect, they are an elaboration of what might be found to be illegal conduct in violation of Section 5 of the Federal Trade Commission Act— unfair or deceptive acts or practices.

Bait Advertising   Bait advertising is a switch scheme. It is an offer to sell a product at what appears to be a very attractive price when the seller has no intention of selling that particular product. The objective is to make contact with buyers interested in a certain type of product and to sell those buyers a higher-priced, higher-profit item. The low-priced special is the lure.

Once a customer has been lured into the store, the job of the salesperson is to dissuade the customer from buying the advertised item and switch him or her to the purchase of an overpriced one. The advertised item will be disparaged; sometimes it will not be available to be shown; perhaps it is "all sold out." An insistent customer may finally be shown a well-used demonstrator. Take the case of an expert in the field who responded to the advertisement of a mattress special by a New York City East Side bedding center. No sign of the advertised special was evident inside the store. After insisting, the customer was finally shown a soiled mattress in the back room that looked like it was ready for a sanitation pickup, although the salesman assured the customer that if she purchased one it would be clean.[12]

If the customer purchases the advertised item, that is not the end of the scheme. The job of the salesperson is then to "unsell" the customer. Perhaps this can be achieved by delivering a defective model or by not making delivery within a reasonable time.

The FTC offers four guides to business to avoid a charge of bait advertising. First, all advertisements must be *bona fide* offers to sell. Second, the advertisements must not create any false impressions as to an item's grade, quality, make, value, currency of model, size, color, usability, or origin. To tell the truth once the customer is in the store does not make it any more legal. Third, the customer should not be encouraged to switch by refusal to show or demonstrate, by disparaging the product, by refusing to take an order for delivery within a reasonable time, by having an inadequate quantity available for purchase, or by showing defective demonstrators. Fourth, switches achieved after a sale are equally in violation of the law. Evidence of such "unselling" can be delivery of a higher-priced or of a defective product, failure to deliver within a reasonable period of time, or disparagement of the guarantee or availability of service or repairs.

Former Price Comparisons   A common business practice is to have sales in which prices are lowered for the sale. This is bargain advertising. It is subject to charges of being misleading, however, if the former price, from which the bargain price represents a reduction, was a fictitious price in some sense.

The former price could have been a higher price for a very short period of time, with the seller knowing that sales at that high price would be minimal. A seller should be able to demonstrate that the product was actively being offered for a "reasonably substantial" period of time during the regular course of business. A former price way back in time, one that was never actively offered to the public, or one that never existed at all, is not a genuine former price.

A price reduction that can justify the nomenclature "sale" must also represent a reduction of some significance. A $10 item reduced a few cents should not be advertised as a "sale."

Comparable Value Pricing   Bargain advertising can take the form of comparing the price of one's own product with that of competitors' prices. One's price can be represented as lower than those being charged by oth-

---

[12]Ralph Blumenthal, "When Buying a Bed Beware," *New York Times*, February 22, 1979, p. Cl.

ers. But who and where are those others? Do they represent competitors' prices on the average, or do they represent a few isolated prices? Are those other prices the ones being charged in the same market? Or are they prices available only some distance away? Furthermore, are those competitive products of essentially the same quality?

The FTC would actually encourage comparative advertising. Price may be only one dimension in which competing products are compared, but any comparisons that provide consumers with fuller market information will enable those consumers to make more rational market decisions and thus contribute to a better allocation of resources. The FTC has issued a policy statement to this effect.[13] And FTC spokespeople have reiterated this in speeches.[14]

Manufacturers' Suggested Prices   Many stores advertise bargains represented by reductions from manufacturers' list or suggested prices. This may or may not represent a true bargain. If most competitors are ignoring the manufacturers' suggested prices, such reductions are not really a bargain. They are closer to the "going" market price. An FTC guide puts the responsibility on the seller to know whether the manufacturers' list prices are or are not the prices being regularly charged in that market. If they are not, then listing a bargain reduction from manufacturer list price is a fictitious bargain.

The problem can become complicated for the seller who advertises and sells nationally, perhaps through catalog sales. Here the seller must act "honestly and in good faith" in quoting a manufacturer's list price in advertising or catalog copy.

A price practice that has been the subject of abuse is the ticketing of a product by the manufacturer itself—so-called preticketing. If the prices printed on the tags in advance by the manufacturer are obviously at a higher level than the prices at which the goods will clear the market at the retail level, clearly the manufacturer has been a party to the deceptive pricing offer. The FTC will hold the manufacturer responsible, even though the act of preticketing is not in itself illegal.[15]

Congress has enacted special legislation to *require* preticketing in the automobile industry. The Automobile Information Disclosure Act of 1958 requires that the suggested retail price of a new automobile and any options included be attached by the manufacturer to a window of the vehicle. Auto purchasers, it was found, were experiencing difficulty in comparing prices of automobiles, especially when dealers were "price-packing," or

---

[13]Statement of Policy regarding Comparative Advertising, 16 C.F.R. 14.15; 44 Fed. Reg. 47328, August 13, 1979.

[14]See, for example, *FTC News Summary*, February 15, 1980, vol. 19–80, p. 2.

[15]*Baltimore Luggage Co.* v. *FTC*, 296 F. 2d 608 (1961), certiorari denied, 369 U.S. 860 (1962).

raising the quoted price to a customer to compensate for giving him or her an overblown allowance on the trade-in of a used car. The Department of Justice opposed such legislation, arguing that it would facilitate resale price maintenance. That argument may have some validity, but experience has shown that when particular models of cars are in surplus supply they are often sold at less than the suggested retail price, and when they are in short supply they often sell for a premium over the suggested price.

The Justice Department's alternative suggestion may have provided a better solution. It recognized the problem but suggested that the price posted on the car should be the price to the dealer. Such a remedy would, of course, give away the seller's reservation price and, therefore, give the customer greater bargaining power.

"Free" Goods   The Commission's guides against deceptive pricing of 1964 and its guide of 1971 warning about the use of the word "free" both cover the problem of possible deception. Seldom is a good literally offered to the consumer free. (A householder may receive free promotional samples in the mail, but such samples are not offers to sell.) More likely the offer is "Buy 1—Get 1 Free" or "2-for-1 Sale." In such instances, there is a tie-in since one unit cannot be purchased without purchasing the other; there is no separate price for the second item.

Two principal problems present themselves. First, is the price of the unit of product that has to be purchased first the actual price at which that product has been moving? Or is it higher than the regular price for the purpose of the sale? If the price of that product has been fluctuating, then what was its "regular" price? If there is a discrepancy between the true regular price and the tie-in offer price, the second unit purchased is in no sense "free."

The second problem is that of explaining to the customer in just what way the merchandise is "free." Both the 1964 and 1971 guides require that the condition or obligation be set forth clearly and conspicuously "at the outset." The 1971 guide states that an asterisk footnote is not enough; the explanation must be in close conjunction with the offer.

Miscellaneous Price Comparisons   A final guide of the FTC on deceptive pricing warns against the use of certain words in conjunction with price. A retailer should not advertise "wholesale" prices unless they are actually the same as prices charged by wholesalers. Retailers should not sell at "factory" prices unless they are the prices actually charged by the factories. They should not offer an advance sale price when they do not plan actually to raise prices at a later date. They should not make a "limited" price offer unless the sale is truly to be limited. Such, states the guide, are typical situations which can be deceptive, but that there are "others too numerous to mention."

REGULATING DECEPTIVE ADVERTISING AND SELLING PRACTICES

The FTC's policies and procedures against deceptive advertising and selling practices have been spelled out in two basic ways. First, it has established a large body of case law through its use of the Federal Trade Commission Act's Section 5 prohibition of unfair or deceptive acts or practices. It has backed up this body of case precedent by a series of guides that represent the FTC's interpretations of what in its view would be Section 5 violations in certain circumstances.

Second, it has promulgated trade regulation rules, which have the full force and effect of law, to control certain practices that had been sufficiently repetitive to warrant special treatment. Some of these rules have applied to particular products, some to particular industries, and others to practices that cross industry lines. The Magnuson-Moss Warranty— Federal Trade Commission Improvement Act of 1975 strengthened this rule-making power of the FTC in terms of authority and procedures.

It has been charged that the FTC has been overly concerned with the "truth" in its principal efforts to protect consumers.[16] If advertising is somewhat misleading but there is no real injury being incurred, why be so concerned? Market forces will take over and, in the long run, the consumer will remain sovereign. Any short-run cost to the consumer could be viewed as a part of the total costs of the equilibrating forces of the economy at work. Suppose, however, that the consumer had been induced to purchase an automobile which turned out to be a "lemon" and the warranty proved to be less than suggested in the sales effort. The costs to that consumer could be very high. What recourse would that consumer have? This has clearly been a serious enough problem to the consumer that Congress required in its 1975 legislation that the FTC promulgate rules to cover warranties, with a special set of rules to cover the used motor vehicle industry.

Procedures in establishing trade regulation rules certainly prevent excesses in the search for truth. Advance notice of proposed rules must be given to the Senate and the House, notice of proposed rules must be published together with any alternatives and the reason for the proposed rule, and hearings must be held. The statement of purpose must include information on the prevalence of the acts or practices that are the subject of the rule, why they are unfair or deceptive, and the economic impact of the rule on both consumers and small businesses. Finally, Congress can veto a rule if both House and Senate adopt resolutions disapproving it.

[16]See the witty comments of a former Federal Trade Commissioner, Mayo J. Thompson, "Government Regulation of Advertising: Killing the Consumer in Order to 'Save' Him," *Antitrust Law & Economics Review*, 8, no. 1 (1976), 81–92.

Section 5 Cases   The basic rule of thumb in utilizing Section 5 against a deceptive act or practice has been that it need have only the capacity or tendency to deceive.[17] An intent to deceive by the seller does not have to be shown.[18] That someone has actually been deceived also need not be shown.[19]

Several practices are to be avoided.[20] Where a term or word is ambiguous, one meaning can be found to be false. An entire representation can be deceptive even if specific claims within it are not. For example, to quote only parts of a magazine article, but not the whole, can create a false and misleading impression not only of what was said in the article, but also of the quality of the product being advertised.[21] Material and necessary qualifications must not be omitted or made too inconspicuous. Deception is illegal even if later clarified. Puffery and spoofing can be legitimate; however, even here a capacity to deceive can still condemn.

The misrepresentation of the real nature and standing of a business has been a frequent object of attack by the FTC. Inclusion of words such as "university," "institute," "federal," and "national" in a business title can be misleading. Firms' representations as to their financial strength, size, volume of business, or years in business have been challenged and prohibited.

Virtues asserted as to the nature and effectiveness of products have very frequently been the basis of cease-and-desist orders. Claims made for products that affect the personal life and ego of the average person have been grossly distorted. Words have been used loosely to describe products without appropriate distinctions, such as the difference between "fireproof" and "heat resistant." The word "safe" has been used without necessary qualifications. Approval by some United States agency has frequently been strongly implied. FTC guides, as well as cease-and-desist orders, have had to be issued to control product endorsements by celebrities and experts.[22]

A variety of unfair selling practices has been covered by Section 5 actions. Shipping goods which have not been ordered and demanding payment, shipping goods inferior in quality to those ordered, the failure to ship ordered goods—all have necessitated FTC intervention. Although

---

[17]*Goodman* v. *FTC*, 244 F. 2d 584 (1957).

[18]*Gimbel Bros., Inc.* v. *FTC*, 116 F. 2d 578 (1941).

[19]*Northern Feather Works, Inc.* v. *FTC* and *Sumergrade* v. *FTC*, 243 F. 2d 335 (1956); *American Life and Accident Insurance Co.* v. *FTC*, 225 F. 2d 289 (1958).

[20]See Sheldon and Zweibel, *Survey*, pp. 29–30.

[21]*P. Lorillard Co.* v. *FTC*, 189 F. 2d 52, 58 (1950).

[22]*Guides Concerning the Use of Endorsements and Testimonials in Advertising*, adopted 1975 and amended in 1980. In 1978, for the first time, a celebrity agreed to pay a percentage of any restitution that might be ordered against the manufacturer and agreed to make a "reasonable inquiry" into the advertising claims for the product being made. The celebrity was Pat Boone, the product "Acne-Statin." *FTC News Summary*, No. 20-1978, May 19, 1978.

precedent has clearly been set determining that the use of lotteries in the selling of goods is a violation of Section 5,[23] the Commission has nevertheless had to issue a large number of orders against the practice.

Trade Regulation Rules   The use of trade regulation rules by the FTC has largely been an effort to codify the consumer protection part of Section 5 law. It is stated within these rules that what is prohibited by these rules or failed to be disclosed as required by these rules is unfair or deceptive in violation of Section 5. The first 13 promulgated (the first in 1963), and 4 others, apply to specific products. Although some may seem to be picky, they undoubtedly were felt by the FTC to save repeated Section 5 complaint filings. These product-related rules are concerned with sleeping bags (size measurement), household electric sewing machines (use of the term "automatic"), binoculars (deceptive as to nonprismatic, partially prismatic, and prismatic), dry cell batteries (deceptive use of "leakproof"), tablecloths and related products (size measurements), waist belts (deceptive as to leather content), used lubricating oils (deceptive in advertising and labeling), television receivers (size measurement), glass fiber curtains and draperies (failure to disclose possible skin irritation from washing), radios (transistor count), extension ladders (deceptive advertising and labeling as to length), quick-freeze aerosol spray products (failure to disclose lethal effect of inhaling), light bulbs (required labeling as to watts, light output in lumens, and average life), amplifiers (power output claims in home entertainment products), textiles (care labeling), and home insulation (required R-factor).

The second group of trade regulation rules, from the late 1960s and into the 1980s, is concerned primarily with particular industries or marketing practices. They apply to retail food store advertising, games of chance in food and gasoline retailing, door-to-door selling (required cooling-off periods), installment sales ("holder-in-due-course rule"), negative option plans ("We'll keep sending more unless you tell us not to"), mail order rules (promptness in shipping), and ophthalmic goods and services (separation of examination and dispensing).

Only two trade regulation rules do not apply directly to consumer protection. One concerns discriminatory practices in the men's and boys' tailored clothing industry (related to Robinson-Patman Act price discriminations). A second rule sets out requirements for dissemination of full information by franchisors to prospective franchisees.

The use of trade regulation rules, with their full force and effect of law, means that this form of consumer protection has become very specific.

---

[23]*FTC* v. *R. F. Keppel and Bro., Inc.*, 291 U.S. 304 (1934). The Supreme Court held that lotteries were a violation of Section 5 not because they were deceptive but because they were unfair. To be a lottery, the device has to involve a game of chance—that is, what is to be received is not known in advance as being directly related to what is paid.

Business is responsible for complying with all the details of such law, and ignorance of such law is no excuse.

Can an FTC trade regulation rule be too constrictive? For example, might the FTC's rule on retail food store advertising and marketing practices that forbids such stores from advertising a bargain if supplies of such products are not "conspicuously and readily available" be deleterious to the consumer, in that the rule might lead to there being fewer bargain sales? There have been some complaints that this rule might add to the costs of the store in the form of higher inventories, more personnel required, and some waste through spoilage.[24] The FTC has risen to complaints such as this by attempting to assess such tradeoffs not only through use of its own personnel, but also through contract consultation.[25] On the other hand, with a "less government intervention in business" philosophy beginning to prevail in the administration and Congress in 1981, there have been some signs that the FTC will tread more lightly on business in these areas.

Warranty Rules Warranties have been recognized as a special source of deception and confusion to the consumer. They have often not been fully understood because their terms had not been fully made available to the prospective purchaser or had not been presented in a clear fashion. Or consumers have made assumptions that warranties have been more complete than they actually were. The FTC promulgated guides against deceptive advertising of guarantees in 1960. Yet in the next 15 years, over 1000 informal cases had to be settled under them.[26] The Magnuson-Moss Warranty Act of 1975 (sometimes referred to as the Consumer Products Warranty Act) was passed to eliminate this confusion.[27]

This federal statute is detailed in spelling out certain basic requirements for warranties. It turns over to the FTC, however, the responsibility for drawing up the rules. It mandates that the Commission prescribe rules requiring that warranty terms be made available to prospective purchasers prior to the sale of the product. It suggests the content of other rules the FTC might prescribe to facilitate the full disclosure of warranty terms and the settlement of warranty claims. It also requires that a set of rules be considered to cover warranties and warranty practices in the sale of used

[24]*Business Week*, March 28, 1977, p. 92.

[25]See, for example, Market Facts, Inc., *A Study of Consumer Response to the Availability of Advertised Specials*, submitted to the Federal Trade Commission, Task Order No. L0221-E-TQ, July 31, 1979. The Commission's use of consumer research increased "dramatically" in the later 1970s, according to its deputy director of advertising practices. Reported in *CCH Trade Regulation Reports*, no. 465, November 24, 1980, p. 7.

[26]*Parts 701 and 702 Staff Report*, Bureau of Consumer Protection, Federal Trade Commission, 1975, p. 9.

[27]Technically, this act is Title I of the Magnuson-Moss Warranty—Federal Trade Commission Improvement Act of 1975.

motor vehicles. Any failure of a warrantor to comply with the terms of the statute or the rules prescribed thereunder by the FTC would be a violation of Section 5 of the Federal Trade Commission Act.

The nature of the problem to be solved through the statute and the FTC rules can be seen by exploring the sources of consumer confusion that led to the passage of the statute. Warranties all too often never fully disclosed all the facts. A product might have a "lifetime guarantee"—but whose lifetime? If it is a five-year warranty, when does the five-year period begin—with the date of purchase or the date of the item's production? A warranty may be offered, but exactly who is the warrantor—the retailer or the manufacturer? If the warrantor is the manufacturer, how is that manufacturer to be reached to make the warranty good? Are all parts, or only certain parts, covered? Is labor covered? Who pays the freight? Is a completed warranty registration card a prerequisite to making a warranty good?

The 1975 statute and the FTC rules on warranties aim to plug all the loopholes in warranty disclosure, clarity, and procedures for making warranties good. They emphasize that full disclosure of the meaning and content of a warranty are to be made available to the consumer prior to purchase. They emphasize that full disclosure be made in simple and readily understood language. They define the distinctions between "full" and "limited" warranties. They try to delineate the consumer's responsibilities. They encourage warrantors to establish mechanisms for informal dispute settlement and provide rules of minimum requirements for any possible informal settlement procedures.

Misrepresentation—Beyond Cease and Desist   The making of representations or claims for a product by a seller carries with it the responsibility of being able to justify those claims if one is to avoid a cease-and-desist order. In 1971 the FTC established procedures under which it might require an advertiser to submit evidence to substantiate its claims with respect to a product's safety, performance, efficiency, quality, or comparative price.[28] An advertiser can be required to submit results of tests or studies, expert testimony, or other evidence to provide substantiation for the claims. Such data must have been gathered and prepared before the advertising claims were made; the firm cannot suddenly prepare any such materials after the fact. Indeed, the FTC can require that substantiation materials be available prior to the making of a claim.[29]

Not just any test or survey can meet the requirements of adequate substantiation; tests and surveys must be scientifically and competently

[28]See Dorothy Cohen, "The FTC's Advertising Substantiation Program," *Journal of Marketing*, 44, no. 1 (Winter 1980), 26–35, for a history and requirements of this FTC program.
[29]*Jay Norris, Inc., Joel Jacobs, and Mortimer Williams v. FTC*, 598 F. 2d 1244 (1979).

conducted. Data should be accurate. No class of products seems to be exempt from possible demand for substantiation. Sellers of autos, auto tires, electric shavers, air conditioners, television sets, denture adhesives, and wrinkle removers have all been required to submit substantiation data.[30] In 1980 the FTC announced it had completed an investigation to determine whether 83 companies were complying with its orders requiring them to substantiate advertising claims.[31]

The ad substantiation program originally had a twofold purpose. One was to be educational, to provide consumers with more precise information about a product so that they might more fully assess the claims made. This objective was, after early experience, found not to be obtainable. Consumers had not availed themselves of the opportunity to study such materials, and when they had, they had often found them too detailed or technical.[32] The second purpose of the ad substantiation program was deterrence. Knowing that advertised claims might have to be substantiated might make the advertiser cautious as to the extent of the claims to be made.

When advertising claims have not been able to be substantiated, the advertiser can be forced in future representations to make amends for the failings of the previous ones. The FTC has long been recognized as having the power to compel advertisers to make affirmative disclosures concerning their products in advertisements.[33] And warning statements about the use of products have also been required where health was involved. But in 1970 the FTC went further and inaugurated a system of "corrective advertising" designed to reverse erroneous impressions left in consumers' minds by misleading or false advertising. The Commission generally followed the principle that corrective ads would be required where consumer research indicated that lasting false beliefs had been created. It pointed out in 1979, however, that the need for corrective advertising could be based on factors other than consumer research, including the degree of exposure consumers had to the advertising, its persuasive character, the manner in which it was presented, and the nature of the audience.[34]

Early "corrective advertising" requirements were embodied in consent orders. The Commission's legal authority to require such remedial advertising was upheld by a court of appeals in 1977.[35] The FTC order to

[30]Cohen, "Substantiation Program," pp. 28–29.

[31]FTC News Summary, vol. 42–80, July 25, 1980.

[32]Federal Trade Commission, Bureau of Competition Staff Report on Advertising Substantiation, May 1, 1972, reported in CCH Trade Regulation Reporter, para. 50,135.

[33]See Marshall C. Howard, Legal Aspects of Marketing (New York: McGraw-Hill, 1964), pp. 115–17.

[34]1979 Federal Trade Commission letter to the Institute for Public Interest Representation summarized by Dorothy Cohen in "Legal Developments in Marketing," Journal of Marketing, 44, no. 3 (Summer 1980), p. 114.

[35]Warner-Lambert Co. v. FTC, 562 F. 2d 749, certiorari denied, 435 U.S. 950 (1978).

Warner-Lambert required in future Listerine advertisements words to the effect that Listerine would not prevent or lessen the severity of colds or sore throats—a claim it had been making for some years.

Typical of corrective advertising have been required statements such as: "No product cures acne,"[36] and "Anacin is not a tension reliever."[37] The FTC order may spell out in detail the requirements of the corrective advertising: time period over which the ads are to be run, the periodicity of the ads, in which newspapers they are to be run, and over which radio or television stations they are to be broadcast. The amount of money to be spent on the advertising in which the corrective statements are to appear may be specified as well.

A further warning to the advertiser who is not careful is the civil penalties which the FTC, since 1975, can seek out in court action if a seller violates a trade regulation rule or a final cease-and-desist order. The party violating the cease-and-desist order need not be the party against whom the order had been issued, provided that party had knowledge that such act or practice was unfair or deceptive. The civil penalty may not be more than $10,000 for each violation, but each day of failure to comply constitutes a separate violation.

Since the passage of the 1975 act specifically giving the FTC power to seek civil penalties, such actions have been quite common. A book-of-the-month club paid $85,000 in settlement of a violation of the negative option plan trade regulation rule.[38] A seller of a weight-reducing product paid $75,000 in civil penalties for violating a 1971 cease-and-desist order with respect to failing to make certain disclosures.[39] A men's wear firm paid $30,000 for violating the Commission's mail order merchandise rule.[40] An automobile tire manufacturer paid $100,000 for violating a 1975 cease-and-desist order involving unsubstantiated advertisements.[41] A magazine subscription company paid $125,000 for violating a 1972 cease-and-desist order not to use certain pretexts to make customer contacts and to cease using certain unfair debt collection practices.[42] And lest the preceding figures seem small, it should be noted that a magazine publisher paid $1.75 million in civil penalties for violating a cease-and-desist order with respect to distributing simulated checks as part of a promotion program.[43]

Finally, a firm that is not alert as to the accuracy of its advertising and

---

[36]*In re Hayoun Cosmetique, Inc., et al. and AHC Pharmacal, Inc., et al.*, FTC File No. 792-3023 (1980).

[37]*In re American Home Products Corp. et al.*, FTC Docket 8918 (1978).

[38]*U.S.* v. *Book-of-the-Month Club* (D.C.-N.Y.), Civil Action No. 78 Civ. 4093, September 8, 1978.

[39]FTC Docket C-2037, March 3, 1979.

[40]FTC File No. 782-3036, January 9, 1980.

[41]FTC Docket C-2734, September 1978.

[42]FTC File No. 782-3035, October 15, 1980.

[43]*U.S.* v. *Reader's Digest Association*, Trade Cases para. 64,247 (1981).

representations may find itself being forced to grant refunds to customers. Vocational schools have been forced to grant tuition refunds to students who failed to land jobs after completing curricula that made false representations as to job opportunities. Nurseries have been forced to give refunds where the advertising had been false as to growth and survival capabilities of the nursery stock. Dance schools have been required to make certain refunds available to customers after having made false representations.

And land sales companies have been forced to give refunds to purchasers because of deceptive sales statements concerning the investment value of land. Interstate land sales has been an industry subject to much misrepresentation. We present here a survey of this industry as a case study.

INTERSTATE LAND SALES: DECEPTIVE SELLING— A CASE STUDY

In the 1970s, especially in the late 1970s, the FTC began to level a series of complaints and issue orders against the deception and fraud in an industry that has come to be known as the interstate installment land sales, or sometimes "lot sales," industry. Operators in this industry purchase large tracts of inexpensive land, subdivide them into small lots of an acre or less, and then sell those small parcels of land at large markups to individuals by such means as telephone, free local dinner parties, and/or mail order. Purchase has been made easy by minimal or nonexistent down-payment requirements. Large tracts of land in the Southwest were being purchased in the 1960s at $100 an acre and being resold to the public at $5000.[44] In the case of one subdivision, the list prices being charged were three to five times the appraised market value of the lots.[45] The FTC has taken action by issuing complaints claiming violations of Section 5 of the Federal Trade Commission Act.

The Industry   This industry is to be differentiated from that which includes firms specializing in construction and community development, whose primary modus operandi is to lay out a complete plan for a full community with all required public utilities, and then build or sell land for building to other builders. In contrast, the installment land sales industry is primarily concerned with selling land. Some of the firms in this latter industry may also do some building, but for the average company 85 percent of its revenue comes from the sale of lots.[46] It is often difficult for the

---

[44]*Business Week*, October 22, 1979, p. 73.
[45]*In the Matter of AMREP Corp.*, Initial decision to cease and desist, July 18, 1979, FTC Docket 9018, *CCH Trade Regulation Reporter*, para. 21,600.
[46]Morton C. Paulson, *The Great Land Hustle* (Chicago: Regnery, 1974), p. 10.

buyer to distinguish between a firm primarily interested in making lot sales and one interested in developing a full-fledged community. This is because an aggressive sales effort emphasizes the increasing investment value of a lot as a community grows and develops around it.

It has been estimated that in 1974 there were more than 10,000 firms in the interstate land sales industry.[47] This number includes large as well as small firms. In 1971, 21 of the 200 largest U.S. corporations were involved in this land selling.[48] The total acreage and number of lots in a subdivision can be of considerable proportions. International Telephone and Telegraph's Palm Coast subdivision north of Daytona Beach, Florida, has 48,000 lots; General Development Corporation's Port Charlotte, Florida, subdivision has 194,000 lots; GAC Corporation's Rio Rico subdivision in Arizona has 34,000 lots; and AMREP's Rio Rancho Estates in New Mexico has 100,000 lots.[49]

Those states with considerable quantities of undeveloped (and sometimes undevelopable) land are the prime sites for such lot sale activity. The states of Arizona and New Mexico have much barren and desolate desert land, yet have the superficial attraction attraction to the unwary of a favorable climate. The mountains of Colorado have their own scenic attraction, although much of this land is unsuitable for home sites. Florida has much in the way of land that can be called "boondocks," but its sunny warmth and blue waters can entice the purchaser who is not cautious. Many of these lands are too dry or too wet or too mountainous or too out of the way. Their seeming potential, however, provides the glib salesperson with potent arguments. Such lots can be sold sight-unseen for considerably more than their true market value.

The Sales Techniques   The appeal of interstate land purchase lies in the rich return it is argued can be obtained from investment in land. Land is limited in supply; its price can only go up. Land is an excellent investment, with little or no financial risk. Resale of lots, at a profit, can be accomplished with ease. The land being sold is usable as home sites. Necessary utilities will soon be forthcoming. If the land is in the Southwest, a comparison with the phenomenal increase in land values in Phoenix and Tucson can be used. If it is in Colorado, ski resorts and condominiums have been rising like mushrooms. If it is in Florida, there is the rapid growth in the population of that state.

Some selling is more directly fraudulent. Land in Florida may be swampy or marshy, yet sold as being high and dry. Lots sold as waterfront properties may never have been cleared for the necessary canal dredging

---

[47]Ibid., p. 9.

[48]Patricia A. Simko, *The Insider's Guide to Owning Land in Subdivisions* (New York: Inform, Inc., 1980), p. 6.

[49]"Buying a Homesite? Beware the Promised Lands," *Consumer Reports,* May 1978, pp. 286–87.

by the Army Corps of Engineers. Lands in the Southwest may be so far
from any center of population that installation of full public utilities would
be prohibitively costly. Or necessary supplies of water may be inadequate.
Or the "roads" constructed may be nothing more than a bulldozed strip
stretching across the desert. Lands in the Rockies may be clearly unsuitable
for a home site.

A come-on of some commission-seeking high-pressure salespeople is
to confide in the potential customer that the property may soon be bought
out by a large corporation that is planning to build a factory on the site. The
resale price of the land, after a holding period of no more than a year, is
sure to be double or triple what the customer has to pay. Another gambit is
that a large corporation may soon be building a new manufacturing plant
nearby, and this factory will require a large labor force. So the demand for
home sites will experience a definite and strong increase, forcing all prices
up. Or a local airport may soon be converted to a major jetport. To sum up,
it may not be very difficult in the lot-sales industry to perpetrate a "vicious
consumer fraud."[50]

Regulation Efforts   State regulation of land sale abuses has been
only partially effective. It has tended to be weakest in those states where
the land hustlers have been most active.[51] Federal regulation of the interstate sale of land was eventually passed in the form of the 1968 Interstate
Land Sales Full Disclosure Act. But, as its title implies, it requires only
disclosure of certain facts. It requires that sellers of 50 or more unimproved
lots register the subdivision with HUD (Housing and Urban Development)
and that the sellers give prospective buyers, prior to purchase, a written
property report containing certain information about the land, such as
availability of present or proposed utilities, any liens on the property, soil
conditions, and distance between the subdivision and nearby communities. It does not, however, require the performance of the salesperson's promises. Nor can it prohibit the sale of any land because it is overpriced. Nor can it assist in the resale of the land. The proof of the ineffec-
tiveness of this federal law lies in the complaints the FTC has found it
necessary to file throughout the later years of the 1970s and into the 1980s.

Consent and cease-and-desist orders have been issued by the FTC
requiring an end to various misrepresentations in the lot-sales industry.[52]

---

[50]See comments of an administrative law judge of the FTC in *In the Matter of Horizon
Corp.*, Initial decision to cease and desist, September 21, 1979, FTC Docket 9017, *CCH Trade
Regulation Reporter*, para. 21,621.

[51]Paulson, *Land Hustle*, p. 168.

[52]See *In the Matter of GAC Corp., et al.*, 84 F.T.C. 163 (1974): *In the Matter of International
Telephone and Telegraph Corporation, et al.*, 88 F.T.C. 933 (1976); *In the Matter of Las Animas
Ranch, Inc., et al.*, 89 F.T.C. 255 (1977); *In the Matter of Flagg Industries, Inc., et al.*, 90 F.T.C. 226
(1977); *In the Matter of Cavanagh Communities Corporation, et al.*, 93 F.T.C. 559 (1979); *In the
Matter of Bankers Life and Casualty Company, et al.*, 94 F.T.C. 363 (1979); *In the Matter of Irving*

These orders have required not only cessation of misrepresentations, but also certain positive disclosures. Individual orders have varied, but certain prohibitions stand out. Lots are not to be sold as good or safe investments. Land prices are not to be touted as always rising. Easy resale cannot be promised. The prospective purchaser is to be advised of the possible high cost of installing any necessary additional utilities. The rate of economic development of the subdivision or surrounding area is not to be exaggerated. The customer is to be advised to consult a registered real estate agent before purchasing the land. Cooling-off periods are to be established, giving the buyer a chance to back out of the purchase after thinking about it for a certain number of days. And, of course, no lies are to be told about the actual nature of the land itself which is up for sale.

FTC efforts have gone beyond cease-and-desist, insistence on positive disclosure, and requirement of "cooling-off" periods. Refunds to purchasers have been ordered.[53] Forfeiture clauses in sales contracts are being challenged.[54] Prices on lots already purchased have been ordered reduced.[55] And land companies have been ordered to improve land that has been sold to make it more habitable.[56]

REGULATING LABELING

The regulation of labeling emanates from several federal agencies. The FTC can use the omnipresent Section 5 of the Federal Trade Commission Act to control labeling where it is an unfair or deceptive practice. The FTC can use trade regulation rules to regulate labeling—as it has, for example, with rules that set requirements with respect to the labeling of light bulbs and home insulation. Congress, in special legislation, gave the FTC the responsibility for establishing labeling rules for wool, fur, and textile garments.

The FDA can establish rules pertaining to the labeling of foods, drugs, devices, and cosmetics under authority granted to it under the Food, Drug,

---

Miller, 94 F.T.C. 1122 (1979). A cease-and-desist order after full proceedings has also been issued in *In the Matter of Horizon Corp.*, FTC Docket No. 9017, *FTC News Summary*, vol. 33–81, May 22, 1981.

[53]*FTC News Summary*, vol. 33-81, May 22, 1981. In one case involving the sale of land in Australia, partial refund of monies to purchasers was consented to and the firms agreed to stop collecting any payments at all. This was because the land could not be resold without the consent of all the other purchasers. *In the Matter of Australian Land Title, Ltd., et al.*, 92 F.T.C. 362 (1978).

[54]Ibid. Also *In the Matter of AMREP Corp.*, Initial decision to cease and desist, July 18, 1979, FTC Docket 9018. A "liquidating damages" clause can force the buyer to give up any right to the land and all cash paid in if he or she falls behind in installment payments.

[55]Settlement filed by the FTC and entered in the Colorado district court against two developments in Colorado. *FTC News Summary*, vol. 4–81, October 24, 1980.

[56]*In the Matter of GAC Corp., et al.*, 84 F.T.C. 163 (1974), and proposed modified order, February 28, 1979, FTC Docket C-2523; *In the Matter of Horizon Corp.*, FTC Docket No. 9017.

and Cosmetic Act. The FDA also controls the labeling of hazardous substances under the provisions of the Federal Hazardous Substances Labeling Act of 1960. The Department of Agriculture regulates the labeling of meat, poultry, and eggs. The Federal Alcohol Administration regulates the labeling and packaging of distilled spirits, wine, and malt beverages. The National Marine Fisheries Service establishes rules pertaining to fish labeling.

The Truth-in-Packaging Act (1966)   The Fair Packaging and Labeling Act of 1966, the so-called Truth-in-Packaging-Act, directed the FTC and FDA to issue certain rules and authorized them to issue certain other rules pertaining to the packaging and labeling of consumer goods. The FDA was to promulgate rules for foods, drugs, devices, and cosmetics. Any violation of those rules would be considered misbranding in violation of the Food, Drug, and Cosmetic Act. The FTC was to promulgate rules to cover any other consumer commodity—those customarily sold through retail stores for consumption by individuals. A violation of these rules would constitute an unfair or deceptive act or practice in violation of Section 5 of the Federal Trade Commission Act.

The basic objective of this 1966 law was to provide the consumer with better information to facilitate value comparisons. Information, on consumer product labels had too often been found to be incomplete, inconspicuous, or confusing. Actual sizes and weights were especially confusing, with a proliferation of fractional weights and quantities. The mandatory labeling requirements specified in the statute were the identity of the product; name and place of business of the manufacturer or distributor; net quantity of contents accurately stated in terms of weight, measure, or numerical count; and where the number of servings is cited, a clear translation of that into terms of net quantity of each serving in terms of weight, measure, or numerical count. The FTC's rules, drawn up to cover these labeling requirements, were 26 in number. It takes a good deal of specification to point out how, where, and in what size print the necessary labeling information can legitimately appear on different kinds of packages.[57]

Upon a finding of need to prevent deception or facilitate value comparisons with respect to any commodity, the FTC and the FDA were given authority to issue rules defining standards for characterizing the size of packages (small, large); regulating labeling implying special lower prices ("cents-off" claims); and requiring labels to show the common or usual name of the commodity and its ingredients. The FTC has found it necessary to issue rules on "cents-off" representations, "introductory offers," and use of the term "economy size."

The FDA had already issued many rules and regulations under its

[57]Federal Trade Commission, *Rules, Regulations, Statement of General Policy or Interpretation and Exemptions under the Fair Packaging and Labeling Act,* issued October 1, 1971.

rule-making authority with respect to foods, drugs, devices, and cosmetics. The requirements of the Fair Packaging and Labeling Act, therefore, fit into its labeling requirement work. And it has been adding new rules of its own from time to time. With respect to foods, for example, it requires on labels the designation of ingredients, in descending order of prominence. It has set standards of identity and quality for given products, such as canned green beans. It has established labeling and composition requirements for foods purported to be for special dietary uses. Labeling rules govern "low-calorie" and "reduced calorie" foods. Certain labeling rules must be followed when claims are made about nutritional quality. Proposals to *require* nutritional labeling illustrate the cost-benefit resolutions that would have to be made. How many consumers would really understand nutritional labeling? And how many of the relatively small food processors have staffs able accurately to apply nutritional labeling requirements?

Textile and Fur Labeling Laws   Three controversial labeling statutes passed by Congress have been the Wool Products Labeling Act of 1939, the Fur Products Labeling Act of 1951, and the Textile Fiber Products Identification Act of 1958. All three of these statutes were placed under the jurisdiction of the FTC for promulgation of any necessary rules, and violations of any of these rules would be considered an unfair method of competition and an unfair and deceptive act or practice in violation of the Federal Trade Commission Act.

The wool statute professed to assist the consumer in knowing, by means of a required label, how much of a wool product was composed of virgin wool and how much of it was made of other fibers, especially reprocessed or reused wool. The FTC promulgated some 35 rules to support this statute. The fur statute aimed to throw light on what kind of fur was actually in a fur product, since a proliferation of brand names akin to real fur names had been confusing the consumer. To supplement this statute, the FTC fashioned some 50 rules and a list of 103 legitimate animal fur names that could be used. The textile fiber products statute was designed to let the consumer know the percentage fiber composition of garments in an age of synthetic fibers. Some 45 rules were promulgated by the FTC to reinforce that statute.

The question has been raised as to whether these three labeling statutes were designed to protect producers more than they were to protect consumers. After all, the competitor who does not label products fully and honestly may obtain an unfair advantage over competitors. In the case of these labeling statutes, the facts show that the legislation was sponsored and urged primarily by industry members.[58] And the prologues of the

[58]Marshall C. Howard, "Textile and Fur Labeling Legislation: Names, Competition, and the Consumer," *California Management Review*, 14, no. 2 (Winter 1971), 69–80; Alan Stone, "Mislabeled Labeling Acts: Economics and Politics in the Wool and Fur Industries," *Antitrust Law & Economics Review*, 7, no. 3 (1975), 46–60.

wool and textile fiber products statutes do specifically state that they are to protect producers as well as consumers.

TEXTILE FIBER PRODUCTS: REQUIRED LABELING—
A CASE STUDY

The Textile Fiber Products Identification Act of 1958 was passed, according to its preamble, "To protect producers and consumers against misbranding and false advertising of the fiber content of textile fiber products, and for other purposes." The basic cause of the envisioned problem was the growing use of synthetic fibers in blends. Even sophisticated consumers could often not identify the actual fibers being used. And producers were finding some synthetics cheaper than natural fibers, and some synthetics cheaper than others, and were making substitutions. A new source of competition had arisen.

The Federal Statute Provisions   Principal supporters of the legislation were the agricultural producers of the natural fibers against which inroads were being made. Cotton producers, wool (sheep) farmers, and fur interests represented vested interests supportive of the statute. Then too, the producers of the more expensive synthetic fibers felt the need for protection from lower-cost synthetics that were being passed off as being more desirable than they were. The argument was also presented that the consumer needed to be protected from deception. Thus, the statute stated that any misbranding or false or deceptive advertising within the meaning of the statute or the rules drawn up to support it was an unfair method of competition and an unfair and deceptive act or practice under the Federal Trade Commission Act.

According to the statute and its rules, textile fiber products must have a label or tag conspicuously affixed to the product which shows the percentage breakdown of constituent fibers by generic name in order of predominance. The label must also show the manufacturer's name or registered identification number. If an imported product, the country of origin must be shown. It must remain attached throughout its sale, resale, distribution, and handling until sold and delivered to the ultimate consumer. The statute, and rules under the statute, also require full disclosure of a product's fiber content in advertising. Invoices must also accurately reflect fiber composition.

The generic names of the natural and manufactured fibers in a textile fiber product must appear on the required label and in their order of predominance by weight. The list of permissible generic names of artificial fibers as drawn up by the FTC in 1960 included 16 terms: acrylic, modacrylic, polyester, rayon, acetate, saran, azlon, nytril, nylon, rubber, spandex, vinal, olefin, vinyon, metallic, and glass. (Three additional names had been added by 1980: anidex, novoloid, and aramid.) Some 700 tradenames which had been in use now had to be placed in one of these 16 categories. A compromise led to the rules permitting the use of a trademark to accompany the generic names on the label, so long as they appear together in immediate conjunction and in type or lettering of equal size and conspicuousness. Thus, Du Pont's Dacron frequently appears in conjunction with the word "polyester."

To enforce the statute the FTC was authorized to make inspections, analyses, tests, and examinations of any product subject to the requirements of the act. The FTC has been criticized for paying too much attention to the minutiae of enforcement of this and the other labeling acts.[59] The resources used to inspect mills and to make spot checks of labels in retail stores might more profitably be used elsewhere. Making an issue of a garment labeled 70 percent polyester when it is actually only 60 percent polyester may not seem to be that important to the ultimate user and thus not the best use of limited resources. This is essentially the same question of priority setting experienced by any enforcement agency.

Content versus Performance Labeling   Two issues of possible consumer confusion have never been fully resolved by the Textile Fiber Products Identification Act. First, how many consumers can distinguish clearly between trade names and the generic names? Second, if they can, of what real significance is it? Required labeling under the 1958 statute is content labeling. The label tells the consumer exactly what the fiber content of a textile product is. Yet performance labeling can be of much greater value to the consumer. This kind of labeling informs the consumer as to how a product should be cared for and how it can be expected to perform in actual use. Years of education and experience may enable more consumers to understand the performance qualities of certain fibers. Still, when a new mixture appears, the consumer may still need more information. It is for this reason that the FTC has gone beyond the statute's requirements and relied on the trade regulation rule to attempt to provide a better resolution of this problem.

In 1972 the FTC promulgated a trade regulation rule entitled "Care Labeling of Textile Wearing Apparel." The rule requires a label or tag to be permanently attached to a finished article of wearing apparel by the maker of that article. The tag must clearly disclose its care and maintenance instructions. This name tag or label requirement also applies to piece goods designed to be converted by the consumer into wearing apparel. Failure to tag or label such articles of clothing or piece goods in the required manner is an unfair method of competition and an unfair or deceptive act or practice in violation of the Federal Trade Commission Act.

Under the rule, the care and maintenance labeling requirements are

[59]See *Report of the ABA Commission to Study the Federal Trade Commission*, pp. 45–49.

those "necessary to the ordinary use and enjoyment of the article." The information carried on the label concerns such operations as washing, drying, ironing, bleaching, and dry cleaning. The information provided should not only disclose what is acceptable care and maintenance, but also warn against procedures that would substantially lessen ordinary use and enjoyment. Consumer confusion concerning new fabrics theoretically is thus lessened through greater knowledge of their performance characteristics. Even professional cleaners and launderers could benefit from the label information, since some had experienced the difficulties of shrinking, stretching, or fading.

The FTC apparently did not believe all consumer problems relating to the proper care of textile products had been resolved through the addition of the 1972 rule. After seeking public comments in 1974, it proposed in 1976 a thoroughly amended trade regulation rule—"Care Labeling of Textile Products and Leather Clothing." This proposed rule, after the close of a period of public comment in 1981, was still under consideration by the FTC in early 1982. This rule is new in several respects. It adds coverage to several other products: leather clothing, draperies, curtains, slipcovers, upholstered furniture, yarn, and carpets and rugs. It is much longer and more detailed and requires the use of specified standard terminology. And it emphasizes the warning approach to care labeling.

The new rule would specify exactly what would form the basis of an unfair or deceptive act or practice. With respect to textile wearing apparel, draperies, curtains, slipcovers, linens, yarn, piece goods, and leather and suede clothing, it would be illegal for a manufacturer or importer (1) to fail to disclose to a purchaser prior to sale the instructions for care procedure necessary to assure "the ordinary use and enjoyment of the product," (2) to fail to warn a purchaser prior to sale when a product cannot be cleaned by any cleaning procedure without being harmed, (3) to fail to warn a purchaser that a procedure a consumer or professional cleaner could reasonably be expected to use would harm the product, (4) to fail to provide care instructions and warnings that can be used by the customer throughout the useful life of the product, (5) to fail to use standardized language in care instructions and warnings, and (6) to fail to possess, prior to the sale, a "reasonable basis" for the care information provided. A long glossary of terms that must be used is provided in an appendix.

Rule-making by a regulatory agency by its very nature makes the law of trade regulation quite specific. At least one commissioner believed the proposed amended rule to be much too specific. Detailed requirements to the point where failure to use particular, standardized terms constitutes a violation of the Federal Trade Commission Act is engaging in an "unnecessary and unduly burdensome form of regulation," according to Commissioner Robert Pitofsky. He would have used guides instead.[60] On the other

---

[60]46 Fed. Reg. 941, January 5, 1981.

hand, the required use of specific terminology can remove the "uncertainties" of law. The apparent "burden" of the law can easily dissipate after a
short period of learning.

SUMMARY

Time and experience have demonstrated that competition is a sufficiently
imperfect process that certain safeguards for the consumer under certain
conditions are desirable. Consumer protection against certain omissions or
commissions on the part of the seller and against buyer lack of full product
knowledge can contribute to more rational consumer decision-making and
therefore a better allocation of resources.

The principal consumer protection agency is the Federal Trade Commission. Section 5 of the Federal Trade Commission Act condemns not
only unfair methods of competition, but also acts or practices unfair or
deceptive to the consumer. A large body of Section 5 consumer protection
case law precedent has developed. The FTC has used the trade regulation
rule since 1963 to supplement and strengthen enforcement of consumer
protection under Section 5. State consumer protection law has tended to
follow this federal precedent.

Certain price advertising practices can be deceptive to the consumer.
The FTC has found it necessary to issue several guides with respect to
some of these practices. Problems can arise because a given pricing practice, such as comparable value pricing, can perform a valuable marketplace
function through informing the consumer of available alternatives, yet the
same practice can be abused.

A host of advertising and selling practices have been abused often
enough to require FTC intervention. The trade regulation rule, with the full
force and effect of law, has been used to an increasing degree in the 1960s
and 1970s. The capability of such rules was strengthened by legislation in
1975. Warranty rules by the FTC were mandated by Congress.

Whereas cease-and-desist has been the usual FTC means for enforcement, that agency has required substantiation of advertising claims
and has embodied "corrective advertising" requirements in orders. It can
also seek civil penalties against violators in the courts and demand refunds
for consumers. The interstate land sales industry has been a target of FTC
action against misrepresentation in sales and illustrates the nature of the
deception and the degree of ability of the FTC to bring some form of
restitution to its victims.

Labeling of products is required by several government agencies and
several different pieces of federal legislation. One of these, the Textile Fiber
Products Identification Act of 1958, illustrates what can and what cannot be
accomplished by different kinds of labeling requirements and how such
requirements make the law more and more specific.

Selected Readings

BRANDT, MICHAEL T., AND IVAN L. PRESTON, "The Federal Trade Commission's Use of Evidence to Determine Deception," *Journal of Marketing*, 41, no. 1 (January 1977), 54-62.

COHEN, DOROTHY, "The Concept of Unfairness as It Relates to Advertising Legislation," *Journal of Marketing*, 38, no. 3 (July 1974), 8-13.

FELDMAN, LAURENCE P., *Consumer Protection: Problems and Prospects*. St. Paul, Minn.: West, 1976.

PAULSON, MORTON C., *The Great Land Hustle*. Chicago: Regnery, 1974.

PRESTON, IVAN L., "The FTC's Handling of Puffery and Other Selling Claims Made 'by Implication'", *Journal of Business Research*, 5, no. 2 (June 1977), 155-81.

SHELDON, JONATHAN A., AND GEORGE J. ZWEIBEL, *Survey of Consumer Fraud Law*. Washington, D.C.: U.S. Government Printing Office, 1978.

9 — Two Selected Issues: Joint Ventures and Commercial Bribery

Certain events occurring in the 1970s threw a spotlight on two particular issues of antitrust and trade regulation. The first was that of the joint venture. Two antitrust guides published by the Department of Justice paid particular attention to this issue. A 1977 guide pertained to international operations.[1] It presented guidelines through the use of 14 hypothetical case examples; 4 of them were concerned with joint ventures. These were actually more than hypothetical, because they represented the pulling together of the Department of Justice's views as represented in pleadings, important cases, and competitive impact statements (which had to accompanying proposed consent decrees).[2] It was not because there was an unusually large amount of foreign antitrust litigation pending that this guide was issued. Rather, there was concern that uncertainty over application of the antitrust laws may have served to discourage international trade and investment. The second Department of Justice guide, issued in 1980, was concerned directly with research joint ventures.[3] It was designed to indi-

[1]U.S. Department of Justice, *Antitrust Guide for International Operations* (Washington, D.C.: U.S. Government Printing Office, 1977).

[2]Douglas E. Rosenthal, Assistant Chief, Foreign Commerce Section, Antitrust Division, Department of Justice, "On the Antitrust Guide for International Operations," Remarks before the Antitrust and Trade Regulation Committee of the United States Chamber of Commerce, Washington, D.C., March 9, 1977, mimeo, pp. 5, 8.

[3]U.S. Department of Justice, *Antitrust Guide Concerning Research Joint Ventures* (Washington, D.C.: U.S. Government Printing Office, 1980).

cate to the business community that a good deal of cooperative research activity to foster innovation could be engaged in without fear of antitrust attack. It too used hypothetical case studies—yet ones that were often based on actual combinations of circumstances.[4]

The second issue, commercial bribery, received conspicuous public attention when Congress passed the Foreign Corrupt Practices Act in 1977. The passage of this trade regulation statute was preceded by bribery scandals involving American corporations doing business abroad. This statute has been criticized as being lacking in clarity and as presenting competitive problems to firms attempting to comply with it. Bills in Congress in 1980 and 1981 were concerned with possible amendments to this statute.

JOINT VENTURES

A *joint venture* is a business organization established by two or more persons or firms that pool their assets and skills. The basic characteristic of a joint venture is joint ownership. In the case of a merger, in contrast, ownership of assets moves from one owner to another.[5] A joint venture need not be a large corporation. It may have a limited objective and be short-lived. It may be transnational in character, with both domestic and foreign corporations joining in the venture. Joint ventures are to be distinguished from pooling arrangements, in which firms in a market collectively determine their operations and pool their profits. Such arrangements pool income, not assets.

The use of joint ventures was fairly limited until the 1950s.[6] But during the 1970s, they occurred at a rate of approximately 10 percent of that of mergers. Joint ventures recorded by the Federal Trade Commission in the years 1972 through 1978 totaled 1083, compared with 11,318 mergers recorded for that same period.[7] The average number per year in those years was 155, with the actual number ranging from 82 in 1975 to 289 in 1972.[8] These joint ventures have had only United States firms as parents or had both United States and foreign firms as parents. It has been predicted that

---

[4]Ibid., p. 2.

[5]See Joseph F. Brodley, "The Legal Status of Joint Ventures under the Antitrust Laws: A Summary Assessment," *Antitrust Bulletin*, 21, no. 3 (Fall 1976), 453–83. He states that a joint venture represents "more than a simple contract yet less than a merger," p. 454. Wilbur L. Fugate would include contractual arrangements but states that the jointly owned corporation is the more frequent form. *Foreign Commerce and the Antitrust Laws* (Boston: Little, Brown, 1973), p. 355.

[6]Stanley E. Boyle, "An Estimate of the Number and Size Distribution of Domestic Joint Subsidiaries," *Antitrust Law & Economics Review*, 1, no. 3 (Spring 1968), 81.

[7]Federal Trade Commission, *Statistical Report on Mergers and Acquisitions 1978* (Washington, D.C.: U.S. Government Printing Office, 1980), pp. 25, 228.

[8]Ibid., p. 228.

the use of joint ventures will increase; it may be a necessary way of entering foreign markets, given foreign nation requirements.[9]

Foreign Commerce Antitrust Enforcement   The antitrust laws specifically apply to foreign as well as domestic commerce. The Sherman Act of 1890 is the antitrust statute that has been chiefly relied upon in reaching unreasonable restraints of trade and monopolies which affect the country's foreign commerce. Sections 1 and 2 apply to trade or commerce "with foreign nations" as well as "among the several states." Likewise, "commerce" is defined in both the Federal Trade Commission Act and the Clayton Act to include commerce with foreign nations.

Two other federal antitrust statutes are applicable to foreign commerce. The Wilson Tariff Act of 1894 contains antitrust provisions; it makes it illegal for importers to restrain trade with respect to imports. Where used, it has usually been in conjunction with Sherman Act charges. The Webb-Pomerene Act of 1918 represents a partial exemption from the antitrust laws. It permits American exporters to get together in an export association to facilitate export sales. It does not permit any restraint by the association on the export business of any domestic competitors or use of the association to restrain domestic competition. The Federal Trade Commission is assigned the task of keeping a record of such associations and maintaining surveillance over their conduct.

In considering the foreign commerce aspects of antitrust, two things should be kept in mind. First, the foreign commerce which is relevant to the antitrust laws of the United States is that of imports, exports, and foreign investment opportunities available to American business.[10] Imports or the price of imports should not be significantly affected by any interference with competition. Similarly, no restraints of any consequence should be placed upon United States exports or private investment overseas. These import-export and foreign investment limits differentiate foreign from domestic commerce antitrust enforcement: "Purely domestic decisions may not be readily generalized to the international context."[11]

The second point of difference peculiar to foreign commerce antitrust enforcement is the problem of the jurisdiction of United States antitrust laws over business activity of American or foreign firms that takes place in foreign countries but at the same time may affect United States commerce. If a foreign firm has an office in the United States or is conducting business in the United States, the problem of jurisdiction is minimized. But suppose the arrangements an American firm has with a foreign firm in a foreign country have an adverse impact on United States exports or imports but

[9]G. Richard Young and Standish Bradford, Jr., *Joint Ventures: Planning and Action* (n.p.: Arthur D. Little, Inc., 1977), pp. 35–39.
[10]U.S. Department of Justice, *International Operations*, pp. 4–5.
[11]Ibid., p. 1, n. 1.

are perfectly legal under the laws of the foreign country? Suppose they were required by a foreign nation's laws? Or suppose those arrangements were with a foreign government-owned firm? Such circumstances might provide a defense against antitrust not only to the foreign, but also to the American firm. Although American courts are generally agreed that there is some extraterritoriality jurisdiction under the Sherman Act, "Even among American courts and commentators, however, there is no consensus on how far the jurisdiction should extend."[12]

Political as well as economic forces have to be considered with respect to United States antitrust enforcement in foreign commerce. The appeals court in the 1976 *Timberlane Lumber Co.* decision said three questions had to be answered: Did the alleged restraint affect, or was it intended to affect, United States foreign commerce? Did the alleged restraint have sufficient magnitude to involve the Sherman Act? And what was the impact on international comity and fairness?[13] International comity, or a mutual courtesy among nations with respect to the different nations' laws, can be a limiting factor as far as United States antitrust enforcement is concerned. Although some nations may be becoming more antitrust-oriented, and international bodies such as the United Nations and the Organization for Economic Cooperation and Development have passed resolutions or declarations in opposition to restrictive business practices, there are limits to the extraterritorial extension of United States antitrust policy. It has been estimated that "blocking" foreign statutes outnumber cooperation agreements 5 to 1 and that instances of diplomatic protests exceed those of express diplomatic support 3 to 1.[14]

Reasons for Joint Ventures   Several reasons have been proffered to justify the creation and use of joint ventures. Some undertakings may be very costly, and a joint venture can spread the cost. The economies of scale present can be too great for any one firm to enjoy by itself. A development project in a developing country may be of immense proportions and beyond the capability of any one firm. Such large projects may also be politically risky, and a joint venture can spread the risks. A joint venture may be the only way an American company can break into some foreign markets, since some nations insist on their own national companies representing at least 50 percent (sometimes 51 percent) interest in a foreign company doing business within their boundaries. Some firms may be lacking in adequate

---

[12]*Timberlane Lumber Co.* v. *Bank of America, N.T. & S.A.,* 549 F. 2d 597, 610 (1976).
[13]Ibid., p. 615.
[14]Joel Davidow, Director of Policy Planning, Antitrust Division, Department of Justice, "Extraterritorial Antitrust: An American View," Remarks before the International Chamber of Commerce Conference on Extra-Territorial Application of Competition Laws, Paris, March 12, 1981, mimeo, p. 4. Blocking statutes can prevent the United States from obtaining documents in a foreign country about a foreign firm even though those documents pertain to the operations of the foreign firm in the United States.

cash, knowhow, or patents and need the resources of another firm before they can begin to engage in certain endeavors. Flexibility in borrowing new capital may be achieved when more than one firm is available to provide guarantees or collateral for loans. Sometimes progress can be more rapid by pooling research and development assets and efforts.

Joint ventures are common in the petroleum industry. Joint bidding for new leases on government acreage has served to share cost and risk. Exploratory drilling projects customarily have several parties contractually tied in to the venture: landowners, drilling contractors, and two or more oil companies (perhaps both small and large). Large, long-distance crude oil pipelines customarily have several large refining companies as co-owners. Joint ownership spreads the costs and provides security of supply to the refiner-owners, no one of which can utilize the capacity of the most economical size of pipe. Large oil refineries in overseas locations may have as co-owners several large American and foreign vertically integrated petroleum firms. Such an arrangement spreads the costs and political risks, and some national ownership may be dictated by the policy of the particular nation.

Other industries also provide illustrations of the use of joint ventures. Joint subsidiaries in the steel industry have been utilized to achieve backward integration into iron ore mining.[15] Joint ventures have likewise been used in silver mining. The petrochemical industry has set up joint asset ownership interlocks between the petroleum and the chemical industries. Large firms in the glass industry have utilized joint subsidiaries among themselves in the production of certain products, especially in foreign countries, and with firms in other industries, such as the chemical industry. Real estate developers have joined with insurance companies on particular projects. French capital and knowhow have combined in ventures with California vintners.

From observing these reasons for use of the joint venture, we can conclude that it can be preferable to an outright merger under certain conditions. First, a firm may have no choice in the matter. If it wishes to do business in a particular foreign country, it may have to enter that business as a co-owner with a firm or national of that country. Second, the enterprise may be short-lived, such as an economic development project like a domestic real estate development or construction of a hydroelectric dam abroad. Once the project has been completed, the firms go their separate ways. Third, a project may be too immense in scope for any one firm, yet each firm may want to retain its own separate rights, as in the Alaska pipeline or joint ownership of massive iron ore reserves. Fourth, a particular project may be so risky that it is advisable to share that risk with

---

[15]See Daniel R. Fusfield, "Joint Subsidiaries in the Iron and Steel Industry," *American Economic Review*, 58, no. 2 (May 1958), 578–87.

others—for example, an oil well drilling project. Joint ventures may also, of course, serve as a vehicle for a restrictive market-sharing agreement.

Joint Ventures and Antitrust　Where the parents of a joint venture are large corporations that have created a joint subsidiary, they may have created a structural market situation, the operations of which may be suspected of restraining competition. The Sherman Act was the only applicable antitrust statute until the Supreme Court ruled in the 1964 *Penn-Olin* decision that Section 7 of the Clayton Act was relevant.[16] Yet the great majority of joint ventures seem not to be in conflict with the antitrust laws. The number of cases has been small. And of the business reviews handed down by the Department of Justice with respect to joint ventures, 90 percent have been cleared.[17] On the other hand, if 10 percent of the number of joint ventures not submitted for review were questionable as to their impact upon competition, there would then be an antitrust problem.

It is clear that there are many variables in the total mix to be considered: the number and size of the competitors involved and of the joint ventures themselves; whether relationships among the members of the ventures are horizontal, vertical, or conglomerate; the relationships of joint ventures to their parents; the existence of potential competition; and the purpose and duration of the joint ventures. The possible combinations of market features surrounding joint ventures is large.[18]

In the sections that follow, certain facets of the joint venture vis-à-vis antitrust have been isolated for presentation. In the case of foreign joint ventures, the venture must have a "substantial and foreseeable" effect on United States commerce no matter where the joint venture operates in order to fall within the jurisdiction of United States antitrust law.[19]

Market Sharing　Jointly owned enterprises designed to be substitutes for individual *horizontally* competitive enterprises and that serve to divide markets and thwart price competition would be clear *per se* violations of the Sherman Act. The *Minnesota Mining & Mfg.* case provides the classic outlines of such market sharing.[20] American manufacturers representing 80 percent of the exports of coated abrasives formed several joint manufacturing subsidiaries in overseas territories through a holding company in the United States. Patents and technology were pooled through

[16]*U.S.* v. *Penn-Olin Chemical Co.*, 378 U.S. 158.

[17]Ky P. Ewing, Deputy Assistant Attorney General, Antitrust Division, Department of Justice, "Federal Antitrust Enforcement: A Partnership with the Private Bar," Remarks before the North Carolina Bar Foundation, Raleigh, N.C., January 19, 1980, mimeo, p. 13.

[18]For a study of various structural conditions and market relationships that come into play in antitrust considerations of joint ventures, see Brodley, "The Legal Status of Joint Ventures."

[19]U.S. Department of Justice, *International Operations*, p. 6.

[20]*U.S.* v. *Minnesota Mining & Mfg. Co.*, 92 F. Supp. 947 (1950).

this holding company. The members agreed not to export from this country to compete in the territories assigned to their jointly owned foreign manufacturing companies. The parents thus agreed not to compete with their progeny and thus with each other, and exports were subjected to a major restraint. It was also felt that the arrangement had the effect of foreclosing from independent exporters some of the market served by the jointly owned foreign companies.

The *Timken Roller Bearing* decision of the Supreme Court provides a similar but structurally different illustration of illegality under Section 1 of the Sherman Act of market division as facilitated by the use of the joint venture.[21] The joint ventures themselves were not under attack; it was the market behavior practiced through the use of joint ventures. Timken held 30 percent of the stock of British Timken, with 24 percent held by a British businessman by the name of Dewar. Timken and Dewar then organized French Timken and jointly held that firm's stock. Beginning in 1928, these three companies and the one individual, the parents and two joint venture children, divided up among themselves world markets for antifriction bearings, of which they had a substantial portion of the world's production. They also fixed prices to be charged in the different territories, cooperated among themselves to eliminate the competition of outsiders or conspired with these competitors to fix prices, and participated in cartels to restrict imports to and exports from the United States. The defense that such restraints "were merely incidental to an otherwise legitimate 'joint venture'" was unacceptable to the Court: "The fact that there is common ownership or control of the contracting corporations does not liberate them from the impact of the antitrust laws."[22] The purpose of the price and market division agreements was to prevent competition among themselves and with others, and court precedent plainly made such agreements illegal under the Sherman Act.[23]

Ancillary Restraints   An agreement not to enter a certain market in direct competition with another joint venturer may, under certain conditions, be a legal ancillary restraint to a joint venture.[24] But in such a case the antitrust authorities would feel compelled to keep a watchful eye. The

[21]*Timken Roller Bearing Co.* v. *U.S.*, 341 U.S. 593 (1951).
[22]Ibid., pp. 597–98.
[23]The district court had ordered Timken to divest itself of its stockholdings and all other financial interests in the British and French Timken companies. 83 F. Supp. 284 (1949). The Supreme Court modified the decree to eliminate the divestment order but enjoined the continuation or repetition of the illegal conduct.
[24]An ancillary restraint is a restraint subordinate or auxilliary to a principal contract itself. In its simplest form, for example, a business with a name, reputation, and clientele may be sold to a buyer who makes the purchase only upon the condition that the seller does not immediately open up a new similar business in competition with him. If the seller had not agreed not to enter the competition anew, the sale of the business would not have been consummated.

Department of Justice has presented as a hypothetical case an American company that feels the need to form a joint venture with a Japanese firm in order to market successfully certain key transistor parts in Japan.[25] Although the third largest producer with 22 percent of the American market, it has been unsuccessful in entering the Japanese market. A joint venture with a Japanese manufacturing company, one of Japan's largest industrial combines, is formed, with the American company holding 49 percent of the stock. The Japanese firm, although producing electronic equipment, has not been familiar with the American company's product. The joint venture will operate using knowhow licensed by the American firm. Penetration into the Japanese market is thus to be achieved.

The American firm is concerned that the joint venture, with lower costs than its costs in the United States, will spoil some of its markets elsewhere in the world. Part of the joint venture agreement is therefore written to limit the Japanese company or the joint venture from competing in certain world markets, including the United States. The question is whether this ancillary restraint built into the joint venture contract is so restrictive as to violate the Sherman Act. The answer given by the Department of Justice is yes and no. It would be legitimate only for a certain period of time, the period of "reverse engineering," or the period over which the Japanese company would have been able to develop the knowhow itself.[26] Since the Japanese company is already in electronics and since technology in that field is changing rapidly, that period would probably not be a long one. To permit this ancillary restraint to continue beyond that period of time would prevent the competition of the Japanese firm with the American firm in the United States and other world markets. But to calculate the actual temporal period for any particular reverse engineering project can be particularly speculative and open to dispute.

The Spillover Problem   If two or more firms in the same industry established a joint venture, for whatever reasons, there is always the possibility that price or output decision-making at the joint venture level may spill over into decision-making pertaining to their common horizontal competition relationships. In the *Minnesota Mining & Mfg. Co.* foreign joint venture decision, Judge Wyzanski observed, "The intimate association of the principal American producers in day-to-day manufacturing operations, their exchange of patent licenses and industrial know-how, and their common experience in marketing and fixing prices may inevitably reduce their zeal for competition *inter sese* in the American market."[27] This dictum

---

[25]U.S. Department of Justice, *International Operations*, Case E, pp. 28–31.
[26]The concept of reverse engineering can involve the taking apart and analyzing of a product to find out how it is put together and how it works. It is a method of obtaining technical knowledge. It is not illegal if patent rights are not infringed upon.
[27]92 F. Supp. 947, 963 (1950).

had no binding force on the decision at hand, but it was clearly suggestive as to a natural danger lurking in a joint venture.

This same fear of spillover was expressed in the Department of Justice's 1977 *Antitrust Guide for International Operations.* In discussing the case of a consortium of large electrical equipment manufacturers and engineering firms for the purpose of submitting bids on an extremely large hydroelectric project in a Latin American country—which was too big to be within the financial or technical capabilities of any one firm or smaller group of firms—it urged the use in such a long-term venture of the joint venture's own separate personnel. This would "reduce day-to-day contact among officials of the competitor-members."[28]

Bottleneck Monopolies   A joint venture can be restrictive and in violation of the Sherman Act when it becomes what the Department of Justice refers to as a "bottleneck monopoly."[29] Such a phenomenon is represented by restricted access to an "essential facility" which is not only important to the members of the joint venture, but to the other competitors in that market. Failure to achieve access to the essential facility can block a firm's ability to move forward in the market toward the ultimate consumer or backward toward sources of supply.

The *Terminal Company* case illustrates the barrier preventing vertical movement forward.[30] The Terminal Company, owned jointly by railroads that controlled all means of railway access to the city of Saint Louis, was found to violate the Sherman Act because this venture could exclude, by any member's vote, any newcomer who might desire use of these facilities. Under ordinary circumstances, new entrants can construct their own facilities and thus bypass a would-be monopoly. But in Saint Louis the geographical and topographical features served as an impossibly costly barrier to such entry. Likewise, the Associated Press was condemned under the Sherman Act.[31] Any member newspaper could prevent a competing newspaper from joining, thereby keeping for itself the exclusive output for AP news in its own local market. Since AP was considered the largest and best source of news, an excluded competitor was put at a competitive disadvantage.

The Department of Justice in its *Antitrust Guide for International Operations* has provided an illustration of a bottleneck monopoly that represents a possible restraint on movement backward toward supply.[32] A joint venture composed of five oil companies is engaged in international operations. Three of the companies are based in the United States and two in Western

[28]U.S. Department of Justice, *International Operations,* p. 20.
[29]Ibid., pp. 20, 59.
[30]*U.S.* v. *Terminal Railroad Association of St. Louis,* 224 U.S. 383 (1912).
[31]*Associated Press* v. *U.S.,* 326 U.S. 1 (1945).
[32]Case M, pp. 57–60.

Europe. The American companies operate concessions in a Latin American country and an African country. The two Western European companies operate concessions in the African country. The objective in using a joint venture is to secure stability of supply of crude oil through strengthening the companies' bargaining power with the foreign governments. The joint venture company provides for reserve supplies for any member through guarantees of a pro rata share of a backup "pool." The five companies, which are dominant firms in the areas concerned, decide to exclude from the joint venture an American firm that has a past record of independent and unpredictable market behavior.

The key question is whether the joint venture truly represents an "essential facility." If this joint venture is just as important in providing security of supply to the fourth American oil company as it is to its founding members, then this American company should be provided access to this joint venture. It does import oil into the United States and compete in the United States market; if it were denied access to the joint venture, it could suffer a competitive disadvantage.

Potential Competition   Where a jointly owned enterprise is organized to enter a new market, a basic question raised is this: Would one or more of the firms combining in the joint venture have entered the new market separately on its own if it had not joined together in the single corporation?

The *Penn-Olin* case, involving the first joint venture challenged under Section 7 of the Clayton Act as well as under Section 1 of the Sherman Act, serves to illustrate this issue.[33] Olin Mathieson Chemical Corporation and Pennsalt Chemicals Corporation, both Fortune 500 companies, formed a jointly owned (50-50) corporation, Penn-Olin Chemical Company, to produce sodium chlorate in a plant in Kentucky. Pennsalt was the third largest of three producers of this product in the country, but its plant was in Oregon. Olin did not produce sodium chlorate but was a large buyer of it (although not from Pennsalt), had expertise in its applications, and had an established salesforce in the southeastern part of the country, a market in which the top two producers accounted for 90 percent of sales.

A joint venture to produce and sell sodium chlorate in the southeastern part of the nation would serve the needs of both corporations. Olin could produce a product it had always purchased for resale. Pennsalt could penetrate the southeastern part of the country with a production plant

---

[33]*U.S.* v. *Penn-Olin Chemical Co., et al.,* 378 U.S. 158 (1964). The district court had dismissed the complaint as to the applicability of Section 7 of the Clayton Act, arguing that it would not apply to a newly formed corporation because it has not been engaged in commerce. 217 F. Supp. 110 (1963). The Supreme Court rejected that position, holding that the test of whether or not it was covered by Section 7 was the effect on competition and that it had been formed to engage in commerce.

better situated vis-à-vis the new market it wished to penetrate and would acquire a salesforce with contacts already achieved. For Olin, the joint venture represented product extension. For Pennsalt, it represented market extension. The district court had viewed the problem as being one of having to show, if the joint venture were to be held illegal, that *both* firms would have entered the market individually on their own. The entry of only one firm is no different from the entry of one joint venture firm in terms of the number of competitors added to the market. Indeed, it might be argued that a joint venture might well be a stronger competitor. The district court did not have evidence that convinced it, however, that both firms would have built their own separate plants, and thus dismissed the antitrust charge.

This reasoning was not satisfactory to the Supreme Court. It applied the principle of "potential competition." Even if only one of the two firms were to enter this market by building a plant, at least the other firm might still be on the edge of the market as a potential competitor that might enter at any time. The threat of this potential competition on the edge of the market would serve to hold down the prices of the product being sold. The Court thus saw the answer as resting on a determination of the reasonable probability that either *one* of the firms would have entered on its own, with the other remaining a significant potential competitor. The Supreme Court remanded the case back to the lower court. It noted the following criteria which the lower court might take into account:

> [T]he number and power of the competitors in the relevant market; the background of their growth; the power of the joint ventures; the relationship of their lines of commerce; the competition existing between them and the power of each in dealing with the competitors of the other; the setting in which the joint venture was created; the reasons and necessities for its existence; the joint venture's line of commerce and the relationship thereof to that of its parents; the adaptability of its line of commerce to noncompetitive practices; the potential power of the joint venture in the relevant market; an appraisal of what the compeition in the relevant market would have been if one of the joint venturers had entered it alone instead of through Penn-Olin; the effect, in the event of this occurrence, of the other joint venturer's potential competition; and such other factors as might indicate potential risk to competition in the relevant market.[34]

Three Supreme Court Justices saw no reason for remanding the case. To them it was obvious that the joint venture was a "sophisticated device"

[34]378 U.S. 158, 177.

to avoid a charge of sharing (dividing up) the market. For the market was a rapidly expanding one, and both firms had adequate resources and knowhow and had at one time or another shown considerable interest in entering that market. Yet the lower court, on remand, did not find any reasonable probability that either firm would have entered, and dismissed the case.[35]

RESEARCH JOINT VENTURES

Joint ventures for research can offer positive advantages for society. Basic research can be especially risky as to the profitability of the outcome, and it can be very costly. A sharing of the risks and spreading of the costs can induce more firms to be willing to engage in research than would otherwise occur. Joint research can thus be a spur to innovation.

Two Hypothetical Cases   Antitrust dangers can be found in research joint ventures. To determine just where the danger may lie, it is necessary to consider several factors. Two polar hypothetical cases may be helpful. In one, a joint venture involving firms from more than one industry is engaged in a fairly costly basic research project designed to unlock the secrets of a particularly critical technological problem. Many possible applications may derive from the project. Any firms wanting to enter as partners can do so. Any resulting patents would be licensed to all outsiders at a reasonable royalty. Such a project would represent a greater research effort than would be likely by individual firms separately, and no one firm or firms in one industry would have the incentive or the ability to slow the research or monopolize the output of the research. All firms would be at the same starting gate as to further developmental work and applications to the marketplace. Such an extreme illustration may seem to be too hypothetical, but it serves to illustrate the benefits of a research joint venture and a situation in which there are no real restraints on competition.

In a second hypothetical case, suppose the joint research venture is one of long standing and is related to product development research that would have been conducted by each participant on an individual competitive basis anyway; is composed of a few large firms in a highly concentrated industry; that there are barriers to entry not only into the industry, but also into the joint research project; and that patent rights to the fruits of the venture are restricted to members of the joint venture on an exclusive basis. This type of research venture could represent a general restraint on competition in that it would tend to strengthen any monopoly position the

[35]246 F. Supp. 917 (1965). The Supreme Court, in a split decision, affirmed. 389 U.S. 308 (1967).

few large firms may have already had. It could even slow innovation, since the firms might find it more profitable to suppress innovations than to create obsolescence of existing fixed assets by introducing innovations. That is, feeling that the loss of value of the existing assets might be greater than the increase in expected profits from the innovation, the few large firms dominating the industry might simply hold back on the introduction of the innovation. In contrast, firms within (or coming from outside) a competitive market structure, without any restrictive barriers to access to the innovation, would introduce the innovation without such a concern.

The first of these hypothetical cases is an ideal, with no restrictions, and with any discoveries flowing freely to society. The second is for all effects and purposes similar to a cartel, with any income gains being appropriated by the monopolists. The structural conditions and any restrictions attached to joint research ventures sought by the joint venturers would undoubtedly lie somewhere between these two extremes. Business, in general, would tend to seek to maximize the financial return it could obtain from whatever investment it may make in the research.[36] Some restrictions would therefore likely have to be built into the contractual agreements surrounding the research joint venture in order to provide the incentive to get the project underway. A basic public policy problem is thus to ensure that the restraints required for the incentives necessary for the research, such as any patent rights and restrictions, are more than offset by any gains to competition.

A second basic policy problem is to ensure that research joint ventures are not a substitute for competitive efforts that otherwise would have taken place or are not a vehicle for nurturing monopoly. Several questions have to be asked, and usually in combination. Is the research joint venture among competitors who were already engaging in the research independently? Is a member of a proposed joint venture one who was a potential competitor in that research—one who had the financial and technical capability and the incentive as well? What is the nature of the market structure, and how would the joint venture affect that structure? Are the firms relatively small or relatively large in terms of market share? Would the research joint venture assist in meeting foreign competition? Would the joint venture permit the continuation of important research that would otherwise have to be abandoned for lack of funds? Is the research basic and of importance to many? Or is it developmental and of particular advantage to a few?

---

[36]The contrast has been made between the university community, which tends to favor full disclosure and nonexclusivity, and the business community, which tends to favor secrecy (at least until patents have been procured) and retention of exclusive control to maximize competitive advantage and financial yield. Joel Davidow, Director, Office of Policy Planning, Antitrust Division, Department of Justice, "Cooperative Research Relationships and the Department of Justice Antitrust Guide Concerning Research Joint Ventures," Remarks before the 42nd Meeting of the Advisory Committee to the Director, National Institutes of Health, Bethesda, Maryland, March 16, 1981, mimeo, pp. 7–8.

What is the duration of the joint research effort—short term to solve a particularly pressing problem, or long term with strengthening interfirm affiliations? Answers to all these questions would be needed before any decision could be made.

Antitrust Application   Research joint ventures can fall within the prohibitions of Section 7 of the Clayton Act or Section 1 of the Sherman Act.[37] The first Department of Justice complaint against research joint ventures, under the Sherman Act, was that in 1969 against the four major automobile manufacturers (General Motors, Ford, Chrysler, and American Motors) and their association, the Automobile Manufacturers Association. It was settled by consent decree.[38] It was alleged that their fifteen-year-old cooperative research program involving antipollution devices for motor vehicles had eliminated all competition among them in the research, development, manufacture, installation, and publicity of these devices. Specific agreements to delay the installation of these devices and to install them as of a uniform date were cited. It was also alleged that there were restrictive agreements on the cross-licensing of patents and on the prices they would be willing to pay for patents developed by outsiders.

The auto manufacturers and their association argued that the research joint venture, through the pooling of research and technical data, was designed to increase the rate of progress in the development of the devices.[39] The Department of Justice argued that the various restrictive agreements which were included dampened competitive efforts at development. If there had been no patent restrictions and no agreements as to when to install the devices, perhaps the auto manufacturers could have made a good case for their joint efforts. Unfortunately too for their position, certain of the auto manufacturers had said that they had been willing to install the devices at an earlier date.[40]

The consent order prohibited any restraints on individual decision-making and on the filing of individual reports to governmental agencies. It ordered the end of agreements on the exchange of confidential information and on the cross-licensing of patents. It enjoined any joint price-fixing of patents purchased from outside. It ordered the end of any combination or

---

[37]U.S. Department of Justice, *Research Joint Ventures*, pp. 4–6.
[38]*U.S.* v. *Automobile Mfrs. Ass'n.*, Civil Action No. 69-75-JWC. Trade Cases para. 72,907 (1969). Named as co-conspirators but not as defendants were Checker Motor Corporation, Diamond T Motor Car Company, International Harvester Company, Studebaker Corporation, White Motor Corporation, Kaiser Jeep Corporation, and Mack Trucks, Inc. Two other Department of Justice complaints against research joint ventures have been issued, both resulting in consent decrees. *U.S.* v. *Wisconsin Alumni Research Foundation*, Trade Cases para. 73,015 (1969). *U.S.* v. *Manufacturer's Aircraft Ass'n.*, Trade Cases para. 60,810 (1975).
[39]*Business Week*, January 18, 1969, p. 28.
[40]U.S. Department of Justice release, January 10, 1969.

conspiracy to "restrain or limit the development, manufacture, installation, distribution or sale" of pollution-control devices.

How is one to know what conditions surrounding research joint ventures would be deemed anticompetitive on balance? The Department of Justice's 1980 *Antitrust Guide Concerning Research Joint Ventures* provided 8 illustrative examples of various possible contextual situations and summaries of 21 research and development joint venture business reviews and clearances between 1968 and 1980. The very fact that it was found advisable to provide guidelines on many possible situations is evidence that different factors and combinations of factors have to be considered in individual contexts.

NEWSPAPER JOINT OPERATING VENTURES—
AN ANTITRUST EXEMPTION

In 1970 Congress passed the Newspaper Preservation Act. It exempted from the antitrust laws certain joint newspaper operating arrangements, provided that they would preserve a "failing newspaper," one which is "in probable danger of financial failure." Two or more newspapers could engage in such joint ventures only so long as only one of them was financially sound. Joint operation of common production facilities, of distribution, of the business department, of advertising and circulation solicitation, and of the establishment of advertising and circulation rates would be permitted. Joint action on revenue distribution would also be tolerated. Editorial and reportorial staffs, however, must function independently. The objective of the public policy was to maintain a newspaper press editorially and reportorially independent and competitive. Joint action on the business side would permit more survival and competition on the editorial and reporting side.

The *Citizen Publishing* Case   The act was passed in response to the Supreme Court's 1969 antitrust decision in the *Citizen Publishing* (Tucson) case, which condemned a joint operating venture in the newspaper business.[41] In effect, it invalidated that decision and exempted the joint ventures in existence in the newspaper industry at that time from the antitrust laws so long as editorial and reporting functions were kept separate. It also cut off in the bud the private treble damage actions that had begun to be filed against such newspaper joint ventures.

The only two daily newspapers in Tucson, Arizona, the *Arizona Daily Star* and the *Tucson Daily Citizen*, had formed a joint operating venture in

[41]*Citizen Publishing Co. et al. v. U.S.*, 394 U.S. 131 (1969).

1940, which agreement was extended in 1953 until 1990. This joint venture was to be owned equally by the two newspapers. The new corporation, Tucson Newspapers, Inc. (TNI), was to manage all departments of the business of the two companies except the news and editorial units. The production and distribution equipment of the two newspapers was transferred to TNI, and they jointly chose its directors. Any commercial competition between the two newspapers ceased; this was the purpose of the arrangement.[42]

The joint setting of subscription and advertising rates was viewed by the Court as illegal price-fixing. The distribution of TNI's profits to the two newspapers according to a prearranged ratio was considered illegal profit-pooling. And an agreement as part of the joint venture that the two companies or their stockholders or officers would not enter into any other business in the same county was considered to be illegal market control. These constituted violations of Section 1 of the Sherman Act. The joint operating agreement constituted monopolization in violation of Section 2 of that act. The Supreme Court upheld the district court, which had decreed a modification of the joint operating agreement to eliminate the price-fixing, profit-pooling, and market control provisions.[43]

Both courts refused to accept the defense that the *Citizen* was a "failing company." It was true that the *Citizen* had been suffering some losses prior to 1940, but there was no evidence that it was about to go bankrupt or be liquidated. There had been no effort to sell the newspaper and there was no evidence that the *Star* was the only possible acquiring company. As a matter of fact, it was the *Citizen* which acquired the *Star*. And why would the *Star* be willing to share its profits with the *Citizen* if the latter were failing?

Consequences of the Newspaper Preservation Act   The act made any existing joint newspaper operating ventures that had come into being because of "economic distress" lawful. There were 22 joint operating arrangements at the time, including that of the Tucson newspapers. The financial status of the newspapers at the time they set up the joint ventures and at the time of the passage of the act were both solicited by the House Judiciary Committee, but the data were never made public because the committee agreed with the publishers concerned to keep all the informa-

---

[42]Ibid., p. 134.

[43]280 F. Supp. 978 (1968). Beyond the joint operating agreement issue there was also a Clayton Act Section 7 stock control issue. As a result of an option in the joint operating agreement, the stockholders of Citizen Publishing, through the vehicle of a new company, the Arden Publishing Company, acquired control over Star Publishing. The Supreme Court upheld the district court's decree requiring Citizen Publishing to divest itself of this control over Star Publishing.

tion confidential.[44] Any new joint ventures or renewals or amendments to existing ones must receive the consent of the attorney general. In the next decade three new applications for approval were filed with the Department of Justice and approved, and a fourth was filed in 1981.[45] But once a joint venture has been approved for "probable danger of financial failure" reasons, it does not have to undergo any further review unless it were to come up for renewal or modification—even if financial conditions were to be changing for the better.

Economies of scale may well be present in the pooling of printing and production equipment and facilities. But the joint solicitation of advertising may raise advertising rates and circulation rates. The Department of Justice had opposed the legislation, but has not made a detailed study of its impact.[46] Probably both the economies of the joint venture and the limits on competition they provide account for the 25 joint operating ventures that existed in 1980 in this industry. Actually most cities are served by only one newspaper. In 1968, of the 1500 cities having a daily newspaper, only 45 cities were served by two or more competing dailies.[47]

COMMERCIAL BRIBERY

There are times and circumstances when sales and business contracts will be allocated not on the basis of arms-length bargaining and competitive efficiency, but through expenditures that represent personal gain to individuals who are in key locations in purchasing channels. Bribes to those charged with purchasing responsibilities or to government officials in positions of influence can be the lubricant that seals a business deal. Bribery may be especially common in doing business in some foreign countries, where the practice is an accepted way of life.

Reports of the bribing of local and state officials to influence the allocation of business to particular firms is not at all uncommon. The business being sought may be insurance contracts, construction contracts, or cable television franchises, for example. The number of federal indictments returned against federal, state, and local public officials on corruption charges between 1970 and 1978 numbered 2622. Convictions were obtained in more than 75 percent of the cases that went to trial in that period.[48]

---

[44]House Report No. 91-1193, Judiciary Committee, to accompany H.R. 279, 91st Cong., 2nd Sess., June 15, 1970, pp. 12–13.

[45]U.S. Department of Justice release, April 10, 1981.

[46]U.S. Department of Justice, *Report of the Task Group on Antitrust Immunities* (Washington, D.C.: U.S. Government Printing Office, 1977), p. 44.

[47]House Report No. 91-1193, p. 4.

[48]U.S. Department of Justice release, May 3, 1979.

Action against commercial bribery can be derived from any number of sources. The FTC can attack commercial bribery as being an unfair method of competition under Section 5 of the Federal Trade Commission Act. Commercial bribery can be a violation of Section 2(c) of the Robinson-Patman Act as bribe monies are paid to a buyer's representative or intermediary, which can include an employee.[49] Bribes may be the basis of charges of fraud. They can violate rules of such federal government agencies as the Internal Revenue Service; the Bureau of Alcohol, Tobacco and Firearms; and the Securities and Exchange Commission (SEC). The Foreign Corrupt Practices Act of 1977 was passed to provide special statutory cover against bribery by American firms attempting to obtain or retain business overseas.

Bribes, payoffs, or kickbacks generally require some kind of falsification of accounting records. One case that reached the front page of *The New York Times* in 1980 was a guilty plea by The Bethlehem Steel Corporation to SEC charges that the company had paid more than $400,000 in bribes to obtain ship repair business.[50] The payoff payments were principally paid in cash from secret accounts in Switzerland. The cash had been generated originally by adding hidden commission charges on repair and maintenance work. The resulting monies were then sent to a sham company in Switzerland.

Reaching the problem of bribery can be complicated by the necessity of drawing the line between a customary granting of gratuities such as liquor, cigars, meals, theater tickets, and entertainment, on the one hand, and more outright bribes, on the other hand. A 1920 court of appeals reversed the FTC in the latter's attempt to include the former category of gratuities as bribery.[51] Nevertheless, the FTC has issued cease and desist orders against commercial bribery as an unfair method of competition since that decision. And in 1978 consent orders with three large aircraft manufacturers, it excluded from prohibited bribes "... normal business expenditures for entertaining, travel or small gifts (the cost of which does not exceed $1,000 per gift) for promotion of respondent's products or services."[52]

Push Money and Payola   One form of commercial bribery consists of financial rewards to the individual salespeople of customers who have the function of making sales to the next buyers. This is sometimes known as

[49]*Ranger, Inc.* v. *Sterling Nelson & Sons, Inc.*, 351 F. 2d 851 (1965), certiorari denied, 383 U.S. 936 (1966). It makes no difference whether the employee turns the bribe monies over to his employer or not.
[50]July 25, 1980. Fines of $325,000 were imposed. *New York Times*, August 26, 1980, p. D1.
[51]*New Jersey Asbestos Co.* v. *FTC*, 264 Fed. 509.
[52]*In the Matter of Lockheed Corporation*, 92 F.T.C. 968 (1978); *In the Matter of The Boeing Company*, 92 F.T.C. 972 (1978); *In the Matter of McDonnell Douglas Corporation*, 92 F.T.C. 976 (1978).

"push money." A key legal issue has been whether the employee receiving the payment does so with the knowledge of the employer. If the employer is aware of these payments, they are not considered illegal.[53] A business, or its salesperson with its consent, has a right to discriminate among the goods it wishes to sell or "push." According to the previously existing trade practice conference rules, the practice would be condemned only where the employer was not aware of the payments, where the grantor of such payments did not make such payments available on proportionately equal terms to salespersons of competing customers, or where a substantial lessening of competition or tendency to create a monopoly was likely to result.

Public attention was attracted in 1959 and 1960 to "payola" in the broadcasting industry. Here the public interest was directly involved. Disc jockeys conducting radio programs featuring recorded music were allegedly receiving monies from record producers to push the playing of certain records. The FTC felt that listeners were being misled into believing that the recordings being played were selected on the basis of merit or popularity. It took the position that a record's popularity was a function of the number of times it was played over the air, and that this was the basic cause of popularity. In 1960 the Commission prohibited this payola in some 80 consent orders, barring such payments as a violation of Section 5 of the Federal Trade Commission Act as an unfair method of competition unless the payola payments were fully admitted at the time of playing a record. A 1960 amendment to the Communications Act of 1934 required that such payments be disclosed by the recipient and be announced on the air.[54]

The payola problem in the record industry apparently persisted, for payoffs began to take on different forms.[55] One was to pay off the publisher of an industry journal, which would then give favorable mention to particular records; this, in turn, would be a guide to a radio station as to what records to play. Another method would be for the record company to purchase expensive airline tickets that would go into the expense accounts but be given to a disc jockey who would cash them in. Another technique would be for promoters to submit bills to record companies from phony limousine rental companies, florists, sound engineers, or advertising or promotion firms. Other variations on this same basic principle of payola were said to be prevalent. In any case, the payors of these monies clearly believe that these payments do influence the popularity of recordings and therefore their sales.

[53]*Kinney-Rome Co.* v. *FTC*, 275 Fed. 665 (1921).

[54]74 Stat. 889. The original act had covered such payments received by the stations but not by the stations' employees or program producers.

[55]Grace Lichtenstein, "Mob-Linked Conduits Get Subpoenas in Payola Case," *New York Times*, June 8, 1973, p. 24. See also Murray Schumach, "19 Are Indicted in Payola Cases," *New York Times*, June 25, 1975, p. 1.

The Foreign Corrupt Practices Act   In 1977 Congress passed the Foreign Corrupt Practices Act (FCPA). This legislation made it illegal for any American business firm (its officers, directors, employees, agents, or stockholders) to pay money or give gifts, or promise to do so, to any foreign official, foreign political party or party officials, or candidates for foreign political office in order to obtain or retain business. The influence being bought covers that used directly to sway particular business deals or indirectly to affect legislation or regulations. Violations could produce a fine of up to $1 million for a firm. Individuals could receive fines of up to $10,000 and/or be imprisoned for not more than five years. Even an executive's "knowing" or "having reason to know" that the illegal payments were being made by the firm's employee or agent is enough to show guilt. The SEC was expected to be the principal investigatory arm and turn any relevant evidence over to the Department of Justice. The attorney general could also bring a civil action to enjoin any such practice.

The use of undisclosed and questionable payments by corporations to foreign government officials was believed to be widespread. SEC investigations had uncovered "corrupt foreign payments" by over 300 American companies involving hundreds of millions of dollars.[56] To the SEC, this represented a breach in its system of required corporate disclosure. The bribery payments had been covered up by the falsification of accounting records, and the records as a result did not accurately portray all transactions. The first substantive section of the FCPA therefore required the use of accounting standards which would ensure that all transactions be fairly reflected.

The Lockheed Corporation scandal was also believed to be a major impetus to the passage of the FCPA. In testimony before a Senate Foreign Relations subcommittee in 1975, it was revealed that Lockheed had paid several millions of dollars in bribes overseas.[57] The revelation of payments to the Office of the Prime Minister of Japan was especially earthshaking. The Department of Justice followed up with charges that Lockheed had violated civil and criminal laws in efforts to conceal certain payments from the Export-Import Bank, which had guaranteed loans secured for the purchase of jet aircraft by All-Nippon Airlines of Japan. The legal charges were wire fraud, making false statements to the U.S. government, and violating customs laws. Lockheed was accused of concealing the payments by false entries in accounting records, backdating agreements, obtaining phony receipts, and using a Swiss bank account. It pleaded guilty in 1979 to concealing $2.6 million in payments between 1972 and 1974 to Japanese

---

[56]Senate Report No. 95-114, Banking, Housing, and Urban Affairs Committee, to accompany S. 305, 95th Cong., 1st Sess., May 2, 1977, p. 3.

[57]U.S. Senate, Subcommittee on Multinational Corporations of the Committee on Foreign Relations, *Hearings, Multinational Corporations and United States Foreign Policy*, Part 14, 94th Cong., 2nd Sess., 1976, pp. 327–91 *passim*.

government and business officials and paid a total of $647,000 in civil penalties and criminal fines.[58]

In more general terms, the issue of foreign bribery payments had come to a head. A statutory statement of public policy on the matter was needed. Maybe bribes to government officials was a way of doing business in certain foreign countries; the initiative may well have originated with a foreign official. But the fact that they were covered up—and therefore implicitly understood to be corrupt—represented a lack of harmony between that way of doing business and certain principles of conduct which were supposed to be, theoretically at least, characteristic of the American system of fair competition. Aside from these theoretical principles, however, these so-called corrupt payments by American business had aroused adverse reaction in such countries as Japan, Italy, and The Netherlands.[59]

The legislative history of the FCPA indicates that a distinction has to be made between bribery payments and extortion. Whereas bribery payments are granted voluntarily, extortion payments are made under duress. A corporation doing business overseas may have to pay terrorists who threaten to blow up plant or equipment. That is extortion, not a bribery payment. On the other hand, the distinction is not always clear. A company having a plant in a foreign country may, for example, subtly, or perhaps not so subtly, be threatened that it may experience difficulties in continuing to do business in that country if it does not make a contribution to the reigning political party.[60]

Competition and Overseas Bribery   The making of payments to foreign functionaries for purposes of obtaining or retaining business a criminal offense has placed American firms at a disadvantage in the competition for some foreign business. Some industrialized countries of the world permit bribery payments to be taken as legal, tax-deductible business expenses.[61] Competing with competitors from such countries may induce American firms doing business overseas to attempt to find ways around the law or to just ignore the law.[62]

The FCPA does not cover payments to employees of foreign governments "whose duties are essentially ministerial or clerical." Certain "grease payments" are a way of getting business done in some countries.

[58]U.S. Department of Justice release, June 1, 1979. See also Judith Miller, "Lockheed Guilty on Payments," *New York Times,* June 2, 1979, p. 29.
[59]Senate Report No. 95-114, p. 3.
[60]See testimony of the chairman of the board of the Gulf Oil Corporation concerning Gulf's 1966 and 1970 contributions to the South Korean government's election campaign in *Hearings, Multinational Corporations and United States Foreign Policy,* Part 12, pp. 9-58, *passim.*
[61]William M. Carley and John M. Geddes, "Payoff Probe," *Wall Street Journal,* February 17, 1981, p. 1.
[62]Jack G. Kaikati and Wayne A. Label, "American Bribery Legislation: An Obstacle to International Marketing," *Journal of Marketing,* 44, no. 4 (Fall 1980), 38–43. See also William M. Carley and Stan Crock, "Payoff Perspective," *Wall Street Journal,* May 20, 1981, p. 56.

Small amounts of money or gifts provided to minor overseas officials are expected in the matter of expediting shipments through customs, securing required permits, or placing overseas telephone calls without undue delay. Are these "lubrication bribes" really exempt from the FCPA? Some firms are not sure and have halted such payments.[63] To help remove such uncertainties, the Department of Justice established a Foreign Corrupt Practices Act Review Procedure in 1980; advice on the legality of prospective foreign payments could thus be obtained.[64] Congressional efforts to amend the FCPA to remove some of its claimed vagueness have been under consideration. Negotiations have also been proceeding within the United Nations since 1976 to attempt to draft a multilateral treaty to resolve the problem of illicit payments.

Efforts to use the antitrust laws as a tool against the use of bribes to foreign officials had been hampered by the need to find evidence that the bribery payments had injured other United States companies.[65] Yet the FTC succeeded in 1978 in obtaining consent orders against three large aircraft manufacturers—Lockheed Corporation, The Boeing Company, and McDonnell Douglas Corporation—which prohibited them from making improper payments to procure aircraft sales abroad.[66] The Commission's position was that these payments represented an unfair method of competition in violation of Section 5 of the Federal Trade Commission Act and price discrimination in violation of Section 2(c) of the Robinson-Patman Act. American competitors were being disadvantaged in the opportunity to compete for such sales. These orders were broader than those possible under the FCPA because the illegal payments were to officials of commercial customers as well as to foreign government officials. In addition, the firms could be liable for civil penalties as high as $3.6 million a year for each violation ($10,000 per day), a greater penalty than the criminal fines under the FCPA.

SUMMARY

A joint venture is a business organization owned by two or more persons or firms that have pooled their assets and skills. The joint owner parents may be only United States or both United States and foreign firms. They are subject to the antitrust laws of the United States even when operating in foreign commerce, and can violate those laws when United States imports, exports, or foreign investment are adversely affected. International comity can serve to limit United States antitrust enforcement efforts.

[63]*Business Week,* April 6, 1981, p. 131.

[64]U.S. Department of Justice, Office of the Attorney General, Order No. 878-80, March 20, 1980.

[65]Burt Schorr, "FTC Staff Action Against Aircraft Firms May Set Precedent for Fighting Payoffs," *Wall Street Journal,* October 18, 1977, p. 2.

[66]See note 52 above.

Joint ventures can create antitrust problems when they affect horizontal competition among competitors, when they create bottleneck monopolies that affect the competition among firms in their vertical relationships, and when they eliminate potential competition. Research joint ventures provide special problems for the application of a rule of reason.

The Newspaper Preservation Act of 1970 is a special exemption from the antitrust laws for newspapers that combine production and commercial operations in a joint venture. The suppression of commercial competition among competing daily newspapers has been permitted in order to preserve "failing newspapers" by permitting the economies of scale supposed to be derived from such joint ventures.

Commercial bribery is a phenomenon as old as business itself. Various statutes, including the antitrust laws, have been invoked to prevent this method of obtaining or retaining business from extending beyond the realm of the customary granting of certain promotional gratuities. It is important to flush out secret bribes and payoffs in order to prevent this unfair method of competition and to preserve the full disclosure and accuracy of accounting records. A special form of bribery is represented by the "payola" payments in the record industry.

The use of bribes to obtain or retain business overseas led to the passage of the Foreign Corrupt Practices Act of 1977. The resulting controls over the use of bribes by American business overseas has put the latter at a competitive disadvantage with firms operating under laws of nations that do not take the same attitude toward bribery and in dealing with customers to whom this practice is an accepted way of life.

Selected Readings

COASE, R. H., "Payola in Radio and Television Broadcasting," *Journal of Law & Economics,* 22, no. 2 (October 1979).

FUGATE, WILBUR L., *Foreign Commerce and the Antitrust Laws* (2nd ed.). Boston: Little, Brown, 1973.

JOELSON, MARK R., AND JOSEPH P. GRIFFIN, "Multinational Joint Ventures and the U.S. Antitrust Laws," *Virginia Journal of International Law,* 15, no. 3 (spring 1975).

MCCLOY, JOHN J., NATHAN W. PEARSON, AND BEVERLY MATTHEWS, *The Great Oil Spill: The Inside Report, Gulf Oil's Bribery and Political Chicanery.* New York: Chelsea House, 1976.

U.S. DEPARTMENT OF JUSTICE, *Antitrust Guide for International Operations.* Washington, D.C.: U.S. Government Printing Office, 1977.

U.S. DEPARTMENT OF JUSTICE, *Antitrust Guide Concerning Research Joint Ventures.* Washington, D.C.: U.S. Government Printing Office, 1980.

Name and Subject Index

Law Case Index

Simplicity Pattern Co., Inc.; FTC v. (1959), 199
Simpson v. Union Oil Co. (1964), 163
Snap-on Tools Corporation; FTC v. (1963), 170
Socony-Vacuum Oil Co., Inc.; U.S. v. (1940), 55–56
Standard Fashion Co. v. Magrane-Houston Co. (1922), 159
Standard Motor Products, Inc.; FTC v. (1959), 196
Standard Oil Co. (Indiana); FTC v. (1951), 182, 195
Standard Oil Co. (Indiana); FTC v. (1958), 197
Standard Oil of California and Standard Stations, Inc.; U.S. v. (1949), 28, 164
Standard Oil Co. of New Jersey; U.S. v. (1911), 24, 46, 124, 137
Sumergrade; FTC v. (1956), 222
Sun Oil Company; U.S. v. (1959), 164
Sunshine Biscuits, Inc.; FTC v. (1962), 196

T

Terminal Railroad Association of St. Louis; U.S. v. (1912), 247
Texaco, Inc.; FTC v. (1968), 165
Texas Industries, Inc. v. Radcliff Materials, Inc. (1981), 43
Texas State Board of Accountancy; U.S. v. (1976), 86
Thatcher Manufacturing Company; FTC v. (1926), 28
Theatre Enterprises, Inc. v. Paramount Film Distributing Corp. (1954), 67
Timberlane Lumber Co. v. Bank of America, N.T. & S. A. (1976), 242
Times-Picayune Publishing Co.; U.S. v. (1953), 155–56
Timken Roller Bearing Co.; U.S. v. (1951), 245
Tingley Rubber Corp.; In re (1980), 202

Topco Associates, Inc.; U.S. v. (1972), 2, 169
totes, inc.; In re (1980), 202
Trans-Missouri Freight Assn.; U.S. v. (1897), 54
Trenton Potteries Co.; U.S. v. (1927), 55
Twentieth Century-Fox Film Corporation; U.S. v. (1978), 157

U

Union Oil Company of California; U.S. v. (1965), 32
United States Gypsum Co.; U.S. v. (1978), 68
United States Steel Corp.; U.S. v. (1920), 123
United States Steel Corp.; In re (1924), 64
United States Steel Corp. v. Fortner Enterprises, Inc. (1977), 154
Utah Pie Co. v. Continental Baking Co. (1967), 187, 190–91, 194

V

Von's Grocery Co.; U.S. v. (1966), 113

W

Warner-Lambert Co.; FTC v. (1978), 226
Westinghouse Electric Corp.; U.S. v. (1977), 69
White Motor Co.; U.S. v. (1963), 169
Wisconsin Alumni Research Foundation; U.S. v. (1969), 252

Z

Zarbock v. Chrysler (1964), 167